BOHEMIA
IN THE EIGHTEENTH CENTURY

BOHEMIA
IN THE EIGHTEENTH CENTURY

A Study in
Political, Economic, and Social History
With Special Reference to the Reign of
Leopold II, 1790–1792

BY

ROBERT JOSEPH KERNER

Professor of Modern European History
University of California

Introduction

by

Joseph F. Zacek

orono, maine

ACADEMIC INTERNATIONAL

1969

THE RUSSIAN SERIES/Volume 7

Robert J. Kerner, BOHEMIA IN THE EIGHTEENTH CENTURY

Second edition 1969

Reimpression of the 1932 edition with a new Introduction

by Joseph F. Zacek

Copyright © 1969 by Academic International

Library of Congress Catalog Number: 74-82895

SBN 87569-007-6

Printed in the United States of America

Address all orders to Academic International/orbis academicus,

Orono, Maine   04473

TO
MY MOTHER
AND THE MEMORY OF
MY FATHER

INTRODUCTION TO THE SECOND EDITION

In the last entry he prepared for *Who's Who in American Education,* Robert Joseph Kerner characterized himself as a "pioneer in America in opening to the Anglo-Saxon world the scientific historical study of Eastern Europe and its Near Eastern and Far Eastern expansions."[1] Despite its somewhat grandiose phrasing, the description was certainly correct, especially as it concerned Eastern Europe. In the latter field, Kerner occupies a secure place among the small group of American scholars who, entirely self-motivated and largely self-trained, first began to introduce the United States to the historical background of those "undesirable immigrants" who had been arriving in growing numbers from Eastern Europe since the late nineteenth century.

Kerner gained his entrée to this esoteric field in the most natural way possible — he was born in 1887 to Joseph A. Kerner and Rose Veselák Kerner, members of the Czech-American community in Chicago. To the advantage of family background he added formal training at Harvard under the patriarch of Eastern European studies in the United States, Archibald Cary Coolidge. He took his Ph. D. in history under Coolidge in 1914, having spent the previous two years on fellowship studying at Prague University and in the archives of Vienna, Berlin, Moscow, and Paris. Three years later, he was placed in a position not merely to record the history of Eastern Europe but to help determine it in a significant way. From 1917 to 1919 he was one of about one hundred and fifty American scholars assembled by Colonel House in "The Inquiry," the preparatory commission directed to study the terms of peace before

1 *Who's Who in American Education,* Vol. XIV (1949-1950), p. 670. Of additional bio-bibliographical value are the Kerner obituaries in *Who Was Who in America,* Vol. III (1951-1960), p. 473, and in the official memorial publication of the University of California, *In Memoriam* (April, 1958), pp. 53-56.

vii

the hostilities of World War I had ceased. Subsequently, he was also made a member of the American staff at the Paris Peace Conference. It is indicative of the embryonic state of Eastern European studies in the United States at the time that Kerner, a thirty-year-old assistant professor barely out of graduate school and the author of a single periodical article,[2] should have become a member — and a highly prized member — of these august bodies. His experience and training, particularly his broad linguistic knowledge, qualified him far above most of the young academic "experts" who were his colleagues. (One of these, for example, was the famous American historian, Samuel Eliot Morison, then a young instructor at Harvard and author of a *Life of Harrison Gray Otis,* who served The Inquiry as a specialist on Finland and the Baltic States!) Kerner's own particular assignment concerned the nationality problems of the Habsburg Monarchy. In this capacity, he ardently and successfully pressed the claims of his personal favorites, the Czechs, Slovaks, and South Slavs.[3]

Until his death of a heart ailment in 1956, Kerner lived the full, busy life of a successful scholar. The first fourteen years of his professional life (1914-1928) were spent at the University of Missouri, where he rose from instructor to full professor of history. The remainder he spent at the University of California at Berkeley where, after 1941, he was Sather Professor of History. In 1948 he organized the Institute of Slavic Studies there, making Berkeley an early center in the United States for the study of Central Europe, the Balkans,

2 "The Foundations of Slavic Bibliography," *The Papers of the Bibliographical Society of America,* Vol. X, No. 1 (January, 1916), pp. 3-39.

3 However, in his many dogmatic reports and recommendations to The Inquiry, Kerner did not support the idea of complete self-determination for the hitherto subject peoples of Central-Eastern Europe. In words strongly reminiscent of the Czech federalist statesman, František Palacký (1798-1876), he feared that, given their independence, these small nations would quickly become the vassals of the neighboring great powers, especially Germany. He urged the United States to work for autonomous status for all nationalities within a federalized Habsburg Empire and a unified, independent Yugoslav state. (Kerner firmly believed that "natural evolution" had already fused the South Slavs into a single nation.) Kerner's activity in The Inquiry is described in Lawrence E. Gelfand, *The Inquiry: American Preparations for Peace,* 1917-1919 (New Haven, 1963), especially pp. 54-60, 200-203, 218-219.

and Russia. An exacting teacher and popular lecturer, he held visiting appointments at Colorado, Iowa, Hawaii, Chicago, Columbia, and the Institute of International Education. He was one of the founders of the *Journal of Modern History* and a member of the editorial boards of *The Slavonic Review* (London), the *Journal of International Relations,* and the *American Historical Review.* Honors came to him in generous measure: at home, from 1920 on, a listing in *Who's Who in America;* several honorary doctorates; election as Faculty Research Lecturer at Berkeley, 1942-1943; and appointment to Unesco's Commission for the Scientific and Cultural History of Mankind. His scholarly and political efforts on behalf of Eastern Europe brought him grateful recognition from that quarter, as well. He was named a member of the Historical Society of Novi Sad (Yugoslavia); the Šafařík Learned Society, the Royal Bohemian Society of Letters and Sciences, and the Slavonic Institute of Czechoslovakia; and the Rumanian Royal Academy. Czechoslovakia awarded him its State Prize for Literature in 1940 and made him a Commander of its Order of the White Lion. Rumania bestowed upon him the Order of the Star of Rumania.

In those halcyon times when rigid and exclusive "area specialization" was still unknown, Kerner could confidently delimit his field of study as "modern European history, with special interest in Central and Eastern Europe, including its Near Eastern and Far Eastern extensions." The list of his major writings — articles, books, and numerous ground-breaking bibliographies — testifies that he did indeed devote himself seriously — though scarcely equally — to all three of these geographical regions. The Slavs were always his chief preoccupation. His *Slavic Europe: A Selected Bibliography in the Western European Languages, Comprising History, Languages, and Literatures* (1918) was the first general bibliographical study published in the United States on Eastern Europe. The Czechs and Russians were the subjects of his two most scholarly works: *Bohemia in the Eighteenth Century* (1932), and *The Urge to the Sea, The Course of Russian History: The Role of Rivers, Portages, Ostrogs, Monasteries, and Furs* (1942). His lifelong Slavophilism also found an outlet in *The Jugo-Slav Movement* (1918) and in the contributions he made to three volumes of the University of California's United Nations Series — *Czechoslovakia* (1940), *Poland* (1945), and

Yugoslavia (1949). (Kerner himself was the general editor of this ten-volume series, 1940-1950.) Kerner's interest in the Near East was peripheral, merely a by-product of his involvement with Balkan-Slavic affairs. In 1930 he compiled his *Social Sciences in the Balkans and in Turkey: A Survey of Resources for Study and Research in These Fields of Knowledge;* six years later, with Harry N. Howard, he wrote *The Balkan Conferences and the Balkan Entente, 1930-1935: A Study in the Recent History of the Balkan and Near Eastern Peoples.* A visit to the Far East in 1931 awakened Kerner's interest in this part of the world, too, and America's vital relationship to it. At Berkeley he subsequently founded and presided over a student-faculty colloquium called the "Northeastern Asia Seminar" and after 1937 edited the university's Northeastern Asia Series. His own chief contribution to the study of the Far East was the two-volume *Northeastern Asia: A Selected Bibliography* (1939).

Kerner's *Bohemia in the Eighteenth Century* originated as his doctoral dissertation at Harvard. It was at once his only serious venture into Czech history, his longest research study, and the only one of his works to involve archival investigations. When it appeared in 1932, it had no legitimate precursors among American publications. American interest in the Czechs and Slovaks had begun only at the very end of the nineteenth century. By Kerner's day, it had resulted chiefly in several popular surveys of Bohemia and the Czechs by sympathetic but hopelessly unqualified authors, such as Robert H. Vickers, Frances Gregor, Charles Edmund Maurice, and Will S. Monroe. Slightly more trustworthy were the many publications of the Czech immigrant, Thomas Čapek, who labored mightily to introduce his countrymen and their history to Americans. The most scholarly English-language study of Bohemian history preceding Kerner's was Count Franz von Lützow's *Bohemia, An Historical Sketch* (1896), a translation of the Czech original. It was based soundly on the major Czech and German historians of nineteenth-century Bohemia but was badly outdated by Kerner's day.

Thus it remained for Kerner and several others, notably S. Harrison Thomson and Matthew Spinka, to begin the scholarly study of Czech and Slovak history in the United States in the interwar period — study by professional historians who were fluent in the languages of the area and who utilized primary and archival sources. Under-

standably, *Bohemia in the Eighteenth Century* was greeted as a
revelation by American reviewers, who praised it uniformly as a
"model," "priceless," "brilliant," and an invaluable reference work
for future researchers.[4] Foreign reviewers, who were far better
qualified to assess its worth, were almost as complimentary. R.
W. Seton-Watson declared it a "penetrating analysis," a "scholarly,
authentic work . . . not likely soon to be superseded."[5] He
especially noted Kerner's fairness toward rival Czech and German
theses on the subject of the historical-political rights of the Kingdom
of Bohemia and the constitutional or unconstitutional character of
the changes wrought by Maria Theresa and Joseph II. On the other
hand, the prominent Sudeten German historian, Josef Pfitzner,
while accepting the book as a valuable study, criticized Kerner's
scant attention to the awakening of national consciousness among
the Sudeten Germans and his use of such "stereotyped concepts"
as "Germanization."[6] Even Czech historians, clannish and traditionally skeptical of the attempts of foreigners at writing Czech
history, gave the work considerable and favorable attention.[7] To be
sure, they received it less as a pioneer work with new insights than
as a careful, comprehensive synthesis of previously published sources
and literature and some valuable archival research by Kerner himself. They especially welcomed the fact that it introduced facets of
Bohemian *domestic* history to Anglo-American readers and the most
important writings of Czech historians on them, rather than the
more dramatic and more widely familiar military, diplomatic, and
religious aspects of the country's past.[8]

4 The most perceptive American review was that of Oscar Jászi in the
American Historical Review, Vol. XXXVIII (April, 1933), p. 544.

5 *The Slavonic Review* (London), Vol. XII (1933-4), pp. 481-482.

6 *Historische Zeitschrift,* Vol. CXLIX (1934), pp. 423-424.

7 See especially the reviews by Otakar Odložilík in the *Český časopis
historický,* Vol. XXXIX (1933), pp. 650-652, and in the *Časopis pro dějiny
venkova,* Vol. XX (1933), pp. 79-81; the evaluation by Josef Šusta in
Posledních deset let československé práce historické (Prague, 1937), pp.
218-219; and the long description and analysis by J. Hanák in the *Časopis
Matice moravské,* Vol. LVII (1933), pp. 306-315.

8 The book seems to have escaped the attention of Austrian reviewers
almost completely. A check of pertinent periodicals, bibliographies, and

The book's importance hinges on the fact that it deals with the crucial century when Bohemia was making the transition from a feudal to a centralized state (or, to use the newer Marxist interpretation, from a feudal-agricultural to a capitalist-industrial economic order). Its core deals with the last phase of the aristocratic opposition to Josephinism as it manifested itself in Bohemia after Joseph's death, during the brief reign of his successor, Leopold II (1790-1792). Kerner details the opposing positions of the Bohemian Estates and the absolutist regime on a wide variety of governmental issues (particularly the Constitution, taxation, and serfdom) and the uneven compromise struck by the two parties — often at the expense of the peasantry — under the threat of the French Revolution. The conclusion emerges that the medieval Estates, with their narrow, selfish class interests, represented as great an obstacle to modern constitutional government in Bohemia as Habsburg absolutism. Only Leopold himself, thoughtful and receptive to sound arguments during his deliberations, appears as a sympathetic participant in the proceedings.

Kerner's primary source base consists of the three *Desideria* composed by the Estates themselves at Leopold's request, together with various related documents (chiefly the *acta* of the Bohemian and Viennese offices which considered the *Desideria*). Some of this valuable archival material was subsequently destroyed by fire in 1927. These sources, together with Kerner's own lengthy introductory chapters and sections, codify the vast changes which occurred in Bohemian internal affairs roughly from the Battle of White Mountain (1620) through the reign of Joseph II (1790). The agreement effected between Leopold and the Estates, in turn, set the fundamental conditions of life in Bohemia for the crucial half-century following, during which the Czech National Revival grew to maturity. The reader is thus presented with a unique English-language summary of the basic developments in every major aspect of domestic life in Bohemia — political, legal, judicial, economic, social, religious, and educational — during more than two hundred years. Kerner here

historical handbooks yielded only an occasional listing of the title. A cursory examination of the as-yet-unorganized fifty cartons of Kerner papers in the Manuscript Division of the Bancroft Library at Berkeley also failed to discover copies of any Austrian evaluations.

exhibits truly remarkable skill in dealing with so many varied aspects of history and in capsulizing his complex material. His treatments of the development of serfdom in Bohemia and of the Bohemian Constitution are invaluable in themselves. Throughout, Kerner is careful to maintain a textbook level of explanation in dealing with basic terms, institutions, and processes, so that his study is able to serve as a reference tool for American scholars working on Czech history, most of whom are necessarily self-taught and have difficulty in finding such systematic expositions even among Czech writings.

In addition to its value as a monograph on the reign of Leopold II and as a survey of Bohemian internal history before 1800, the *Bohemia* may also be viewed as an introduction to the history of the famous Czech National Revival in the late eighteenth and early nineteenth centuries. The nucleus of the book is a case study of what is traditionally considered the first stage of this phenomenon — the development of a Bohemian *Landespatriotismus* among the Bohemian nobility as a reaction to Joseph's attempts to centralize and Germanize his entire realm.[9] However, there is scant mention in the book of the seeds of the second stage — a popular resurgence of Czech culture — which were also planted in Joseph's reign: his easing of serf burdens and espousal of religious toleration released a vast reservoir of Czech national feeling by giving mobility to the most nationally-conscious stratum of the Czech population and permitting it renewed contact with the stirring Hussite past. Kerner also devotes little attention to the links between the aristocratic and popular movements such as the noble patronage of nationalist historians and scholars and the founding of patriotic institutions and societies. He does, of course, underline one important connection, the opposition of the Estates, particularly the clergy, to the Germanization of the educational system.

Unlike many of the older historical works currently being reprinted, then, Kerner's *Bohemia in the Eighteenth Century* is not merely an antiquated "classic." As a detailed examination of the Bohemian

9 Kerner, of course, accepts the general pre-Marxist Czech interpretation of the National Revival. The complete range of variations in this interpretation is discussed in Albert Pražák, *České obrození* (Prague, 1948), pp. 63-110. Josef Kočí, *Naše národní obrození* (Prague, 1960), pp. 5-24, also includes Marxist interpretations.

Desideria, it is still unique in any language, even among Czech historical writings.[10] In his extensive bibliography, Kerner did not see fit to include a single English title on Bohemia. Even today only two, both monographs on economic history, are worthy of addition for the eighteenth century: Herman Freudenberger's *The Waldstein Woolen Mill: Noble Entrepreneurship in Eighteenth Century Bohemia* (1963) and William E. Wright's *Serf, Seigneur, and Sovereign: Agrarian Reform in Eighteenth Century Bohemia* (1966). (The latter work has an excellent up-to-date bibliography on Bohemia and the Habsburg Monarchy in this century.) Anglo-American scholars working on the region have concentrated upon the fifteenth, nineteenth, and twentieth centuries — upon the Hussites, the National Revival, the independence movement in World War I, the Sudeten German problem, Munich, and the Communist takeover —but have almost completely ignored the eighteenth.

The dearth of writings in Kerner's day on the life and reign of Leopold II has now been significantly ameliorated by the researches of Ernst Wangermann, Heinz Holldack, Denis Silagi, and Adam Wandruszka, especially the latter's *Leopold II: Erzherzog von Öster- reich, Grossherzog von Toskana, König von Ungarn und Böhmen, Römischer Kaiser* (2 vols., 1963-5). But it is really only the broad background sections of Kerner's study that require serious updating in text and bibliography since 1932.[11] In general, the reader will find it profitable to consult the more recent constitutional and administrative histories of Austria by Friedrich Walter, Otto Stolz, Ernst C. Hellbling, Otto Brunner, and *Die Entwicklung der Verfassung Öster- reichs vom Mittelalter bis zur Gegenwart* published by the Institut fur Österreichkunde in Vienna (1963). The two crucial reigns pre- ceding Leopold's have been heavily and fruitfully researched and

10 It is accepted as such, for example, in František Kutnar's standard univer- sity text, *Přehled dějin Československa v epoše feudalismu, IV: Doba národního obrozenf, 1740-1848* (Prague, 1963), p. 81.

[11] Recent American and Austrian publications on the Habsburg Monarchy are systematically recorded in the *Austrian History Yearbook* edited by R. John Rath at Rice University (Vol. I, 1965- ; previously the *Austrian His- tory Newsletter,* Nos. 1-4, 1960-1963). There are excellent selected biblio- graphies on the Monarchy in Erich Zöllner, *Geschichte Österreichs von den Anfängen bis zur Gegenwart* (1966), and in Hugo Hantsch, *Die Geschichte Österreichs* (2 vols., 1959-1962). Czechoslovak historical writing

continue to attract new investigators. On Maria Theresa, one should primarily consult such authors as Willy Andreas, Heinrich Kretschmayer, George Peabody Gooch, and Friedrich Walter; on Joseph II and Josephinism, Saul K. Padover, Paul P. Bernard, Ernst Benedikt, Eduard Winter, Fritz Valjavec, Ferenc Fejtő, Ferdinand Maass, Herbert Rieser, and Henrich Benedikt. Franco Valsecchi's several works, in Italian, on Enlightened Absolutism in the Habsburg Monarchy are also of great value. As for monographic research by Czech scholars on Bohemian history during the period from 1620 to 1790, it is impossible to make even a basic selection here from the vast number of titles that have appeared since 1932.[12] Broad surveys of this period, on the other hand, are quite few. The chief of these is Kamil Krofta's *Nesmrtelný národ: Od Bílé Hory k Palackému* (Prague, 1940). Krofta's comprehensive history of the Czechs and Slovaks, *Dějiny československe* (Prague, 1946), includes a masterfully selected list of books and articles on Bohemian and Czechoslovak history by the well-known bibliographer, Josef Klik. Detailed and authoritative is the historical volume of the Czechoslovak encyclopedia entitled *Československá vlastivěda* — Volume IV (*Dějiny*, Prague, 1932) and its first supplement (*Doplněk* I, Prague, 1933). The contemporary Marxist version of this historical period is codified in the official history published by the Historical Institute of the Czechoslovak Academy of Sciences: *Přehled československých dějin*, Vol. I (Prague, 1958).

Joseph F. Zacek

State University of New York at Albany

is recorded comprehensively in two serial bibliographies, the *Bibliografie české historie* (1904-1941) and the *Bibliografie československé historie* (1955 -). The gap between them is bridged by the long bibliographical essay, *Vingt-cinq ans d'historiographie tchécoslovaque*, 1936-1960 (Prague, 1960). The only significant attempt to record American writings on Czech and Bohemian history is included in *The American Bibliography of Russian and East European Studies* (1945-), published by Indiana University.

12 Cross sections through the sources and literature, including archival holdings, are given in Josef Kočí and Jiří Kořalka, "The History of the Habsburg Monarchy (1526-1918) in Czechoslovak Historiography Since 1945," *Austrian History Yearbook*, Vol. II (1966), pp. 198-223; in Arnošt Klíma, *Příručka k dějinám Československa v letech 1648 až 1848* (Prague, 1963), pp. 73-88, 119-129; and, for the later eighteenth century, in Kutnar's text (mentioned above), pp. 12-18, 74-82, 149-156.

PREFACE

To understand contemporary conditions in Central Europe one must go back to the Eighteenth Century. Besides the history of the central government of the Habsburg Monarchy, the histories of the two countries most important for this purpose are those of Hungary and Bohemia. The former has already been analyzed in a remarkable monograph by the noted Hungarian historian, Henry Marczali.[1] It is the purpose of the present study to do much the same thing for Bohemia.

Intensive archival research in both cases has revealed the dominant forces at work in the internal history of the Danubian Monarchy. In the case of Bohemia, it has exposed a national reaction led by the half-medieval nobility which was just strong enough to check the centralizing and Germanizing tendencies of Vienna, but not strong enough to prevent the triumph of the modern state over the medieval.

No part of the Eighteenth Century is so important for the study of this clash of forces, modern and medieval, centralizing and decentralizing, denationalizing and nationalizing, as the reign of Leopold II (1790-1792). It coincides in time with the French Revolution, which came near having a side-show in the Habsburg Monarchy. After the manner of the French in their *Cahiers*, the Estates in Central Europe presented their *Desideria* and demanded many changes. It is from this material that much insight may be obtained in regard to existing conditions, the functioning of government, the character and plans of the Estates, and public opinion, such as it was. No single source for the study of Eighteenth-Century Bohemia is comparable to the bulky archival materials that accumulated around the *Desideria*. To a large extent these materials

[1] *Hungary in the Eighteenth Century* (Cambridge, 1910).

have not been utilized. Certain general characteristics have been culled here and there, resulting in over-emphasis on the Monarchy as a whole. On the other hand, some research has been done along specialized lines of development. The present volume offers the first intensive study of the innumerable and complex details of the *Desideria* as a whole, so far as they concern Bohemia.

In the maze of Eighteenth-Century bureaucratic scribbling interesting problems in the history of the Czech nation constantly protrude. Here is to be seen the struggle, largely theoretical and academic, to preserve the semblance of the independent Bohemian State in the midst of the highly practical attempts by Maria Theresa and Joseph II to weld the Habsburg Monarchy into a single, modern German state. Here the forces of weak Czech nationalism and powerful German imperialism, of medieval political conceptions and modern centralizing tendencies, are seen in conflict. Strife in politics is usually proof that in the economic and social spheres of daily life warfare is rampant. But the issues are more complex and confused. In the case of Bohemia the vast mass of the population favored the economic and social reforms of Maria Theresa and Joseph II, but the Estates representing the old order did not. There was, however, one exception to this. The Czech nation as a whole, where it expressed itself, was opposed to the Germanizing tendencies of Vienna. Here are found the roots of that Czech national revival which resulted four generations later in the Czechoslovak Republic.

This study was begun independently by the author as a result of an examination of the archives of Vienna and Prague just before the World War. Presented originally as a doctoral dissertation at Harvard University, it has been revised as a result of later researches. Some of the material on which the study rests has since been destroyed in street riots in Vienna, giving this analysis of it some value for that reason.

To the late Professor Archibald Cary Coolidge of Harvard University I owe many suggestions and criticisms from his ripe

knowledge and abiding interest in the history of the Habsburg
Monarchy. I am indebted to the directors of the archives
mentioned in the study and to numerous librarians for their
unfailing kindness. Acknowledgment is also made to Mrs.
Emily D. Wilkie, of the University of California Press, for
skillful editorial assistance in preparing the manuscript for
the press. To my parents, one of whom did not live to see
the publication of the study, is due my sincere appreciation
for their sympathetic interest and their kindly encouragement.

ROBERT J. KERNER.

ABBREVIATIONS

AKÖG	*Archiv für Kunde österreichischer Geschichtsquellen.*
AÖG	*Archiv für österreichische Geschichte.*
BGB	*Beiträge zur Geschichte Böhmens.*
BGW	*Die böhmische Gesellschaft der Wissenschaften.*
ČA	*Česká Akademie Císaře Františka Josefa pro Vědy, Slovesnost, a Umění.*
ČČH	*Český Časopis Historický.*
ČMKČ	*Časopis Musea Království Českého.*
ČMM	*Časopis Matice Moravské.*
Č N M Archiv	Český Narodní Museum Archiv.
DKAW	*Denkschriften, Kaiserliche Akademie der Wissenschaften, Wien.*
FIGÖ	*Forschungen zur inneren Geschichte Österreichs.*
FRA	*Fontes Rerum Austriacarum.*
GFDWKLB	*Gesellschaft zur Förderung deutscher Wissenschaft, Kunst, und Literatur in Böhmen.*
H H S Archiv	Haus- Hof- und Staats-Archiv.
H K Archiv	Hof-Kammer Archiv.
KAW	*Kaiserliche Akademie der Wissenschaften*, Wien.
KČSN	*Královská Česká Společnost Nauk.*
M I Archiv	Archiv des Ministeriums des Innern.
MIÖG	*Mittheilungen des Instituts für österreichische Geschichts-Forschung.*
MVGDB	*Mittheilungen der Verein für Geschichte der Deutschen in Böhmen.*
PČA	*Pojednání, České Akademie.*
S Archiv	Statthalterei Archiv.
SKAW	*Sitzungsberichte, Kaiserliche Akademie der Wissenschaften, Wien.*
SMSG	*Schriften der historisch-statistischen Sektion der k. k. mährisch-schlesischen Gesellschaft zur Beförderung des Ackerbaues, der Natur- und Landeskunde.*
S V Archiv	St. Vitus, Cathedral Archive.
VČA	*Věstník, České Akademie.*
VKČSN	*Věstník, Královské České Společností Nauk.*
Z Archiv	Zemský Archiv—Landes-Archiv.
ZVMS	*Zeitschrift des Vereins für die Geschichte Mährens und Schlesiens.*
ZČA	*Zprávy o Zasedání—České Akademie.*

NOTE.—In the Eighteenth Century the Austrian florin (60 kreuzers) fluctuated on the London Exchange from 9 florins to 9 florins 4 kreuzers for 1 £ sterling.

CONTENTS

VIII. FINANCE AND TAXATION   226
       I. The Financial Policy of the Habsburgs in Bohemia in
       the Eighteenth Century; II. The Land Tax in Bohemia in
       the Eighteenth Century; III. The Financial Policy of the
       Estates and the Government under Leopold II; IV. Ques-
       tions Pertaining to Taxation.

  IX. SERFDOM   273
       I. The Introduction; II. Serfdom under Leopold II; III.
       Revolt or Passive Resistance? IV. Civil or Military Rule
       for the Serfs? V. The Penal Code; VI. Was Robot to Be
       Abolished? VII. The Serf and the Bohemian Diet.

                        PART IV—SOCIAL

   X. RELIGION   309
       I. The Domination of the Jesuits; II. The Dawn of
       Toleration; III. The Question of Religious Toleration be-
       fore the Diet and the Government under Leopold II;
       IV. Other Religious Questions.

  XI. THE SCHOOL SYSTEM, GERMANIZATION AND THE CZECH
       REVIVAL   344
       I. The System of Education and the Progress of Germani-
       zation; II. The Attitude of the Diet and of the Govern-
       ment on the Question of Schools and of Germanization
       under Leopold II.

                           PART V

 XII. CONCLUSION   367

                           PART VI

       BIBLIOGRAPHY   375
       I. Bibliographical Guides and Publications; II. Sources in
       Manuscript and Print; III. Secondary Authorities: A. His-
       toriography; B. Political; C. Law and Judicial System;
       D. Economic; E. Social: 1. Religion; 2. Schools and Ger-
       manization.

       INDEX   407

PART I

INTRODUCTION

CHAPTER I

BOHEMIA BEFORE AND AFTER WHITE MOUNTAIN

THE golden age of Bohemia's history falls in the Fifteenth and Sixteenth Centuries. The government was medieval in structure and the power of the ruler was limited by a constitution. Protestantism was the religion of the very large majority of the Czechs, though Catholicism was tolerated. The Czech language was the official language of the government. Following the Battle of White Mountain (1620) and for a century thereafter, the government was partly absolute in form, it was intolerant of any creed other than Catholicism, and it was officially bilingual, Czech and German. When Joseph II died in 1790, the government was modern and absolute in form, tolerant in religion, and officially German.

To trace this remarkable evolution will be the task of this chapter, because a clear understanding of the main forces in Bohemian history is necessary to a comprehension of what happened in Bohemia and elsewhere in the Lands of the Habsburg Monarchy under Leopold II (1790-1792). This monarch came to the throne after his unfortunate brother, Joseph II (1780-1790), had died of a broken heart, despairing of the welfare of his possessions. He left behind him a costly war with Turkey and along with it the dangerous enmity of Prussia, a serious rebellion in the Austrian Netherlands, an almost similar movement in Hungary, and great unrest in other Lands belonging to the dynasty. An empty treasury, defiant Estates, and a restless peasantry were the heritage of Leopold II. Confronted with such a state of affairs, Leopold II issued Patents in all his Lands calling together their legislative assemblies to discuss the situation and to offer suggestions

3

and remedies. In Bohemia, this call was announced by the Royal Rescript of May 1, 1790.[1] Three great questions were to be treated by the assembled Diet, the question of the Constitution, of taxation and serfdom, and of all other grievances whether political, judicial, financial, or social. This was the origin of the three Desideria which were composed by the Bohemian Diet under Leopold II and which form the best basis for a knowledge of his reign and of the one that preceded it. They remind one of the French *Cahiers* of 1789 which, however they may have been composed, led to great things. It is in the light of these ideas that we shall pause to pick up a few threads of Bohemia's past.

I

BOHEMIA BEFORE WHITE MOUNTAIN

Under Charles IV (1346-1378) Bohemia became the leading state in Central Europe and Prague (Praha-Prag) the capital of the Holy Roman Empire. Latin was the official language of this cosmopolitan empire, Roman Catholicism its creed, and the increasing exaltation of the Estates or castes, accompanied by the gradual enserfment of the population, its apparent future development. Bohemia began to oppose these unmistakable tendencies a little more than a generation after the death of Charles IV, who had done so much for his adopted country. For two centuries the central thread of Bohemian history is a violent struggle for religious and intellectual freedom, a struggle for freedom from the shackles which the Holy Roman Empire had welded upon Central Europe. Necessarily the political, national, and social elements were nicely interwoven in this all-absorbing conflict which began with the burning of Hus at Constance (1415) and ended with the triumph of the Habsburgs and Jesuits at the Battle of White Mountain in 1620.

[1] M I Archiv, Carton 516. The document is printed in Kalousek, *České státní právo*, 2d edition (1892), p. 490.

Bohemia had obtained the leadership of Central Europe; it was incumbent upon it to bear the chief responsibility in the decisive events of the future. Twice Bohemia led in the struggle for religious and intellectual freedom [2]—in the wars waged by the Hussites (1414-1436) and in the Thirty Years' War (1618-1648). The former secured religious toleration for Bohemia long before it existed in any other state in Europe, but exposed it to a pernicious internal strife for two hundred years thereafter. Meanwhile, within the political and social fabric of Bohemia, the exaltation of the Estates and the degradation of a vigorous peasantry proceeded with an even faster stride because of the exhaustion of the peasants as a result of the Hussite wars. The fact that Bohemia had fought against the Catholic world—for the Holy Roman Empire in an effort to save its unity had sent its crusaders against the Hussites—in turn produced an unhealthy reaction against foreign influences which hardened the young nationalism of the Czechs. Thereafter Bohemia sought to isolate itself from the great currents which swept over Western Europe. With the discovery of the Americas came the shift of economic forces from the Mediterranean to the Atlantic, from Southern Europe to Western Europe, from Italy to Spain, England, and France. New ideas, culture, and wealth thenceforth came from the West instead of the South. It is a decisive but unfortunate fact that just at that moment Bohemia shut its doors to the West.[3] The result was momentous. Žižka and his embattled Hussites managed to defeat a crusading, though somewhat indifferent, Europe. The feudal Bohemian army which assembled on the slopes of White Mountain two centuries later, however, was no match for the newly equipped warriors of the West led by Maximilian of Bavaria. Bohemia had been absorbed too much in theological controversy, had tried

[2] See Palacký, *Geschichte von Böhmen*, (Prague, 1867) V, II Abt. Introduction v-vi. Palacký explains that thereafter in the West the Bohemians were hated, while in the East, Olešnický of Poland destroyed a budding Panslavism (vol. III, part III, 335-337).

[3] Rezek, *Dějiny Čech a Moravy*, 1648-1657, pp. 3-21. The introduction is excellent.

to isolate itself too much. The contrast was apparent not alone in military science, but in many other things. All their intellectual activity engulfed in sterile religious strife, the Czechs, in splendid isolation, looked down with disdain upon the great progress which Western Europe was making in the arts and sciences and in the material things of this world. Their narrowed struggle for intellectual freedom tended to develop into pettiness of ideal, their young and vigorous nationalism into haughty, disdainful pride and oversensitiveness, and their political constitution, till then bearing the earmarks of a strong kingship and a virile Bohemian peasantry, thenceforth took on more the garb of Poland and of Hungary, rather than that of France or England. These were the larger characteristics of Bohemia's historical development during the two centuries designated in the rest of Europe as those of the Renaissance and the Reformation.[4]

Looking more closely at the condition of things in Bohemia we are impressed with the power and the resources of the king in the Bohemian Constitution.[5] He had both a private and a royal income. Before the Battle of White Mountain he was private landowner of about one-ninth of the land of Bohemia.[6] His royal income, which the Diet could not touch in any way whatsoever, consisted of various incomes from the cities, from regal rights such as customs, mines, the salt monopoly, and the Jews, and finally from escheats and confiscations. A reasonable estimate has it that the king's income amounted to about one million florins yearly, four-fifths of which declared Stránský, a Seventeenth-Century Bohemian

---

[4] Ernest Denis, *La Bohême depuis la Montagne Blanche*, volume I, as well as his other works, *Hus et les Guerres des Hussites*, and *Fin de l'Indépendance de la Bohême*, 2 vols. (Paris, 1890). See further the works by Helfert, Bezold, Loserth, Höfler, and Count Lützow on the questions of Hus and the Hussites. For English readers Count Lützow's *Life and Times of Master John Hus* and his *Hussite Wars* are to be recommended.

[5] For the best account of Bohemian constitutional history see Kalousek, *České státní právo*. Fundamental documents may be found in *Böhmische Landtagsverhandlungen—České Sněmy*, II-V, and Jireček, *Codex Juris Bohemici*, II-V.

[6] A. Gindely, *Geschichte der böhmischen Finanzen von 1526 bis 1618* (*KAW*, 1868, pp. 12-24).

publicist, was enough to support both royal court and state administration. The king could well have lived 'on his own,' but in addition the Diet voted yearly large grants of taxes.'

The legislative power the king shared with the Diet. Alone he had no lawmaking power, except the right to issue ordinances through the Chancellery in executing the laws made by him and the Diet. He could summon, adjourn, and dissolve the Diet and the assemblies in the circles. He could make treaties concerning his dynasty, but those which in any way touched the public or private law of Bohemia required the consent of the Diet. In the performance of the duties with which the Bohemian Constitution intrusted him, he was assisted by certain institutions designated as royal in contrast to others over which the Diet had control.

The king of Bohemia directed the activities of three of the great feudal courts, the Court of the Treasury, the Court of Fiefs, and the Appellate Court. The Diet controlled the Court of the Land, namely, the supreme court of Bohemia, the Land Tables, and part of the Chancellery, as well as the courts of first instance on the manors of the Estates. The king's officials were placed over the Treasury, over the Court of the Fiefs of the crown of Bohemia, over a part of the Chancellery, and over the Subtreasury which ruled the financial destinies of the royal cities. The Great Officials of the Land, in other words the great feudal officials of Bohemia, were the Chief Chamberlain, the Chief Justice, the Chief Chancellor, the Chief Secretary, etc. These officials were under the direction of the Diet and were chosen from its members. Together with the judges of the Court of the Land, they made up the Royal Council which advised the king in the matter of appointments to the offices just named.* Thus in every field of activity, executive, legislative, and administrative, the Estates and the king each shared a part, the institutions under the care of the Estates being designated as belonging to the "Land," those under the king as being "Royal."

[7] Kalousek, *České státní právo*, 280-287.   [8] *Ibid.*, 364-379.

The Bohemian Diet in fable traces its origin to the story of Princess Libuše and her assembly held on the banks of the Elbe. Membership in the Diet was based on membership in the Estates, which meant Bohemian citizenship and the ownership of land. With the Hussite wars the clergy practically ceased to be an estate, the cities becoming legally the Third Estate, the nobles and the knights making up the other two. Besides the Great Diets, there were assemblies held by the Estates in the twelve local districts of Bohemia.[9] These were attended largely by the gentry unable to be present at the Diet at Prague, and there often the program of the latter was threshed out and deputies elected to represent the local gentry in the Great Diet.

It was the fundamental right of the Bohemian Diet to grant or to refuse to grant taxes. This ancient custom had been assured to Bohemia by the famous Great Privileges of King John in 1310.[10] In theory, the king was to live 'on his own,' from the revenues, of which we have already spoken, and this was designated as his Ordinary Income. What the Diet voted was, in theory, called the Extraordinary Income, although the Habsburgs soon made it "Ordinary" in practice. In the Fourteenth and Fifteenth Centuries this exclusive basis was abandoned and other taxes such as the house, capitation, chimney, and hop taxes, and the excises on wines, beer, and provisions were added. It has been calculated that about five per cent of this amount was spent for Bohemia and the rest, about ninety-five per cent, went to support the armies which had to win back Hungary for the Hungarians from the Turks.[11]

Legislative initiative belonged both to the king and to the

[9] Rieger, *Zřízení krajské v Čechách*, I, 96-166. This is the standard work on local government in Bohemia during this period.
[10] See the document in Kalousek, *České státní právo*, 563-65. "Collecta generalis quoque, quae vulgariter berna dicitur, nec per nos nec per successores nostros reges Boemiae ipsi regno debet imponi vel recipi, nisi in duobus casibus infrascriptis: ad coronationem videlicet regis, et ad quamlibet regis filiam maritandam. . . ."
[11] Gindely, *Gesch. der böhmischen Finanzen*, 17. See also Kalousek, p. 317, and Bachmann, *Österr. Reichsgeschichte*, 253.

Diet. An attempt in 1547 to make a conclusion of the Diet legal by a mere majority without the signature of the king ended in failure, although in 1609, after the disposal of the king's demands or postulata, it was voted that other matters, not in the postulata, should be considered.[12] The joint legislative power possessed by the king and Diet is best seen in their coöperation in drafting the constitution and in compiling and codifying the laws. King John in 1310 had issued the Magna Charta of Bohemia providing that taxes should be levied only with the consent of the Diet and that no law, whether public or private, could be changed without calling the Diet. Charles IV, in 1355, failed to secure the consent of the Bohemian Estates for his constitution and code, *Majestas Carolina,* which aimed to codify law and custom in Bohemia. Later on commissions elected by the Diet, in coöperation with the king prepared the Land Ordinances of 1499, 1549, and 1564. These contained the public and private law of Bohemia and come nearest to what are nowadays called constitutions, although it was the custom then to put into them a great deal of private law.

Local administration at this time was but little developed. It consisted of a knight and a noble, as captains of each of the twelve circles (counties), together with a very small *état.* The circle assemblies, already referred to, were very busy meetings and perhaps more truly represented the nation than the Diet itself. We shall hear of them again.[13]

From this very brief sketch it will be seen that the Bohemian Constitution was not what the Polish Constitution became, nor what the English was. It would easily have worked like the latter under a virile monarch who had no other country over which to rule. It gave just enough power to the king to make his influence a real one; it gave the Estates room enough, in case the king were weak, to plunge Bohemia into anarchy similar to that of Poland. Besides the personality of the ruler, geographical conditions were a factor

[12] Kalousek, 325-50.   [13] Rieger, *Zřízení krajské v Čechách,* I, 96-166.

in molding the future of the Czech people. Bohemia was placed in the very center of Europe—it was the crossroads of Central European politics. Here was no English channel to protect it from an invading foe and to transform the second generation of a foreign dynasty into natives; nor was the Bohemian Constitution saved as was Hungary's by its relations with Turkey. And finally, although the political genius of the English and Hungarian gentry was undoubted it does not seem clear that the Bohemian statesmen or diplomats of that day were in any way decidedly inferior to their contemporaries.

Like all medieval kingdoms, Bohemia had its share of foreign kings after 1306 when the native Přemyslides died out. The Luxemburgs, the Jagellonians of Poland, and the Habsburgs of Austria succeeded each other. So it came about that the Estates managed to secure the Magna Charta of 1310 when the Luxemburgs came to the throne. They increased greatly their power under the Jagellonians, and obtained the Five Articles of 1526 when the Habsburgs definitely linked their destinies with Bohemia and Hungary after the Jagellonian king, Louis, lost his life at the disastrous battle of Mohacs against the Turks. As long as the rulers down to Ferdinand I of Habsburg (1526-1564) were indifferent in the matter of religion or even were Utraquists as was George Poděbrad, it did not matter. But the definite accession of the Habsburgs under Ferdinand I distinctly altered the situation.

The Habsburgs brought with them three things of the greatest danger to Bohemia. They were absolutists, while Bohemia was a constitutional state; they were strong Catholics, while two-thirds of Bohemia was Protestant; and they were German, while two-thirds of Bohemia was Czech. Moreover, Ferdinand I was also ruler of the Habsburg Hereditary Lands and King of Hungary. The relation of the Catholic Austrian Habsburgs to the Catholic Spanish Habsburgs and their adherence to Rome was not likely to help a Protestant Bohemia. Ferdinand I became the father of Austrian centralization when he created the Secret Council, the Central Treasury, and the War Council, which in course of time became respectively the State Council and later the Cabinet of Ministers, the Ministry of Finance, and the Ministry of War of the entire Habsburg state.[14] In accepting election by the Diet (and at that time the Bohemian Diet refused to accept his claims of heredity through his wife, Anna, of the Luxemburg line[15]), Ferdinand I in 1526 confirmed the Compacts of Basel (1437) as the basis of the religious situation. These provided that communion "both in the flesh and blood of God" should be allowed the Bohemians by the Roman Catholic Church.[16] Thus Bohemia for nearly a century had existed in religion, Utraquist and Catholic, as it had long been in nationality, Czech and German. Meanwhile, during this time the Bohemian Brethren had been formed, and they clamored for a legal position.[17] Ferdinand I failed in 1537 to secure the union of the Old Utraquists (as the Hussites were called in distinction from the Bohemian Brethren) and the Roman Catholics. By this time also the Lutherans and the Calvinists were asking for legal recognition in the toleration which the two old religions enjoyed. Finally, in 1556, came the Jesuits and the various religious camps armed for the struggle, at first in the legislative halls of the Diet, and a half century later on the battlefield.[18] An attempt by the Bohemian Estates in 1575 to secure the confirmation of the *Confessio Bohemica*, the Bohemian Confession, more closely allied to the teachings of Calvin and the Bohemian Brethren, resulted only in the practical legal acceptance of the Lutherans. The union of the remains of the Old Utraquists and the declining Roman Catholic Church in Bohemia was consummated in

[14] Rosenthal, "Die Behördeorganisation Kaiser Ferdinands I" (*AÖG*, 1867, XIX, 51-144).

[15] Kalousek, 202 ff.

[16] Count Lützow, *Bohemia*, 174, gives the conclusion as follows: " . . . the Bohemians and Moravians who received the flesh and blood of God in both kinds were true Christians, and genuine sons of the Church."

[17] See Gindely, *Gesch. der Böhmischen Brüder* (Prague, 1857) and Gindely, *Quellen zur Gesch. der Böhmischen Brüder*, II.

[18] Rezek, *Gesch. der Regierung Ferdinands I in Böhmen.*

1593. In spite of this union, two-thirds of Bohemia was
Protestant, respectively Lutheran, Bohemian Brethren, and
Calvinist in point of numbers. The Protestants were pre-
ponderantly Czech. The other third was Roman Catholic,
mostly German in speech. It became imperative for a Protestant country ruled by a Catholic sovereign in an intolerant
age, that this condition *de facto* should be recognized *de jure*.
Finally, after long and intricate negotiations, in which Václav
Budovec distinguished himself, the famous Letter of Majesty
of 1609 was wrung from the unwilling and imbecile Rudolph
II (1576-1612).[19]

The Letter of Majesty confirmed the Confession of 1575
and gave to the Bohemian Estates, then Protestant, the
right to supervise the University of Prague and to elect and
oversee the members of the Protestant and Catholic-Utraquist
consistories. An Agreement signed at the same time between
the Estates sub Una (Catholics) and the Estates sub Utraque
(Protestants) guaranteed full religious freedom, in which even
the serfs were to share. Full rights were given to Protestant
landlords to appoint priests to livings in their gift and both
parties were to be allowed to build churches and to worship
freely on the lands belonging to the crown.[20] Thus a complete
religious toleration was secured on paper, but in reality this
signified only a truce. The last provision gave occasion for
new friction. The Catholics gained courage when they re-
flected that the intolerant Ferdinand II (1618-1637), then
Archduke of Styria, was heir to the throne. The way in which
he had brought Styria back to the bosom of the Church of
Rome inspired the little band of Jesuits who were stronger
than their numbers showed. After the "confirmation" of
Ferdinand II as King of Bohemia, it was only a matter of

[19] Gindely, *Geschichte der Ertheilung des böhmischen Briefes,* and K.
Krofta, *Majestat Rudolfa II* (Prague, 1909). In addition, see Gindely,
Rudolph der Zweite und seine Zeit (1600-12), 2 vols. (Prague, 1862-68) as
well as Czerwenka, *Geschichte der Evang. Kirche in Böhmen,* I, last five chapters, and Glücklich, "Václav Budovec z Budova. Korrespondence z let
1579-1619" (*Historický Archiv,* no. 30).
[20] Gindely, *Rudolph der Zweite und seine Zeit,* I, 68 ff.

time when the misunderstandings would turn into an armed conflict. It was the struggle of a constitutional state against the new absolutism, of a weak and necessarily disunited Protestantism against the reformed Catholic Church marshaled by the Jesuits, of a Slavic nation against a German dynasty. History knows few contrasts more interesting than this.

II

THE BATTLE OF WHITE MOUNTAIN AND THE LAND ORDINANCE OF 1627

The Czechs lost the Battle of White Mountain [21] on November 8, 1620, isolated in the game of diplomacy and poorly led by their new king, Frederick of the Palatinate, whom they had elected in the place of the dethroned Ferdinand II. It was a battle of the kind which decide the fate of nations, and "the destiny of the country was henceforth in the hands of foreigners, who had neither comprehension nor sympathy with its former institutions." [22] So complete was the victory of the Catholic forces and so absolute the moral imbecility of many of those who posed as the leaders of the cause of Bohemia, that in a very short while that country was deserted by the Estates who had brought about the troubles. The punishment fell on the people, the loyal Catholics and the serfs, who for the most part had little to do with them. [23] Within a few hours after the Battle of White Mountain, Ferdinand II was master of Bohemia. In 1627 he issued the Reformed Land Ordinance, and the Treaty of Westphalia in 1648 adjudged the Czech émigrés to perpetual exile. In a little over a generation Bohemia had lost its most important political rights, three-fourths of its nobility, its most eminent citizens, its schools of learned men, and practically its independence.

[21] Krebs, *Die Schlacht am weissen Berge*, 35 ff.
[22] Gindely, *Geschichte des Dreissigjährigen Krieges*, IV, or *Geschichte der Gegenreformation in Böhmen*, p. 83.
[23] See the Desideria on the Constitution, 1790, M I Archiv, Carton 516.

It would be digressing too much to relate in detail the course of events in that generation, but a few of the most important facts may be noted here. The punishment meted out to Bohemia was as decisive as it was severe. About three-fourths of the manors of Bohemia were confiscated—their value amounted to more than two hundred and fifty millions of dollars in our money.[24] It has been estimated that over 30,000 families fled from Bohemia immediately after the Battle of White Mountain and that after the Thirty Years' War but 900,000[25] inhabitants remained in a country where formerly about 3,000,000 had made their homes. The wealth thus confiscated was given to the conquering warriors and to the zealous Jesuits and priests who had made up the imperial army. From that time down to the end of the third quarter of the Eighteenth Century the Jesuits held a predominant position in Bohemia. To them and to other religious orders, together with the coöperation of the new Bohemian nobility, was entrusted the task of reconverting that part of the Protestants, which had been left in Bohemia. The Jesuits were given charge of the University and the care of the gymnasia, while the Piarists took over for the most part the lowest schools. To them in the course of the next century is attributed chiefly the destruction of the Czech literature and the downfall of the language.

But that was not all of the punishment.[26] The Constitution

[24] See the standard source work on the confiscations: T. V. Bílek, *Dějiny konfiskaci v Čechách po r. 1618*, 2 vols. (Prague, 1882-1883). Introduction I, 1-cl. On page cxlvii Bílek states that out of 926 manors 491 were confiscated completely, 253 partially, and only 182 left wholly untouched. See also C. d'Elvert, *Die Bestrafung der böhmischen Rebellion*, for the years 1620-1629, Krones, *Handbuch der Geschichte Oesterreichs*, III, 439, and Toman, *Schicksal des böhmischen Staatsrechtes in den Jahren 1620 bis 1627* (Prague, 1870).

[25] See Pekař, *Kniha o Kosti*, II, 161 ff. F. A. Slavík, "O popisu Čech po třicetileté valce" (*Zprávy Zemského Archivu Království Českého*, III, Prague, 1910) has much that gives light on the situation in Bohemia after the war. Tomek, *Sněmy české*, 19-21, calculated it at 800,000.

[26] The two most reliable accounts of the punishment which was meted out to Bohemia are to be found in Kalousek, *České státní právo*, 391 ff. and in Gindely, *Geschichte der Gegenreformation* (Leipzig, 1894). Many of the documents are to be found in the appendix to Kalousek and in the *Obnovené právo a zřízení zemské dědičného království českého—Die Verneuerte Landes-Ordnung des Erb-Königreichs Böhmen*, 1627. Hermengild Jireček, editor. (Prague, 1888).

of Bohemia had as yet been untouched in this wholesale destruction and confiscation of all material and spiritual things that had been Czech. The punishment must be made lasting, therefore not only the lucky Ferdinand II but his allies took counsel as to just what was to be done. Maximilian of Bavaria's reward was the vote of the Electorate of the Palatinate, so he was called on for advice in regard to the fate of political Bohemia. The Spanish Court, with which Ferdinand II had just made a treaty of inheritance by which the Spanish Habsburgs were to inherit the Lands of the Austrian Habsburgs on the dying out of their line, had subsidized Ferdinand II's army and pensioned his Secret Council, because they hoped some day to ascend the throne of Bohemia. This could hardly be done unless Protestantism were uprooted and the Constitution thoroughly reformed. The Court of Rome, which had laid a tithe on church property in Italy in order to aid Ferdinand II, was ready under Nuncio Caraffa for a fight to extermination. Ferdinand II needed the support of both, in the first place to retain Bohemia, and in the second place to make headway in the Holy Roman Empire against the Protestants. Had he been left to himself Ferdinand II would very likely have been less severe, because it was an undeniable fact that within a short time after the Battle of White Mountain he was punishing those who had not rebelled. How, for instance, would a patriotic Czech, loyal to the Habsburgs, view his open destruction of Bohemia's political liberties? To such a man it was enough to banish the Protestants and to confiscate their material wealth. Why should he suffer the loss of political rights? This and the uncertainty of the contest of Catholicism against Protestantism outside of Bohemia caused Ferdinand to work in secret to reform the Constitution and to reserve the publication of this reformed land ordinance until the triumph of the Catholics in Central Europe was certain.

For three years after the Battle of White Mountain Bohemia was subjected to military rule. In the years between 1620 and 1625 enormous taxes were gathered by virtue of royal

patents issued contrary to the letter of the Constitution. The
Council which collected them asked when Ferdinand II intended to call the Diet, since he had already, by a document
written into the Land Tables, confirmed the continuity of the
Constitution and had promised to call the Diet.[27] He asked
them to have patience, at the same time stating that the Constitution would have to be reformed. In 1625 a Commission
made up of six Germans and two Czechs was appointed for
this purpose. The famous adventurer Wallenstein, better
known for his brilliant military exploits than for his Czech
patriotism, and Prince Lichtenstein, a noble of undoubted
loyalty to the Habsburgs, were the two Czechs on the Commission. But they were not always present, and it is clear
that the result was almost wholly the work of Germans. The
deliberations of this Commission were secret. Only a few of
the government officials of Bohemia knew exactly the status
of the work, and they knew it only indirectly because they
were asked to give their opinions on the faults of the Bohemian Constitution.[28] In April, 1626, Wallenstein defeated
Mansfeld at Dessau, over-ran Silesia, and together with Tilly,
who had just triumphed over Christian of Denmark at Sutter,
brought Holstein, Schleswig, Jutland, and Mecklenburg into
imperial nands before the summer of 1626. Thus a Czech
adventurer helped to make the emperor's triumph complete,
and made possible the wholesale confiscation of Bohemia's
constitutional liberties. The Battle of White Mountain had
resulted in the material and spiritual subjection of Bohemia,
the victories of Wallenstein and Tilly opened the way for its
political subjection. Toward the end of 1626 the contents of
the Renewed Land Ordinance of Ferdinand II were made
known to the loyal government officials in Bohemia. They
were horrified. The theory of state rights lost by conquest
was stamped numberless times within the document, and, as
one authority stated, the punishment of the rebels literally

[27] See Kalousek, *České státní právo*, 399 ff.
[28] *Ibid.*, 423.

stares one in the face. It was exacted from the very population which had remained loyal to the dynasty.

In glancing briefly at the contents of the Land Ordinance of 1627, as this document was called, we shall understand why it was a penal document. The Estates in 1790,[29] pointing to the century and a half of tried loyalty which Bohemia had given to the Habsburgs, asked in their Desideria on the Constitution, that such parts of this famous state paper as showed that it was penal in motive be abolished "as unfit for a brave and a loyal people."

On May 10, 1627, Ferdinand II promulgated the "Renewed" Land Ordinance by means of a royal patent, without the consent or advice of the Estates.[30] It was an act of absolutism, not constitutionalism. Fearing, however, that his loyal Catholic Bohemians might cause trouble, Ferdinand II issued on May 29, 1627, the Confirmation of Privileges in which, with certain exceptions, he confirmed the ancient liberties of Bohemia.[31] On reading the Patent of Promulgation, the Land Ordinance, and the Confirmation of Privileges, one is at once face to face with a difficult problem. The Patent, after discoursing in general that Bohemia had rebelled *in forma universitatis,* makes certain remarks on changes in private law (as distinguished from public or constitutional law). Inserted among these changes is a statement to the effect that the sovereign reserved to himself the right to make and change laws (*jus legis ferendae*).[32] In this connection it would evidently refer to private law. In the Land Ordinance under article VIII in the last of the articles on the power of the Bohemian Diet, the right of legislation (*jus legis ferendae*) is reserved to the sovereign and his successors. In the Confirmation of Privileges, with two exceptions, Ferdinand II

[29] The Desideria on the Constitution, 1790. M I Archiv, Carton 516.
[30] Jireček, *Obnovené právo,* pp. 1-7.
[31] Kalousek, *České státní právo,* Appendix, pp. 600-62.
[32] Jireček, *Obnovené právo,* p. 5. The German text runs: "Auch darbey Uns nicht allein die königliche Macht, solche Unsere Landes-Ordnung zu mehren, zu ändern, zu bessern, und was sonst das Jus legis ferendae mit sich bringt, vorzubehalten. . . ."

confirmed the ancient rights, privileges, and liberties of the
Bohemian Estates. The two exceptions were the two diplomas, the Letter of Majesty and the Agreement already mentioned above, forced from Rudolph II and the statement that
anything in the ancient liberties of Bohemia contrary to the
Land Ordinance was null and void. Thus with these two
exceptions one may say that hereafter the Bohemian Constitution was the Land Ordinance of 1627 and the old political
rights not contrary to it. The question naturally arises
whether the sovereign had reserved to himself merely the right
to legislate in private law or to make and alter the Constitution also at his own will. Over this question a great controversy has been waged, and it remained a live issue[33] until the
establishment of the Czechoslovak Republic in 1918.

The Czechs have argued that only private law was meant
and not constitutional law and that the great changes carried
out by Maria Theresa and Joseph II were therefore wholly
unconstitutional. The Germans for the most part have held
that the reservation extends to constitutional law, that in
reality, indeed, no constitution existed; there were no such
things as historic Bohemian constitutional rights—all depended on the will of the sovereign. The former read the documents literally and gave them the strict construction. The latter, interpreting the Constitution broadly, put greater weight
on Ferdinand II's supposed intentions and on the actual practice of the Habsburg sovereigns. The situation was the result
of Ferdinand II's personal character. He would have destroyed
the Bohemian State entirely, had he been sure that the war
in its course would not have undone his work. Instead of that

[33] Gindely, "Vznik obnoveného zřízení zemského" (*Právník*, XXXIII,
17-94) and his *Geschichte der Gegenreformation in Böhmen*, state the point of
view which German writers without exception accept. V. V. Tomek, *Sněmy
české dle obnoveného zřízení zemského Ferdinanda II* (Prague, 1868), Kalousek, *České státní právo*, and Baxa, *K dějinam veřejného práva v zemích
koruny České* (Prague, 1906) best state the Czech point of view. The clearest
of the latter is Kalousek against whom particularly Gindely wrote the first
article mentioned above. L. Eisenmann, *Le Compromis austro-hongrois*
(Paris, 1904), has assumed neutral ground and so in general has E. Denis,
La Bohême depuis la Montagne Blanche, I (Paris, 1903). Such writers as
Luschin v. Ebengreuth, Huber-Dopsch, Adolph Bachmann, Veith, Kostetzky
and Winter support the German view, while Rieger, Čelakovský, Toman and
Kapras stand by the Czech point of view.

it was better to leave matters as veiled as he did. He could count on holding in line the new cosmopolitan nobility which were his creatures. So far as we are interested in the subject, it is important to note that before 1791 and for a half century thereafter no one, either of the Estates or of the scholars, appears to have pointed out this question. If the Estates of 1790 knew of the difficulty, they were too tactful to state it. Instead of arguing with the king whether, by the documents promulgated by his predecessors, he had the right to change the Constitution without their consent, they demanded among other things that a new constitution be drawn up. At least the old one was to be reformed so that the Estates should be consulted in the legislation. Some members of the Estates, we shall see, demanded that all laws, constitutional and private, should receive the consent of the Estates before having validity.

The actual changes carried out by the Land Ordinance of 1627 were of a lasting and radical character. The Bohemian kingship became hereditary in both male and female branches of the Habsburg family, and the old custom of "accepting" or "electing" the king was done away with.[34] The king named the date of coronation, and called and adjourned the Diet. The clergy were restored to the number of the Estates and given first place before the nobles.[35] Before 1620, each Estate had one vote, i.e. they voted entirely by colleges (*curia*); after 1627 in many deliberations each member of the Estates of the clergy, the nobility, or the knights had one vote, while the City Estate in practice had one vote altogether. All religious toleration was done away with, and the Estates through the clergy became active agents in the conversion of the people of Bohemia. All Protestants who did not allow themselves to be converted, were ordered out of the country. The Roman Catholic faith was declared the "only reigning" faith.[36] In political matters the king was an absolute monarch. He re-

[34] Jireček, *Obnovené právo*, A I-III.
[35] *Ibid.*, A 24.
[36] *Ibid.*, A 23. See Czerwenka, *Geschichte der Evangelischen Kirche in Böhmen*, II (1870), 576-622, 631 ff.

served to himself the legislative power and the initiative.[37] In the case of government officials great changes were also made. All officials—and that included the officials who had charge of the institutions heretofore under the control of the Diet and who had been called Officials of the Land—became officials of the king, i.e. Royal Land Officials. The two Castle Counts of Karlův Týn (Karlstein), who had guarded the crown jewels and the archives, were suppressed, and the incomes from their offices and lands were turned into the royal treasury. In the appointment of officials, Ferdinand II bound himself to get due report about the candidates, but all officials upon entering into office were to take the oath to the king and not, as heretofore, to the country. In other words, the government officials became the servants of the dynasty and not of the country.[38]

The Court of the Land ceased to be the supreme court of Bohemia—that is, the court of last instance. The question of life and death was especially reserved for the sovereign and nearly all cases could be appealed to him. Neither could this court hand down decisions which would in the least legislate as well as adjudicate. The decisions of all of the courts of Bohemia were delivered in the name of the king and not, as heretofore, in the name of the country. Judicial procedure instead of being oral and public was henceforth secret and written. The king took upon himself the complete right of granting Bohemian citizenship, i.e. the *inkolat*, a right which had previously belonged to the Estates, although he had always had the right of ennoblement. The German language was made officially the equal of Czech in the government offices and courts of Bohemia.[39] In substance all other ancient

[37] Jireček, *Obnovené právo*, A VIII.
This article reads as follows in the German text: "Wir behalten auch Uns und Unsern Erben, nachkommenden Königen, ausdrücklich vor, in diesem Unserm Erb-Königreich Gesätz und Recht zu machen, und alles das jenige, was das Jus legis ferendae so Ihnen als dem König allein zustehet, mit sich bringt."
[38] *Ibid.*, A, IX, XXXIX, XLII-XLVII; the implication is that only Bohemians were to be appointed to offices. They could hold them only for five years and not for life as before.
[39] *Ibid.*, A X, F 75, 82, D 49, C 1, B 4, A 20, B 12, C 2-5, D 47, F 4, J 6. See Kalousek, *České státní právo*, 443 ff.

rights and usages were confirmed—but we may add that it is not easy to find them, so completely did the Land Ordinance legislate in all directions in its three hundred odd printed octavo pages.

Among these may be mentioned, however, the following. The State still had its being and it will hereafter be noticed in what a crippled manner it eked out its existence. The relations to the Holy Roman Empire were left untouched, and while that empire existed, the Bohemian State necessarily had to be continued, for it gave the Habsburgs a vote in the election of the emperor. The right of electing a sovereign after the complete dying out of the Habsburgs was left to the Bohemian Diet. The Bohemian Royal Treasury, the Chancellery, the Mint, and the Fiefs—for Moravia and Silesia belonged to the Crown Lands of Bohemia—were left untouched. In such matters, the Bohemian Diet remained the guardian of the Bohemian Crown Lands, and treaties disposing of parts of these, to be legal, were always submitted to it for ratification. In other words, the existence of the Bohemian State was undoubted, although its liberties had been much curtailed and for a century and a quarter after the Battle of White Mountain no thought was given to amalgamating the administration which existed under the Bohemian Crown with that of the Austrian Hereditary Lands.[40] Remarkable among the privileges allowed to the Estates may be mentioned that, both in the Land Ordinance and in the Confirmation of Privileges, Ferdinand II promised to take no taxes except such as were granted by the Diet.[41] This remained the greatest power, perhaps the only real one, which the Bohemian Diet retained after the Battle of White Mountain.

Thus in a little less than a decade a complete transformation in the government of Bohemia had been effected. In public or constitutional law absolutism was stamped on every page of the Land Ordinance of 1627. In private law, the Roman spirit superseded the slow process of amalgamation which had been going on between Slavic country law and German city

[40] Kalousek, 449 ff.   [41] *Ibid.*, appendix, 602.

law. In the former the political rights of the Czechs were destroyed, in the latter their spiritual and social privileges were canceled. "The short dream of glory of the Protestants" was over, and the fury of the Jesuits freely took its course.

III

BOHEMIA AFTER WHITE MOUNTAIN

The central thread of Bohemian history from the Thirty Years' War to the death of Joseph II (1790) is financial and political oppression under German domination. Down to the accession of Maria Theresa in 1740, Bohemia was handed over to the taxgatherer, to the recruiting officer, and to the Jesuits. Its treatment resembled that which Turkey often bestowed upon a conquered province. After 1748, when the Habsburg dynasty had lost Silesia to Prussia, there were several reasons why Bohemia should be better treated. There was the necessity of preserving the Lands of the Austrian Monarchy against Prussia, of rehabilitating and increasing the revenues of the State, and of atoning for the sins which the Habsburgs had committed in Bohemia in the days of White Mountain and after.

The treatment which Bohemia received at the hands of the Habsburgs during the first century after the Thirty Years' War brought agony to patriotic Czechs and disgust to loyal Germans. The history of the Bohemian Diet which met annually during this period is repeated and wearisome monotony, for, having broken the power of the Estates in Bohemia, the Habsburg dynasty busied itself in wars with Turkey and France, and especially in the conflict for the Spanish Succession. In this state of affairs Bohemia became a province and was neglected. The membership of the Diet fell off to one-half, even to one-fourth, of those who had attended before 1620.[48] Circle assemblies were discontinued by the dynasty;

[48] See M I Archiv, Carton 534, IV H. 3. Böhmen in genere, to 1692, Landtags Postulata. See the document dated January 18, 1677. The Diet of

they were regarded as hotbeds of revolution."⁴² Instead of short Diets (which were inexpensive to the Estates), the regular Diets tended to extend into many months, so that only the richest of the Estates could attend them, and they were generally well filled with government officials.⁴³ Ferdinand III in 1640, after the Diet had existed thirteen years without legislative initiative, gave it that right. In minor matters "which do not encroach upon our person, authority, and regalia," stated the document, "the Estates with the consent of our Diet commissioners, may have the right to propose and to decide." ⁴⁵ Had the old nobility been in the Diet to take hold of matters, perhaps this right might have been used with effect, but ennui was too much the order of the day. In 1714 Charles VI established the Permanent Executive Committee (*Zemský Výbor-Landes-Ausschuss*) in order to bring order out of the Diet's chaos. This Committee was to be composed of two members elected from each of the four Estates. Its duty was to look after that part of the administration which was entrusted to the Diet consisting for the most part of collection of the taxes.⁴⁶ It may have served as a powerful lever in the hands of the nobility, but at the same time it offered the government an opportunity to control the affairs of the Diet through the control of the elections to this Committee. It was easy to see which would win out—an apathetic, disinterested, unnational nobility or a quasi-absolute monarchy.

Before such a nobility the Pragmatic Sanction was laid for approval. The consent came without the slightest opposition,

---

1627 was attended by seventeen prelates, seventy-two nobles, fifty knights, and the representatives of the cities. In 1651, twelve prelates, twenty-four nobles, and twenty-four knights were present. In 1671, thirteen prelates, eighteen nobles, and fifteen knights attended the Diet, while the session in 1720 which accepted the Pragmatic Sanction consisted of eighteen prelates, twenty-three nobles, eighteen knights, and twenty-three deputies from the cities, a total of eighty-three.

⁴³ Rieger, *Zřízení krajské*, I, 270-282.
⁴⁴ Tomek, *Sněmy české*, 96-106, and fn. 1.
⁴⁵ Kalousek, *České státní právo*, Appendix, 618.
⁴⁶ M I Archiv, Carton 590, Ständische Verfassung, contains the instructions of this committee. See also Flieder, *Zemský výbor v království českém, jeho organisace v letech 1714-1783*, 1-22.

so much so that one is almost tempted to say that its importance was misunderstood.[47] This famous document which was accepted by the Bohemian Estates in 1720 changed the union which had previously existed between the lands of the Habsburgs from a personal to a real union and the succession was settled once and for all as indivisible and in both sexes. It was the foundation stone of the Habsburg Monarchy thereafter, and was the first step toward the great centralizing reforms of Maria Theresa and Joseph II.

If we examine the course of events in other matters during this century of punishment we shall find the same inability on the part of the Estates to stem the tide of centralization and Germanization. The serf belonged to the rebellious race. By the Land Ordinance of 1627 he was all of a sudden subjected to the full force of the enslaving Roman law.[48] Furthermore, he fell into the hands of a lord who did not know his language and cared less about it. The patriarchal care that his old lord had given him was abruptly changed into economic oppression. His new master wished to get rich quickly.[49] Conditions became so bad that in 1680 the Bohemian peasant revolted. The revolt was put down by military force, and the first of that series of disastrous serf patents was issued. This, at one fell swoop, canceled all the rights which the serf possessed before the Battle of White Mountain. "It codified the conditions brought on by force and out of the injustice of the lord created justice."[50]

On this legal basis the monarchy of Charles VI, Maria

[47] See Landtagsschlüsse 1720, and for the significance of the Pragmatic Sanction for Bohemia and for literature on this subject see: Baxa, *K dějinam veřejného práva v zemích koruny české*, Prague, 1906, pp. 8 ff.

[48] Ott, *Beiträge zur Receptionsgeschichte des röm-canon. Processes in dem böhm. Ländern*, VII, 259 ff.

[49] Pekař, *Kniha o Kosti*, II, 112 ff.

[50] Grünberg, *Die Bauernbefreiung*, I, 75-130. Pekař, *Kniha o Kosti*, II, 89 ff. The Patent of 1680 is printed in Grünberg, *Die Bauernbefreiung*, II, 3-5. The most important passage is ". . . wollen wir derentwegen hiemit durchgehend statuiret und verordnet haben, dass auf keine Privilegia deren unterthänigen Gemeinden, Bauernschafften, oder Unterthanen in diesem Unsern Erb-Königreich Böhmen Reflexion zu machen, welche sie vor der Zeit der abscheulichen Rebellion gehabt oder genossen, sondern, dass dieselbe für allerdings abgethan, aufgehoben, und cassiret zu achten. . . ."

Theresa, and Joseph II built its legislation. The serf was to render regularly three days of *corvée* (*robot*) weekly, besides an unlimited amount in special cases. But even this sweeping document which literally took everything away from the serf and substituted almost unmitigated slavery was a dead letter, for down to 1736 not one case was brought by the government against the oppression of the lords in the few cases where the Patent allowed such action to be brought. This punishment was heaped upon all serfs, even those who had not rebelled in 1618 or 1680. The attempt to regulate the conditions of serfdom in 1717 ended in a rehash of the Patent of 1680. The Patent of 1738, called forth because the peasantry was falling in arrears in paying the government taxes, was a very important step backward. The first two patents were indefinite and allowed an interpretation in some places favorable to the serf. The Patent of 1738 codified all that the lord could desire, as sharply and as clearly as possible. The reign of Charles IV (1711-1740) ended with a third, but likewise unfortunate attempt to regulate the relations between the lord and the serf. This lends belief to the interpretation that it was the State which brought about the social and economic ruin of the Bohemian peasant and not the landlord. All of these patents were issued by the sovereigns themselves, the Diet had nothing to do with them at all.[51]

Closely connected with the welfare of the State, of the landlord, and of the serf was the question of taxation and the granting of taxes by the Bohemian Diet. What the Diet in Bohemia granted was of course determined largely by the amount that the sovereign wished to get from all of his territories. So far as the Lands of the Bohemian Crown and the Austrian Hereditary Lands were concerned a certain "ratio" existed. As early as 1541 the Bohemian Lands paid two-thirds and the Austrian one-third, and the arrangement of 1682 lightened the Bohemian Lands by one-fourth of a point out

[51] Grünberg, *Bauernbefreiung*, I, 134-141; II, 13-38. See also Pekař, *Kniha o Kosti*, II, 161 ff. and Rieger, *Zřízení krajské v Čechách*, II.

of eighteen because of the loss of the Lusatias. The ratio, therefore, stood at 11¾ to 6¼.[52] One-half of the former quota was paid by Bohemia, one-sixth by Moravia, and one-third by Silesia. In other words down to 1748, Bohemia alone was paying 32.6 per cent of the total tax quota of all the Bohemian and Austrian Lands. For military aid alone Bohemia was paying much more than Hungary and that did not include the rest of the income from the provincial and royal revenues of Bohemia of which total only about 5 per cent was spent in Bohemia. It is an undoubted fact that Bohemia, in spite of the neglect and shabby treatment it received during this period, was the richest and most steady source of revenue which the Habsburgs had in the first century after the Thirty Years' War.[53]

In order to raise the huge sums which the Habsburg Monarchy needed, the king demanded ever greater amounts, and the Estates were forced to increase the rate of taxation. In this is not reckoned the vast revenues which the king obtained from the sources which we have mentioned above, such as customs, mines, salt, tobacco, etc., which in this period amounted to about one-third of the gross revenue annually gotten from Bohemia at this time.[54] With this the Bohemian Estates had really nothing to do. That was the business of the king, and we shall see that, as the Eighteenth Century progressed, the shrewd Habsburg monarchs increased the revenue over which the Diet had no power at all until in 1790 it almost equaled that obtained from the taxation to which the Diet subjected Bohemia.

[52] M I Archiv, Steuer-Fusses, Fasc. (Carton) 576, 71 ex Jänner, 1748, Carton 575, 5 von J. 1691, Böhmische Landtagsverhandlungen, I, 532 ff. In secondary accounts one may get the general outlines of this matter in Huber-Dopsch, Österr. Reichsgeschichte, 211-212, Mensi, Österr. Finanzgeschichte, 13-14, as well as in Toman, Das böhmische Staatsrecht, 96 ff.; D'Elvert, Finanzgeschichte, XXV, 222 ff.

[53] Compare for instance the statements in Huber-Dopsch, Österr. Reichsgeschichte, 211-212, on Hungary: H K Archiv, A B 218 D. 1760-1763, Nos. 105-127, H S S Archiv, Staatsrat Akten 2510 in 1780 on Netherlands and Hungary with M I Archiv, Carton 575, 5 vom Jahre 1691 and Carton 576, 71 ex Jänner 1748.

[54] Based on a calculation in the documents cited fn. 53. See the Chapter on Finance.

In Bohemia, before the Battle of White Mountain, the lord paid as much in taxes as the serf, a great contrast to the condition of things in Poland and Hungary.[55] After that event, however, it became more and more the custom to heap all on the serf. In 1627 Ferdinand II, instead of asking for certain taxes, which were often difficult to collect, requested outright a stipulated sum—800,000 florins. Thereafter down to 1740 the bargaining between the king and the Estates was not in taxes but in amounts of money. The Estates after the conclusion of each bargain would divide it up into taxes and then collect them. The amount asked by the kings of Bohemia grew enormously during the course of this period. During the first generation after the Land Ordinance generally between five and eight hundred thousand florins were demanded and less than five hundred regularly obtained. At the end of the Seventeenth Century about a million and a half were asked and obtained, and in the War of the Spanish Succession and the Turkish War (1736-39) the four million mark was often reached.[56] The Land Tax was the most important tax and this brought in about three-fourths of the amount the Estates had to raise or about fifty to fifty-five per cent of the total revenue of Bohemia down to 1748. The remainder of the amount—or one-fourth—was brought up by the taxes and excises on beer, persons (*capitation*), houses, chimneys, mills, food provisions, liquors, fish, meat, and wool.[57] In all this extra-regal revenue, the administration and collection was in the hands of the Bohemian Diet and more directly in the hands of the Permanent Executive Committee created in 1714. In just the same way as the Estates bargained with the monarch as to the amount they must take for taxation, so too they assumed debts contracted by him, although a regular

[55] See Pekař, *Kniha o Kosti*, II, 170-172.
[56] Tomek, *Sněmy české*, 17 ff. H K Archiv, 1763-1791, Finanzen 229 D 1735 Repartitions Tabelle auf das Sommer Halbjahr von Mai bis Ende Oktober. M I Archiv, Carton 576, 71 ex 1748 contains a table: Billanze zwischen denen sammentlichen österr. und böhm. Landesverwilligungen 1716-1739. There is, of course, naturally the series of Landtagsschlüsse, 1627-1740.
[57] Calculate figures presented in documents cited in footnote 53 and in M I Archiv, Ständische Ausweis, Carton 518, 239 ex Augusto 1791.

financial agreement, as that of 1748 and thereafter, was not arranged as yet.

The political and financial oppression to which Bohemia had been subjected was almost equaled by the religious persecution of the Protestants which was carried out by the Jesuits. It is an undeniable fact that Ferdinand II and his allies took such vengeance upon the Czechs because the king was a Catholic and the Czechs Protestants who wished to deprive him of his crown, and not because they were Czechs, although that fact did not help them with a German master.[58] In 1655 the Bishopric of Litoměřice (Leitmeritz) was established and, in 1660, that of Hradec Králové (Königgrätz) to help in the work of conversion, for the Treaty of Westphalia in 1648 had forever banished the Bohemian émigrés. No exceptional position was given the Protestants in Bohemia as was given those in Silesia by the Dresden Accord of 1622 and the Treaty of Altranstadt of 1707 forced upon Austria by the Protestant Charles XII of Sweden.[59] The Czechs, in the meanwhile, had shifted their hopes from the Saxon electors to the kings in Prussia. Thousands fled to found colonies elsewhere. Meanwhile, within, the burning of Hussite literature and the persecution of Protestants continued with certain intermissions throughout this period. It drove many into exile and the rest into secret sectarianism. Under Joseph I (1705-1711) and Charles IV (1711-1740) persecution was carried almost to the extreme of the Spanish Inquisition. A Protestant became a criminal and Protestantism a crime. So acute did the situation become that on the appeal of the Bohemian Protestants, Frederick William I of Prussia, through his ambassador at Vienna, imparted to Charles IV in 1735 the draft of a rescript which he intended to issue to the Imperial Diet, publicly declaring that he stood on the side of the Protestants

[58] See Rezek, *Dějiny prostonárodního hnutí náboženského v Čechách od vydání tolerančního patentu až na naše časy*, I, 18-19 (Prague, 1887). Tomaš V. Bílek, *Reformace katolická neboli obnovené náboženství katolického v království českem po bitvě Bělohorské* (Prague, 1892), 176 ff.

[59] Rezek, 32 ff.

in Bohemia. That year the persecution was abandoned, and henceforth the Bohemian Protestants were exiled to Transylvania instead of outside the Habsburg Monarchy. Among the ruthless tamperings with a nation's spiritual well-being, the treatment of Bohemia in matters pertaining to religion stands unique in the annals of history.[00]

From all this we are able to discern the position which the Bohemian Estates and Diet assumed in the general tendency of events. In legislation, even after a slight initiative power was restored, the influence of the Diet was small. True, as time went on, it legislated on what was later called internal economy—on the machinery of the administration of taxation, on forestry, courts, police protection and thievery, the repair and upkeep of roads, the regulation of prices of products, navigation of rivers, the care of schools, the propagation of the Catholic religion, and public health. Perhaps, in reality, if we had more accurate knowledge of the exact dealings of the Diet we should find out that its influence was even more extended. The legislation however was wholly provincial. But when all is said, the difference between the legislation before White Hill and that for a century after it, is very great. Just as great was the difference between the work of the crippled Bohemian Diet of 1627 to 1740 and the phantom ceremonial Diet of 1740-1790. In finance, wherein lay its greatest powers, it was reduced to unsuccessful and often unfortunate bargains, because, beyond haggling over the amount, it had nothing else to hold back or to bargain about. To make a bargain one must have alternatives. In social and religious matters, naturally the interests of the monarchy and of the Estates were one—both were Catholic, both wished to keep down the rebellious serf and to exact from him all they could. This alliance was dissolved in the course of the next half

[00] Rezek, 52-60, 82, 89 ff.; Bílek, *Reformace katolická*, 269-83 and 289; Gindely, *Die Processierung der Häretiker in Böhmen unter Karls VI* (*Abhandlungen, B G W*, 1887, VII, class 2). Hřejsa, *Česká Konfese* (Prague, 1911) is also of considerable use in this connection; it is the most recent scholarly work on a part of the subject.

century but for the present the truth of the old Czech proverb
was only too evident, "one hand washed the other." In the
second half of the Eighteenth Century and thereafter, the
Habsburgs reaped the harvest of their work in Bohemia.

Two months after Charles VI died, Frederick the Great, by
his invasion of Silesia in December, 1740, proved that the
Pragmatic Sanction was only so much paper. A year later
when Charles of Bavaria invaded Bohemia and had himself
crowned king of that country, two of the richest and most
highly developed provinces of the Austrian Monarchy were
on the verge of being lost. It was only by heroic work that
the twenty-four-year-old Maria Theresa was able to save
Bohemia. Silesia, however, was lost, and its loss was felt in
many ways. What irritated Maria Theresa in regard to Bohemia was the fact that nearly the whole Bohemian nobility
swore homage to Charles III.[61] The loss of Silesia brought a
wound to the treasury which could not be readily closed up.[62]
Furthermore, the loss of Silesia presaged a revolution in the
economic life of the Habsburg Monarchy. For the enmity of
Prussia and later of Saxony closed the Elbe and the Oder
rivers to free transportation, and Austrian export, which heretofore went north down the rivers, had to seek another outlet.
The outlet was found at Trieste. Thus the currents of commerce and trade were reversed from a northward to a southward flow.[63] For Bohemia this economic revolution was of the
highest importance. Heretofore Bohemia had been on the
highway of commerce and trade, thereafter it was farthest
from the port of export. Economic depression, as the result of
the downfall of commerce and trade and of industry, was

[61] Arneth, *Maria Theresias erste Regierungsjahre*, II, 221 ff.
[62] M I Archiv, Carton 575 Steuer-Fusses, Wenn also das Gesambte . . .
document; *ibid.*, 6 von 1747 Böhmen. M I Archiv, Carton 577, 27 ex Marcio
1749.
[63] Beer: "Die handelspolitischen Beziehungen Österreiches zu den Deutschen Staaten unter Maria Theresia" (*AÖG*, 1892, LXXIX, 542 ff.).
    Fournier: "Handel und Verkehr in Ungarn und Polen um die Mitte des
18ten Jahrhunderts" (*ibid.*, LXXIX, 339 ff.). See later the Memoir of the
Estates on the National Bank and that of Schulstein on Commerce and
Industry. One may trace the first steps in closing up the north in Srbik,
Der staatliche Exporthandel Österreichs von Leopold I bis zu Maria Theresia,
399-407.

Bohemia's lot in the second half of the Eighteenth Century.[64] It was under these circumstances that Maria Theresa began her reforms in government following the treaty of Dresden in 1745, by which Silesia and Glatz, comprising about one-third of the Lands of the Bohemian Crown, were given to Prussia.

The great reforms of Maria Theresa, nearly all of which came in the decade, 1746-1756, were measures forced on her by the stern necessity of self-preservation. In that respect they differed from the reforms of Joseph II, with whom reform was a theoretical indulgence, rather than a necessary duty. Maria Theresa was reluctant to reform; Joseph II was zealous to topple over and build anew—he was, properly speaking, nervously zealous. If Maria Theresa reformed in order to preserve the Habsburg inheritance and prepare the way for a state capable of regaining Silesia, Joseph II, while not giving up the hope of winning back Silesia, extended further the work of centralization and consolidation, with the idea of trading the Netherlands for Bavaria. Maria Theresa centralized in order to regain Silesia, of which she thought an unrighteous Frederick had deprived her; Joseph II consolidated for conquest in other directions, in Bavaria or the Balkans, and, as well, for the satisfaction of having a smoothly running, bureaucratic machine. The great ideas of unity and centralization which the monarchs of the Habsburg dynasty of the Eighteenth Century sought to realize may be said to have begun with Charles VI in 1720 when he put through the Pragmatic Sanction in Bohemia. From that date Bohemia was an hereditary Land, indivisible from all the other inheritances of the Habsburgs, in both male and female lines. Maria Theresa strove to put alongside of this unity of succession, unity of administration and law. Joseph II strove for a single nationality and for the economic unity of his many territories. Meanwhile throughout the century the "alone-dominating"

[64] See the Third Desideria, Vorschlags zur Errichtung einer Leihbank für die Hochlöbl. böhmischen Landesstände, M I Archiv, Carton 518 (July 3, 1790: 239 ex Aug. 1791) and the Schulstein Memoir: Unmassgebige Gedanken über die Mängel der Industrie und des Kommerzes im Königreiche Böhmen und einige Mittel demselben abzuhelfen. 207 ex Julio 1791, M I Archiv, Carton 516.

Catholic religion represented unity of faith in the lands of the Habsburgs.

Let us glance, therefore, at the various ways in which Maria Theresa endeavored to bring about the unity of administration and of law by means of her reforms, discussing in turn the political and legal, the financial and economic, and the religious and educational features of the program. That they were practical and therefore necessary will be at once recognized.

It was natural that these reforms should vitally concern Bohemia, because that country had very nearly shared the fate of Silesia. The disaffection of the Bohemian nobility in 1741 in swearing homage to Charles III of Bavaria was never forgotten by Maria Theresa. Many were let off with light punishments, but this clemency weakened their resistance to Maria Theresa's reforming activity, so that, just when their resistance to onslaughts on the Bohemian Constitution should have been strongest it was weakest: they played the part of children just pardoned for a sin and tried to show their gratefulness by accepting meekly whatever Maria Theresa ordered. Furthermore, the desertion of the Estates of Bohemia, although it had brought tears to the noble queen's eyes, later earned her just contempt when she was sure that Bohemia was saved. During her coronation in 1743 she talked of the Bohemian crown as a "fool's cap." With these circumstances made clear one can imagine very easily why two such reforms as the Financial Recess of 1748, of which more hereafter, and the abolition of the Bohemian Court Chancellery and Bohemian Statthalterei in 1749 were carried out without great opposition.[55]

The political and legal reforms of Maria Theresa consisted of a separation of the functions of government into two

---

[55] Rieger, "Dílo centralismu v 18. Století" (Osvěta, 1888: 1, 193, 289). There is a passage in Folkmann, Die gefürstete Linie Kinský, p. 59, which shows that Maria Theresa would rather have seen all the Hungarians sacrificed before she would give up Bohemia. "La resolution de mon côté est prise, qu'il faut tout risquer et perdre pour soutenir la Bohême, et sur ce système vous pouvez travailler et faire les dispositions." This letter was sent to Count Kinský.

branches, the political and the legal, the financial going with
the political. Moreover, there was the program of codification
of law, which was never carried out. On May 1, 1749, Maria
Theresa abolished the chancelleries of the Bohemian and
Austrian administrative units as well as the Bohemian Statthalterei and created a new institution, the Directorium in
Publicis et Cameralibus, which was to control all political and
financial matters of government. At the same time the Supreme Court was established at Vienna—a court to which
cases from the provincial courts of all the Bohemian and
Austrian Lands could be appealed. Thus at one stroke of the
pen, and without consulting the Estates in the least, Maria
Theresa had centralized the various institutions of the separate
states into two highest central offices which ruled over them
all. The creation of the State Council in 1760 completed the
hierarchy of the new centralizations, and it proved to be an
institution which commanded great influence in the reign of
Maria Theresa. In 1762 the Directorium was suppressed, and
political and financial matters were separated. The Bohemian-
Austrian Court Chancellery took charge of political matters
and taxation (contribution), the Court Treasury taking charge
of the mint and mining together with auditing, and the Vienna
City Bank, the quasi-public banking institution. In 1782,
Joseph II undid this administrative organization and combined all three into the "United Bohemian-Austrian Court
Chancellery, Court Treasury, and Ministerial-Bank Deputation." A decade later Leopold II again separated the political
from the financial administration. By these reforms of Maria
Theresa the Lands of the Bohemian and Archducal Crown
became one unit, thus imperiling, if not totally destroying, the
independent statehood of Bohemia, and Vienna became the
capital of the new fictitious central state, while Prague and
Bohemia were relegated to the respective status of provincial
city and province.[66]

[66] See Baxa, *K dějinam veřejného práva v zemích koruny české*, pp. 15 ff.
The Patent of May 1, 1749 is printed in Maasburg, *Geschichte der obersten
Justizstelle*, 2d edition, 347 ff. The efforts to codify law under Maria Theresa
can be found so far as Bohemia is concerned in Čelakovský, *O účastí práv-*

Necessarily, such reforms in the center meant others in the "Lands" or "provinces" as they were generally called thereafter. After the abolition of the Statthalterei and Court Chancellery in Bohemia all political and financial matters were handed over to a bureaucratic council, the Representation and Treasury (*Kammer*) and all the judicial powers of the old Statthalterei Council to a Committee (*Consessus*) made up of the Chief Land Officials under the presidency of the Chief Castle Count of Prague. At the same time that the political and financial administration was separated in the central offices, in Bohemia (1763) the three functions, political, financial, and judicial, were merged into one by the abolition of the Representation and the Committee and by the creation of the Gubernium. For nearly a decade this institution existed, but in 1771 the Gubernium Council was divided into the political and the judicial senate, the Chief Land Officials being retained only in the latter. From that time to the accession of Leopold II, the Chief Land Officials were banished from the political affairs of Bohemia. Joseph II took away even their few remaining judicial functions.

In 1751 the local administration of Bohemia was reformed and reorganized. Instead of twelve circles, sixteen were mapped out. Heretofore, there were two circle captains for each circle, a noble and a knight. By this reform one captain was designated in each. He received a respectable salary and was given a better *état*. He was made a royal official and freed from the oversight of the Estates, who may be said to have controlled the local administration of Bohemia down to Maria Theresa. Thus during the decade of peace from 1746-1756, the central, provincial, and local administration became bureaucratic. These reforms were so far-reaching that in reality they were left untouched down to 1848, except for minor details and a change of name here and there.[67]

Thus far we have discussed reforms in the political, finan-

níkův a stavů, ze zemí českých na kodifikaci občanského práva Rakouského (Prague, 1911).
[67] See Rieger, *Zřízení krajské v Čechách*, II, pp. 1-15; Toman, *Das böhmische Staatsrecht*, 149 ff.; Kalousek, *České státní právo*, 479 ff.

cial, and judicial administration. We shall now turn to the concrete financial and military reforms carried out by Maria Theresa's "Iron Chancellor," Haugwitz, in 1748. One of the reforms was the Recess or Financial Contract of 1748, the first of its kind which really succeeded. The plan of Haugwitz was to create a standing army of 108,000 men and to secure an annual revenue of 14,000,000 florins to pay for the military. It would lead us too far into detail to show just how he carried this plan through over the heads of the Estates. In the first place, the decreased financial income entailed by the loss of Silesia had to be made up. Silesia had paid 21 per cent of the total quota for the Bohemian and Austrian Lands and after 1742 only one-fifteenth of Silesia remained.[68] Then, too, the government had contracted enormous debts and these in some way had to be partitioned and distributed among the provinces. And finally, in order to secure its safety, the new central state of Maria Theresa had to have control of the army, to recruit, to house, and to equip it. Haugwitz carried through successfully all of these matters. Beginning with the easiest, Silesia, he next put the bargain through in Moravia. In Bohemia the light-hearted disaffection of 1741 permitted the Estates only a meek opposition, although Counts Harrach and Kinský opposed the plan tooth and nail, because of its constitutional features and because the quota which Haugwitz desired to exact from Bohemia was unjust. Nevertheless the deal went through.[69]

It appears that the loss of Silesia meant a 10 per cent increase in the revenues for the military in all the Lands including Hungary. But it took the Bohemian nobility almost ten years to discover that they were made to pay about 35 per cent of the total loss, a large part of which fell on the serf. The new inter-Land financial ratio called on the Bohemian Lands for 55.7 per cent of the total for all the Bohemian and Austrian Lands, and on the Austrian Lands for 44.2 per cent.

[68] See fn. 62.
[69] See besides fn. 62, H K Archiv, A B 218 D, 1760-1763, Landtagsschlüsse, 1747 (xvi-xvii), and 1748, xxiii ff., M I Archiv, Carton 576: 18 ex Augusto 1748; Ständische Ausweis, 1749-1790 in Carton 518, 239 Ex Augusto 1791.

This meant that from 1748 on Bohemia was to pay 40.16 per cent of the grand total for the Monarchy. Concretely, Bohemia agreed through her Estates to pay yearly 5,270,488 florins into the treasury for ten years, of which 4,200,000 went for the military alone, and to assume a debt of eight and a half million florins. Such was the unfortunate Financial Recess of 1748, no matter how legal it may have been since it was accepted by the Diet. Bohemia, which had suffered most in the war of the Austrian Succession, was now meekly accepting the heaviest part of the resulting burden. Other Decennial Recesses were carried through, each time more easily because the Bohemian Diet was becoming more and more a phantom; they came in the years 1757, 1767, 1775, 1785. It is of importance to notice here that in 1748 the Bohemian Estates assumed 53,050 tax units in the land tax at 60 florins each. When they came to distribute this amount they discovered that only 41,850 taxable units could be found. Thus they had assumed 11,200 more units than they should, and this load they carried down to 1790.[70]

In the financial history of the Habsburg Monarchy it is most important to note that, in the Seven Years' War, Bohemia of all the Lands was most devastated by the military expeditions yet at the same time paid into the coffers of the Treasury the largest sums of any state then belonging to the Monarchy. Besides carrying between 32 and 40 per cent of the ordinary public revenue of the Monarchy, Bohemia alone contributed four times as much as all the Hungarian Lands, and, if both the ordinary and the extraordinary war revenues were counted, it contributed between 20 and 40 per cent more than the Netherlands, the next richest source of revenue. Such facts are astounding. They also account, perhaps, for the famine and misery and commercial depression which came upon Bohemia after the Seven Years' War.[71]

[70] Reckon figures given in the documents fn. 62 and 69. See also S Archiv, Landtagsschlüsse, 1747, 1748, 1748-1775.

[71] H K Archiv, A. B. 218 D. Staats Inventory. Haupt Billanze, 1760-1763, Nos. 105-127. Tabella Was zur Bestreitung des Extraordinairii beym letztern Krieg für gratis Beyträge, auch freywillig und angesonnene Anticipationen mit baarem Gelde, Naturalien, und ausgestelteren Papieren auch weme geleistet

There remains for us to glance at the social reforms carried out by Maria Theresa in religion and education. The Catholic Church could hardly have found a more staunch believer than Maria Theresa to continue the persecution of the Protestants. In 1752, she declared that it was a capital offense for one to declare himself a Protestant, and this crime—for Protestantism had been made a crime by Charles IV—was named alongside of treason and rebellion. This was the acme of paper legislation against the Protestants in Bohemia. Already the new Protestant colossus of the North, Prussia, was giving heart to the secret sectarians of Bohemia. And, too, though much against her will, Maria Theresa was obliged to prepare the way for the Toleration Patent of 1781 of Joseph II. In 1773 the State Council had urged a milder treatment of the Protestants, presenting the very practical question, what would happen if all the secret non-Catholics were punished? Incidentally, the efforts of Maria Theresa for centralization and absolutism led her to exclude the Pope and the Church of Rome from the internal affairs of the Monarchy. In this sense, no bulls of the Pope could have validity after 1767 in the Habsburg Monarchy without the Placet of the monarch. In the next year no excommunication in private heresy could be declared by the Church of Rome without the permission of the sovereign, and six years later the clergy could no longer correspond directly with the Church at Rome. In 1774 the Jesuits, the order most responsible for the conversion of Bohemia, lost their power in the Lands of the Habsburg Monarchy. And finally, the Peasant Revolt of 1775, in which the motives of economic oppression and religious persecution were blended, convinced Maria Theresa that persecution was useless. It was only a matter of time when toleration would come—and that time was to be when the monarch felt that the Protestants would be loyal to the dynasty.[72]

worden. Verfaszet mit Ende Mai, Anno 1763. See also Ausweis, M I Archiv, Carton 518, 239 ex Augusto 1791.
[72] Czerwenka, *Geschichte der Evangelischen Kirche in Böhmen*, II, last two chapters; Rezek, 104 ff.; Frank, *Toleranz-Patent Kaiser Josephs II,* 1-19; Karel V. Adamek, *Listiny k dějinam lidového náboženského hnutí na českem východě v XVIII a XIX věku*, I, 1750-1782 (Prague, 1911), p. 23.

The Jesuits had had charge of the educational system of Bohemia down to their abolition in 1774. During the century and a half of their domination the excellent school system for which Bohemia had been so noted sank into decay. The Jesuits taught the sciences. Their theology was dominated by scholasticism and casuistry, and their philosophy—peripatetic philosophy—was about one hundred years behind the times. Medicine and law were professions only for the earning of one's bread; history, natural sciences, and other liberal arts were unknown. The system itself was cumbersome and mechanical, and the University of Prague, as also those in other Lands of the Habsburgs, had fallen behind the Protestant universities of Germany.[73] In this, Maria Theresa found Gerhard Van Swieten, of the Austrian Netherlands, a ready reformer. It was owing to his labors that university education in the Habsburg Lands was reformed in 1749-1753. He died in 1773, a year before his enemies, the Jesuits, were banished from active public life. In 1774, the universities, the gymnasia, and the lower schools throughout the Bohemian and Austrian Lands underwent a thorough reform. To the new plan of educational reform, which, by the way, was none other than the plan of the noted Bohemian scholar, Comenius, of the Seventeenth Century, was added the idea of Germanizing the school system of Bohemia. But as yet under Maria Theresa, Germanization had made little progress and it would have succumbed to the inevitable had not Joseph II taken up the idea of linguistic unity and tried to spread it in the public offices and schoolrooms of not only Bohemia but other Slavic Lands and in Hungary.[74]

The creation of the central organs of government in political and judicial matters handed the chief offices of government in the Bohemian and Austrian Lands over to the bureaucrats

[73] Wolf, *Das Unterrichtswesen in Österreich unter Kaiser Joseph II* (really Joseph v. Sonnenfels' report of 1785) (Vienna, 1880), pp. 5 ff.
[74] Helfert, *Die Gründung der österreichischen Volksschule durch Maria Theresia* (Prague, 1860), 49 ff.; Kink, *Geschichte der kaiserlichen Universität zu Wien*, I, 432 ff.; also Tomek, *Geschichte der Prager Universität* (Prague, 1849).

and banished the Estates from them forever. The financial and military reforms took out of the hands of the Estates, for ten years at a time, their greatest power, the control of the purse and their administration of things pertaining to the military. The religious and educational reforms separated the Estate of the Clergy from much which they had considered their own. Henceforth the Catholic Church was not to be Roman, but Habsburg, the teachers not priests, but trained laymen. By the great Urbarial Patent of 1775, issued in behalf of the Bohemian serf, one may say that many of the rights given to the landlords in 1738 were withdrawn, and the first gun fired in the battle between the landlords and the government over the possession of the serf. There had been many accounts of the frightful condition to which the Bohemian serf had been reduced during the first twenty years of Maria Theresa's reign. But it was not until the report of the War Council in 1771 that action became critically necessary. Agriculture was neglected, government taxes were left unpaid, children were lamed from robot and grew up misshapen men and women; insobriety and idleness, famine and disease—all of these were written bold in the report.[75] The government was well aware of the frightful condition of things and was preparing a law to meet the situation when the Peasant Revolt of 1775 broke out. In fact, just as the ink of the document was drying, the insurrection flamed up. After military force had put down the revolt, a new Patent was issued. It did not set aside the law of 1738 but legislated more accurately in favor of the serf in certain details of the law. It divided the serfs into classes and set a standard day's work. Moreover, extraordinary robot, except for one class, was entirely set aside. The "Gordian knot" was cut.[76] The same power which by the law of 1738 had given rights to the nobility, withdrew these rights in 1775 and dissolved the alliance of White Mountain. Henceforth, the struggle between the Estates, i.e. the

[75] M I Archiv, Carton 449; Volkszählung, 219: 17 Sept. 1771. Vortrag die in dem K. Boheim vollendete Seelen- und Zugviehs-Conscription betreff.
[76] Grünberg, *Bauernbefreiung*, I, 222 ff. See the Patent, II, 257-267.

landowners, and the government was keen; each fought to preserve its revenues. For us the Patent of 1775 is important in that it became the basis to which the government returned after the reform legislation of Joseph II. It really remained the basis of serfdom down to its total abolition in 1848.

We shall see presently how closely Joseph II followed in the footsteps of his mother. But we must not forget that there was a difference in the way he followed over the path which the able empress had pointed out. She acted from necessity, tactfully, calmly, and only when absolutely forced to do so. He acted from theory, tactlessly, impatiently pushing on and on the theories of reform, although his intentions were nearly always noble and his heart yearned for the general welfare of mankind.

In dwelling here on some of the larger features of the reign of Joseph II which interest us most, we must always bear in mind that he belonged to that class of men who loom up better in the light of what they intended than what they really achieved. He fought for freedom in all its aspects, but his reasons were very practical ones. He hoped to free the Protestants and the Jews from persecution so as to invite them into the Monarchy, because of their advanced ideas in trade and industry. He intended to free the peasant from serfdom so as to free labor for other purposes; for example, industry and occupations other than agriculture. He hoped to free commerce and industry within in order to make them independent without. He yearned to make all equal before the law and in taxation, so that the burdens of the state and the responsibility for them might fall where they belonged. His destruction of the remaining political, economic, and social power of the Estates was only one consequence of all these hopes and intentions. Leopold II gathered in the harvest of the ideas that Joseph II sowed. Catholics will not cease to hate him for his tolerant spirit, nor Protestants to praise him therefor.[77]

[77] Compare Jäger, *Kaiser Joseph II und Leopold II, Reform und Gegenreform,* 1780-1792 (Vienna, 1867) and Frank, *Das Toleranz-Patent Kaiser Josephs II* (Vienna, 1881). See also the satirical chronicle by the Bohemian Monk, Locatelli.

Those who believe in castes and Estates will not forget to revile him for his desire to level all. Constitutionalists will point him out as the soul of despotism,[78] and absolutists as the prince of rulers. And the great mass of the people, remembering tales of the rule of the Jesuits, handed down from parent to child, keeping in mind his righteous endeavors for equality, for emancipation from serfdom, and for just taxation, will continue to call him the great Joseph II.[79] All of these were right. He was at one and the same moment as hasty, just, cruel, and tyrannical as he was loved and adored. His life was the strangest combination of impatient, undue haste united with an earnest desire to make application of theory without allowing the elements with which he dealt time for adjustment thereto. The results were therefore necessarily always only half complete, and a stubborn opposition often blocked further fulfillment.

The reforms of Joseph II in matters pertaining to religion consisted in the proclamation and maintenance of toleration, in the suppression and reduction of monasteries, and in the reform of theological education. The spirit of liberalism in all things which swept over Europe in the Eighteenth Century, destroying the decayed remnants of the old Counter Reformation and of the old Protestantism, was called Deism in England, Encyclopædism in France, and Rationalism in Germany. As the Jesuits had been the champions of the Counter Reformation, so now the Freemasons became the warriors of the new liberalism. And it interests us to know that it was the celebrated Comenius (Komenský), the best known Czech of the Seventeenth Century, who gave the impetus which led to the founding of the first lodge of Freemasons in England in 1717 and in Bohemia nine years later.[80] This helped to restore once more the tendency to intellectual union between England and Bohemia which had become so notable since the days of

---

[78] Mitrofanov, *Joseph II, seine politische und kulturelle Tätigkeit* (Vienna, 1910), I, 81 ff.

[79] The tendency of more recent Czech historians, Novotný, *České dějiny*, I, Chapter I and fn. and Pekař, *Kniha o Kosti*, II, in the chapter on serfdom.

[80] Svatek, *Obrazy z kulturních dějin českých* (Prague, 1891), 260 ff. See also Vlček "Z doby Josefinské" (*ČČH*, 1900, VI, 15, 97, 313).

Wycliffe and Hus. Jansenism within the Catholic Church, as also Pietism within the Protestant Church, shook the foundations on which rested both of the old churches. The suppression of the Jesuits in Austria in 1774 marked the dawn of the Eighteenth Century there.[81] It was in this atmosphere that Joseph II, speculating on how to attract Protestant colonists and trusting in the loyalty of his Protestant subjects, issued the Patent of Toleration, October 30, 1781.[82] It granted right of private exercise to three religions, the Lutheran, the Calvinist, and the Ununited Greek Orthodox. The Roman Catholic religion, however, was expressly designated as dominant and was alone allowed the right of public worship. Joseph II issued this Patent for Bohemia, as he did for his other Lands, over the protests of Gubernium Councillor Rottenhan and State Councillor Hatzfeld. Both predicted endless trouble and the downfall of the Catholic Church. In fact, so far as Bohemia was concerned few adherents of the three reformed religions declared themselves but there were thousands of Hussites, Taborites, Deists, and Israelites. This was a remarkable phenomenon. At first, officials endeavored, but without success, to class some of these as Lutherans, and the Israelites, if circumcised, as Jews. Now although Joseph II had proclaimed toleration, he had allowed it only to three religions. He persecuted the sects—and these were overwhelmingly Czech.[83] There may have been some fifty thousand non-Catholics in Bohemia in 1790.[84]

Maria Theresa had pointed out, in Lombardy, the way to a suppression of monasteries and Joseph II in the spring of 1781 declared that they had long ago demonstrated "they

[81] Novotný, České dějiny, I, I, 28 ff.; Goll (ČČH, IV); Hanuš (ibid., XIV, 141-152, XV, 277, 425, XVI, 306-315); and Kraus, Pražské Časopisy, 1770-1774, a české probouzeni (Rozpravy, ČA, 1909, III, 31).
[82] Frank, Das Toleranz-Patent Kaiser Josephs II, 1-20, 37 ff. See Chapter X in this study.
[83] Ibid., 44, 47-50; Hock, Der österr. Staatsrath, 343-344. Kressel wrote, "es sei notorisch dass in Böhmen weit mehr Hussiten als Protestanten des Augsburg. und Helvet. Bekenntnisses vorhanden wären." See also Adamek, Listiny, 145 ff., and Czerwenka, Evangelische Kirche, II, 662 ff.
[84] See Chapter X on Religion.

were useless and not pleasing to God." There were then 154 monasteries belonging to 25 orders in Bohemia. In the course of his reign, he suppressed 39, reduced 31, scheduled 14 more for reduction, and left unmolested 67.[85] Their wealth was turned over to the Religious Fund created for charitable religious purposes. In 1782 Joseph II forbade the appeal of cases to Rome thus cutting off foreign influence over native orders and monasteries. The visit of the Pope ended in dismal failure that very year. Meanwhile within, thousands of priests and monks were rendered homeless and the clergy deprived of a steady stream of candidates by the abolition of the seminaries attached to the monasteries and by the creation of general seminaries controlled by the State. Many minor measures assailed the fast sinking Church from all sides, and when Joseph II died he had succeeded in educating the younger part of the clergy to obey, while the older clergy hated in silence and awaited the time of revenge.[86]

The reforms pertaining to religion gave the inhabitants a certain freedom of conscience. The reforms connected with serfdom aimed to free the serf economically and socially. When Joseph II had hinted to the Estates his desire to change the condition of serfdom then existing in Bohemia (1781), he was met with meek assent in theory and stubborn resistance in practice and detail. When the Estates were through with the proposals of Joseph II, only the name of serfdom remained changed, none of its essential content.[87] On November 1, 1781, Joseph II, of his own authority, issued the Emancipation Patent. The serf was free to marry whom he wished, he might devote himself to handiwork, arts, or sciences as he desired, and he might move from place to place. The consent of the landlord was merely formal and without cost to the serf. The compulsory service of children at the court of the lord

[85] M I Archiv, Carton 513: 104 ex Aprili 1791: Extractus Protocollis, 15. März 1791: Verzeichniss der aufgehobenen, reduzirten, wie auch annoch beibehaltenen, allerlei Gattungen, Klöster, und Stifter.

[86] Hock, Österr. Staatsrath, 409-440, 456, 486 ff.

[87] M I Archiv, Carton 2485, 464 Junio 1781. Grünberg, Bauernbefreiung, II, 373-378.

was abolished with certain limitations. Nevertheless for all else—for robot and for debts—the Robot or Urbarial Patent of 1775 and its supplements were to remain law. By the establishment of trained justices of the peace on the manors and the Penal Patent of September 1, 1781, legislation for the serf as a human being in society was rounded out.[88]

These reforms touched largely the economic and social bond which held the lord and the serf as man to man. Joseph II planned, by the new taxation and urbarial system completed late in October, 1789, to treat of the relations between lord and serf so far as the holding of land was concerned. Necessarily this involved the taxation which the State laid upon the land and the robot and other obligations which the landlord exacted. Bohemia, as we have already noted, was paying far more than its quota.[89] Clever landlords, however, concealed from government taxation 36 per cent of all the productive land of Bohemia while the serf was taxed far beyond his ability to pay.

The investigation carried out by Joseph II had proved this conclusively. This truth, combined with ardent championship of the physiocratic theories of the French, led him in 1785 to issue the Patent on the new taxation and urbarial system whereby all income-bearing land and property were to be sought out and registered in the new survey. Its "grain product" was to be estimated according to the producing power of the land. All property owners, whether landlords or serfs, were to be treated by the same standards. A hard and fast rule was laid down that seventy out of every hundred florins worth of produce were to be declared free to the serf. Of the thirty florins, the State was to take 12 florins 13½ kreuzer for the land tax and the landlord 17 florins 46-2/3 kreuzer for serf obligations. Peasants who paid 2 florins yearly in state taxes were exempted from giving robot. To carry this out 184 tax

[88] Roth-Blasek, *Auszug aller im Königreiche bestehenden Gesetze und Verordnungen*, 6 vols. *Handbuch der Verordnungen und Gesetze unter Joseph II*, I, 65-79.
[89] Grünberg, *Bauernbefreiung*, I, 314-331.

districts were created, and tax collectors, this time state officials
not landlords, gathered in the taxes. By this means many
feudal tax units were swept out of existence, and the justice
of the peace and the tax collector became the "two eyes" of
government in the countryside.⁹⁰

One can hardly understand the significance of these two
great reforms unless one follows the increase in the population
which henceforth devoted itself to industrial and handiwork
occupations. During the reign of Joseph II this population
doubled in number. One must also remember that between
1721 and 1736—let us say in the first half of the Eighteenth
Century—the State, the landlord and the church took about
73 per cent of the serf's income; in the Twentieth Century
the State takes about 22, and the peasant keeps 77, per cent.
The magnitude of the revolution which Joseph II tried to
carry out during his decade of power is truly impressive.⁹¹

We now come directly to questions bearing on the economic
condition of the country as a whole and to commerce and to
industry in particular. The seizure of Silesia and the enmity
of Prussia, together with the Seven Years' War, had as their
aftermath a tariff war with Prussia and Saxony which had
shut off Bohemia from free transportation of its goods on
the Elbe and the Oder. The revolution in economic conditions
thus made necessary has already been mentioned. Trieste became the outlet of the Habsburg Monarchy, not Hamburg at
the other end of the Elbe River.

Tariff war with Prussia soon led to a policy of high protection in an endeavor to build up home industry and to bring
Prussian Silesia to economic ruin.⁹² This explains also Maria
Theresa's encouragement of industry during the decade of
peace, 1746-1756.⁹³ The Seven Years' War (1756-1763), how-

⁹⁰ *Ibid.*, Rieger, *Zřízení krajské*, II, 483 ff. and 526-528.
⁹¹ Pekař, *Kniha o Kosti*, II, 195ff.
⁹² Fechner, *Die handelspolitischen Beziehungen Preussens zu Österreich
während der provinziellen Selbständigkeit Schlesiens, 1741-1806* (Berlin, 1866),
last chapter.
⁹³ Fournier, "Maria Theresia und die Anfänge ihr. Industrie und Handelspolitik" (*Historische Studien und Skizzen*, II Reihe, Vienna, 1908), also in
AÖG, 1887, LXVII, 341 ff.

ever, had left Bohemia exhausted financially and economically. Besides warfare, mercantilism had in many countries closed home markets to Bohemia. New processes of manufacture cost it others.[94] In the course of time came the Tariff of 1774—an admission that the high protective idea was failing in Austria. The Habsburgs had discovered that, because of their high protective tariffs, they were able to make commercial treaties with Bavaria and Russia only. Nevertheless, the process of unification went on within the Monarchy. In 1775 the Bohemian and Austrian Lands constituted for the first time one customs unit, and another "foundation stone in Austrian politics" was laid.[95] If Joseph II had not feared for the ruin of the Bohemian and Austrian peasant at the hands of the Hungarian peasant with his cheaper grains, he would have made all the Bohemian, Austrian, and Hungarian Lands one customs unit in 1784 when he promulgated the highest protective tariff of the Habsburgs in the Eighteenth Century—a tariff of 60 per cent with many outright prohibitions.[96] Efforts were not lacking to create anew the industry which had declined in the Seven Years' War and especially to reinvigorate the old Bohemian industrial enterprises in glass, cloth, and paper. Joseph II really had some measure of success if one takes into account the amount, not the quality, of the product and the increase both of industrial enterprises and of industrial classes. The high protective tariff made trade with regions outside the Monarchy almost impossible, and these opportunities significantly decreased during the reign of Joseph II. Meanwhile he worked feverishly within the Monarchy so as to increase commerce and trade between

[94] M I Archiv, Carton 449:219:17, Sept. 1771. Die in dem K. vollendete Seelen- und Zugviehs-Conscription; Bartenstein Denkschrift of 1760 in H H S Archiv, 29 and Salz, *Geschichte der böhmischen Industrie in der Neuzeit* (München und Leipzig, 1913), pp. 269 ff.

[95] Beer, *Die Zoll-Politik und die Schaffung eines einheitlichen Zollgebietes unter Maria Theresia* (*MIÖFG*, XIV, 262 ff.; 304-305). Galicia was included with Bohemia and Austria in 1778, but under Maria Theresa, Transylvania, Noaquisita and the Temesvar Banat were not a part of the Hungarian customs district.

[96] Hock, *Österr. Staatsrath*, 549 ff.

the various parts of his possessions. In this hope he abolished in 1786 all guilds and monopolies and increased still more the quantity of industrial labor. This is very evident when one considers that in 1788 there were twice as many "masters" and one and a half times as many industrial undertakings as there were in 1761.[97]

The Financial Recesses of Maria Theresa had bound Bohemia to a very unjust annual burden and to a huge debt. It is to Joseph II's credit that he sought to reduce the annual quota Bohemia paid, but the debt remained unpaid, because the government used the money, which should have gone into the interest and sinking fund, for the Turkish war in 1787.[98] It is a fact in the financial history of Bohemia in the Eighteenth Century that by the middle of that century the highest amount that could be got from land taxation was reached. Thereafter, with the wars which followed, it was impossible to increase it. This was however the part of the revenues of Bohemia which was controlled by the Estates in their Diet and the Recesses covered this. In 1748 the relation of the land tax to the other taxes then in the hands of the Estates was as 4 is to 5 or about 45 per cent of the total revenue, provincial and royal, of Bohemia. And at that time the relation between the royal and provincial revenue of Bohemia was as 1 is to 3 or thereabouts. Being unable to increase the revenue through the land tax because, with the old style of taxation, it meant the ruin of the agricultural serf, the government began to develop the royal revenues from salt, tobacco, liquors, and other commodities over which the Estates had no control whatsoever. Thus when Joseph II died the relation of the royal to the provincial revenue was as 3 is to 4. Within the budget of the provincial revenue the land tax had reached a height of 87 per cent as compared to the other part of the provincial

[97] Příbram, *Geschichte der österr. Gewerbe-Politik*, I, 359-60 and 408 ff.
[98] M I Archiv, Carton 517. An E. M., unterthänigste Vorstellungen der böhmischen Stände über die bedenkliche Lage des unter ihrer Garanzie bestehenden Aerarial-Kreditgeschaftes. 29 Jan. 1791. Gubernium opinion, 22 Feb. 1791, *ibid.*

revenue, which had dwindled because of the bargains made with the sovereign. In 1781 the land tax was about one-half of the total provincial and royal revenue of Bohemia. The Monarchy was steadily gaining on the Estates.[99]

In order to make over the feudal Habsburg Monarchy into a modern state, a reform of law and justice was absolutely necessary. The central reforms in the system of justice carried out by Maria Theresa in 1749 still remained. The activity of Joseph II was confined to the reorganization of the lower instances in the provinces. The codification of law, begun by Maria Theresa and wisely laid aside by her as untimely, was fresh in the memory of Joseph II as he came to the throne. Maria Theresa had put the idea of codification on a broader basis than had her predecessors, who had in mind the making of a new Land Ordinance of public and private law on Ferdinand II's pattern for Bohemia alone. She planned to make a great universal code for all the Bohemian and Austrian Lands.[100] Joseph II took up the threads of reform just at the point where Maria Theresa had become convinced it was time to halt. He refused to be guided by the experience of three decades and, after toying for a while with the idea of promulgating a complete code, he decided to launch it under the guise of partial codes and separate laws at various times. At this point natural law came in for its share alongside of old Czech, German, and Roman law. The mass of laws which Joseph II promulgated in the course of the decade of his reign, proclaimed in direct contrast to the legislation of Maria Theresa, which was drawn up in the spirit of the Estates, equality of all citizens before the law, the destruction of the judicial and the legal privileges of the Estates, and many other radical changes. These changes sank deeply into

[99] Compare Ständische Ausweis, 1749-1790. M I Archiv, Carton 518, 239 in Augusto, 1791, with H K Archiv, D. 227, 1763 and D 227, 1763-1791. Finanzen A/D Erforderniss and Bedeckung, Aufsatz der gesamten Staats-Einkünfte und Ausgaben für das Militärjahr, 1791.

[100] Čelakovský, *O účastí právníkův a stavů ze zemí českých na kodifikaci občanského práva rakouského*, 15 ff.

the political and social structure of Bohemian and Austrian life in the Eighteenth Century.[101]

Joseph II declared that the great land trusts (the *Fidei Commisse*), could be allodialized and debts to one-third of their value made on their security. By the partial emancipation of serfdom (incorrectly called *Leibeigenschaft*) on October 1, 1781, Joseph II had given the serf a larger legal personality. The Toleration Patent of November 13, 1781, had given the Protestants the right to public office and to hold property. Marriage was made a civil contract. The equality of male and female inheritance was proclaimed, and the right of inheritance was extended in full to illegitimate children. The spendthrift was practically deprived of a legal personality and all laws on usury were abolished. The exclusive privileges of the Estates to purchase certain kinds of property were done away with and the peasant was allowed to divide his holdings. These and other similar laws serve to indicate the nature and character of the legal reforms of Joseph II.[102]

Joseph II indisputably reorganized in an excellent way the entire system of justice in Bohemia. He established the Royal Court of Appeals in 1783 as the court of the second instance for all the civil and criminal courts of Bohemia. The civil court of the first instance was the Court of the Land, which was assisted by the magistracies of Prague and of other cities, by the courts on the manors, and by the Mining Courts of Jáchymov (Joachimsthal), Příbram, Kutná Hora (Kuttenberg), and the like. The criminal courts of the first instance consisted of the magistracies of some fifteen cities. In civil procedure, therefore, a case went from a manorial court, or magistracy, or the Court of the Land, as the first instance, to the Royal Court of Appeals in Prague as the second instance, and to the Supreme Court in Vienna as the third instance. In criminal cases the suit started in the criminal courts of

---

[101] Domin-Petrushewecz, *Neuere österr. Rechtsgeschichte* (Vienna, 1869), 45-88, a good account of the significance of the codifications.
[102] *Ibid.* and fn. 100. Beidtel, *Österr. Staatsverwaltung*, I, 330-363.

the fifteen cities and was appealed in turn to the Royal Appellate Court and to the Supreme Court. The theory of three instances both in civil and criminal cases was preserved.[103]

Joseph II may be said to have continued the reform of the educational system as begun by Maria Theresa. This meant a closer imitation of the teachings of Comenius (Komenský) and of his German Protestant disciples; it also meant Germanization. The universities, the gymnasia, and the lower schools were overhauled and imbued with the practical spirit. Instead of being feeders for the clergy, they became the source of supply for public officials. Everywhere in the universities and gymnasia, and even in the lower schools, tuition fees were exacted, and as many students as possible were discouraged from attending the two higher schools. Theological seminaries were changed into general state seminaries, and the number of candidates for the clergy was cut down considerably. Industrial schools were encouraged. The practical and material nature of the instruction repeatedly stares one in the face. The system was simple but far too mechanical, and it was under the tyrannical will of the son of the old Van Swieten. He was called in derision the "University Pasha." [104] The slow progress of Germanization initiated by Maria Theresa in 1774 in the gymnasia and in the lower schools was quickened by several radical measures which Joseph II carried out in his usual way. Down to 1780 Czech had been tolerated in the gymnasia, but after that it was not, and from 1784 on the lectures in the University of Prague, with the exception of a few in Latin, were given in German. In the lower schools also much practical progress was being made. In fact, when the reign of Joseph II ended the Czech language had been banished from the schools of Bohemia. In the same way the "national" language, as it was even then called, was banished from the offices of government. The great centralizing measures of 1748 and 1749 brought a horde of German public offi-

[103] Adler, *Das adelige Landrecht in N. und O. Österreich und die Gerichtsreformen des XVIII. Jht.*; Toman, *Das böhmische Staatsrecht*, 115 ff.
[104] Wolf, *Das Unterrichtswesen*, 7-8; Kink, *Universität Wien*, I, 580-588.

cials into Bohemia, and important government correspondence was carried on more and more in German. Patents were printed in both languages, as the Constitution called for, down to 1788, but after that, with some exceptions, in German only. Thus, when Joseph II died, in the schoolroom and in public office, Czech was no longer the language of instruction or of official business, although two-thirds of the inhabitants of Bohemia still spoke it.[105]

By means of these momentous changes the Bohemian Constitution was altered radically. The legislation on matters pertaining to religion had sorely wounded the Estate of the Clergy and had taken from its hands much of the oversight it formerly had over the religious welfare of Bohemia and over the schools of theology and the lower public schools. The legislation on serfdom had deprived the landlord of the right to hold and to determine the character of his labor and forced him to pay higher prices for it. The new taxation system, made without the coöperation of the Estates, took out of their hands what little financial power the ill-fated Financial Recesses had left, and it almost crippled the only power which the Diet retained after the Battle of White Mountain, namely, the right to grant taxes. In the new system, the Estates had nothing to do with the distribution or collection of taxes. Tariff legislation had dissolved the economic unity of Bohemia, and the legislation of Joseph II had all but ruined Bohemian commerce. The new laws and the new judicial system completely destroyed the old codes and the old judicial system as outlined in the Land Ordinance of Ferdinand II (1627). And finally the policy of Germanization was a direct violation of this document where it was expressly affirmed that the Czech and the German languages were both official languages in Bohemia. These were some of the powerful blows with which the old Bohemian Constitution was assailed from without.

[105] Rieger, "Z Germanisačního Úsili" (*Osvěta*, 1887, 389 ff.); Denis, *La Bohême depuis la Montagne Blanche*, I, 597 ff.; Rieger, *Zřizeni krajské*, II, 44-45.

From within the process of destruction went on at even a more terrific pace. In 1782 the Judicial Committee of the Gubernium, in which the Officials of the Land sat, was dissolved and their offices were either suppressed or declared honorary. In the next year, the Permanent Executive Committee, instituted by Charles VI in 1714, was abolished and the entire administration which had been in charge of the Estates was united with the Gubernium. Thereafter the Bohemian Estates had no administration and no patronage. With the exception of two members of the Diet in the Gubernium, whose election the government controlled, before 1790 the Estates had been banished from the entire central and local administration. Only their private meetings as individuals and their ceremonial Diets as Estates were left to them. But in 1788 Joseph II forbade even the private meetings and informed the Diet that thereafter it would not be called annually, but only when the sovereign decided there was something important to be laid before it. Thus the last trace of the Constitution was obliterated: Joseph II had made the Diet useless and had destroyed the Constitution.[106] In 1789 Bohemia was totally in the hands of the bureaucrats; it was officially German, tolerantly Catholic, and wholly absolute in form of government.

[106] Desideria on the Constitution, M I Archiv, Cartons 516, 517.

CHAPTER II

BOHEMIA IN 1790

I

LEOPOLD II AND THE BUREAUCRACY

HAD a traveler wandered into the domains of the Habsburg Monarchy in 1790, he would have found a bureaucratic government working in two huge departments, the political and the judicial. The political branch of the government consisted of the administrative, the executive, and the legislative. The judicial department functioned unusually well with its three instances. When Joseph II died in 1790 there were really four great territorial units which had this twofold organization. There was the heart of the Monarchy consisting of the Lands of the Bohemian Crown, of the Austrian Hereditary Lands, and of the Polish Lands.[1] All of these were governed by the Bohemian-Austrian Court Chancellery in the political affairs of government and by the Supreme Court at Vienna in the judicial. There was the unit which might be called Hungarian, which consisted of Hungary, Transylvania, Croatia, and Slavonia. Each formerly had institutions peculiar to itself, but Joseph II had centralized all into the two categories, the Hungarian Court Chancellery and the Supreme Court. The other two territorial units, the Austrian Netherlands and the Italian Possessions, were likewise centralized.

[1] The Bohemian Crown Lands were Bohemia, Moravia, and Silesia; the Polish, Galicia and Lodomierz; the Austrian, Upper and Lower Austria, Tyrol and Voralberg, Carinthia, Carniola, Görz, Gradisca, Trieste, etc. Bukowina was likewise administered from Vienna. There remains an excellent opportunity to write the history of the Austrian and Bohemian Court Chancelleries before and after their union. No one in Bohemia had so thoroughly imbibed the Josephinian idea of the two parts of government as Lamoth. See his Besondere Meinung on the Second Desideria referred to in Chapters IV and V.

Doubtless Joseph II was anticipating the last few steps in the unification of his possessions when he died. First should come the union of the Bohemian-Austrian with the Hungarian chancelleries and supreme courts. Then, if the Austrian Netherlands could be exchanged for Bavaria, the territory made up of Bavaria, of the Bohemian, Austrian, and Hungarian Lands, and of the Italian Possessions would be one solid and continuous realm. Provincial distinctions would be erased, and this colossal German Viennese Empire would then be divided up into a hundred odd circles administered by circle captains or intendants appointed from Vienna. While the provinces still existed, however, each was to have a separate political and judicial organization. The political half of the business of government was to be operated by the Governor and a Gubernium Council, for short called Gubernium, and this Council was to administer the executive, administrative, and legislative branches of public life, while the provincial Court of Appeals, as a court of second instance, was to look after judicial matters. The former worked through the circle or local administration, the latter through the courts of the first instance on the manors and in the cities. All offices of the government were to be operated by trained servants whether sons of butchers or of princes. The whole idea had in it the germ of simplicity and of logic.

At Vienna, besides these two great vehicles of government activity, there were several supplementary central organs which breathed added energy into this bureaucratic structure. At the very summit of the hierarchy sat the monarch, the last instance of resort, representing in his person the supreme instance both political and judicial. His word and decision were absolute law. He could arrest the machine anywhere in its progress and examine the question before it went farther or he could ignore it after it had gone through miles of bureaucratic red tape, when a single sheet of paper had become a lusty archive, fresh from Eighteenth-Century scribbling. In turn, each office or commission, within the sphere of its influence, administered, executed, legislated on, and adjudged all that came before it. The great Diets of Bohemia and Hungary, which had humbled countless monarchs, had by 1790 so shriveled into insignificance that no account was taken of their existence. The royal postulata were turned out and approved by them with mechanical regularity, amid, it is true, a few concealed growls. But in 1790 bureaucracy was supreme.

The central hierarchy consisted of the sovereign, the State Council, the commissions temporarily or permanently appointed, the Bohemian-Austrian Court Chancellery, assisted by the Treasury and the Auditing Bureau nominally amalgamated, and the Supreme Court.

Leopold II, the third son of Maria Theresa and Emperor Francis, was forty-three years old at his accession in 1790.[2] When Tuscany had been changed from a province of primogeniture to a province of secundogeniture, Leopold II was married to the Spanish Infanta, Marie Louise, the daughter of Charles III. For a generation he had been the ruler of Tuscany. He found it a weak disorganized state fallen into the decay which often befell provinces which were not the centers of a court life and an active policy. Leopold II gave Tuscany the best government in Europe in the Eighteenth Century, a government which concerned itself only with internal politics, for the army had been disbanded and the navy beached or sold, and the little state was governed by police. The finances were rehabilitated, the judicial system reorganized, and complete modern freedom of trade within the province secured. The Church was nationalized and the bishops were exalted as much as possible. The serf was assisted and given an opportunity such as he had not had before. In this

[2] P. Mitrofanov, *Leopold II Avstriiskii. Vnieshnaia Politika*, I, 1, pp. 1-34, 35-134. See also Hirsch, "Leopold II als Grossherzog von Toskana" (*Historische Zeitschrift*, 1878, XL, 433 ff.). There is no adequate life of Leopold II nor even a respectable history of his remarkable reign. One may find something in Reumont, *Geschichte Toskanas seit dem Ende des florentinischen Freistaates*, II, and some general facts in G. Capponi, *Storia di Pietro Leopoldo*. Wolf-Zwiedineck-Südenhorst, *Oesterreich unter Maria Theresia, Joseph II, und Leopold II, 1740-1792*, pp. 319 ff. sums up most of this literature, as does Mitrofanov.

and in many other things, Leopold II followed the precepts of his imperial mother and of his zealous brother Joseph II. But if he was autocratic, he was and intended to be constitutionally so, whereas Joseph II was despotically autocratic. Leopold II had toyed with the plans of a constitution for Tuscany built upon the general ideas outlined in the Virginia Constitution of 1776.[3] In this, then, he essentially disagreed with and differed from Joseph II. He favored an agreement with the Netherlands and a different policy in Hungary. He believed that the war with Turkey was ill-advised, and he desired a *rapprochement* with Prussia. In the end, Joseph II, discovering that Leopold II disagreed with his policy, both external and internal, left him in Florence in ignorance of the course of things, abandoned even by his own son Francis, whom Joseph II dominated at Vienna.[4]

In this state of affairs, Leopold II was called to the inheritance of the Habsburgs. He took his time about reaching Vienna in order to test the strength of public opinion which under the driving omniscience of Joseph II had exposed itself only in out-of-way places and in the secret whisperings and correspondence of the members of the Estates. For weeks he did not let himself be seen, and, immersed in work, his first year showed what a prodigious laborer he was. Being personally of a very weak physical make-up, he was subject to melancholia. He suspected and distrusted everyone about him. He was calm and reasonable, where Joseph II had been zealous and hasty. He was tactful but firm, where his brother had been tactless and brutal. Though outwardly cool, his own inward nature was gentle and warm, and his family circle

[3] Zimmermann, *Das Verfassungs-Projekt des Grossherzogs Peter Leopold von Toscana.*

[4] One can get glimpses of his opinions on the politics of the day in such collections of his correspondence as Wolf, *Leopold II and Marie Christine, Ihr Briefwechsel (1781-1792);* Beer, *Joseph II, Leopold II und Kaunitz, Ihr Briefwechsel;* Schlitter, *Briefe der Erzherzogin Marie Christine, Statthalterin der Niederlande, an Leopold II, März 1780 bis 1792 (FRA,* 1869, XXXXVIII); Huber, *Die Politik Kaiser Josephs II beurtheilt von seinem Bruder Leopold von Toscana.* Leopold's ideas on government come out well in the letter of January 25, 1790 to Marie Christine, Wolf, *op. cit.,* pp. 84-86.

was always delightful. He did not introduce the police into
the Habsburg Monarchy, he merely gave it Italian *finesse*.
This has given him the "secret-police" reputation and misled
some historians into ascribing to him the basest and most
concealed of motives. He hunted little, played less. He was
rather the scholar as is shown by his support of the first
Italian Encyclopedia and the historical archive at Florence.
If he went to the theater, it was to hear tragedies; they were
fit companions to his cold seriousness.[5] One can say that in
the main his ideas and his principles were straightforward,
but in the age of the "cabinet noir" and of ciphered diplomatic correspondence, his own real ideas have been shrouded
in a veil of mystery. He was a statesman who believed in a
policy of peace and friendship without, and tactful government within. That does not mean that he was not firm. Just
the contrary. His firmness was of the kind which great statesmen
possess. Besides that, he saw clearly the new dawn
breaking over the political horizon. It was the dawn of the
new state in Europe, which was to be based on the absolute-
monarchy type of government with legal constitutional limits
in which the people were to be consulted. He had not promulgated his Tuscan-American constitution, because he
judged that the time had not yet come for it. He believed in
the theory of it, yet not in its expediency. And he went farther
than many another "Enlightened Despot" in his belief that
in practical government the inhabitants of the state over
which he ruled should have a share in the government. Only
those who have read his straightforward and laconic decisions

<hr/>

[5] Various accounts, though panegyric, may be found in the cheap popular
lives of Leopold II which appeared at that time. Oehler, *Skizze der Lebensbeschreibung Leopold des Zweiten,* is only fair and so is Alxinger, *Ueber
Leopold den Zweyten.* Very poor is the *Biographie Kaiser Leopolds des
Zweyten Königs von Ungarn und Böhmen, Erzherzogs von Österreich,
Grossherzogs von Toscana.* The same is true of Hegrab, *Versuch einer kurzen
Lebensgeschichte Kaiser Leopolds II bis zu dessen Absterben.* A pamphlet
in German and Latin, hostile to Leopold II, and laudatory of Joseph II may
be found under the title: *Gespräch zwischen einem durch Ungarn reisenden
Fremde und einem unparteyisch denkenden Ungarn über das Ende der
Regierung weiland Kaiser Josephs des Zweiten und über die dermalige des
Kaisers und Königs Leopold des Zweiten* (1791) (Library of the Abbey of
Strahov).

can comprehend the keenness and the conciseness of his states-manship. His resolutions stand out in contrast to the lengthy and egoistic rulings of his unfortunate brother.

The State Council,[6] since its creation under Maria Theresa in 1760, had much influence, in fact, often decisive influence, over matters both political and judicial, and except for the sovereign, it was the highest central office. Men from varied stations of life were called from time to time to take part in its deliberations, or "paper votes." Its regular method of operation was less by oral proceeding than by the "paper vote," by which a sheet of paper was circulated containing the subject matter on which the vote or decision of each council-lor was required. These councillors were very often the high-est officials in various organs of government, but not necessar-ily so. In the last years of the reign of Joseph II and during the two years of the rule of Leopold II this great council consisted of Count Charles Frederick Hatzfeld, Prince Kaunitz, Baron Kressel, Baron Reischach, Baron Martini, Frederick Eger, and Baron Izdenczy. Of these, three be-longed to the Bohemian nobility, one was a Swabian, another a Tyrolian, still another an Austrian, and the last a Hungarian.

Count Hatzfeld was born in Bohemia in 1718, and since 1771 had been the Bohemian-Austrian Chief Chancellor. He was a disciple of Maria Theresa with a leaning toward the Estates, but of such a temperament as to be obedient to Joseph II. Baron Kressel came from the Bohemian nobility. He served as Second Chancellor during the years, 1789-1792. Baron Simon Thaddäus von Reischach, a Swabian by birth, was really a minister without portfolio in the decade, 1782-1792. Baron Martini, the tutor of Joseph II and Leopold II, was reporter or referent in the Bohemian-Austrian Court Chancellery on educational matters. Frederick Eger was the son of a petty bureaucrat of Lower Austria. He was of that

[6] Hock, *Österreichischer Staatsrath*, 105 ff.

extreme type which most appealed to Joseph II, who entrusted to him the colossal labor of putting the new system
of taxation into being. Baron Izdenczy was a Hungarian
noble of Josephinian tendencies who sat in that council from
1785.

In one sense this council was really a board of ministers. It
gave its advice mostly on paper, thereby continuing the time-
honored Eighteenth-Century custom of overscribbling, but
also preserving to us the great secrets of the reforms of the
Habsburg Monarchy. Joseph II did not take the advice of his
council when it did not fit in with his ideas. Often he set it
to work on ideas of his own. Unlike his mother, he was complete master of his council. Leopold II did not give them his
confidence during the first year of his rule, but he fell back
on the second grade of the hierarchy, the Court Chancellery
and the Supreme Court, and on his commissions. There was
a commission for the new taxation system, a commission for
educational matters, another for religious affairs, and later
one for the codification of law. When Leopold II ascended
the throne, he abolished the first of these and created a new
one which was to decide on the Desideria. This was presided
over by the Archduke Francis and attended by members of
the Court Chancellery and the Supreme Court.

This hierarchy was dominated by two currents of opinion,
the Theresian and the Josephinian. The Josephinian was the
stronger in the State Council and was represented in an extreme form by Eger. Count Hatzfeld was his sturdiest opponent. Prince Kaunitz wished to stand as mediator and gave
his closest attention to foreign policy. The Theresian Party
was stronger in the Court Chancellery, where Count Leopold
Kolovrat had much influence. At the beginning of the reign
of Leopold II, it looked as though the Court Chancellery and
the Supreme Court were about to quarrel over their newly
won power, the confidence of the sovereign, but happily they
made compromises. In the second year of his reign, Leopold

II gave the State Council his confidence, doubtless for several reasons.[7] In Bohemia and in the Austrian Lands, the reaction was gathering momentum whereas, by a clever interplay of military force, of tactful foreign policy and of native dissatisfaction, the Monarchy was solving its problems in Hungary and in the Austrian Netherlands. The time had come for Leopold II to counteract this reaction. In the meanwhile, the State Council had atoned for its previous behavior. There was also the constant jealousy of the heads of the various organs of government who strove for royal favor. By the end of his short reign, Leopold II, so far as his internal government was concerned, was giving the forces of the Josephinian group more field in which to play.

In Bohemia,[8] the political hierarchy consisted of the Governor and of the Gubernium Council. They were assisted by several commissions like those on military matters, taxation, education, and religion, by the chief chamberlains of the royal and dower cities, by the half-extinct Diet and its insignificant administration, and by the local administration divided up into sixteen circles or districts. The other branch of government consisted of the Bohemian Court of Appeals of the second instance and of the Court of the Land and its Auxiliary Courts of the first instance.

The Governor, Count Ludwig Cavriani, who was not of Bohemian birth, had been presiding officer of the Gubernium Council and of the Bohemian Diet since 1788. He was also chairman or protector of the military and religious commissions and of the Patriotic Economic Society of Bohemia. He came from a family originally Italian, which later settled in Austria. He was a thorough Josephinian bureaucrat, and we shall have plenty of opportunity to watch him in action in the Diet and Gubernium. His advisers were the Josephinians, Baron Lamoth and Joseph von Smitmer, the go-between

---

[7] Haus- Hof- und Staats-Archiv (hereafter cited H H S Archiv), Staatsrat Akten 3553 in 1791.

[8] *Schematismus für das Königreich Böhmen,* 1789, 1790, 1791. These handy booklets always contain full lists of state officers.

bureaucrat, and Knight John Marcel von Hennet, Count
James Cavriani, Baron William Hugo MacNeven and
O'Kelley von Aghrim,[9] the warm defenders and representatives of the Estates. More interesting than the prolific and
office-seeking Lamoth was Baron MacNeven of an old Irish
family which came to the Continent with James II. He was
only one of the numerous Irish who were to find new homes
in the domains of the Habsburgs. The O'Donnells, O'Kelleys,
O'Briens, and O'Gilvys all fought in the armies of Maria
Theresa.[10] Baron MacNeven's father had been a professor of
medicine at the University of Prague, and his son had received
a legal education there. He was thoroughly conversant in the
Czech language, something which proved useful to him in
his official duties. He was always a seeker after office and
yet ever ready to fight "agin' the government" when promotion was not forthcoming. Besides administering several
lucrative positions to which the Estates had elected him, he
was also their representative in the Gubernium. In the meetings of the Diet he distinguished himself by writing large
parts of the Desideria and by reporting for the Executive
Committee during the sessions of the Diet. He was voluble in
speech and copious on paper. Leopold II never forgave him
for the part he played in composing the Desideria, and when
the Diet voted him a pecuniary gift for his "fatiguing" labors,
Leopold II refused to confirm the grant.

The sixteen circles (counties) which composed the local
government of Bohemia were each ruled over by a circle captain. He in turn was assisted by three circle commissioners,
a school commissioner, a secretary, the circle physicians and
surgeons, and the bureaucratic personnel. Up to the reign of
Maria Theresa, the circle captains were always nobles or

[9] *Schematismus*, 1791, pp. 34-35. MacNeven was born in 1734 and died in
1814, leaving three sons and one daughter. His father was born in Ireland in
1714 or 1715 and came to Prague from Vienna in 1749. He died professor
of medicine at the University of Prague in 1787. See Popisní Úřad Prahy
(City Archive).
[10] Wurzbach, *Biographisches Lexikon des Kaiserthums Oesterreich*, vol.
XXI.

knights, after that, civil officials raised to the nobility or knighthood or plain bureaucrats.

The other organs of government were likewise honeycombed with bureaucrats. The President of the Court of Appeals of Bohemia was Count John James Spork and the Vice-President, Count Štampach. These and their ten [11] councillors were members of the Bohemian Diet, and they often took part in its proceedings. The Court of the Land was headed by Count Prokop Lažanský, a very capable public servant with Josephinian leanings, who later became Governor of Bohemia and then Chief Minister of the Bohemian and Austrian Lands under Francis I. He was assisted by four councillors who likewise attended the Diet.[12] The "General Field Marshal and Commander-General in Bohemia" was Count Michael Wallis, a noble of English extraction. The great feudal offices, such as the Chief Chamberlain, Chief Steward, and the like, were either left vacant or were suppressed by Joseph II. By way of exception, Count Adalbert Černín still retained his Chief Land Master Huntsmanship.[13]

In general, the bureaucracy of the Austrian Monarchy of the Eighteenth Century was un-national and wholly subservient. We say "un-national," because if Joseph II had decreed Latin or Spanish or Turkish to be the language of Austrian officialdom, his officials would have submitted without a murmur. To them Germanization was only a means to a practical end. It was not the Germanization of the Nineteenth Century in which sentiment and imperialism dominated. In that sense of the word, then, these officials, from the three Bohemians in the State Council down to the meanest local official, had no nationality and felt none. They were the loyal

---

[11] *Schematismus*, 1791, pp. 129-131. The Councillors in the Court of Appeal were Baron Adam Escherich, Baron Leopold Sternegg, John von Ehrenberg, Baron Philipp Sweerts, Count Kaspar Künigl, Baron John Běšín, Baron John Janovský, Baron John Dubský, Count Philip John Sweerts and Spork, and Baron Wittorf-Hohendorf.

[12] *Ibid.* The Councillors of the Court of the Land were Count Rudolph Morzin, Count Leopold Spork, Knights von Hennet and Losenau together with the "asculants," Karl Štepanovský and Count Joseph Auersperg.

[13] *Ibid.*, 44-45.

servants of the House of Habsburg and went where they were led. Leopold II managed to change a few features of this hierarchy, and the story of these changes is the task of the following chapters.

II

THE ESTATES

Such was the hierarchy which governed Bohemia and the other Lands of the Habsburgs. What was the population that they governed? The Habsburg Monarchy ruled over some twenty-four millions of people, if we include the two millions in the Austrian Netherlands and the one and three-tenths millions in Italy. France and Russia had approximately the same population. Prussia with one-fourth the number of inhabitants had an army proportionately four times as great as any of these three powers. Again France had one and two-third times the revenues which the Habsburg Monarchy enjoyed, but Austria had almost twice the income of Russia and about three times the income of Prussia. On paper, Austria seemed the strongest military power (excluding Russia), but it was actually the weakest.[14] In France and in Russia the government was highly centralized and the country unified in speech. This was not true of Prussia which had added many thousands of Poles in the first partition of Poland, and still less true of the Habsburg Monarchy. Under the Habsburgs there lived at least seven large national groups besides the Germans. These were the Bohemians and Poles, the Magyars and Roumanians, the South Slavs and Italians, and the French. The Danubian Monarchy was about one-half Slavic, and the bond which held it to the Holy Roman Empire was loosening every day. Nevertheless, the period of which we speak, namely, the end of the Eighteenth Century, was the epoch in the history of the Habsburgs in which the domination of the Germans was undoubted. It is an interesting fact that the large number of Slavs in the lands of the

[14] *Schematismus*, 1789, II, 3, and 1791.

Habsburg Monarchy, even in 1791, was a subject of serious discussion. In a lecture delivered in the presence of Leopold II, the noted Bohemian scholar, Dobrovský, asserted with good ground, that of the twenty-one millions of population under the ægis of the Habsburgs (not including Netherlands and Italy) almost one-half were Slavs. They were about twice as numerous as the Hungarians. Commenting on their relations to the Habsburgs, he emphasized the fact that of all his peoples the Slavs were the most loyal to the dynasty which he represented. These Slavs, however, did not speak the same Slavic language, but at least five, and in 1790 they were even more disunited politically and insignificant for their numbers than at any time before or later.[15]

Census or conscription statistics of the Habsburg Monarchy in 1791, excluding Netherlands and Italy, gave the total population as twenty and eight-tenths millions, Bohemia counting about two and eight-tenths millions within her limits.[16] Then as now about two-thirds of this number were Czechs, namely, one and eight-tenths millions, and one-third were Germans, namely, a little over nine-tenths of a million. The outer rim of Bohemia, the mountainous region, was inhabited by the Germans, while the interior and the south and east were inhabited by the Czechs. The Germans devoted themselves more to industry, trade, and to public service, the Czechs were farmers and artisans.[17] Many of the cities were German.

[15] See *Krameriusowy Cýs. Král. Wlastenecké Nowiny,* January 7, 1792. "O stale wěrnosti, kterauž se narod Slowanský domu Rakouského po wssecken čas přjdržel." Translated from Dobrovský's lecture given in the Bohemian Society of Sciences in the presence of Leopold II, September 25, 1791. Dobrovský's total, excluding the Slavs in Styria, Carinthia, and Carniola, which he could only estimate, was 9,200,796. In this he counted Galicia at 2,580,795, almost 700,000 too low. The Croats were estimated at 367,000, the Illyrian Slavs at 253,000, the Bohemians and Slovaks at 6,000,000. *Schematismus,* 1791, II, 144.

[16] The best statistics are to be found in the Archive of the Ministry of the Interior (cited hereafter M I Archiv) Volkszählung, Carton 449. For 1790 the best table and document is 172 ex 1792.

[17] See Schreyer, *Kommerz, Fabriken, und Manufakturen;* Hartig, *Kurze historische Betrachtungen über die Aufnahme und den Verfall der Feldwritschaft bey verschiedenen Völkern,* pp. 386 ff.

Prague, in high society, was German, but the vast majority of its population spoke Czech.[18]

The area of Bohemia was 951 square geographical miles which meant that on an average it had one manor to a square geographical mile.[19] In 1790, Bohemia was proportionately the most thickly inhabited state of the Habsburgs. Within its boundaries the population had increased forty-two per cent in little over a generation and the increase of births over the death rate amounted to almost fifty thousand yearly.[20] A contemporary, who had a hobby of comparing the various parts of the population, stated in 1792 that the manufacturing part of the inhabitants of Bohemia produced goods to the value of some thirty-five million florins, about five millions more than the 950 odd manors could produce in natural products.[21] Yet the ratio of the population employed in industry could not have been so much as one is to five. Land was owned by the Estates and by the government to the amount of about forty-two per cent of the taxable lands. The serf held approximately fifty-eight per cent.[22] As we shall see later in greater detail, the heaviest financial burdens of the entire Monarchy were laid upon Bohemia. In spite of this fact, the Bohemian nobility shared proportionately more of these burdens than the nobility in other provinces.

Not counting Galicia, Bohemia had ten per cent of the area of the Austrian Monarchy proper, contained fourteen per cent of its population, and paid in between twenty-five and thirty per cent of the revenue. In other words, Bohemia was one-fourth the size of Hungary, contained one-third of its population, and contributed far greater sums to the Treasury

[18] Riegger, *Archiv*, I, for population of Prague.
[19] Kostetzky, *Die Verfassung des Königreichs Böhmen*, pp. 73-74.
[20] M I Archiv, Carton 449; 172 ex 1772. In 1762 the population was 1,640,600, in 1790 over 2,800,000. In 1786 the births registered 127,748, the deaths 81,026. See also 207 Dec. 1763 and Table D.
[21] Kostetzky, 222. See also *Die österreichische Monarchie in Wort und Bild, Böhmen*, II, 464 ff.
[22] *Ibid.*, 270 ff.

down to the time of Joseph II. It was one-half as large as all the Austrias, contained one-half of their population, and brought only a little less into the government coffers than all of these provinces. Such facts are often lost from sight unless they are brought together, and they demonstrate that, in 1790, excluding for the moment the rebellious Netherlands and the Italian Possessions, Bohemia was proportionately the richest, the most populated, and in spite of the great changes in the channels of commerce and trade, economically the most advanced state of the Habsburg Monarchy.[22]

What was the character of the Estates themselves? There were five Estates in Bohemia, the nobles, the knights, the clergy, the inhabitants of the cities, and the common people, i.e. the farmers, the farm hands, and the lowest industrial and artisan classes. Each had some rights and peculiarities in 1790 in spite of the great reforms of Joseph II.

The character of the Bohemian nobility has been one of the most important factors in Bohemian history since the Battle of White Mountain (1620). Before that momentous event took place, the Bohemian nobility was far more numerous than at any time thereafter. One account states that there were 254 noble and 1128 knightly families and that the latter, by means of local diets held in each circle, as in the county in Hungary, were more powerful than the nobles. At that time the Estates were overwhelmingly Czech. In order to become a member of an Estate in Bohemia then, the consent of both the Diet and the king was necessary. This was

[22] In area—geographical square miles of that day—excluding Italy and the Netherlands, the Habsburg Monarchy made up 11,172 square miles. Of this number Hungary composed 3,610, Galicia 2,427, Bohemia 951. See Kostetzky, *op. cit.*, 73-74.

In population (1790), Moravia had 1,350,000, Silesia 300,000. The Austrias (including Carinthia, Carniola, Görz, and Gradiska) had 2,725,000, Galicia, 3,224,000, Tyrol and Voralberg 656,000, Hungary together with Croatia and Slavonia 7,020,000 and Transylvania 1,500,000. See M I Archiv, Carton 449. Likewise in 1805—the relation was proportionately the same as in 1790— Bohemia with 951 geographic sq. m. had 3,722 inhabitants to a geographic square mile; Lower Austria had 3,105, Moravia 3,067, Galicia (East) 2,338, (West) 1,489, Hungary (alone) 1,842. Kostetzky, *ibid.*

called the granting of the citizenship, the *inkolat*.[24] The Land
Ordinance of Ferdinand II, seven years after the Battle of
White Mountain, gave the right of granting citizenship to
the king alone. This became the source of much evil as it
placed control of the membership of the Estates largely in
the hands of the king.[25] The Bohemian nobility fled from the
country after the Battle of White Mountain, though not without hope of returning. The Peace of Westphalia in 1648
ended that hope forever, and the Protestant Bohemian
émigrés were banished for good. Between two-thirds and
three-fourths of them had left and their estates were confiscated. Their manors were given away to the conquering warriors, or to the priests then with the army, or sold to faithful
Catholics.[26] The Bohemian nobility has never recovered from
the blow which was dealt to it in the Seventeenth Century.
The few Catholic Czechs left in the nobility were not strong
enough to give the new nobility their language or their character, although, on the other hand, it was almost a century
before they themselves submitted to the Germanizing influence of the government, the court, and the majority of the
nobility.

Under Leopold I (1657-1705) there appear to have been
four hundred forty-one noble families, of which ten were
families of princes, one hundred ten counts, eighty-three
barons, and two hundred twenty-eight knights.[27] Here we
see the new subdivisions from the simple classes noted above.
Also, the great decrease in the number of knights is apparent
at once. Among this motley assortment of nobles, many were
descended from European adventurers who came from all
parts of the Continent. Before the Battle of White Mountain,

[24] Schlechta-Wsserdsky-Wssehrd, "Die Entwickelung des böhmischen
Adels" (*Österreichisch-Ungarische Revue*, 1890, Neue Folge, IX, 81-114,
265-302).
[25] See Gindely, *Die Entwickelung des böhmischen Adels und der Inkolats-
verhältnisse seit dem 16. Jahrhundert*, and the more recent work by Baxa,
Inkolat (A Indigenat) v zemích koruny české.
[26] Bílek, *Dějiny české konfiskace*, pp. 25 ff.
[27] *Verneuerte Landesordnung des Königreichs Böhmen, 1627*, A 20, 24.

the Bohemian nobles, far famed in diplomacy and in war, had considered themselves the equal of the German nobility of Central Europe and by intermarriage with Spanish and Italian families had attained a distinguished position in the international politics of the Sixteenth Century. After 1620, the German and foreign nobles who made their homes in Bohemia called themselves "Counts" (Grafen), while the Czechs of noble origin had previously called themselves "Barons" (Svobodný Pani or Freiherrn). The foreigners immediately interpreted this as a sign of the native nobility's inferiority.

The composition of the new Bohemian nobility was a strange one. Nine of the very old Czech families remained in Bohemia after the Battle of White Mountain. They were the Černíns (Czernins), the Kinskýs (originally Vehynskýs), the Kolovrats (Kolowrats), the Kaunitzes (Kounics), the Lobkovices (Lobkowitzes), the Šliks (Schlicks), the Sternbergs, and the Waldsteins (Wallensteins). There were also other Czech families such as the Běšíns, the Bubnas, the Čejkas, the Dohalskýs, the Dubskýs, the Hřebenařs of Harrach (Haroch), the Choteks (in some lines German), the Lažanskýs, the Nostices (Nostitzes), the Voračickýs, and the Janovskýs. German or of doubtful nationality were the Lichtensteins, the Proskovskýs, the Andritzkýs, the Bechyněs, the Hartigs, the Hennigers, the Hochbergs, the Schirmdings, and the Štampachs (Bohemianized for Steinbach). Of four hundred forty-one families, from one-eighth to one-fifth had belonged to the old Bohemian nobility both Czech and German.[28]

The new nobility can almost be detected by its names. Here we find the Wallises from England, the O'Kelleys, the Taaffes, and the MacNevens (Macnevens or Maknevens) from Ireland, the Buquoys (Bouquoys) from France and the Desfours from Lorraine. The Schwarzenbergs, the Rottenhans, the Fürstenbergs, the Bartensteins, and the Götzes

[28] Vlasak, Der Altböhmische Adel und seine Nachkommenschaft nach dem Dreissigjährigen Kriege, 6-109.

came from various parts of Germany. The Auerspergs were Carniolan Slavs, the Trautmannsdorfs came from Austria proper, the Sterneggs from Styria, and the Rummerskirchs, the Vrbnas, the Hartigs, the Unwerths, and the Haugwitzes from Silesia.[29] This new Bohemian nobility very likely used Latin as the common literary language and may have spoken bad German at the beginning of its stay in Bohemia. The new nobility was therefore not national in origin, but cosmopolitan, with a decided leaning toward German, because its members were the creatures of the Habsburgs. Furthermore, it was not the result of slow infiltration, but of an abrupt change.[30] Its various components it is true gave up their former nationalities, yet had little desire in Bohemia save to get rich quickly. Meanwhile the Bohemian peasant, bound in serfdom, was forced to submit to these new masters who were separated from him not only by social position but henceforth by language also. The serf paid for the sins of his former masters. The denationalization of the Bohemian nobility as a result of the Battle of White Mountain has remained until this day the decisive factor in the history of Bohemia and of Czechoslovakia.

Upon this foundation the Habsburg dynasty continued to build further. In the place of Latin, German was encouraged, thanks to the complete destruction of the Czech literature by the Jesuits. And down to the middle of the Eighteenth Century, the new nobility was still called the "Bohemian Nobility." It knew no other name. But in 1752 Maria Theresa created a new diploma for her nobility. In the future if a person were created a noble he received his diploma of ennoblement in the Bohemian-Austrian nobility. This was one of the items in the measures of centralization which Maria Theresa promulgated in the ten years of peace, 1746-1756. It foretold the end of a distinct Bohemian nobility. Of equal importance was Bartenstein's teaching inoculated in Joseph II in the days

[29] Meraviglia, *Der böhmische Adel*, pp. 188 ff.
[30] See Gindely, *Die Entwickelung des böhmischen Adels*, 8 ff., and Baxa, *Inkolat*, pp. 4 ff.

of his youth, that it should be the cardinal principle of the policy of the Habsburg dynasty to promote the settlement and intermarriage of Austrian nobility in Bohemia and of Bohemian nobility in Austria. Thus was weakened nationalism, as well as provincialism.[31]

In 1789 the semi-official *Schematismus*[32] for Bohemia enumerates one hundred and seventy-four noble family names, of which fifteen were princely, seventy-nine noble, forty-four baron, and fifty-one knightly. Three of the fifteen princely families were of Czech origin; they were the Kinskýs, the Lobkovices (Lobkowitzes), and the Příchovskýs, of which one was then the Archbishop of Prague. Of the rest little can be said of their national feeling, either German or Czech. The majority perhaps had none; they were what the dynasty was. In general, men like the Kinskýs, the Sternbergs, and the Janovskýs were proud of their Czech extraction and helped to uphold and later to revive the Czech language. But they were rare men. Few stood out as active champions of the fallen nation. Those who might have played a public rôle in 1790 were either bound by their political positions to do otherwise or at least to be neutral, or were too timid to make an effective appeal on the question of nationality. When Baron Janovský, in the Diet of 1790, remarked, with a cynical sneer, that of the many that were clamoring for Bohemia's ancient rights, there were few whose forefathers had helped to secure them, he excited amusement rather than reflection.[33] The Bohemian clergy feared for their fold, and so they were insistent that the Czech language should not suffer so much in the future as it had in the past. This was the very clergy, which, under the leadership of the Jesuits, had done most to bury the language by the destruction of the literature of the Czechs and by their failure to produce another in its place.

Men like Prince Kaunitz, Count Leopold Kolovrat, and Baron Kressel, who held some of the highest positions in the

[31] H H S Archiv, Bartenstein Memoir—Denkschrift über die innere Verfassung Böhmens, Mährens und Schlesiens, 1759. No. 29.
[32] *Schematismus*, 1789, I, 290 ff.
[33] C N M Archiv, Sternberg Diary, November 27, 1790.

new Bohemian-Austrian State, could not be counted as Czechs, nor even as Bohemians, though they belonged to the Bohemian nobility but rather as "Habsburgians," the loyal disciples of the House of Habsburgs. Having attained to the great offices created by the union of the two sets of crown lands, the Bohemian and the Austrian (and later the Galician), they found it to their obvious material interest to oppose nationalization, or as they called it in the Eighteenth Century, provincialization. The trend of economic forces strengthened the hold of the Monarchy. Landholdings grew ever larger, and the noble became a landholding magnate, and magnates were always likely to be more dependent on an all-powerful sovereign. Thus, by the time of Maria Theresa, the princes held property to the value of 465 million florins, the counts 119 millions, the barons 10.1 and the knights only 7.5 millions. Even foreigners held land in Bohemia to the value of 22.4 million florins, and the State about 8.3. Thus, the barons and the knights, or the small landowners, were decidedly losing out in the struggle. The Schwarzenbergs were the richest of the princes, holding 14.4 millions worth; the Lobkovices then held about 7.9 millions worth.[34] Of the sixty-two great land-trust holdings (the *Fidei Commisse*), whose aggregate value was at least 26.4 millions, the Buquoys, the Kinskýs, the Martinitzes, the Morzins, and the Černíns possessed the greater portion.[35]

The Estate of the Clergy gives evidence of equally momentous changes. Down to the end of the reign of Charles IV the clergy composed an Estate, although attendance in the Diet then, as later, depended on the holding of land and the possession of the inkolat. The Hussite wars broke down this custom, and it was not until Ferdinand II made the clergy the first Estate in the Land Ordinance of 1627 that the Church recovered what it had lost in those times of agony after the burning of John Hus. The spirit which guided the Estate of the Clergy in Bohemia after the Battle of White Mountain was

[34] Prášek, *Joseph II*, II, 137.
[35] Riegger, *Archiv*, I, 426-432. Verzeichniss der böhmischen Fidei Commisse, 1787.

that of the Jesuits. In every Diet after the end of the Seventeenth Century they brought in a report on the condition of
the Catholic religion in Bohemia, which was formally accepted by the three remaining Estates. The suppression of
the Jesuits in 1774 took away much of the clergy's spirit and
led to rapid demoralization. The Edict of Toleration in 1781
and the suppression and reduction of the monasteries were
blows too powerful for the Church to withstand in its weakened condition. By these suppressions and reductions 1934
monks and nuns were forced to seek other livelihoods. There
remained 63 monasteries and 847 clergy in the orders. Twenty-
two Jesuit monasteries were suppressed and six hundred of
their members turned out into the world.[36] The clergy which
in 1763 numbered 6510, in 1786 was reduced to 5392, scat-
tered over about twelve hundred parishes.[37]

At the head of this hierarchy was the Archbishop of Prague,
Prince Příchovský. The three bishops of Litoměřice (Leitmeritz), Hradec Králové (Königgrätz), and Budějovice
(Budweis), whose sees were created after the Battle of White
Mountain, were the dignitaries who shared the highest honors
with him. The Cathedral of St. Vitus, on the beautiful
Hradčany, had a prior, a dean, and an archdean, who had
been important factors in Church politics. The commander of
the Crusaders of the Red Star and the landowning abbots of
the Benedictines, the Praemonstratians, the Cistercians, and
the Augustinians likewise sat at various times in the Diet.
The dean of Vyšehrad also came in for his share. The Arch-
diocese was divided into six districts; the Diocese of Litoměřice
(Leitmeritz) embraced the circles of Litoměřice (Leitmeritz),
Boleslav (Bunzlau), and Žatec (Saatz), and the diocese of
Hradec Králové (Königgrätz) was made up of the circles of
Hradec Králové (Königgrätz), Bydžow (Bidschow), Chru-
dim, and Čáslav (Czaslau).[38]

The clergy was itself divided into two camps, the one for a
very limited toleration, consisting of the young clergy, which

[36] Riegger, *Materialien*, IV, 719-740.
[37] M I Archiv, Carton 449, 207 Dec. 1763.
[38] *Schematismus*, 1790 or 1791. See also Second Desideria, Carton 517.

Joseph II himself had educated, and the other against toleration, composed of the old clergy, which could not adjust itself
to the new conditions. Fortunately, the former were still too
young in the Church to cause great friction. Doubtless both
would have combined to limit Josephinian toleration, in their
effort to control the theological schools, and their desire to
save the Bohemian language in the public schools. Joseph II's
theological schools would have turned out a German-speaking
clergy unable to preach to the vast majority of its church
members. In this the Catholic Church saw the downfall of the
Catholic religion in Bohemia.[39] In 1790 the Catholic Church
of Bohemia was morally shattered,[40] but it nevertheless remained a power in the Diet. Eventually it withstood the
inroads of rationalism, as shown in private life by the Freemasons and in public life by the bureaucrats representing the
Enlightened Despotism. It represented, however, an intolerant past which was afraid to repent, and it was at a decided
disadvantage because it faced an equally sinful dynasty and
a nobility which had the courage to repent.

The Estate of the Cities consisted of the property owners
in the cities, just as the other Estates were made up of owners of land in the country. The attendance of the Bohemian
cities in the Diet dates back to the time of the Přemyslides
in the Twelfth Century.[41] Before the Battle of White Mountain (1620), Prague and thirty royal cities were represented
in the Diet. Unfortunately, the Bohemian cities were filled
with Protestants, and this brought down on them the wrath
of the Habsburgs. By various measures, too detailed to mention here,[42] the cities were limited in their autonomy and
compelled to pay pecuniary fines to the monarch. By the

[39] M I Archiv, Carton 585, Steuer-Fusses (1714).
[40] Riegger, *Archiv*, I, Verzeichniss der Herrschaften und Güter in Böhmen
nach dem Werthe derselben—Verfaszet von M. C. . . . Rektificaturs v. Regis-
trator, 574 ff. The church owned 26.4 million florins worth of property under
Maria Theresa and perhaps 20 to 25 millions under Leopold II.
[41] Čelakovský, "Postavení vyslaných král. Měst na sněmech českých a
spor měst Hory Kutné, Plzně, a Českých Budějovic o přednost místa a hlasu
na sněmě" (*ČMKČ*, 1869, pp. 115, 243, 307).
[42] Falk, *Die landesverfassungsmässigen Verhältnisse der königlichen Städte
als vierten Standes im Königreiche Böhmen.*

Land Ordinance of 1627 only six cities had the right to attend the Diet. They were the four cities of Prague, Kutná Hora, Plzeň (Pilsen), and Budějovice (Budweis). The last three had been loyal during the rebellion, and it was impossible to keep Prague out of the Diet. So thoroughly, however, had the Habsburgs discouraged the cities that a century later they still slept within their feudal walls and worried over their microscopic local markets while Western Europe entered into commerce and industry on an imperial scale.

After 1755 Prague alone represented the Bohemian cities in the Diet and the others sent deputies only when the royal *Postulata* (demands) were read and approved. It does not appear that they even voted.** At any rate, the Estate of the Cities seems to have done nothing else in the century and a half which came after White Mountain but fight among themselves for second place, the first being reserved to Prague without dispute.

A table of statistics preserved in the archive of the Ministry of the Interior states that there were 244 cities, 307 market places, and 11,322 villages in Bohemia in 1790.** Prague then had a population of over 70,000 and Plzeň (Pilsen) perhaps between 8,000 and 12,000, while all other cities were still under 6,000.** Bohemia, even with these insignificant cities, had a greater urban population for its size than Hungary; in 1790 no city in Hungary had a population larger than 29,000.** Vienna, thanks to centralization the largest city in the Habsburg Monarchy, had about 270,000.**

Joseph II, by the legislation of 1784, had changed the officials who ruled over the cities from men chosen out of the

** Čelakovský, *op. cit.*, 312.
** M I Archiv, Carton 449, 172 ex 1792.
** Riegger, *Materialen*, III. See also MSS book in Archiv of Abbey of Strahov: Dominien in den K. Boh-b. nach alphabetischer Ordnung und denen Freysten dann—wie viele Meilen, etc. *Reise von Wien über Prag, Dresden, und durch einen Theil der Lausitz nach Berlin und Potsdam* (Leipzig, 1787).
** Grellmann, *Statistische Aufklärungen über wichtige Theile und Gegenstände der Österreichischen Monarchie*, II, 275.
** *Schematismus*, 1789, II, 3 ff.

locality to officials proposed by the government and selected
by a special election committee.[48] It was a blow at the autonomy of the cities, although the smaller cities in the country were less affected owing to the fact that in each merely
one official, a justice, was placed. There were three classes
of cities in Bohemia, the royal, the dower, and the serf, cities.
Neither the dower,[49] nor the serf, cities had any representatives in the Diet after 1627; the former since 1625 had been
the "table" cities of the queen, from which she raised certain
funds for herself; the latter belonged to the lord who owned
them. The royal cities[50] were of two kinds, those which sent
representatives to the Diet, and those which were not allowed
to do so. The subject (serf) cities had formerly been entirely
in the power of the lord, but under Joseph II they were almost entirely taken from their lords. The dower cities, as
well as the royal cities, were under the care of the two subtreasurers (thereby showing their fiscal traditions), Count
John Sternberg for the former and Knight Marcel von Hennet
for the latter.[51] They were governed by a mayor and a body
of magistrates. In theory, before the Battle of White Mountain, the officials of a city had the right to attend the Diet.
But the expenses of such a representation were too great and
so deputations were not generally sent. Some idea of the size
of the Estate of the Cities can be had by noting that in 1790
about 80,000 people were "citizens" and about 135,000 artisans. Not including the last-mentioned class, all three of the
higher Estates, the city populations, and the foreign trades-

[48] Toman, *Das böhmische Staatsrecht*, 169.

[49] The Dower Cities were Melník, Hradec Králové (Königgrätz), Chrudim,
Vys. Mýto (Hohenmauth), Polička (Policzka), Jaromeř (Jaromierz), Trutnov
(Trautenau), Dvůr Králové (Könighof), and Bydčov. Riegger, *Materialien*,
XII, 187 ff.

[50] The Royal Cities were Ústí n. Labe (Aussig), Beroun, Most (Brüx), Č.
Brody (Böhmischbrod), N. Brody (Deutschbrod), Milbohov (Elbogen), Ml.
Boleslav (Jungbunzlau), Boden, Karlovy Vary (Karlsbad), Kauřim, Klatovy
(Klattau), Kolin, Louny (Laun), Litoměřice (Leitmeritz), Stříbro (Miess),
Nymburg, Pelhřimov (Pilgram), Písek, Rakovník (Rakonitz), Rokycany
(Rokizan), Žatec (Saatz), Sušice (Schüttenhoben), Tábor, Domažlice (Taus),
Čáslav, Vodňany (Wodinau). *Schematismus*, 1789, II, 144.

[51] *Schematismus*, 1790.

men in Bohemia numbered 120,000.[52] Excluding Vienna, even with this small urban population, Bohemia had the most numerous and most advanced city population for its size in the Habsburg Monarchy proper.

The agrarian population made up the Fifth Estate in Bohemia. It had known better times, as when, in the days of the Hussites, it could bear arms. Archival statistics show that between 2.3 and 2.6 millions of people in Bohemia were country folk, the most oppressed of all.[53] Under Maria Theresa the Habsburg Monarchy began to undo the unfortunate legislation it enacted against the serf after White Mountain, and Joseph II's emancipation edict gave the serf the right to migrate, to marry of his own free will, and to learn whatever trade or profession he cared for. This loosened somewhat the bonds which had held agrarian labor together for several centuries. For this legislation the Bohemian nation has to thank Joseph II, who, in spite of his efforts at Germanization, was much lamented by the common folk of Bohemia when he died. He was at once the avenging justice and the executor of the judgment. The reform legislation of these years had established the rule that if a serf paid two florins yearly in state taxation he was a peasant. In 1790 there were 122,291 such peasants and about 441,990 sons and farm hands.[54] It may be estimated that about 82 per cent of the population was surely agrarian, and that about 18 per cent belonged to the cities and to the other Estates.

In spite of the fact that the central government, by means of its tax collector, its justiciar, and its schoolmaster, was penetrating ever nearer to the serf, agrarian life in Bohemia at the end of the century was still manorial. Each manor was a little economic and social world to itself. When the conscription, the state tax, and the schoolmaster were taken care

[52] M I Archiv, Carton 449, Table 1790 and Kostetzky, *Die Verfassung*, 222. Strahov MSS. note 45 above.
[53] *Ibid.*
[54] M I Archiv, Carton 449, 171 ex 1792.

of, the peasant became indifferent to everything else, except perhaps to the amount of the *robot* he had to render his lord or what he had to pay in money in its place.

III

CULTURE AND SOCIETY

Bohemian society in 1790 presented many resemblances to our own times. There was the same cry of the high cost of living, the "high-hat" question, painted women, and inflated manners. In a ball in Prague where six hundred people amused themselves in dancing, during the course of the evening only three or four women could be found unpainted, the rest looked like "painted" masks.[55] The women wore hats which could not go through the doors, and their choice of colors in dress was as shocking as their taste in hats.

Society adhered closely to the lines laid down by the political Estates and congregated in exclusive balls and in coffee and wine houses. The upper Estates, namely the great magnates, the counts, and a few of the barons, moved in the highest society, whose chief sin was extravagance in all conceivable lines and especially in the breeding of horses. There were some who maintained more than forty horses and were willing to ruin themselves to secure more. As a result, Prague was overfilled with equipages which made the night hideous as they rattled over the cobblestones of its hilly streets. Militarism held the upper Estates entirely in its grasp. To be an officer in the army admitted one into the highest society and made possible such unthinkable miracles as that "the son of a butcher could lead a countess under his arm." The feeling of caste was so strong that only militarism could overcome it. The pride and the vanity of the Bohemian noble was as far-famed as his irreligiousness, which he took as a sign of free-

[55] There is no better description of Prague by an impartial traveler than is to be found in *Beobachtungen in und über Prag* (Prague, 1787), pp. 121 ff.

dom from bigotry. To show this, he would talk long and loud. As a matter of fact no one could be more bigoted than he, nor more responsible for his subjection to the usurer, than he himself. The lower nobility, a few barons, the knights, and the higher state officials composed the second grade of society. The third consisted of the petty officials, the educated élite, both scholarly and professional, and the better merchants. The final and lowest grade consisted of the rest of the urban and all of the agrarian population, although a real peasant was always a little lord in miniature in his microscopic domain.[56] All loved to eat well and to drink their fill, and extravagance was as much in evidence with the insignificant peasant or tradesman as it was with the prince.

In such a society everyone, whether German or Czech, who did something for Bohemia, was a "patriot." He might build a theater, found a library, write a book about the country's glorious past or in defense of its ancient rights, or praise it with pen or brush. German domination was complete and unquestioned, therefore it was liberal. Herein also lies the explanation of the fact that the Germanization of the Eighteenth Century was not of the kind that the Nineteenth Century was to know. German was spoken poorly even by the higher society, but Czech was not banished and under Leopold II it was heard very audibly in the antechambers during the coronation ceremonies. Joseph II had spoken Czech poorly, but Leopold II had studied it with diligence and had no hostility toward it. The theater which Governor Nostic built in Prague presented Italian operas, for Prague above other European cities had an especial taste for music and the Czechs are a people noted for musical talent. The Casino in the Palace of the Thuns was a happy meeting place for the nobles. Here in the winter of 1786 a company of actors played several dramas in Czech, "in der nationalen Sprache," and thereafter in this

[56] Č N M Archiv, *Vavak Memoirs*, 1789-90. The manuscript copy was used in this study. For the published version, see P. J. Skopec (ed.), *Paměti Františka Vavaka*, 3 vols. (Prague, 1914-16).

theater and in others, Czech plays were on the billboards, and theaters were for once really full and became profitable investments. The mass of the population was Czech and the mere business acumen of the theater promoters led them to see that it was "better for the people to express themselves freely in their own language than stiffly in another." One contemporary remarked, "I know no land where a national drama would be easier to present and where it would find a higher support." [57] That was saying much for 1787, just at the time when Joseph II had about completed the official Germanization of Bohemia. These two forces, the Bohemian revival and autocratic Germanization, met in the last years of the reign of Joseph II, and in the reaction the revival triumphed.

Political discussion busied itself with the terrific slaughter caused by the Turkish war, the fall of the Bastille, the serail of the Turks, and the like. Stories of Turkish harems outnumbered disputes over the Bohemian Constitution. The age was too material, too practical to think of abstract political theories; it was indeed too lazy to think at all. Nevertheless Voigt wrote in the spirit of Montesquieu about law and the Bohemian Constitution, and Pubička and Dobner and Dobrovský and a group of others were busy composing the history of Bohemia or of its literature or trying to show in more ways than one that the Czech nation, although it had fallen low, was a nation with a proud historic past. They were furnishing the fuel to a future generation which would catch fire from a Slavophil Russia and a romanticist Germany.[58]

In cultured circles, the French Encyclopædia was a prize preserved and used with great care. A native thought it one of the proudest moments of his life to be able to show some intimate friend a Voltaire or a Rousseau or a Hussite Bible which had escaped the Jesuits or the censors. Czechs often wrote in

[57] *Beobachtungen,* 140.
[58] Novotný, *České dějiny,* I, Chapter I.

German rather than in Czech because they were sure to get a reading public, which after all was not small. Prague had two newspapers, bi-weeklies, a German and a Czech.[59] Both were typical of the journalism of the day. As they existed only on the grant of a government license, patriots were often constrained to write in the manner of Montesquieu in the *Lettres Persanes* or of Havlíček, the Nineteenth-Century journalist, in his letters about Ireland. Nevertheless it may be truthfully asserted that many of the scribblers of that day deserved even a stricter censorship than Joseph II provided. That hardly applies, however, to the average Bohemian who was ready to honor a Maria Theresa, to worship a Joseph II, and to respect a Leopold II.

In the country, the rôle of justice of the peace was a source of inspiration to the peasants. His "learning" and often his personality caused him to be much admired, and he was generally the natural leader of peasant revolts. Many of them were loyal patriots like Vavak, whose memoirs are the best individual source for the social life of the Bohemian peasant in the Eighteenth Century.[60] Social unrest, when it occurred, was usually caused by famines, the result of bad harvests. It is clear, however, from the evidence that has been handed down to us that except for several years such as those of 1770, 1771, 1775, and 1780, the peasants lived quietly and even in a rude splendor.[61] Vavak's memoirs show that in spite of the terrible harvest of "King Robot," merriment and even comfort were not lacking. The Bohemian peasant was a lord in comparison to the average Polish or Hungarian peasant, and if he was restless it was rather because he was better off than anything else.[62] In years when famine or drought struck Bohemia, misery was quickly apparent. Bohemia's population grew so very rapidly that production of grains did not keep up with consumption, and the government had not as yet

[59] *Prager Oberpostamtzeitung* and *Krameriusowy Wlastenecké Nowiny.*
[60] See *Vavak Memoirs*, 1789-90.
[61] Riegger, *Archiv*, I, 136-169; Wander, *Magazinirung.*
[62] *Vavak Memoirs*, 1789-1790, especially pp. 70, 115, 145, 159.

carried through any definite plan for the storage of grains nor perfected a complete system of transportation and of good roads.

It was a strange coincidence that, together with the political crisis described in the preceding chapter, the year 1790 witnessed a great drought and a partial famine. This must be kept in mind when making an estimate of the conditions under which Leopold II came to the throne.

CHAPTER III

THE LITTLE BOHEMIAN DIET UNDER LEOPOLD II

I

The Habsburg Monarchy at the Accession of Leopold II

The reforms of Maria Theresa and of Joseph II had profoundly changed the political structure of the Bohemian State, but had left society still separated into Estates.[1] The same was true in the Austrian Netherlands, in Hungary, and in the other possessions of the Habsburg dynasty. The government was modern, but the Estates were medieval. The absolute monarchy wished to turn its back upon the past and pointed hopefully to the future. The Estates looked to the past and desired to change the present so that the evident future, which meant their complete destruction, might not be fulfilled.

On January 1, 1787, Joseph II promulgated in the Austrian Netherlands the form of government described in Chapters I and II, and within a few months the old existing constitutions had been abolished and the new administration was completely established. The Estates of the various provinces opposed him at every step and sought to cripple the new administrative machine by withholding grants of money. For nearly three years threats, negotiations, and partial settlements followed one another until on December 12, 1789, revolt broke out. On the one hand, the government was handicapped by incapable and timid civil governors and by rash military commanders. The Turkish war and the hostility of Prussia did not ease the situation, which grew rapidly more and more acute. On the other hand, the opposition which

[1] See Mitrofanov, *Joseph II,* I and II, and by the same author, *Leopold II Avstriiskii, Vnieshnaia Politika,* pp. 1-34; 135-460.

Joseph II had aroused in the Netherlands, though temporarily united against him, consisted really of two distinct parties. Van der Noot led the clerical party, which desired to bring about a revolution for the benefit of the aristocracy, i.e. of the Estates, and to recover the old rights of the provinces of the Netherlands. This was the more numerous party, and it dominated a vast number of Belgians by its religious fanaticism. Vonck was the leader of the democratic party, which desired a constitutional government and, among other things, the extension of suffrage and the suppression of the privileges of the Estates. The two parties, at bottom in direct opposition to one another, made a compromise and declared the independence of the United Belgian States, a republic, by the Act of Union, January 20, 1790. This was the clearest proof that Joseph II had failed as a ruler. The democratic party was his natural ally, and yet he had so managed his affairs as to throw it into the opposition.

But his successor saw this blunder. On March 1, 1790, Leopold II offered the Estates of the Netherlands a compromise whereby the principles of the Act of Union and his own ideas of government were harmonized. On the whole, it was a great concession. The Catholic party, however, went over into extreme opposition, hoping for foreign aid, and in this the followers of Van der Noot were disappointed. But the Vonckists, realizing that the compromise offered by Leopold II was the best they could get, by July, 1790 began to forsake the opposition. Six months later, Leopold II put down the revolt in the Netherlands with armed force.[2]

[2] The Joyeuse Entrée, paragraph 59 of the constitution of Brabant is in *Goettingisches Historisches Magazin*, 1787, I. See also Arendt, "Die Brabanter Revolution" (*Historisches Taschenbuch*, 1843), Lorenz, *Joseph II und die Belgische Revolution* (1862), Juste, *La révolution brabançonne* (1887), Deplace, *Joseph II et la révolution brabançonne* (1880), Schlitter, *Die Regierung Josephs II in den oesterreichischen Niederlanden* (1900) I, and other works by the same author, Verhagen, *Le cardinal de Frankenberg* (1891), Zeissberg, *Zwei Jahre belgischer Geschichte, 1791-1792.* 2 vols. (1891), Wolf-Zwiedineck-Suedenhorst, *Oesterreich unter Maria Theresia, Joseph II und Leopold II* (1884), who uses the MSS memoirs of Duke Albert Saxe-Teschen ,and Sorel, *L'Europe et la révolution française*, I, 137 ff., who draws some interesting conclusions from the course of events.

The course of events in Hungary was not dissimilar. As in Bohemia, so in Hungary, the reforms of Joseph II had made the State modern, but left the Estates medieval. In contrast to Bohemia, Hungary possessed a national nobility and a virile local self-government. The Hungarian gentry met in their local diets (*comitate*-counties) down to the accession of Joseph II. It was here that the Hungarian nobility of 1790 had learned practical politics, for the Hungarian Parliament had not met for twenty-five years. Bohemia's nobility was unnational, at best neutral, and its circle (county) diets had been discontinued by the Habsburgs before the end of the Thirty Years' War.

In the winter of 1788 and 1789 the Hungarian Estates prepared for an armed resistance, which Joseph II hoped to overawe with a successful campaign in Turkey. At the same time, the Hungarian, Baron Hompesch, negotiated at the Court of Berlin for Prussian aid for the new Hungarian State whose independence was soon to be declared. It was hoped that Charles August, Duke of Weimar, the friend of Goethe, would be persuaded to accept the crown of Hungary.[3]

Joseph II had refused to acquiesce in the demands of the Belgian Estates, but the case of Hungary was different. The Netherlands were separated from the rest of the Monarchy, and it was to the advantage of England and Holland that they should remain Austrian. Matters could take their course there. But Hungary's refusal to give its quota for the support of the army and the continuance of the war with Turkey and the enmity of Prussia forced Joseph II into another policy with regard to Hungary. This state was far more vital to the Habsburgs than the Netherlands. Consequently Joseph II vaguely promised the calling of a Parliament, and when the reaction grew stronger issued the Patent of January 30, 1790,

---

[3] See Wertheimer, "Baron Hompesch und Joseph II" (*MIÖG*, 1901, VI, Ergaenzungsband), and his "Magyarország és II Frigyes Vilmos Porosz Kíraly" (Hungary and Frederick William II of Prussia) (*Budapesti Szemle*, 1902). Marczali has written on this subject in *Literarische Berichte aus Ungarn*, 1878, II, 28 ff.

whereby he abolished the new administration as well as all other reforms except those on toleration, on parishes, and on serfdom. The Patent did not satisfy everybody, but it broke the force of the opposition. During the next five months there was much preparation for this revival of feudal Hungary. Leopold II staunchly held to the rights which the Pragmatic Sanction of 1723 had given him, and he worked for an understanding with Prussia. The Hungarians put on their national dress, their poets wrote of Hungary's ancient glory, and their political thinkers discussed plans for a new constitution.[4] On June 8, 1790, the Hungarian Parliament began its first session.[5]

The Bohemian and Austrian Lands were likewise restless. They did not go to the extreme of desiring to break loose from the Habsburg dynasty as did the Netherlands and Hungary, but they had definite demands to make notwithstanding. They planned—and in this Bohemia led—to hold the monarch to a guaranty of the privileges which his ancestors had confirmed on numerous occasions. Furthermore, they did not seek to gain foreign aid, but expected their loyalty and the constitutional inclinations of Leopold II to assist them in accomplishing their purpose. Necessarily, they were at a greater disadvantage when it came to bargaining, even though in some ways they were as firm and daring in their demands as their sister Estates in the Netherlands and in Hungary.

On his way from Florence to Vienna, Leopold II had an opportunity early in March, 1790, to gauge the extent and volume of the reaction in the home of the dynasty. He was met at Bozen by the Estates of Tyrol, in Bruck an der Mauer

[4] For political literature see Concha Győző, *A Kilenezvenes Évek Reformezmei és Előzményeik* (The Reform Ideas of the 90's and their Origin) (Budapest, 1885). Marczali, "Alkotmány Ternezetek 1790—ben" (Proposals of Constitutions, 1790) (*Budapesti Szemle*, 1906) discusses the constitutional plans of this period.

[5] For the course of events in Hungary, see Adler, *Ungarn nach dem Tode Kaiser Josephs II* (Vienna, 1907), Marczali, *Der Reichstag von 1790-1791*, 2 vols. (1907), and his two other works: *Magyarország Története II. Joseph Korában* (1885) in 4 vols. and *Hungary in the Eighteenth Century* (1910). Useful for Transylvania is Zieglauer, *Die politische Reformbewegung in Siebenbürgen in der Zeit Josephs II und Leopolds II* (1881).

by the Styrian Estates, and in Vienna by those of Lower Austria. Each came forward with their complaints in a tactful, but firm, way. Thereupon, Leopold II issued on May 1, 1790, a Patent which summoned Diets in Bohemia, Moravia, Silesia, Upper Austria, Styria, Carinthia, Carniola, Görz, Tyrol, and Lower Austria. It was in these assemblies that the Austrian Desideria were composed. They differed essentially from the French *Cahiers* in that they accepted, with certain exceptions, the firm basis of absolutism and endeavored to fit the medieval structure which guaranteed their rights, into the new absolute state.

II

Bohemia in the Spring of 1790

Keeping in mind the course of events elsewhere in the Danubian Monarchy, we shall now turn to Bohemia. The Bohemian Diet had been reduced to such a political phantom that in 1790 the records of the Diet of 1789 could not be found! The institution then possessed only two functions. It might assemble when Joseph II thought it necessary, and it might elect its two representatives who sat in the Gubernium Council. It is not known whether Joseph II thought it still necessary to call the Diet to ratify the royal demands or postulata, so unchangeable were these financial agreements in the course of the six years previous to his death. To all intents and purposes, therefore, Joseph II had all but destroyed the Bohemian Diet.

But the Bohemian nobles met in secret in the long winter months when Joseph II's health was failing. These clandestine meetings were attended by a few bold souls like Counts Buquoy, Francis Kolovrat, and Adalbert Černín, who worked like "patriots" for the welfare of the "Estates," which they honestly mistook for the country and its people. It was in these meetings that the *Puteani Memoir,* the first paper of the Bohemian Estates on the question of the new system of taxation and serfdom, was composed. It was not long, however, before these secret meetings became public. On February 20, 1790, Joseph II died, and two weeks later the Court Chancellor was empowered by Leopold II to call a "Little Diet" in Bohemia, that is, a diet hurriedly called together and consisting of those nobles who happened to be in Prague. Thus, the Bohemian Estates renewed a tradition which Joseph II had labored so strenuously to annihilate.[6]

The Little Diet opened on March 7, 1790, with an attendance about three times as large as the regular Diet under Joseph II.[7] Twenty-one new members, mostly nobles, took their seats in the Bohemian Diet for the first time in this session. This large number of participants, however, did not represent even all the members of the Diet who then happened to be in Prague, and no attempt at all was made to summon those who were away from the city.[8] After Chancellor Kolovrat's communications of March 2 and 5 had been read, the Governor, Count Ludwig Cavriani, presented the twofold order of the day, first, the election of the "Reinforced" Executive Committee of sixteen, and then, the preparation of the memoir of the Bohemian Estates containing their com-

[6] See S Archiv, Journal of the Diet, 1790, which contains a few remarks under the year headed "1789"; M I Archiv, Carton 546: 72 ex Augusto 1790 and V. H. K. IV H 3, Zur Sitzung 4. Julius, 1790 and in Second Desideria, see the chapter on the Constitution. For the secret meetings see: *Sammlung einiger Schriften welche von den königl. böhmischen Ständen über das neue Steuer und Urbarial-System veranlasst worden.* Published in Dresden between April 6 and April 27, 1790, pp. v-vi. There is a copy of this remarkable pamphlet in the library of the Bohemian Museum which contains contemporary annotations of some value. Toman, *Das böhmische Staatsrecht*, 189, citing Pelzel's, Joseph II, MSS, states that on February 11, 1790, 60 members of the Estates signed a memoir which was handed to Joseph II on his deathbed.

[7] *Sammlung einiger Schriften*, pp. viii-ix. See S Archiv, Journal of the Diet, March 7, 1790, ff. The number present in the session of March 9 was 62; March 22, 76; March 30, 75. The nobility made up respectively 48, 58, 58 of this total. There is a document in the Land Archive at Prague which gives a list of those who attended the Bohemian Diets from 1783-1793. The average between 1783 and 1790 is something like 20 to 24 for each session and three-fourths of those present were public officials of Bohemia.

[8] See the diary, St. Vitus Cathedral Archive (cited, hereafter, S V Archiv) Kurze Anmerkungen, March 7, 1780: ". . . weilen er ordentlich nicht ausgeschrieben, sondern nur die in Prag befindlichen Herren Stände, ohne dass sie noch alle erschienen, für geladen worden. . . ."

plaints against the new system of taxation.[9] The result of the
first session was a lively debate over the contents of this first
Desideria. Many members of the Diet wished to present grievances other than those which they had against taxation, and,
as one contemporary put it, "especially as the other matters
pertaining to the country were just as important." By this
they meant "the abolished constitution, the suppressed rights
of the Estates, . . . the ruined financial credit of the country,
the insignificant trade, the decreased business, and agriculture
impoverished and exhausted by taxation and recruiting. . . ."
But "these patriotic efforts of the Estate of the Nobles" were
in vain, because the other Estates, and particularly the clergy,
would not support them.[10] The Governor therefore won his
first, incidentally his last, victory over the nobles, and the
Diet proceeded to the election of the "Reinforced" Executive
Committee of sixteen.

The election of this Committee, which was to draw up the
complaints of the Estates and otherwise wield much influence
in the affairs of the Diet, was of considerable importance. At
once the question arose whether the head of each Estate
should name the members who were to represent that Estate
in the Committee, or whether they should be chosen by the
Estate itself, or whether the entire Diet should choose them,
voting "promiscuously." The last method of election would
throw the Diet into the hands of the nobility, who had a large
numerical majority, and would nullify the hard-earned victory
just won by the Governor.

The Archbishop of Prague, as head of the Estate of the Clergy,
proceeded to name four of his colleagues in spite of the desire
of the majority of the Diet to the contrary. The Governor,
as head of the Estate of the Nobility, wished to do likewise, but
hesitated, and finally declared he would consult Vienna!
Then, after a consultation between him and the Estate of the
Nobility, the Governor "with all noble condescension for that

[9] S Archiv, Journal of the Diet, March 9, 1790.
[10] Sammlung einiger Schriften, Introduction, 9-10, MSS annotated edition.

one time only" dispensed with "his" right and allowed the
nobility to choose their four members of the Committee.

When it came to the election of the knights, it was discovered that only two were present in the Diet. Many of them
were off with the army on the Turkish frontier. Others were
engaged as government officials in distant parts of Bohemia or
elsewhere. As we have already noted, a number of them eked
out an impoverished existence as small landowners in the
country. The two knights who were actually present in the
Little Diet were so "new in the affairs of the country" that
the three other Estates "assisted in proposing the four committee men" who were to represent the knights. The Mayor
of Prague, as head of the Estate of the Cities, named himself
and three city councillors to represent that Estate.[11]

The main business of the "Reinforced" Executive Committee was to prepare the complaints of the Estates on the
question of taxation and serfdom and to present them for
approval to the Diet. One is surprised to read in the instructions to this Committee, that "they were to make a formal
reservation of the rights of the nation and insert also a petition to the king to restore them completely very soon." This
was the work of the nobility who insisted on this throughout,
and it shows that in this matter at least they and the Governor
had compromised.[12]

At this time a number of Bohemian noblemen happened to
be in Vienna. Under the guidance of Count Chotek, they
drew up a memoir on the new system of taxation, which considerably affected the action of the Estates in Bohemia. After
being transmitted to Prague it was compared with the memoir

[11] S Archiv, Journal of the Diet, March 9, 1790; S V Archiv, Kurze
Anmerkungen, *ibid.* The Archbishop named the prelates Krieger, Herites,
Bubna, and Suchánek. The nobles elected Prince August Lobkovic, Count
Prokop Lažanský, Count John Buquoy, and Count Francis Novobrodský
Kolovrat. The Diet selected for the knights, Knight Francis Hanisch, who
was present, and Knight Hynek, the Subtreasurer, Knight Joseph Leiner and
Knight Joseph Müllersdorf. The Mayor of Prague, Scheiner, selected, besides
himself, the city councillors, Štepanovský, Fischer, and Slívka.

[12] *Sammlung einiger Schriften,* Introduction, 10-11. "Im Schlusse . . . eine
förmliche Reservation der Rechte der Nation, und eine Bitte an den König
dieselben ehestens vollständig herzustellen, einzuschliessen."

by Puteani. Count Lažanský then prepared a third by revising these two papers. It was his work that was sent to the Court of Vienna as the opinion of the Bohemian Diet, while the Chotek Memoir was sent along as a minority opinion. The Estates expected that the two documents would be immediately sent to Vienna by the Governor. But he delayed. One contemporary complained that

Bohemia among all the countries was the last which sent in its complaints . . . it was by far the most oppressed, it was most imposed upon in all changes of government, and complained last. To stay in this unfortunate condition, it would be the last to be heard, and apparently the last to be helped out.[13]

In the meanwhile, the central government abolished, on March 22, 1790, the commission which was administering the new system of taxation as well as the horde of new officials whom it had called into existence. A week later the Bohemian Diet decided to send a deputation to Vienna. The instructions of this deputation ordered its members to congratulate Leopold II on his accession to the throne, to present the wishes of the Bohemian Estates that he allow himself to be crowned king of Bohemia, and to ask that the former constitution be restored and that the Executive Committee be reëstablished legally and with its former powers. The Estates asked also that the village judges who were created to help raise the taxes be abolished. After electing alternates for the deputation, the Diet adjourned.[14]

The fact that the Governor of Bohemia held back the Bohemian Desideria had an important result.[15] The Estates of Lower Austria had already demanded and received the monarch's sanction for the abolition of the new system of taxation, and his permission to return to the old basis of taxa-

---

[13] *Ibid.*, Introduction, 12, lxiii M S notes, and S Archiv, Journal of the Bohemian Diet, March 22, 1790.

[14] See the S Archiv, Journal of the Diet, March 30, 1790. S V Archiv, Kurze Anmerkungen, March 22, 1790.

[15] S V Archiv, Kurze Anmerkungen, April 3, 1790, and the *Sammlung einiger Schriften*, Introduction, 14.

tion after May 1, 1790. The Court Chancellor thereupon sent a note to the Governor of Bohemia hinting that "the Estates, in the present critical condition, should agree to like sacrifices in favor of the serf," i.e. the taxes which were due should be paid on the new basis until May 1, 1790, and that certain increases in the proportion which the serf had heretofore paid should be shouldered by the Estates. The letter of the Chancellor suggested that a deputation of two members from each Estate be sent to Vienna to act in conjunction with two of the Bohemian noblemen staying there. For this reason the Little Diet assembled once more on April 3. The Bohemian Estates decided after much debate that a deputation of two nobles, Counts Lažanský and Buquoy, should be sent to Vienna to coöperate with Counts Chotek and Leopold Clary then in Vienna. Instead of sending the congratulations, however, as earlier decided, a letter of thanks and good wishes was declared to be sufficient. The Diet decided, further, that the case of Lower Austria, which the Chancellor had cited, "did not yield enough to serve as a guide." [16]

The deputation of nobles, thus chosen, went to Vienna and carried on negotiations there for about a month. Count Chotek did not accept his nomination because he had already served on the committee which drew up the Desideria of Lower Austria. But Count Clary accepted the nomination, and he and Counts Lažanský and Buquoy sat with various commissions appointed by Leopold II to investigate the questions of taxation and serfdom, held conferences with the Chancellor, and concluded a bargain. The Estates agreed that for the year 1790 they would assume 244,000 florins of the amount of taxation which would naturally fall to the serfs when the government went back to the old basis on May 1, 1790.[17] In other words, in going back to the old basis, which was more favorable to the landowners than the new basis, the Estates agreed to take over that amount of the total increase (perhaps twice as large) which the serf would have to pay.

[16] *Ibid.*, Introduction, 14.   [17] *Ibid.*, p. 15.

The deputies did not have full powers to negotiate with regard to a settlement on the conditions of serfdom, and so this matter was postponed. Just as it had suggested the agreement of the Estates of Lower Austria in the matter of taxation, so now the government advised the Bohemian Estates to accept the Moravian agreement with regard to serfdom. The government was getting a tighter grip on the course of events.

In the meanwhile, Leopold II issued the Patent of May 1, 1790, whereby the Diets in the Bohemian and Austrian Lands were convened to consider questions of taxation and serfdom, of the Constitution, and of all the other grievances. These Diets began to assemble in the next two months and some were intermittently in session for over six months thereafter. On May 9, 1790, while the conferences of the Bohemian Deputation at Vienna were drawing to a close, the emperor issued a Patent which abolished the new Josephinian system of taxation. The old basis of taxation as it existed down to October, 1789, was provisionally adopted. In the matter of robot, the government allowed free bargaining between the landlord and serf, expressly stating, however, that the transaction should be watched by the officials of the circles.[18]

In order to show their esteem for Leopold II, the "Reinforced" Executive Committee made a grant in kind (grain) for the army,[19] and on May 30 or the next day it held a meeting to receive the report of the deputation from Vienna. The task of the deputation would not have been difficult had it been united. Counts Buquoy and Lažanský continued their rivalry begun in the Diet's earlier meetings and complained one against the other in the Diet. Count Buquoy wrote that Count Lažanský was too anxious to get back to his judicial

---

[18] The Patent of May 9, 1790 is printed in Grünberg, *Bauernbefreiung*, II, 458-62. For the Patent of May 1, 1790, see M I Archiv, Carton 513, 234 in May, 1790.

[19] *Sammlung einiger Schriften*, M S notes, 9-16. The amount was "300,000 Metzen von Hafer"—300,000 measures of oats.

duties in Bohemia and that he unduly hastened their work. The Estates openly derided the misunderstanding between two of their ablest members, and even the government was anxious that their quarrels should not disrupt the Diet. Otherwise, the report of the deputation was accepted. The Diet regretted very much that the government did not proceed to more vigorous measures against the serfs. But the rescript to punish obstinate serfs, such as refused to pay for or render robot, was being planned at Vienna. It was understood that they were to be drafted into the army so that their stubborn spirit might be broken.[20]

The "Reinforced" Executive Committee then prepared the program of the Big Bohemian Diet, which by the Patent of May 1, 1790, was to meet very shortly. This Committee issued a printed notice, certainly the first of its kind since the Battle of White Mountain, in which the matters which were to come before the Diet were announced. The three great headings, taxation and serfdom, the Constitution, and all the other grievances occupied a conspicuous part in the announcement. Under the heading of taxation and serfdom, especial care was to be taken as to how robot might best be turned into a money payment. Under the third heading, the Estates were to be given an opportunity to present grievances peculiar to their own class. This announcement was printed in the form of a circular and included, in addition to the subjects enumerated under the three headings, a number of matters which the Executive Committee itself desired to take up immediately. These referred to the prerogatives and the privileges of the Estates in judicial matters, to the taxation of liquors, and to mining. Usury was to be attacked by allowing free investment of Church money. Obstinate and rebellious serfs were to be punished more severely, and the justices of the peace were to be limited in their activity. These and other matters the

[20] Č N M Archiv, Sternberg Papers; Buquoy, Gehorsame Relazion, May 31, 1790, M S.

Executive Committee reserved to itself for preparation. They were later brought into the Diet and revised "over and over again."[11]

III

THE END OF SPRING, 1790. RESULTS

When we contrast the condition of things in the Habsburg Monarchy at the end of February, 1790, and at the end of June, the same year, we see that much progress toward a pacific solution of the internal problems had been made. When Joseph II died there was restlessness and confusion in every province, in addition to a war with Turkey and the enmity of Prussia. The summer, however, opened with Leopold II much more firmly in control. In the Austrian Netherlands Leopold II had once more separated the democratic from the clerical party and prepared the latter's downfall by isolating it from any aid by a foreign state. In Hungary, the Emperor was prepared to make certain concessions but stood up for the essential rights of the House of Habsburg as guaranteed by the Pragmatic Sanction. In allowing the Hungarian Parliament to assemble on June 8, 1790, he was giving the Hungarians an opportunity to air their grievances. Incidentally, he knew full well he would find allies within its membership and when worse came to worse he could delay action by negotiations. He took their minds off military preparations while he pushed the negotiations for an agreement with Prussia.

One bargain followed another between the government and the Estates in the Bohemian and Austrian Lands. In this process the Bohemian Estates were at a disadvantage for two reasons. Prague was then at least two days' distance by stage coach from Vienna, and Count Ludwig Cavriani, the Governor, refused to make any compromises whatsoever. The

[11] The circular was headed: Ex Deputatione D. D. Statuum in Regno Bohemiae, Prague, Die 31 Mai. 1790. S Archiv, Fasc. Diaet. 40: 1; 16293 ex 1790.

enmity between the Governor and the Estates increased daily. In contrast, the government at Vienna pursued a very clever policy. It struck a bargain with one province, preferably a smaller one, and then it used that as a precedent in its dealings with another. In this way it tried to have the Bohemian Estates accept the settlement which Lower Austria made with regard to taxation and that of Moravia with regard to serfdom. The Estates refused both, and, more than any other Estates of the Bohemian and Austrian Lands, tried to get a hearing for their constitutional grievances. In this they were more like Hungary.

Just as it was the policy of the government to separate the parties within the Austrian Netherlands and then isolate the province from without, to separate Hungary from Prussia and to make an end of the Turkish war; so, too, it was the aim of Leopold II to keep apart the Lands of the Bohemian and Austrian crowns and to find allies within each province. The government would have nothing to do with a congress of the provinces—its policy was to isolate them individually and then strike bargains with them. In Bohemia, the Governor made an alliance at the beginning with the clergy, the knights, and the burghers, and confined the Estates to a consideration of taxation and serfdom only. The Diet itself was not working together properly. Misunderstanding and suspicion between Estates, as between individuals, was the order of the day, and, had the Governor been more clever, any success at all of the Bohemian Estates with such a bad start would have been out of the question. The government delayed using force against the obstinate serfs as long as possible in order to have them on its side in case the Estates became too restless. Without the serfs, against whom the Estates in 1790 were urging coercive measures, the Bohemian nobility could not threaten rebellion. The crown of St. Václav, therefore, rested safely on the head of Leopold II.

PART II
POLITICAL

CHAPTER IV

THE BOHEMIAN CONSTITUTION UNDER LEOPOLD II

(PART I)

By the end of spring, 1790, Leopold II had transformed the perilous unrest in all the Habsburg domains, except one, from a latent desire for armed resistance into a peaceful discussion of grievances in legislative assemblies. The lone exception was Belgium, but we have already seen that the opposition there was dissolving, leaving only the clericals who had little hope of aid from without. There remained the urgent necessity of giving some sort of satisfaction to Prussia, for that Power was already mobilized on the northern frontier. And the war with Turkey still dragged on giving Prussia an excuse for mobilization and for treating with the Hungarians and the Belgians.

Leopold II sought for an understanding with Prussia—an understanding which both Maria Theresa and Joseph II refused for half a century to the detriment of their own just interests.[1] After several months of negotiation, Prussia and

---

[1] The foreign policy of Leopold II has been the cause of considerable controversy. For the best work on this subject see P. Mitrofanov, *Leopold II Avstriiskii, Vnieshnaia Politika*, I, 1, pp. 1-68; 135-220. The opposing views are sharply stated by Sybel, in *Historische Zeitschrift* (1863, X) and Herrmann, *Die Österreichische-Preussische Allianz vom 7. Februar, 1792 und die zweite Theilung Polens. Eine Streitschrift gegen H. v. Sybel* (Gotha, 1861). Sybel is inclined to picture Leopold II as having only the best intentions toward France and as defending the integrity of Poland. Herrmann looked at Leopold II as the head of the Italian secret police whose real aims lay hidden deep in his cold personality. The whole matter has been discussed since then, and Leopold II seems to have gained thereby. Ranke (see fn. 2) took a favorable attitude toward him, also Schultze, *Kaiser Leopold II und die französische Revolution* (Leipzig, 1899); Wolf, *Leopold II und Marie Christine. Ihr Briefwechsel* (1791-1792) (Vienna, 1867); and Schlitter, *Briefe der Erzherzogin Marie Christine, Statthalterin der Niederlande an Leopold II.*

Austria signed the Convention of Reichenbach on July 25, 1790.[2] Austria renounced any and all desires she may have had to gain by her conquests in the war with Turkey. Prussia gave up meddling in Hungary and the Netherlands. This convention led to three important results. In the first place, from the end of July, 1790, the armed resistance in the Netherlands was doomed to failure, and Hungary was wholly isolated in its hopes for independence.[3] In the former, Leopold II could proceed with armed forces to overcome resistance, in the latter he could take his time in outwitting the Parliament. The Convention of Reichenbach, in the second place, led to the peace with Turkey concluded at Sistowa, August 4, 1791, guaranteeing the status quo before the war.[4] And in the third place, it led to an entente between Austria and Prussia agreed upon more formally in the Declaration of Pillnitz, August 27, 1791. The two monarchs, Leopold II and Frederick William II, declared that they would help Louis XVI of France and his wife, Marie Antoinette, the sister of Leopold II, "to secure a monarchical government, which was equally fitted to the rights of the sovereign and the interests of the nation." This action resulted eight months later in a war between France and Austria, which

Nebst einer Einleitung: Zur Geschichte der französischen Politik Leopolds II (FRA, XLVIII); all tend to clear him so far as France is concerned. It is very likely that Leopold II wished only to secure the personal safety of Louis XVI and Marie Antoinette, although the contagion of the French Revolution was decidedly dangerous to the Habsburg Monarchy in the condition in which it found itself under Leopold II. Zimmermann, *Das Verfassungs-Projekt Leopold von Toscana*, gives Leopold II's views on constitutional government. The view that Leopold II was a real friend of Poland is gaining ground constantly.

[2] See Ranke, *Ursprung und Beginn der Revolutionskriege 1791 und 1792*, (Leipzig, 1875, 2d ed., 1879); and Glagau, *Die französische Legislative und der Ursprung der Revolutionskriege, 1791 bis 1792* (Berlin, 1896).

[3] For Belgium see fn. 1; for Hungary: Adler, *Ungarn nach dem Tode Kaiser Josefs II* (Vienna, 1907); Wertheimer, "Baron Hompesch und Joseph II" (*MIÖG*, 1901, VI Ergb.), and his "Magyarország és II. Frigyes Vilmos Porosz Király" (Hungary and Frederick William II, King in Prussia) in the *Budapesti Szemle*, 1902. See the Hoffmann Memoir in Sebastian Brunner, *Die Mysterien der Aufklärung in Oesterreich, 1700-1800* (Mayence, 1869), for the activities of the Freemasons.

[4] See Lampl, *Thronbesteigung Leopolds II und dessen Friedensverhandlungen mit der Türkei* (Pardubitz, 1891). The work is written in Czech also.

soon became a conflict between France and Europe.[5] The Convention of Reichenbach, therefore, had far-reaching consequences both within and without the Habsburg Monarchy. Before another half-year had passed Leopold II had recovered the Austrian Netherlands, tamed the Hungarian Parliament, true, at the price of concessions, and secured a lasting peace in the home of the dynasty, in the Bohemian and Austrian Lands.

Leaving aside the details of external politics under Leopold II and the course of events in the Netherlands, Hungary, and the cther possessions of the Habsburgs, we shall now consider in detail what happened in Bohemia.

I

THE BIG BOHEMIAN DIET, 1790-1791

The Big Diet, whose writ of convocation has been discussed in Chapter II, assembled on July 12, 1790, in the royal palace on the beautiful heights of Hradčany after attending a solemn Mass and hearing the "Veni Creator" in the chapel of the castle.[6] After the introduction of twenty new members, Count Ludwig Cavriani, the Governor of Bohemia and the presiding officer of the Diet, made a short speech and ordered the royal rescript calling the Diet to be read.[7] The Estates were asked to hand in their grievances in writing on three main subjects, taxation and serfdom, the Constitution, and all other matters pertaining to government. Ultimately these emerged from the legislative chambers of the Diet as the First, Second, and Third Desideria respectively.

Not since the days before the Battle of White Mountain (1620) had the Bohemian Estates had such an opportunity. This Diet was the first legal assembly of the Bohemian Es-

[5] See fn. 1 and 2, and Rose, *William Pitt and the National Revival* (London, 1911), pp. 674 ff.
[6] Č N M Archiv, Sternberg Diary, July 12, 1790.
[7] S Archiv, Journal of the Diet, July 12, 1790.

tates since 1627 in which the Royal Commissioners did not appear and give their permission to the legislation which was to be introduced.* It was also the first in which newer ideas of parliamentary procedure, such as voting as an entire house and not as Estates, and the initiation of legislative bills, were introduced. Finally, it was the largest Diet which had assembled since the days of White Mountain. More than one hundred members of the Estates attended its first meetings, and of this number five were princes and more than two-thirds nobles.*

Governor Cavriani was a serious-minded Josephinian bureaucrat to whom legislation by the Diet was loud talk and useless scribbling. Himself a better administrator than orator, he read nearly everything he had to say in the Diet. When called on as the Diet's presiding officer to make, on the spur of the moment, an important decision, he vacillated or acted so tactlessly that he gave the opposition many opportunities to make his seat uneasy. The Governor learned by sad experience that ordering and administering a Josephinian government by paper decrees and ruling an assembly of Estates by means of his voice and personality were two very different things.

In the first session, that of July 12, Count Künigl and the Governor fell out over a question which the former raised as to how many times the "Reinforced" Executive Committee should read before the house the proposals, or bills, it had to take care of. Count Künigl wanted them read at least twice. The Governor became excited and declared, with some heat, that the "Directorium," by which he meant himself, would not allow itself to be dictated to by individual members of the

* See M I Archiv, V. H. K. IV H. 3 Ministerialschreiben (Kolovrat to Cavriani): Da es übrigens bey dem auf den 12. Julius ausgeschriebenen allgemeinen Landtag sich um keine Postulata handelt, desfalls im Namen S. M. den Ständen keine Proposition zu machen ist, folglich auch keine königl. Kom'säre dabey einzutreten haben.

* S V Archiv, Kurze Anmerkungen, July 12, 1790 and S Archiv, Journal of the Diet, ibid.

Estates. Count Künigl's effort fell through because nobody supported his proposal, which he perhaps got from his Masonic experiences, for he was one of the leading Masons of Prague. Count Wallis moved, just as the first session was coming to a close, that the journal of the Diet for the day be read in order that it might be corrected and properly preserved.[10] The Diet decided that a journal should be kept and that it be read at the beginning of each session and corrected by eight elected "correctors," who would assist the two secretaries of the Diet. The importance of this decision is evident when one considers that not since the Battle of White Mountain had a journal of the Diet been kept. The Diet ordered that copies of the journal were to be kept in the Royal Land Tables, and the bills before the "Reinforced" Executive Committee were to be copied, registered, and exposed to view in the four rooms of the Estates, which were also used both for the special meetings of the separate Estates and as lounging rooms.[11] On July 14 the Diet debated the question of the value of their daily decisions. Some members contended that the journal which contained them was read only to make sure that it was written up in the "true sense" of the action taken by the Diet. Others declared that a bill or a conclusion of the Diet should have three readings and the assent of the majority, before it could be called the formal conclusion of the Diet, as was the case with "bills in the English Parliament." Count Lažanský was in favor of allowing the Diet to change its decision when it changed its mind, and there were many who supported him in this. But the Governor remarked that this would produce many complaints, and every absent member on coming to a future session might ask the Diet to open an old subject up once more when the decision had not been to his taste. The Diet ruled that a conclusion once taken was not to be changed unless some new phase of it came up.[12] The question was not

[10] Č N M Archiv, Sternberg Diary, July 12, 1790.
[11] *Ibid.*, July 13, and S Archiv, Journal of the Diet, *ibid.*
[12] *Ibid.*, July 14, 1790.

settled at this time, however, and it remained a thorny one throughout the proceedings of the Diet. Nor was the rule thus laid down strictly adhered to.

The manner in which the Estates treated legislation becomes clear when one examines the journal for the session of July 17, 1790. Proposals and bills were given by members of the Diet to the "Reinforced" Executive Committee which, after registering and numbering them in order of receipt, brought them up for discussion in one of the following sessions through its committee reader (referent or reporter), who was generally Baron MacNeven. On the day of which we especially speak here, more than a hundred bills were brought before the house, about seventy-five of which were later actually incorporated into the Desideria, the greater number of them making up the Third Desideria.[13] In voting on questions before the Diet, except in the election of important committees, each member stood up and publicly cast his vote, making a speech at the same time, if he so desired. Only in the election of important committees and deputations was voting by ballot. As time went on, there was less and less voting by Estates, and before the Diet realized it, at the instigation of the government it was voting as an assembly and not as four separate Estates. The meetings of the Diet were not open to the public, although Count J. Dillon O'Kelley warmly advocated this. Owing to the fact that it was expected that the entire legislation would later be sifted out and the important "deeds" handed down to posterity, no public documents were printed. Count Joseph Černín unsuccessfully advocated that the Diet publish a gazette for the benefit of the public, which was not admitted. The Diet, under the influence of the government, showed itself adverse to informing the public, in any way whatsoever, what the "fathers of the country" were doing in the Diet. To do so suggested too many analogies to French conditions.[14]

[13] *Ibid.*, July 17.
[14] See Z Archiv, Abschrift der Beschreibung jener Ceremonialien, welche vor der Landtags-Proportion über die von Sr. M. dem König in Böhmen durch

So much for the manner in which the Bohemian Diet conducted its business in the days of Leopold II. From July 12 until September 6, 1790, its first term, it was in session nearly every other day. After seven weeks of recess, the Diet reassembled on October 27, 1790, and remained in session exactly a month. It then adjourned for the holidays and met on January 17, 1791, for a short term of two weeks, adjourning permanently on January 29 after having completed the last of the Desideria and their supplements. On May 10 and 11 two sessions were held to consider some of the royal decisions on the Desideria and in June, 1791, the royal Postulata of the year 1792 were brought forward. In 1792 the Diet met on January 9, and was still in session when Leopold II died.

We have already noted that the Diet of July 12, 1790, opened without the presence of the royal commissioners and without the presentation of the royal Postulata. There is good reason to believe that the government and some members of the Estates wanted to be ready to present the Desideria to the king at the end of the first term in September. That they were not ready was the result of the work of Count Buquoy and his followers who wished to do the best they could with the Desideria. Count Buquoy could marshal as many as forty votes at times, and he ultimately secured the enactment of many things that he advocated. He and his followers represented the opposition against the government and against the reforms of Joseph II. Other members, like Count Leopold Clary, were willing to bargain with the government. Count Lažanský, although a government official, was also labeled "a patriot." He managed to reconcile the complaints of the Estates and the just interests of the government. Thus he made proposals, but if they were not accepted

---

Ihr k. k. Kommissäre von den Höchlöblichen Herren Ständen alljährlich zu fordernden Landtags-Postulata, bis zum hierab absassenden und zur Publikazion gelangenden Landtagsschlüsse nach der von alters herabgebrachten, und eingeführten Gewohnheit beobachtet werden. Exped. 26 October. Cavriani, (Date perhaps 1790—but surely between 1787-1791) Ledwinka, Secretary. See also Č N M Archiv, Sternberg Diary, November 10, 1790.

by the government, he meekly let them drop. His propositions were well chosen, and they definitely prove that he had an excellent knowledge of Bohemia's past history. His case, however, was that of a capable man who did not wish to inconvenience the government of which he himself was a servant.

Because of the very large number of nobles, the nobility were opposed by the other three Estates on many questions when the voting was by a simple majority and not by Estates. In general, the nobility had the strongest leanings toward reëstablishing the Constitution. When once the subject of religion was discussed, no Estate was so reactionary as the clergy. Here the three other Estates joined to save private religious toleration. Both the nobility and the clergy outwardly pitied the knights for their insignificant numbers, but both were really glad that the knights were so powerless. In turn the three upper Estates opposed themselves flatly to the City Estate; and the more so as time went on and exposed the trend of the French Revolution, which fell at last into the hands of the city mob. Some members of the nobility and of the clergy were willing to give the cities a slightly better representation, but only as a matter of expediency, not as a matter of right. The Governor and the government supported the Estate of the Cities whenever they got a chance and often bewailed the weakness of the knights. As between the clergy and the nobility, the government was more likely to make concessions to the latter than to the former, especially in questions of religious policy. From all this it is clear that unity in the Bohemian Diet was a myth, and had the government of Leopold II been entrusted to a cleverer governor, things would have come out differently, especially if one considers that the government possessed a weapon against the Estates even greater than their own disunion, namely, ninetenths of the population of Bohemia, the serfs.

The second term of the Diet of 1790 opened on October 27. It had two tasks to perform on both of which it worked but both of which it left uncompleted for the next term. The first was the completion of the Desideria and their supplements, and the second was the passage of the royal Postulata for the next year, 1791.

On November 10, 1790, the royal commissioners came to present the royal Postulata in the ancient ceremonial way. The traditional formalities which such an event called for are of interest. The Principal Royal Commissioner and his two colleagues, after receiving their credentials from Vienna, sent them to the Registrar of the Estates,[15] who in turn fixed the date of their call on the Governor. On the day set aside for the audience the two commissioners called on the Principal Commissioner in a six-team equipage. The Principal Commissioner took his seat among his colleagues and two empty six-team coaches proceeded along behind them on parade, with flambeaux and men in liveries, to the palace of the Governor. As they arrived before the palace, the Governor in gala attire attended by his "house officers" and liveried servants came forth to the carriages to meet them, and led them into the palace. After the three commissioners had taken their seats opposite the Governor, the Principal Commissioner presented his credentials and those of his colleagues as well as the Royal Rescript. In the same way that they came, they then departed for their lodgings. The Governor on his return to the palace opened the documents and sent them to the Secretary of the Diet and ordered the commander of the military in Prague to give the commissioners the guard of honor.

Then came the ceremonial in the Diet. The Secretary in open session gave the documents entrusted to him to the Governor, and the four heads of the Estates named two members from each to introduce the royal commissioners. This delegation of eight rode to the lodgings of the officials to fetch them to the Diet. The two burghers rode standing in their coach and had their own livery. The two knights rode in the coach of the Secretary of the Land, one of the head officials

---

[15] Ständische Aktuar—Perhaps Registrar or Archivist. See fn. 14 for the ceremony.

of the Land. The two members of the clergy and the two nobles went in the Governor's "four-seated gala wagon" accompanied by the Governor's liveries, and after them came others wearing the liveries of state. They arrived at the lodgings of the Principal Commissioner, where the other two commissioners were ready to receive them. After exchanging compliments, in much the same way as already described they drove to the Diet chambers in the royal palace. They entered the Diet, the Estates rising to greet them. The Principal Commissioner made his speech in Czech. The Secretary of the Diet read the credentials and instructions of the royal commissioners in both Czech and German, *a pertis valvis*, whereupon the Governor received the documents, transmitted them to the Secretary of the Land Tables, the legal depository, and thanked the commissioners. The Diet then adjourned and the Principal Commissioner invited guests to dinner where he drank to the health of Leopold II and gave the toast *Augustissima Patronanza* amid the blare of trumpets. The nobility amid a like blare of trumpets then proposed a toast to the commissioners.

The clergy next presented its special report on the state of religion, which ever since the end of the Seventeenth Century had been incorporated in the conclusions of the Bohemian Diet. The Diet approved it and also the royal Postulata, which under Leopold II were none other than the amounts asked of Bohemia by Joseph II before he introduced his new system of taxation. This accomplished, the commissioners were once more called into the Diet. Each Estate assembled beforehand in its own lounging room. After the nobles had been led into the Diet chamber, two deputies from the clergy entered with the *Geistliches Votum*, as their special report was technically called, and one of them read it, gave it to the Governor, and retired. The nobles then sent two deputies from their midst to lead the Estate of the Clergy into the chamber. When the two Estates had taken their places on the benches, four deputies, two from each Estate, were sent to call in the knights who in the meantime had been given time to think over the report. Soon two knights came back, and with thanks returned the Votum to the Governor, whereupon the Estate of the Knights was introduced into the chamber. In turn the City Estate was invited by six deputies and was in like manner introduced into the Diet. On entering the chamber, it was the custom of the Estate of the Cities to exclaim in Czech, "Wydite a Poyte" (enter and come in). When all were seated the Secretary of the Diet read the report of the clergy and this together with the rest of the "conclusion" received the seal of the officers of the Diet and of the royal commissioners. This act was called "sealing the conclusion of the Diet" and after the monarch had signed it, it became law in Bohemia. The session ended with the members of the Diet calling witness to their approval and seal with the Czech words, "Příznavam se" (I acknowledge myself). Further banquets and gala rides were indulged in until finally this parliamentary holiday remained only as a pleasant memory for the Eighteenth-Century noble, who, with his long Desideria and endless scribbling, had worn out everybody but himself.[16]

The Desideria prepared by the Bohemian Estates were delayed for six months for two reasons: (1) Buquoy and his friends deliberately prevented quick action; and (2) when soon after the middle of August, 1790, they were ready to present the two Desideria on Taxation and Serfdom and on the Constitution, the government was not willing to receive them.[17] The fact was that in the trying days before the Convention of Reichenbach (July 25, 1790) the government wished to have a solid front in case of a disagreement with Prussia. After the Convention was signed, this need was no longer urgent and Buquoy and his young enthusiasts "with a

[16] A ceremony similar to this took place at the publication of the conclusion of the Postulata of 1789 in the Session of January 17, 1790. See Č N M Archiv, Sternberg Diary for that date.

[17] S Archiv, Journal of the Diet, August 14, 1790, and Č N M Archiv, Sternberg Diary, ibid.

dangerous spirit of innovation" were allowed to go on with their work. The imperial election in October (1790) and the suppression of the revolt in Belgium in November followed in quick succession. Meanwhile, the government, in order to gain time, dallied with the Estates for several months on the question of instructions (on the Desideria) to be given to the deputation which had been elected early in September. In short, the government wished the deputies to come to Vienna with full power to negotiate and agree on the points at issue after the manner of the little province of Görz! The Estates, mindful of the fate of previous deputations, pointed out, perhaps erroneously, that the 11,000 additional tax units heaped upon Bohemia in 1748 and 1757 and paid regularly since then were the result of the dealings of such a deputation. The instructions of January 14, 1791, gave the deputies no power to negotiate otherwise than in the terms stated in the Desideria.[18] All other propositions were to be referred to the Diet.

The Third Desideria was discussed throughout the second term of the Diet (October 27-December 27, 1790). Late in December, 1790, the government suddenly desired to see the end of the Diet.[19] The imperial election had gone through properly, Belgium was once more under the rule of the Habsburgs, and peace with Turkey was in sight. There was no reason why the government could not settle the Desideria of Bohemia and the demands of Hungary in the spring (1791) before events in France should lead to serious consequences. But by this time the diets everywhere in the Bohemian, Austrian, and Hungarian Lands had come to like the idea of

[18] H H S Archiv, Staatsrat Akten, 2333 in 1790. Alleruntertänigste Nota, August 2, 1790, contains two letters of Count Leopold Clary (July 24 and 27, 1790). He describes Buquoy's followers as "nur wenige junge unerfahrene, wiewohl talentirte Männer überlassen sich einem inneren Besonnensgeiste und in gegenwärtige Lage gefährlichen Neuerungsgeiste. . . ." But they managed to get forty votes together and it was necessary to get the Archbishop to cast his vote to make a majority of one on the question that no ordinance of the king was law until it had received the consent of the Estates. In the Instructions given to the Deputation, they were ordered to stand by the Desideria, "ohne Rückfrage nicht abzuweichen."

[19] M I Archiv, Carton 513, 173 ex Dec. 1790, 147 ex Jan. 1791.

remaining in session. The government, however, anxiously watching the course of the French Revolution, was beginning to fear lest the populations of the cities, especially the urban centers of Bohemia, which were dissatisfied with the treatment accorded to them in the Diet, might become restless. In a fiery speech on November 27, 1790, the mayor of Prague asked for more rights and for a better representation of the Estate of the Cities. A year later the actual attempt of the Bohemian peasants to send deputies to the Diet indicated the spirit of those who felt oppressed.[20] The Governor, and finally the Diet also, promised to bring the legislature to a close at the end of January, 1791.[21] Precisely on January 29, 1791, the Bohemian Diet completed the Three Desideria and their supplements, composed the instructions of the deputation which was to convey their literary labors, and adjourned.[22] Thus closed the most important Diet held in Bohemia since the Battle of White Mountain. When Governor Cavriani laid down the gavel on January 29, 1791, he knew he had ended his days of usefulness in Bohemia. The nobles, in spite of his autocratic behavior, had succeeded in shaping large parts of the Desideria to suit themselves. They had defeated him on countless occasions by majority voting, and once had made it so unpleasant for him that he was forced to retire for several sessions because of illness. Whether from jealousy or for some other reason, he had quarrelled with Count Leopold Clary, thus losing the support of many followers and helping to throw the Diet into the hands of Count Buquoy. He had vacillated where he should have been firm, had acted brutally where he should have been tactful. In the spring of 1791, Count Cavriani was "promoted" elsewhere, and Count Rottenhan was made Governor to the entire satisfaction of the

[20] See Č N M Archiv, Sternberg Diary, November 27, 1790, and the chapter on serfdom.

[21] See especially, *ibid.*, November 3, 1790, and the Instructions of the Deputation. Sternberg Papers, December 2, 1790, Court Chancellery note. The early correspondence can be found in M I Archiv, Carton 513, 160 ex Augusto 1790.

[22] S Archiv, Journal of the Diet, January 29, 1791.

Estates. He possessed those qualities which Cavriani lacked, namely, a glib tongue to lull the Estates and tact to soothe them into believing that the government was going to do something entirely different from what it intended.

The Desideria were passed upon by various organs of government. They always went to the Gubernium first, then to the Court Chancellery, to the Commission on Desideria presided over by Archduke Francis, and finally to the State Council. In the case of the Third Desideria, the Court Chancellery asked the opinions of the Commission on Religion, the Supreme Court, and the Treasury. In general, the decision of the Commission on Desideria was most important, although in the consideration of the Third Desideria the Supreme Court and the Treasury played important rôles. The royal decision on the Constitution was published August 12, 1791, at the time of the coronation of Leopold II as king of Bohemia. The negotiations with regard to the restoration of the crown jewels had been successful and with the renewal of the old Bohemian Constitution on the basis of 1764 there was much jubilation at Prague. The main decisions on the Desideria on Taxation and Serfdom and on the Third Desideria were published in the Decree of October 28, 1791, a few odd decisions coming later in various decrees. The meetings of the Diet held May 10 and 11 and June, 1791, were only echoes of what had gone before. The Diet of January and February, 1792, considered various parts of the Desideria left over as unsettled, but no definite conclusion was arrived at in these matters during the lifetime of Leopold II, and few results were obtained in the first years of the reign of Francis II.

II

THE ESTATES AND THE GOVERNMENT INTERPRET THE
BOHEMIAN CONSTITUTION

Nothing in the deliberations of the Bohemian Diet is so interesting as what was said and done in its interpretation of

Bohemian constitutional history. The Second Desideria, or the Desideria on the Constitution, contains a long introduction in two parts in which is embodied what the Estates considered had been the Constitution of Bohemia down to 1627. The first part of the introduction extends from the origin of the Diet down to the Sixteenth Century. It was written by Baron MacNeven and called the "Historical Exposition." [23] The fact that it went so far back in its narrative of Bohemian history opened it to criticism as violating the Rescript of Leopold II to describe the Bohemian Constitution as it was under Maria Theresa. After some discussion, the Diet accepted the work of Baron MacNeven, and thanked him for his "fatiguing and fundamental . . . exposition of 'Fatherlandish' history." The Protocol of the Diet expressly stated that the "exposition" was to be used as a basis for comparison with their former condition "from which the Monarch could convince himself of the moderation and reasonableness of their desires." It was also stated that not all of the former rights and powers spoken of as then belonging to the Diet and Estates were appropriate in 1790, nor did the Estates demand them. Their real desire was "to show the origin of the Estates by means of this exposition." [24] The second part of the introduction to the Desideria on the Constitution was written by the "Reinforced" Executive Committee. It dealt with the period be-

---

[23] MacNeven's "Historische Darstellung" can be found at the beginning of the Second Desideria, M I Archiv, Carton 517. It bears the date September 4, 1790.

[24] S V Archiv, Kurze Anmerkungen, August 28, 1790. "Per unanima mit wenigen conträren Stimmen von der Geistlichkeit, diese Schrift (MacNeven's) dem K. vorzulegen . . . mit diesem lediglichen Insatz, dass gleich Anfangs dieser historischen Darstellung beizusetzen sei, dass die hhly. Stände alle diese Vorrechte und Privilegien als denen dermaligen Zeiten nicht passende von darum nicht aufführen, gleichsam sie anwiederum in derselben Besitz zu gelangen wünschten sondern Ihr. Maj. nun die eigentliche ständische Entstehung dadurch beweisen wollen, welches ohne dies aus dem Schlusse dieser Schrift Sr. Maj. erkennen werden." See Bohemian Diet, Official Journal, August 28, 1790: ". . . dass dieses keineswegs in der Absicht, um hiernach die ständischen Schlussbitten auf den Stand jener früheren Zeiten auszudehnen sondern, nur ihrem gütigsten Monarchen durch den Vergleich ihres vorigen Standes, aus jenen, den so von seiner Gerechtigkeit, und Gnade ganz von der Mässigkeit und Billigkeit ihrer Bitten zu überzeugen, gemeint seyn."

tween the Battle of White Mountain (1620) and the death of Joseph II (1790).

Count Ludwig Cavriani, the Governor of Bohemia, in a letter accompanying the Constitutional Desideria and the opinion of the Gubernium Council, stated that the introduction of the Desideria should have gone back only to the times of Maria Theresa or at most to Ferdinand II, because under the latter the form of government "was an unlimited monarchy and the succession as well as the structure of government were not in the least doubt." [25] It was, therefore, useless to examine the rights which the Estates had before Ferdinand II. As an answer to the work of Baron MacNeven, he had secured a memoir on the same subject from the Gubernium Councillor, Joseph Anton von Riegger, the famous statistician of Bohemia. Baron MacNeven, after reading the Riegger memoir, wished to reply to it, but the Governor refused to "have things spread out still more." Two views on the constitutional history of Bohemia are presented in the two memoirs. Baron MacNeven's "Historical Exposition" presented the side of the Estates, while Riegger's "Historical Elucidation" gave the government's point of view, incidentally that of the Habsburg dynasty.[26] By examining both we shall be able to understand more clearly the constitutional theories existing in Bohemia in the Sixteenth, Seventeenth, and Eighteenth Centuries.

It was Baron MacNeven's object to treat of "the real sphere of activity of the Estates and the extent of their influence on the administration." He discussed in all eight subjects, such as, the election of the king and the influence which the Estates exerted on the elections; questions of regency; matters pertaining to interregna; the limits of royal power and the relations between king and Estates; the influence of the Estates on administrative and military institutions; the

---

[25] Cavriani to Court Chancellery, January 5, 1791. M I Archiv, Carton 517.

[26] Riegger's Memoir is entitled: Historische Erläuterung des historischen Theils der böhm. Ständischen Dedukzion. 239 ex Augusto 1791, November 11, 1790. M I Archiv, Carton 517.

power of the Estates in the internal administration of Bohemia; the Diet and lawmaking; and finally, the influence of the Estates on taxation. Baron MacNeven's chief source was Hájek's *Bohemian Chronicle,* a work highly favorable to the Estates. It was written in 1540 when the Estates were still at the height of their power. It is needless to say that the early account which it gives of the first Diets and even down into the Fourteenth Century is inaccurate, as Riegger well pointed out. After the Fourteenth Century, while not inaccurate, Hájek is still partial to the Estates. Riegger in his memoir followed MacNeven step by step. In contrast to MacNeven, the lawyer bureaucrat, Riegger was a statistical and cultural historian who had kept in touch with the march of historical research under Maria Theresa and Joseph II, and who, by using the works of Dobner and Pubička (Pubitschka), was able to point out the unreliable character of Hájek's early account as well as his later partiality, and to base much that he wrote upon such chronicles as those of Cosmos, Pulkava, St. Ludmila, and others.[27] With this in mind we shall glance briefly at the contents of these two memoirs.

The first three questions were at bottom really one, namely, was the Bohemian Monarchy hereditary or elective? Baron MacNeven concluded that the Bohemian monarchs had always been elected by the Diet, that the Estates and the king in coöperation had made the fundamental laws, that the Diet had settled the succession, appointed regents, even administered the regency in the absence of the monarch, and decided on war and peace. From 822 down to 1306, that is to say, from the first Přemyslid down to Václav III (Wenzel or James), the kings had always been freely elected by the Diet. The succession, settled under Charles IV, allowed the free right of election after the dying out of his line, the Luxemburgs. In 1278, 1281, 1423, and 1441 MacNeven claimed that the Estates controlled matters pertaining to the regency and that this practice was expressly confirmed in the Letter of

[27] See fn. 23 and 24.

Majesty of 1508 and declared a part of the Constitution, i.e. a fundamental law, by the Diet of 1526.[28]

In his "Historical Elucidation" Riegger warned against incautious generalizations. To say that Bohemia was always an elective or always an hereditary kingdom was too sweeping. The facts differed with the epoch and with the circumstances. So far as he was concerned, he could see no signs of the dominating influence of the Estates in the government, such as the Estates had outlined from the beginning of Bohemian history down to the Sixteenth Century. He was convinced that down to 1306, that is, until the accession of the Luxemburgs, the government of Bohemia was monarchical. The word "election," as pointed out in the early chronicles, did not have the same meaning that it acquired in later medieval times. The chronicles spoke more of a ceremonial accession and not of an election; in other words, the Monarchy even in its origin was hereditary rather than elective. It was true that the Břetislav Law of the Seniorat of 1055 had been violated many times, but there was always an hereditary successor. From about 1216, the eldest son generally succeeded. Even in the case of the accession of the Luxemburg line heredity counted, for John married the daughter of Václav II. Riegger stigmatized the Hussite Wars as times of great anarchy and sought to point out that whenever the succession in Bohemia was clearly hereditary and not in doubt Bohemia enjoyed peace. He admitted that after the dying out of the line of the Přemyslid kings, the activity of the Bohemian Diet increased, and the Estates as representatives of the people acquired a greater influence in the choice of their kings and in the government.

From the time of Vladislav II (1471-1516), continued Riegger, it was "indisputable that the Bohemian Estates asserted more and more the rights they had already acquired and strengthened them or won new ones." With singular patience Riegger pointed out that MacNeven had written of the meeting of Diets (as he found them in Hájek) whereas re-

[28] Second Desideria, M I Archiv, Carton 517.

search had demonstrated that none had taken place. Entering into detail on the election of Bohemian kings, he pointed out that Seventeenth-Century historians and publicists of Bohemia, such as Stránský and Balbín, collected evidence to show that the Monarchy was elective, while Goldast and Glassey wrote pamphlets to prove it was hereditary. Of course, Ferdinand II, by the Land Ordinance of 1627, made it forever hereditary. Riegger implied, therefore, that in earliest times election in the modern sense of the word was ceremonial rather than actual; that down to 1306 the government of Bohemia was distinctly monarchical, and not by the Estates; that in the succession of the Luxemburgs heredity in the female line was taken into account; that, in the Fifteenth and Sixteenth Centuries, although the power of the Estates increased, it was never so great as the Estates claimed; and, finally, that times of the greatest power of the Estates were also times of the greatest disorder. In short, with certain reservations, Riegger placed himself on the side of those who claimed that the Monarchy was hereditary. He was unable to overcome the argument of the Estates as to the interregnum of 1526 and declared that the Revers (or Receipt-Act of Confirmation) then issued by Ferdinand I, which confirmed the previously existing state of affairs, was executed "in ignorance of legal basis." He contested the argument of the Estates on the question of regency and declared that the Letter of Majesty of 1508 and the legislation of 1526 were not parts of the Constitution. If they had been parts of the Constitution, they had ceased to be so under Ferdinand II.[29]

The next subject was the "real" limits of the power of the king and the relations between the king and the Estates. MacNeven, in favor of the Estates, named among others the Revers of Sigismund in 1435, the Capitulations of Vladislav in 1453, and the legislation of 1526 which received the consent of Ferdinand I. He made most of the last document in which it was confirmed that the king could not control the Land

[29] Riegger, Historische Erläuterung, M I Archiv, Carton 517.

Tables where all the laws of Bohemia had been registered and where records of landed property and titles of nobility were kept, and promised that he would not insert anything therein against the liberties of the kingdom; that no office or power could be delegated by him without the advice and proper knowledge of the Chief Officials of the Land; that only native Bohemians were eligible to office; that no Bohemian could be haled before a court outside Bohemia, and finally that the king must live in Bohemia and rule with the advice and consent of the Diet.

Riegger, in reply, argued that examples taken from the Hussite Wars did not prove anything, nor did the agreements of Sigismund. The example of 1453 had a certain appropriateness, but it merely showed the poor condition of Vladislav. These were all merely facts, not law. As for the situation in 1526, Riegger believed as pointed out above, that Ferdinand I had acted in ignorance. Moreover he did not fail to show that in 1547 Ferdinand I had visibly weakened the power of the Estates by his treatment of the cities.[30]

MacNeven next pointed out that the influence of the Bohemian Estates on military and administrative institutions was not insignificant. In 1541 the Diet had decided that the army against the Turks should be called out only by the Diet, and that the Estates should muster, equip, and choose leaders for it from the highest officials of Bohemia. In 1588 the Diet had concluded that no war could be undertaken by the king of Bohemia without the consent of the country. After correcting a few dates, Riegger admitted these arguments without comments.

As regards the influence of the Estates on the internal administration of Bohemia, MacNeven pointed out that no one could be received into the Land or acquire the right of citizenship except with the consent of the Diet. This meant that the Diet controlled its own membership, for owners of landed

[30] Second Desideria and Riegger, Historische Erläuterung, M I Archiv, Carton 517.

property could attend the Diet. Here again Riegger admitted the memoir was right.

MacNeven declared that the power to make laws was divided between the Estates and the king and no laws could be promulgated by the latter without the consent of the Diet. He declared that he could prove joint legislation in matters of public and private, penal and political, law, and he cited numerous examples of this. A detailed discussion of these would lead us too far from our main subject. Suffice it to say that Riegger refused to accept illustrations based on Hájek down to the Fourteenth Century, but admitted the validity of later ones. He agreed that the Land Ordinance of Ferdinand I had really been made "with the help of God and of all the nobility and the knighthood." The Estates, he affirmed, had administered justice, although the king had presided in the Court of the Land; justice was rendered, however, in the name of the king (erroneously); and laws were made with the consent of the Estates, although the king's signature was always necessary to make valid a conclusion of the Diet.

Finally, came the question of the influence of the Estates in matters pertaining to taxation. MacNeven maintained that no other taxes or impositions could be taken except such as the Estates granted in the Diet. He cited many cases beginning with the reign of King John (1310-1346), and dwelling at some length on the Revers of 1323 in which John especially confirmed the rights of the Diet. In 1526, Ferdinand I confirmed these rights. Riegger, in answer, pointed out that the Revers of 1323 spoke of taxes on the occasion of royal family marriages rather than of taxes in general, and declared that it could not be proved from the Revers cited by MacNeven that the "consent of the Estates was necessary for the levying of a tax." The language used in these documents referred to the duty of granting the taxes rather than to the right of doing so. Admitting that with Vladislav II these rights really came more and more into the hands of the Estates, Riegger argued that the historical background should be taken into account.

One wonders how the lawyer, Baron MacNeven, could have passed by the great Diploma of 1310 [31] which expressly confirmed the rights he was defending.

In general, we may say that the Estates claimed that the Monarchy was elective and that the government was carried on by both the king and the Estates, while the government claimed that the Monarchy was hereditary and the State essentially absolute. Riegger's contention, so far as the earlier history was concerned, rested on a distinctly more scientific basis. The government of Bohemia in early times was monarchical, and recent historical research has shown that the so-called early elections of kings or dukes were confirmatory, rather than actual. [32] Riegger repeatedly pointed out errors in dates in Baron MacNeven's paper. He also showed more moderation by limiting his generalizations. Baron Mac-Neven's errors were chiefly due to ignorance, while Riegger's occasional silence and veiled expressions, as well as his smooth passages, do not always indicate the impartiality which he declared was his aim. Riegger was a public official of the enlightened despot type. If MacNeven erred in seeking to expand the power of the Estates into earlier times, Riegger was guilty of trying to explain away too often the weakness of the king, attributing, for instance, the action of Ferdinand I in 1526 to ignorance. The Estates were on solid ground after the Fifteenth Century, and had Baron MacNeven been an historian, he would not have exposed his paper to ridicule by so closely following Hájek whose early tales are mostly legends.

Baron MacNeven's account ended here. Then began the second part of the introduction composed by the Executive Committee and dealing with the rest of Bohemian history down to 1790. The work of the Executive Committee being based on firmer ground, is more accurate, and Riegger was forced to admit great parts of it without comment.

[31] *Ibid.* See also for the Capitulation or Magna Charta of 1310, Kalousek, *České státní právo,* Appendix, 563-565.

[32] See Novotný, *České dějiny,* I, I, *passim,* and Bachmann, *Geschichte Böhmens,* I, *passim.*

The Estates deprecated the unrest which led in 1618 to religious and political troubles and ended in a civil war which had been put down by force. Their interpretation here is interesting. Emperor Ferdinand II, according to them, had come to the rescue of the "greater part" of the Bohemian Estates and of the nation which had recognized him as the lawful king. Together they had taken up arms against "the other but smaller" part of the nation which had been misled by false religious zeal. Thus did the Bohemian Estates in 1790 interpret conditions at the time of White Mountain (1620) and of the promulgation of the Land Ordinance of Ferdinand II. Historical research has now made it clear that the majority of the Estates and of the Czechs were Protestant and that they sympathized with, if they did not actually participate in, the "rebellion." Nevertheless the descendants of the Estates which in 1627 had profited by the Land Ordinance of Ferdinand II, wished, as we shall see, that all appearances of punishment should be removed from that document and that certain provisions should be excluded from it.

Riegger advanced the theory that Ferdinand II had conquered Bohemia and, in accord with the doctrine of rights lost by conquest, could do what he wished with it. Nevertheless he had shown forbearance and moderation not only by his Confirmation of Privileges of 1627, but also by the Land Ordinance which bore his name. The Estates themselves partly recognized this moderation. They admitted that the king had reserved to himself alone the right to make all private and public and constitutional laws, whereas formerly this right rested in both king and Estates together.[33] Further, the Estates were inhibited from making proposals in the Diet, this power being given to the royal commissioners of the king.[34] Finally, the right of granting citizenship was taken away from the

[33] Second Desideria, M I Archiv, Carton 517 and Jireček, *Verneuerte Landesordnung*, 1627, A 8 G 10. See also Novella Declaratoria C c 5 and Rescript promulgating the Land Ordinance.
[34] *Ibid.* and Tomek, *České sněmy dle obnoveného zřízení zemského*, and Kalousek, *České státní právo*.

Estates and given to the king and the famous Letter of Majesty of Rudolph II was withdrawn.[85] All other rights and privileges not contrary to the Land Ordinance (1627) were sanctioned in the Confirmation of Privileges which Ferdinand II issued on May 29, 1627, and which contained also the article that no tax or contribution should be levied in Bohemia without the consent of the Estates.[86] All this Riegger admitted and recent research confirms.

The Estates contended that, in spite of all they had lost, they still retained under Ferdinand II a fairly extended sphere of activity. They pointed out that up to that time no legislation had been promulgated on the succession, or on constitutional law or general law of the country, without consulting the Estates beforehand. Ferdinand III, they argued, had fully recognized this and allowed the Estates a limited legislative initiative. Charles VI (1711-1740) had confirmed this right and in 1720 submitted the Pragmatic Sanction to the Bohemian Diet for a "virile" vote, i.e. a vote by majority, not by colleges or Estates. The Estates also showed that, in the period between 1657 and 1740, no taxes were levied except those which were permitted by the Diet. Likewise between 1627 and 1714, the Estates declared that they administered their own offices and collected the taxes. In 1714, when a change in the collection of taxes was made, the work was assigned to the newly created Executive Committee.

When Maria Theresa came to the throne she took an oath, the exact copy of the oath taken by Charles VI, with certain unimportant additions, thus confirming all the rights which the Estates had enjoyed down to 1740. But in spite of the reconfirmation of these rights in the Recesses of 1748 and 1775, certain very vital changes in the Bohemian Constitution were made during her reign.[87] The Bohemian Estates singled out three of these for mention. In 1749 Maria Theresa had abolished the Statthalterei and substituted in its place the

[85] Land Ordinance A 6; A 20; Novella Declaratoria, A a 18, 19.
[86] *Ibid.*, A 5.
[87] Second Desideria, M I Archiv, Carton 517.

so-called "Representation and Treasury" by which the administration of the central government was taken from the Chief Officials of the Land and entrusted to civil officials. She had already so limited these same officers in the Committee for Judicial Matters as to reduce them to nullity. In 1771 Maria Theresa had partly, and Joseph II in 1783 had completely, abolished the Judicial Committee, and thus the Chief Officials of the Land were deprived of all direct influence on the central administration of Bohemia. Secondly, the Court Commission in 1770 had introduced a new system of taxation and auditing whereby the auditing of the Domestic Fund (another name for the Treasury of the Estates) was put under royal supervision. And finally, in 1775, without consulting the Estates, Maria Theresa had issued the famous Fourth Robot Patent which deprived many of the landlords of a considerable part of their income "all at once without any compensation." [38]

The Estates then proceeded to describe in detail the exact character of the actual influence left to them under Maria Theresa.[39] Incidentally thereby they carried out the wishes of Leopold II as expressed in the Rescript of May 1, 1790. We shall mention here only a few of the rights which the Estates claimed came into their scope of activity then: the granting and collection of taxes and impositions, the administration of offices of the local government other than those of captain and commissioner; operations involving the credit of Bohemia; compensation for losses from fire, weather, and war; the administration of the Treasury of the Estates, and various administrative departments entrusted with carrying out the financial agreements of 1748, 1757, 1767, and others which will be discussed later.

Joseph II restricted, in fact destroyed, even this limited activity, asserted the Estates. By the Rescript of May 7, 1782, he ordered that payments out of the Treasury of the Estates (Domestic Fund) be suspended, thus practically abolishing it.

[38] *Ibid.*   [39] *Ibid.*

By the Rescript of October 27, 1783, the constitution of the Estates was radically changed. So far as the Diet was concerned only the power to pass on royal postulata (royal demands for money) was left; the Permanent Executive Committee, which had been established in 1714, was abolished; and two representatives of the Estates were allowed to transact the business of the Estates with the Gubernium Council. All the administrative offices of the Estates were abolished or united with other royal offices. By the Decree of May 26, 1786, the last officials named by the Estates, namely the physicians of the circles, were henceforth to be appointed by the government although their salaries were paid out of the Treasury of the Estates. On September 25, 1788, the Executive Committee, which had lived an empty existence for four years, practically deprived of all activity, was abolished. The Diet had become "an empty shadow." [40] It had lost even the right of meeting annually,[41] although in theory it still had the right to grant taxes. In practice, however, this had been violated by Joseph II, when, on February 10, 1789, he promulgated the new system of taxation. Thus the last important right of the Diet, the right to grant and collect taxes, was finally lost.[42]

III

CONSTITUTIONAL REMEDIES

Having related their constitutional history, with its list of grievances and wrongs, the Bohemian Estates took up the question of remedies. They did not doubt the honest intentions of Joseph II, but felt that he had been misled by wicked advisers. Therefore they asked for a confirmation of all the

[40] Second Desideria, M I Archiv, Carton 517, ". . . und zu einem leeren Schatten, von dem, was sie vormals gewesen, geschwunden war. . . ."
[41] Ibid.: ". . . bei Fürgängen dieser Art konnte die Versammlung der Stände wohl nichts anders, als wirkungslose Ceremonie seÿn. . . ."
[42] Ibid.: ". . . So wurde das letzte Überbleibsel Ständischer Rechte zertrümmert und die Stände sahen sich von aller Wirksamkeit, von allem Einflüsse auf die Geschäfte, die das Land betreffen, entfernt. . . ."

rights which they had enjoyed down to the time of Joseph II. They went farther than that. The Land Ordinance of Ferdinand II, in their opinion, contained certain clauses which were inserted under pressure of the conditions in Bohemia immediately after the Battle of White Mountain (1620). Conditions since that time had changed much, and these clauses now were, in the opinion of the Diet, "unnecessary, unsuitable, or insulting, and in part had become harmful to the character and force of the Constitution itself." [43] The Bohemian Estates therefore deemed it their duty to plead that, for the sake of the general welfare, these limitations should be abolished. Farther on, in the text of the Second Desideria were enumerated the clauses of the Land Ordinance of Ferdinand II, which they expressly wished expunged and which we shall presently discuss. It is important to note here that, in expunging parts of the ordinance, the Estates were taking as a model the condition that existed before the Battle of White Mountain.

The Bohemian Diet proposed therefore three concrete changes in the old Bohemian Constitution. In the first place, parts of the Land Ordinance were to be abolished; in the second place, the part which remained was to be sworn to by the sovereign; and, in the third place, certain new clauses were to be added and sworn to by the monarch. The new document was to be called the Reformed Land Ordinance of Leopold II. He himself should be crowned king of Bohemia at the time of the promulgation of this Land Ordinance, which was to be "the foundation stone of the future happiness of the Bohemian State." In case the new land ordinance was not finished in time for the coronation, the Bohemian Estates proposed that Leopold II swear to an agreement or "pragmatical" containing the most important rights that they asked for. In any case, the Bohemian Diet wished to make sure that Bohemia would receive a new constitution.

The Gubernium treated these demands of the Estates with

[43] The Second Desideria, M I Archiv, Carton 517.

irony." That council quoted several passages of the lengthy
Land Ordinance of Ferdinand II (1627) and admitted rather
dryly that many changes had taken place since that time.
They noted that this was especially true in the case of constitutional law, but at the same time they stated that they had
no desire that any laws should be made which would endanger
the position of the king. Nor did they see any objection to
the monarch's oath being sworn to a new land ordinance
inasmuch as Joseph II had sworn to the old. They might have
added that it would not bind Leopold II any more than the
old one had bound Joseph II. But they had definite objections
to the pragmatical, perhaps fearing that this might turn into
the capitulations of the Middle Ages. "Why should his majesty," the Gubernium Council declared, "allow such a serious
limitation, which was without analogy?" The Gubernium
councillors, Count James Cavriani (not the Governor but his
kinsman), Baron MacNeven, and Baron Sweerts, who handed
in a minority report on many points with regard to the Constitution, argued that this was no serious limitation, nor a
check upon the king's absolute power. They declared the
pragmatical did not infringe upon the rights of the sovereign,
but, quite to the contrary, it promoted the welfare of the
country. The Governor, Count Ludwig Cavriani, in the letter
which accompanied the opinion of the Gubernium, wrote that
he considered the Land Ordinance of Ferdinand II a fundamental law or constitution. "Bohemia was happy under it."
He pictured the industrial prosperity which that country enjoyed as a result of its benign influence. His was a thoroughly
Josephinian argument. "I do not see why we should depart
from the Land Ordinance. I do not see how we can depart
from it, because it contains the rights of the royal successor."
Continuing, he advised strongly against radical changes in
the Constitution—changes might bring woe to "a great and,
in other respects, blooming kingdom." Thus the Gubernium
and the Governor were in the queer position of defending the

    " Gubernium Bericht, December 26, 1790. M I Archiv, Carton 517.

Land Ordinance when the Estates wished to change it, and of cursing it when the Estates asked that certain of its provisions, abolished by Joseph II, be restored!

The remaining organs of government then gave their opinions on the question at issue. In turn the questions of Bohemia's constitutional history and of a new constitution and pragmatical went to the Court Chancellery, the Commission on the Desideria, to the State Council, and finally to Leopold II. All of these offices were impressed with Councillor Riegger's "Historical Elucidation" and refused to hear anything about a "pragmatical." The referent or attorney before the Commission on Desideria,[45] after expatiating at great length on Riegger's memoir, remarked that what the Estates wrote about the "pragmatical" was only in the nature of an introduction. By this he meant that they were not at all serious in their request, and so might be pardoned for so audacious a demand. This Commission voted that the deputies whom the Diet sent to Vienna to defend the Desideria, were to be informed that "the standard of the future constitution of the Estates would be the year 1764 of the reign of the blessed Maria Theresa," and that the Commission could not go back farther than that. Nevertheless, the Commission continued, "his majesty would be inclined to give an ear to their proposals of reform which, without misleading the administration in its dealings, would rather give it guidance to conduct the government with responsibility and confidence to the satisfaction of the country and of the Estates."

It was during one of the meetings of this conference, held March 12, 1791, that Count Leopold Clary, one of the deputies of the Bohemian Estates, proposed that the year 1745 be chosen as the normal, standard year upon which the constitution should be patterned. This was a highly advantageous proposal for Bohemia and its Estates, for that year was the most favorable to the Bohemian Constitution after Ferdinand

[45] Protokoll über die Konzertazion, welche über die Zweite Abteilung der böhmischer Stände, deren Organisirung betreffend, abgehalten wurden 12ten März 1791. 239 Aug. 1791. M I Archiv, Carton 517.

II and before the great reforms of Maria Theresa in 1746-1756.

Later on when someone asked—and the questioner was no less than Leopold II himself—why the year 1764 was taken as a standard or normal year, nobody in Vienna appeared to know exactly why.⁴⁶ It became evident, however, that the attorney had in mind the condition of things in Lower Austria when he argued so strongly for that date. This did not prevent the central offices in Vienna from urging Leopold II to adopt it also for Bohemia and Leopold, without any special comment, for here as always he was very laconic, accordingly so designated the year 1764.⁴⁷ Thereby was saved only that part of the Constitution which existed after the Statthalterei, the Chancellery, and other institutions had been abolished, and after the Gubernium, from which the Estates had been excluded, and many royal institutions, as well as the financial recesses together with the reforms in the local administration, had become realities. The Estates had failed to secure the new basis for which they had asked, or even that of 1627 or 1745. Leopold II said nothing in his decision about a new land ordinance or a "pragmatical"; that idea had been lost from sight long before it reached the monarch through the clever manipulation of the central offices. Nevertheless, the Estates did gain something, for the decision to take 1764 as a standard meant that all changes in the Constitution in the twenty-five years which followed were to be abolished. It meant more active diets, a real executive committee, and practically all the rights which the Estates so painstakingly enumerated as having been theirs under Maria Theresa (see p. 23 and fn. 37). It was on the whole a compromise such as Leopold II loved to make. It was just enough to satisfy the Estates.

The Bohemian Estates next asked in the Desideria on the Constitution that the legislation contained in the Land Ordi-

⁴⁶ See M I Archiv, Carton 690.
⁴⁷ Protokoll über die Konzertazion, 12ten März 1791, 239 in Aug. 1791, M I Archiv, Carton 517 and H H S Archiv, Staatsrat Akten, 1775 in 1790.

nance of Ferdinand II be abolished with respect to four subjects: (1) the monarch's sole right to legislate; (2) the nature of the ordinance so far as it bound the king; (3) the right to make public and private law in Bohemia; and finally (4) citizenship. We shall discuss each one of these in turn.

The monarch's sole right to legislate went back to the famous clause "to supplement, to change, and to reform the laws" contained in article A 8 and most clearly stated in the Patent which promulgated the Land Ordinance. It has already been pointed out that one school of Czech historians claims that this refers to private law only, therefore not to the Constitution. But the Bohemian Estates in 1790 and the government in Vienna interpreted it to refer to the Constitution. At any rate, the Estates wished to take that power out of the hands of the king. The Gubernium replied very curtly that this was calculated to lessen the legal rights of the monarch. The three members of the Gubernium, who handed in their dissenting opinion on this point, declared that it was not the object of the Estates to limit the rights of the sovereign but merely to give a lasting form to a constitution once adopted by the monarch. They were referring to the new Land Ordinance whose compilation they hoped that Leopold II would permit.

The attorney for the Commission on Desideria declared that the Estates wished to "erase" A 8, the very root of royal power. Since Ferdinand II, no one except the monarch had the right to change the fundamental law or constitution; to him alone belonged that exclusive right. The attorney further advised that the Estates had no direct influence on lawmaking except such as was permitted by the monarch himself out of the fullness of his power.

Leopold II ruled that the Estates should be consulted in cases involving changes of important laws. "The Estates might make suitable representations, but these were to have no suspensive effect" whether in interpreting or in changing the Constitution, or in regard to laws "which were about to be introduced or against all other laws, even when they have received my sanction." In other words, the emperor reserved to himself the exclusive power to make laws, which the Land Ordinance of Ferdinand II had given him, but allowed the Estates to make "representations" or protests on any law already promulgated or about to be promulgated. He did not give the Estates the right to legislate on such matters in co-operation with himself, but merely the right to petition, to make desideria at any time.[48]

In the consideration of the second subject, the nature of the ordinance so far as it bound the king, the Bohemian Estates advanced the theory of compact government, an idea of Rousseau. They maintained that "The constitution of a state and its fundamental laws, on which it rested, was a treaty (*Vertrag-compact*) or agreement between the sovereign and the nation which . . . must bind both parties equally," and asked that in the future no fundamental law be made without the consent of the Estates. In other words, just as in respect to the monarch's sole right to legislate, the Estates wished to obtain a share in making the constitution, so they desired also to bind the monarch to the constitution thus made. In their opinion a fundamental law was a contract between the king and the Estates, which both were to live up to.

The Gubernium likened this wish of the Estates to a "capitulation"—a severe limitation on the absolute power of the king. If the principle were recognized, "an aristocratical form of government would be introduced." The rebellion of Bohemia under Ferdinand II, maintained the Gubernium, brought with it the loss of the former rights of the kingdom. The Land Ordinance (1627) had legally settled all this, they claimed, and "the undisputed and practiced absolutism" (*Alleinherrschaft*) ran counter to any such suggestions on the part of the Estates. The three dissenting members of the Gubernium declared that the Estates desired neither a kind

[48] Protokoll über die Konzertazion, 12ten März 1791, 239 in Aug. 1791, M I Archiv, Carton 517.

of "capitulation" nor a change in the form of government and they tried, though illogically, to show that the Estates recognized the unlimited power of the king and desired this concession not as a "right but as a favor." The Gubernium was the more logical; an absolute monarch could not make contracts or compacts because these immediately limited him *ipso facto*.

The attorney for the Commission on Desideria argued that Bohemia's form of government had long been recognized as absolute. Bohemia was an unlimited monarchy and the theory of compact government could not be applied to it. He maintained also that the Estates could no longer be taken as representing the entire nation, for the greatest number of the citizens, namely the peasants and the inhabitants of the cities, were not represented in the Diet, and did not share in the rights and privileges of the Estates. Thus he attacked the principle of Rousseau as a doctrine not applicable to the absolute rule of the Habsburgs in Bohemia, and then, for sake of argument admitting the principle, showed that it was to be applied between the king and the nation and not between the king and the unrepresentative Estates. Leopold II passed over this subject without comment.

With regard to the third subject, the right to make public and private law in Bohemia, a majority of one of the Bohemian Diet asked that articles A 8 G 10 of the Land Ordinance of Ferdinand II and C c g of the additions of Ferdinand III be modified so that the Estates be allowed to hand in their opinions on every law, whether public, private, political, or penal before it was promulgated. But in the Diet itself on July 21, 1790, Count Buquoy and twenty-one other members handed in a dissenting opinion in which they declared they "wanted . . . an indestructible constitution." They asked that the king declare that "he would not depart from it without the consent of the Estates and that without their consent he should never make a law or change an existing one which had anything to do with the welfare of the country as a whole, the security of persons, or the property of the inhabitants of the kingdom. He and his associates pictured the fate of a land under an absolute monarch "to whom law was not holy, civil freedom a monstrosity, and whose will alone appeared to him to be something important." The time to prevent such a future calamity was under the good and wise Leopold II."⁹ This was by far the boldest document presented in the Diet. Among its signers could be found the foremost champions of the Estates and almost half of the number were descendants of the old Bohemian nobility who could point with pride to ancestry before the disastrous battle of White Mountain.

On July 24, 1790, Count Chotek produced another minority opinion signed by fourteen members of the Diet and sent to Vienna as Supplement B. Its signers asked that all such laws before they received validity be submitted to the Estates, and if they did not meet with their approval, they were to be suspended for twelve months so that the Estates might have plenty of time to make a second representation on the subject to the monarch, who, if still unpersuaded to the contrary, might after the expiration of one month publish the law.

Thus we see that on these all-important subjects—the right of legislation and the power of the Estates with regard to it— there were really three views in the Bohemian Diet. The majority of the Diet—and it was only a majority of one— wished to get the right to petition or protest in the making of laws. Count Chotek and his friends wished to give the Estates the right of suspension in legislation whereby they could retard legislation by a year and a month, if they so desired. Count Buquoy and his associates were more radical. They wished to make the consent of the Estates obligatory for the

⁴⁹ Second Desideria, M I Archiv, Carton 517, Beilage A. See Sternberg Papers. Erklärung welche die unterzeichneten Stände in der Landtagsitzung vom 21 Juli zu Protokoll gegeben, die Wünsche zur Erlangung eines Anteils an der Gesetzgebung enthaltend. Those who signed this document were: Counts Buquoy, Millesimo, Fr. Jos. Kolovrat, Taaffe, O'Kelley, Hartmann, Harrach, Paar, Wrbna, Joseph Černin, Francis Sternberg, Francis Joseph Černín, Rudolph Morzin, Joachin Sternberg, Johann Unwerth, Frederick Nostic, Voračický, Adalbert Černín, John Pachta, Lanjus, Michael Kaunitz, Henniger.

validity of any law—in other words, they were recalling the days before White Mountain. The Chotek memoir is remarkable also because of the reflections it contains on the Constitution and the Estates in general. It called the Land Ordinance of Ferdinand II by its very origin "a penal sword still reeking with the blood of the nobility." The country in 1620 had fallen under the suspicion and disfavor of the court. "Such a document," i.e. the Ordinance, continued the memoir, "is nothing but the instrument of an avenging king grasping after unlimited power and not an agreement of a nation with its sovereign." It contended that the Land Ordinance was in no way a fundamental law, an inviolable constitution, for the king had taken it upon himself alone to change it at his will. This, the memoir contended might be done "daily." If the Estates of Bohemia had enjoyed more than was given in the ordinance, that was due to the wisdom and favor of the monarch and such favor was not at all binding on the monarch. If some had forgotten their duty toward their sovereign in 1620, one hundred and sixty years of loyalty had made up for it. The Chotek memoir declared also that if the Estates had been the true representatives of all parts of the nation, it would have advocated that full legislative power be given to the Diet and that the compact theory be fully enforced. But since the Estates were only a small part of the nation and no other form of representation was as yet in use, the memoir urged a compromise whereby the Estates should have the right to suspend temporarily the laws obnoxious to them. On the whole, this memoir was one of the most remarkable papers presented before the Diet, and is a good illustration of the best political thinking done in the Habsburg Monarchy in 1790.[50]

The Gubernium pointed out, with much satisfaction, Count

[50] The document is printed in the appendix of Čelakovský, *O účasti právníkův*, Appendix, 49-58: Abegesonderte Meinung der Unterfertigten Ständischen Mitglieder über den Punkt des Einflusses der Stände in die Gesetzgebung." July 25, 1790. It was signed by Prince Joseph Schwarzenberg, Count Joseph Nostic, Count Leopold Spork, Count Chotek, Count Francis Příchovský, Count Wenzel Cavriani, Baron Hochberg, Count Joseph Sweerts, Baron MacNeven, Count Ernest von Goltz, Count Philip Sweerts-Spork, Count Christian Philip Clam von Gallas.

Chotek's statement that the Estates did not properly represent the "nation" and suggested that perhaps some "special favor" might be shown by his majesty to the Estates in this matter. The attorney for the Commission on Desideria saw no reason for making concessions to the Estates. He argued that they desired to take away "the most important rights and the essential constitutional prerogatives of the king, which are (by their nature) incapable of a change."

On this subject also Leopold II rendered his decision briefly and to the point. He did not believe that the Estates as they were composed in 1790 represented the "nation." Therefore he would not consent to give them rights which they might use only for themselves or even against the great mass of the nation. That would mean only a division of government between the ruler and the Estates. Enough is to-day known of Leopold II's constitutional plans for Tuscany to make it certain that he knew what modern popular representation meant and was in favor of it, even if he did not consider it the proper time to inaugurate the new era. He stated, therefore, that he would allow the Estates to petition and to bring forth plans of legislation at any time whether in the case of old or new legislation; but he would not allow, as Count Chotek proposed, the Estates to have a suspensive veto, nor, as Count Buquoy proposed, would he permit the Estates the right to make legislation valid by their consent.[51]

The fourth subject dealt with the question of citizenship. By articles A 20 of the Land Ordinance and A a 18 and 19 of the Additions of Ferdinand III, the right of granting citizenship was wholly in the hands of the king. The Bohemian Estates asked that these articles be abolished and the right be returned to them.

The Gubernium saw no reason for the suppression of this part of the Land Ordinance. They argued that, if he saw fit, the monarch might show special favor to the Estates on this

---

[51] Protokoll über die Konzertazion, 12. März, 1791. M I Archiv, Carton 517. See Zimmermann, *Das Verfassungs-Projekt Leopolds von Toscana.*

subject, although the ultimate decision in matters pertaining to citizenship should rest with the sovereign. The attorney for the Commission on Desideria argued that this clause, as well as all the others before it, stated an essential prerogative of the Bohemian king. For that reason the wish of the Estates could not be granted.

Leopold II in his Decree of August 12, 1791, refused to grant the Estates the right to determine citizenship in Bohemia. Doubtless he realized that the power to determine who should be a citizen of Bohemia was important. By this means the Germanization and Austrianization of the Bohemian nobility was furthered, since a monarch with this power could prevent people obnoxious to his interests from settling in Bohemia.[52]

The Estates had asked that in respect to the four subjects mentioned above the Land Ordinance of Ferdinand II be abolished. They now asked that one important clause be reconfirmed. That was Article A 5 of the ordinance, which was expressly sanctioned in the Confirmation of Privileges of 1627 and in the Financial Agreements of Maria Theresa. The article declared that grants of taxes must have the consent of the Diet and must then be accepted formally by the assembly. The Estates wished to make it clear that not only the regular contribution was to be understood by this, but that all other supplementary taxes were to be included. All these were to be "written out" regularly in the royal Postulata presented to the Diet before any attempt was made to collect them.

The Gubernium was willing to accept this with the limitation that in pressing cases the monarch should be able to "write up" the taxes without waiting for the approval of the Diet. The minority in the Council of the Gubernium declared the words "no contribution" in the documents meant precisely

[52] Protokoll über die Konzertazion, 12. März, 1791. M I Archiv, Carton 517. See also the Court Decree of August 12, 1791. The entire question of the *Inkolat (Indigenat)* or right of citizenship, has been treated in a scholarly way by Baxa, *Inkolat (a Indigenat) zemích koruny české, 1749-1848*. See also H H S Archiv, Bartenstein Memoir on Bohemia, 1759-60.

what they said.[53] The attorney for the Commission on Desideria was in favor of acceding to the wish of the Estates.

Leopold II in the Decree of August 12, 1791, ruled that "everything which up to that time had been inserted in the Royal Postulata was to be put in them in the future." In unusual and urgent circumstances, however, and especially in times of war, this could not be allowed. In such a case the Estates still had left to them the distribution and the collection of this special tax as well as of the remaining ordinary levies.

[53] The word "Keine"—"Žadne" is found in the Confirmation of Privileges, 1627.

CHAPTER V

THE BOHEMIAN CONSTITUTION UNDER LEOPOLD II
(PART II)

EVEN more interesting than the constitutional theories and remedies of the Estates and the government was their attitude with regard to the organs or institutions of the Constitution. By these they meant the Diet, the Executive Committee, the old Chief Officials of the Land, and the Treasury. We shall take up each of these in turn.

I

THE DIET

After discussing the composition of the Estates and the history of the Diet as an institution,[1] the Estates formulated, in the Desideria on the Constitution, eighteen demands, which if accepted by the monarch should form a sort of constitution or statute for the Bohemian Diet.[2]

The Estates asked first that it be constitutionally determined that the Diet be called in the spring of each year. They advocated the springtime because it was the quiet time of the year and because the Postulata of the king could be accepted and the taxes written out before the beginning of the fiscal year. The Gubernium opposed this because it meant a "diminution of the king's prerogatives."[3] By the Land Ordinance of Ferdinand II the sovereign had the right to determine the

[1] See Chapter II, Bohemia in 1790.
[2] Second Desideria, M I Archiv, Carton 517. Also Journal of the Diet. Č N M Archiv, Sternberg Diary, S V Archiv, Kurze Anmerkungen for August 4, 7, 9, 11, 14, 16, 18, 28, 30, September 1, and November 27, 1790.
[3] Bericht des böhmischen Landes-Guberniums, 18. Feb. 1791. M I Archiv, Carton 520.

time of meeting and the frequency of the sessions to suit himself. The Diet heretofore had been held in the fall, and the commissioners attended it in the spring.

The attorney for the Commission on Desideria, in the session of March 12, 1791,[4] agreed that the Diet could be held more suitably in the spring, but he would not think of binding the king constitutionally to that effect! The deputies of the Estates present at the hearing asked that this provision for calling the Diets in spring be inserted in the rescript calling the session of the Diet. Count Chotek spoke up in the conference and declared he did not see "why an upright and illustrious sovereign . . . could not declare this or that article, which after ripe consideration he had found necessary for the welfare of the state . . ., constitutional and allow it to be drafted into the future reformed land ordinance." He openly deprecated the timidity and lack of decision among government officials.

When the report of the Commission on the Desideria reached Leopold II, he wrote out his decision without any comment whatsoever, doubtless disgusted with the puerility of his officials. He ruled that Diets could be held in the months of May or June annually, but his decision gave no hint of enacting this into a part of the Constitution.[5]

In the next place, the Estates asked that the Chief Count of the Castle (another name for the Governor) or the next Chief Official of the Land in rank be allowed to summon the Diet without the consent of the king, but with the consent of the Executive Committee. The Gubernium opposed this on the ground that it ran counter to the Land Ordinance of Ferdinand II and besides was neither "necessary, nor wholesome." The attorney for the Commission on the Desideria waxed warm against this demand as encroaching upon the rights of the sovereign "under high penalty." He would not allow any other way than that prescribed in the Land Ordi-

---

[4] Protokoll der Konferenz, 12. März, 1791, M I Archiv, Carton 517.
[5] Court Decree of August 12, 1791, M I Archiv, Carton 517.

nance. On this point, Leopold II stood by the attorney and the Commission and declared that the Estates could not have this right.[*]

In the third demand the Estates asked that in case of a very urgent matter which concerned them all, they be allowed to give their opinions to the Executive Committee and to move that the Governor call the Diet. The Gubernium did not oppose this, taking the ground that everyone had the right to bring complaints before the proper officials. The Court Chancellery quoted the minority opinion of Baron Lamoth of the Gubernium, who argued that the Estates did not differ from any other citizens of the state and could bring their complaints or proposals before public officials. The attorney of the Commission again fell back on the Land Ordinance as modified in 1640 whereby some rights of legislation were allowed to the Estates and pointed out that nothing was to come before the Diet unless it received the preliminary sanction of the royal commissioners. Leopold II did not give a decision on this question, but indirectly he sided with the Commission.

In their next demand, the Diet asked that in calling that assembly, at times when there was no special urgency, at least fourteen days should be given to the Estates to arrive at Prague; in cases of urgency, five days. The announcement of the session of the Diet was to contain the exact date and the reasons for calling it. This was to be sent to all the members of the Diet or to their proxies, and the material prepared by the Executive Committee was to be accessible to the members a number of days before it was presented. The Gubernium agreed to the last point but not to the other three. Heretofore patents had been printed calling together the Diet, and nothing else had been or would be necessary, argued the Gubernium. It also declared that a time limit was not practicable. The attorney for the Commission on Desideria opposed the demand of the Estates on similar grounds. The

[*] See fn. 2-5 inclusive.

emperor ruled on August 12, 1791, that in the future the custom of printing the patents should be continued. He considered this to be the better way of calling the Diet, for the officials of the circle could take care of this very easily. The remaining requests of the Estates on this question were passed over without comment.[7]

Under the eighth heading the Estates asked that forty members should constitute a quorum of the Diet, authorized to give validity to its conclusions. These should be members of the Estates properly registered in the Land Tables. The provision shows that the government must have been accustomed to control the Diet in the past and must have made use of the small attendance to gain its own ends. The majority of the Gubernium refused to give assent to both of these propositions on the ground that no such limitation was prescribed in the Land Ordinance, and that this would work to the "greatest disadvantage of the Estates and to the country." Three dissenting members of the Gubernium, however, declared that this would force the Estates to assemble in larger numbers and the effect would be salutary and very beneficial to discussions on important matters. The attorney for the Commission declared in the session of March 12, 1791, that no stipulated number should be set for the Big (or Regular) Diets, but "for all other assemblies," thirty might make up the quorum. Leopold II inquired first what was meant by the phrase "for all other assemblies." He was informed that it meant "Little Diets" like the one in the spring of 1790. He ruled, therefore, that at these "Little Diets" thirty members present should constitute a quorum.[8]

The Estates, in their ninth demand, took up the question of membership in the Diet. Those who had already got into the Diet, whether in violation of the Land Ordinance or not, were to be allowed to stay. But in the future no one should be allowed to sit and vote in the Diet unless he were himself

[7] See fn. 5.
[8] *Ibid.* See also Abgesonderte Meinung der Referenten Cavriani, Mac-Neven, Sweerts, M I Archiv, Carton 516.

an owner of property registered in the Land Tables and an inhabitant of the country, or the son, or the direct ward of such a person. In this way the Estates hoped to prevent the government from packing future Diets.

The Gubernium interpreted the Land Ordinance differently. The possession of land, it argued, was not the only basis of right to attend the Diet. Ability, industry, and business acumen might justify such right. Should the Estates be successful in their plea, then the knights, formerly so numerous, having lost their lands, wholly or in part, would be excluded from the Diet. Even then only ten knights were present in the Diet in 1790-1791. The same rule as to owning property would also apply to some inhabitants of the cities, who aspired to become members of an Estate. The three dissenting members of the Gubernium discovered in article A 24 of the Land Ordinance that "no one who was not an inhabitant of the country should be admitted into the Diet" and this referred, not to the clergy alone, as the majority of the Gubernium contended, but to all the Estates.[9] They pointed out that this clause was inserted in the paragraph on the clergy, but that it was included in parentheses.

The attorney for the Commission on the Desideria agreed with the Estates. The unpropertied people might some day outvote those who had property—men who really had the welfare of the state at heart—this was his contention. Leopold II this time sided with the Estates. Henceforth those who were not inhabitants of the country would not have the right to a seat and a vote in the Diet.[10]

In their next wish, the tenth, the Estates asked that a part of Article A 6 of the Land Ordinance and Article A a 9 of the additions to it be entirely suppressed, so that in the future every member of the Estates would be allowed to bring forward proposals or complaints in the Diet without obtaining the preliminary consent of the royal commissioners. In

[9] See Jireček, Die Verneuerte Landes-Ordnung, A. 24.
[10] Court Decree of August 12, 1791, M I Archiv, Carton 517.

other words, the Bohemian Diet asked for the right of the initiative in legislation.

The Gubernium argued that this did not have the importance which the Estates attached to it. The royal commissioners really helped to expedite business and often saved much time by deciding what propositions by their nature might come up before the Diet. The Gubernium advised that the old practice be adhered to. In urgent cases, however, it considered that a member or members having such a proposition might speak to the Governor, and (if time was not pressing) to the Executive Committee, who would bring up the proposition in the Diet. Baron Lamoth, a member of the Council of the Gubernium, objected to this being done. He had no use for legislative assemblies or for the Executive Committee. The more the Diet mixed in legislation, the more, he thought, was time wasted.[11]

The attorney for the Commission on Desideria was in favor of allowing the Executive Committee to take care of such matters. Leopold II decided, on August 12, 1791, that the old law of submitting to the royal commissioners all proposals presented for consideration by the Diet should remain as before. But if anyone had anything to propose "for the good of the country," this might be laid before the Executive Committee so that the matter might be brought up after the royal propositions.[12]

In their eleventh demand, the Estates asked that they should not be forced to reach conclusions on important matters in the same session but that they might be allowed to postpone them for deliberation to a future one. The Gubernium completely agreed to this wish of the Estates. The attorney for the Commission on Desideria recommended that this should not be allowed in case a majority could be found to conclude on a matter which had already been sufficiently discussed. Leopold II agreed with the attorney but made no

[11] Votum Separatum des Freiherrn von Lamoth, M I Archiv, Carton 517.
[12] See fn. 10.

statement as to the number of those who were to be present in order to make a conclusion valid.

The next three wishes of the Estates had to do with the keeping of the Journal of the Diet, regulating its correctors, accepting the Journal in the sessions, and keeping copies of it for legal reference. Concretely the Estates asked that a Journal of the Diet be kept which eight elected correctors (two from each Estate) were to examine and approve but not change. After the reading of a conclusion it was to be considered "unchangeable." Two copies of the Journal were to be kept, one in the Court of the Land in the Land Tables, the other in the Registry of the Estates. One realizes the importance of this proposition when one notes that since the Battle of White Mountain no journal of the Diet existed. Only the dry conclusions of the Diet were printed after that assembly's yearly sessions. Beginning with 1789, however, a journal was kept.[13]

The Gubernium had no objection to these proposals. Baron Lamoth thought that two copies were unnecessary and considered that too much faith was put in the Governor and the correctors. The Governor feared cabals and was opposed to making a conclusion, which had been read and corrected, "changeable." The attorney for the Commission on Desideria agreed with Lamoth and strongly supported his contention that the Journals were invalid from a legal point of view until they had received the king's sanction. Leopold II accepted this statement of the Commission and added that in the matter of the improvement of the Journals, only corrections of actual mistakes should be made, and in no wise any change of the conclusion of the Diet. These Journals were then to be submitted to him for approval and having received it were to stand as law in Bohemia.

The Estates also asked that during the recess, when the Diet was not sitting, they be allowed to address their com-

[13] Č N M Archiv, Sternberg Diary, November 27, 1790. See the speech of the Mayor of Prague.

plaints directly to Leopold II or to the Court Chancellery
without first submitting them for examination on the part of
the central offices (the Gubernium) in Prague. This was allowed to every citizen of the State and to Estates in other
lands. They asked also that they be permitted to send a delegation made up of Estates at Prague or of those present in
Vienna without necessarily seeking permission in each specific
case. Such a delegation was to have the confidence of all the
Estates and to be elected by them.

The Gubernium considered itself attacked here, for it
aspired to the control of all the correspondence of the Estates.
The recent Decrees of August 26 and September 30, 1790, gave
the Gubernium this right. In tracing the right historically, the
Gubernium pointed out that the Statthalterei, the forerunner
of the Gubernium down to 1749, had controlled all the
correspondence of the Estates.

We must point out here that the Statthalterei at that time
was not a bureaucratic institution, but made up of the Estates
some of whom were members of the Executive Committee of
the Diet.

The attorney for the Commission on Desideria flatly opposed the wishes of the Bohemian Estates. All correspondence
should go through the Gubernium and permission to send delegations was to be preliminary to any action whatsoever.
When it was a matter of private business, that could be taken
care of in the old way.

Leopold II cast aside the objections of the Gubernium and
of the Commission and ordered that opinions written up in
the Diet might be sent through the Gubernium or directly to
him. The Estates could send a delegation directly to him
when they had elected it regularly. But it was to be well
understood that the delegation should take care of matters
pertaining only to the general welfare of the Estates and of
the country and not to private matters. The expenses of the
delegation were to be paid by the Estates, and not by the
country. And finally, although the Gubernium's consent was

not necessary in order that the delegation might come, yet that institution was to be informed that the delegation intended to go to Vienna.[14]

In their last two demands, the Estates took up the question of the election of the deputies or delegations which were to be sent to the monarch when occasion demanded. The Diet decided that henceforth the election of these delegations should be by all the Estates assembled and voting individually and not as colleges. The Estate of the Clergy protested against this in a minority opinion[15] supported by thirty-six signatures. From the names of those who supported this minority opinion we can see that the three Estates, the clergy, the knights, and the Estate of the Cities joined once more against the nobility to protect themselves against overwhelming numbers. The three Estates realized that the nobility could always put through its candidates even though it had to pick them from the other Estates, for deputations generally contained an equal number from each Estate, however unequal they might be in actual numbers. The minority opinion did not insist that in all elections voting should be by Estates, but merely in the election of the Executive Committee and important delegations, where the rights and privileges of the separate Estates were at stake.

The Gubernium sided with the nobility, although it implied that the Estate of the Cities should be better taken care of. That Council declared that it was true that the heads of the Estates in times past had named committees and stated that in committees on unimportant matters this custom might con-

[14] See fn. 2-5.
[15] Besondere Meinung der anwesenden geistlichen Stände und verschiedener anderer Mitstände über den gemachten Antrag, die Ausschussmänner promiscire zu wählen, als ein Votum privatum der minderen Stimmen. Beylage "C" to Second Desideria, M I Archiv, Carton 516; 239 ex Augusto 1791. The original document was signed by Bishops Schulstein and Prelates Krieger, Herites, Suchánek, Jacobus of Branau, Mayer, Ebel, Winkelburg, Vesely, Werner and Novák; by the nobility: Count Adalbert Klebelsburg, Prince August Lobkovic, Count Francis Nostic, Count Leopold Clary, Count Louis Hartig, Count Henniger, Count Carl Clary, Count Joseph Canal, Count John Anton Schvinding; by the knights: Hennet, Leiner, Rosenthal, Hanisch; by the city Estate: Steiner, Štepanovský, Fischer, Slívka.

tinue unmolested. In cases where important action was to be taken, the whole Diet should participate in the choice of its representatives. The Gubernium opposed the use of the secret ballot and advocated the old practice of publicly registering each vote. Leopold II, in the Decree of August 12, 1791, decided in favor of the nobility. The election of the deputies should take place in full Diet and by ballot. In case no majority was attainable, the officer who presided over the Diet was empowered to cast the deciding vote.[16]

II

THE PERMANENT EXECUTIVE COMMITTEE

The Estates next repeated the story of the Permanent Executive Committee, and on the whole correctly. Charles VI had established the Committee by the Rescript of October 4, 1714[17] according to the documents the Estates submitted to the government. The reason for its creation was the great disorder into which the business of the Bohemian Diet was falling, and the need for a more unified administration. Charles VI placed at the head of this Committee the Chief Count of the Castle (later called the Governor) and eight members of the Estates. Two members were elected from each of the four Estates, voting as colleges, and for a term of two years.

The first election, according to the Estates, was held on October 10, 1715. At that time the Royal Instructions were accepted and put into force. The new institution had divers activities.[18] Among its important duties were: the prepara-

---

[16] See in turn the Second Desideria, M I Archiv, Carton 517, Bericht des böhmischen Landes-Guberniums, 18. Feb. 1791, Carton 520, Protokoll der Konferenz, Carton 517, Court Decree of August 12, 1791, Carton 517.

[17] See the Series Allegatorum, 19, attached to the Second Desideria, M I Archiv, Carton 517.

[18] *Ibid.*, Series Allegatorum 20. The Instructions gave the activity of the Executive Committee as follows: (1) die Landesökonomie zu besorgen; (2) den Steueramts-Direktor zum Vollzuge der Schlussfassungen anzuhalten; (3) die monatliche Repartizions-Eintheilung nach Verschiedenheit der Monate den Ständen vorzubereiten, und im Landtage vorzulegen; (4) Die Repartizion der Diätalverwilligungen zu adjustiren; (5) Die Ansässigkeitsveränderungen und Beschwerden zu beurtheilen und zu entscheiden; (6) Die Militär-Dis-

tion of the legislative work of the Diet, the care of that part of the central and local administration entrusted to the Estates as well as their own administration; and the representation of the Estates before the government when the Diet was not in session. Necessarily much of its work was administrative, as the Estates pointed out. During the first half of the Eighteenth Century, before the era of great reforms began, the direction of the collection of the taxes voted by the Diet, the authorization of financial and credit operations, and the conduct of the administration of the Estates, were in themselves of vital importance. In very important matters or on special occasions two members of each Estate were added to the eight already elected and the Permanent Executive Committee was called the "Reinforced" (der Verstärkten) Permanent Executive Committee. Often the Chief Officials of the Land deliberated with it in this form, thus constituting a grand council, representing both the king and the Estates.

The Estates then described the administrative activities of the Executive Committee just before it was abolished in 1783 by Joseph II. They enumerated seven departments in all: namely the chief office, the tax personnel, the treasury, the credit treasury, the pay department, the domestic (or Bohemian) auditing department, and the credit auditing department. This meant a civil list of sixty-six positions with a total in salaries amounting to 34,161 florins yearly. Together with the local administration, various other officers of the Diet, and the members of the Executive Committee, the civil list ran up to 153 positions at an annual expense of 69,594 florins.[19]

The Diet also pointed out that besides these permanent

---

lokazion zu entwerfen; (7) Das Steueramt in guter Ordnung zu erhalten, die Offizianten desselben den Ständen in Vorschlag zu bringen, und darüber im Landtage einzeln zu votiren; (8) Die Zustandbringung der Rechnungen über das diätaliter verwilligte *Militare ordinarium* zu besorgen, solche zu adjustiren und vierteljährig mit dem Aerario Abzurechnen; (9) Die Präliminar-Entwürfe zu verfassen in den Ständen vorzulegen; (10) Die Ständischen Darlehen und ihre Rückzahlung zu besorgen.

[19] M I Archiv, Carton 690: 752 ex Julio 1794. See also Series Allegatorum, 22.

officials and bureaus, there were special commissions appointed by the assembly such as the "Rectification Commission" (like our Equalization Board for Taxation) which had as its object the establishment of the tax quota and the revision of the land survey. Tax commissions of several kinds were also appointed. In 1759 the Inheritance Tax Fund was created to pay the debts incurred in the Seven Years' War, and later the collection of the Inheritance Tax was entrusted to the Estates and therefore to the Executive Committee. The Estates also told the story of the dissolution of the Committee by Joseph II. On October 27, 1783, Joseph II abolished the Permanent Executive Committee and united its administrative offices with those of the Gubernium, two representatives of the Diet being allowed to sit in that Council. In the course of the next year the Governor of Bohemia, Count Nostic, tried to revive the Committee but even that phantom of its former self was completely abolished in 1788. The Estates, in the Desideria on the Constitution, September 4, 1790, asked for the complete restoration of the Permanent Executive Committee on the basis of the Instructions of 1715.[20]

The Gubernium remarked that it was very evident that the Permanent Executive Committee was in no way an institution provided for in the Land Ordinance of 1627, which to the Gubernium was, for sake of argument, the Constitution of Bohemia. It was a creation of Charles VI. Joseph II had reformed the government of Bohemia, continued the Gubernium, and "so it came to pass" "that the committee had become unnecessary." The Gubernium next raised the question as to whether it should be restored and after sifting a few of the arguments pro and con determined that the Executive Committee was a useful one, for the business of the Diet must be prepared, credit operations superintended, and some committee handy during the recess of the Diet. Councillor Baron Lamoth violently opposed the restoration of the Committee on the ground that the concentration of institutions by

[20] Second Desideria, M I Archiv, Carton 517.

Joseph II into two great branches, the political and the judicial, gave government business "a much faster tempo." In his opinion the two representatives of the Estates, who sat in the Council of the Gubernium, were sufficient to carry on their business.[21]

The attorney for the Commission on Desideria and the Commission itself completely agreed that, whereas Leopold II had allowed the Estates of Lower Austria to have an Executive Committee, he could not very well refuse to allow Bohemia to have one.

Leopold II decided that the Bohemian Estates should have a Permanent Executive Committee, but that its constitution should be based on conditions in the year 1764 and not on the Instructions of 1715. The Estates were ordered to hand in a description of the activities of the Committee in 1764 and the central government was to take up the matter once more in complete detail after that. Later it became known that there were no instructions for the year 1764 extant and that the year 1779 should have been selected, for in that year Maria Theresa had issued a new set of instructions for the Executive Committee.[22] Of course, this was less favorable to the Estates than those of 1764.

Next came the question of method of election of the members of this Executive Committee. The Estates, under the influence of the nobility, asked that the committeemen be elected by ballot of all members of the Diet, not voting by colleges, and not "as used to be the case by the heads of the four Estates." The Estates, in discussing the Rescript which called the Executive Committee into life (1714), declared that the four heads of the Estates by custom had a right to designate matters to be brought before the Committee and

[21] Besondere Wohlmeinung des Referenten Freiherrn von Lamoth in M I Archiv, Carton 518: 239 ex Augusto 1791.
[22] See especially Protokoll der Konferenz, March 12, 1791, M I Archiv, Carton 517. Carton 790 ex j. 1764 has this annotation: Die Instruktion des böhm. Landesausschusses v. J. 1764 nach welcher so oft gefragt wird scheinet nie bestanden zu haben, sondern es wurde jenen v. j. 1779 als letzte emanirte bestimmt. See 214 ex Janis 1792, V B12.

to appoint unimportant committees themselves. They stated the reasons why the Committee should be elected by the entire Diet and not by colleges. It represented the welfare of the whole state, not of a single Estate. Its members were not allowed to work in behalf of their particular Estate so much as for all the Estates, and it should be elected by all of them, in order that everybody might have confidence in its acts. Finally, no Estate would be injured, for two members would be elected from each, even if election were by the whole Diet.

Once more the three other Estates, the clergy, the knights, and the Estate of the Cities handed in a minority opinion opposing "promiscuous voting," as they called it, for members of the Executive Committee and of deputations, and asked that in such cases voting by Estates be substituted. But both the majority and the minority of the Diet were agreed that the Heads of the Estates should be deprived of the right of electing these committees.

The Gubernium declared that the abolition of the Executive Committee in 1783 had severed its traditions. Therefore the custom of the nomination of committees by the Heads of the Estates had been done away with. The two members of the Diet representing that body in the Council of the Gubernium were elected in full Diet and thus since 1783 had established a new precedent—a new custom. The Gubernium was opposed to putting so much power in the hands of four persons and advocated the stand taken by the nobility for an election of the committeemen in full Diet. It further explained that the nobility had this large majority in that Diet, because so many new nobles, men whose ancestors had never sat in the Bohemian Diet, had taken their seats for the first time. Otherwise, the Gubernium thought the other Estates could have mustered enough members to balance the nobles. The Gubernium, however, refused to allow voting by ballot. The nobles wished to have the election carried out by secret balloting, but the Gubernium wished to know its friends and its enemies and declared unequivocally for public and oral voting.

The attorney for the Commission on Desideria differed from both the Estates and the Gubernium and his view was accepted by the Commission and by Leopold II. The emperor ruled that the members of the Permanent Executive Committee should be chosen by each Estate in full Diet by ballot. Only those who were actually present in the Diet could vote, no proxies were to be allowed. In case of a deadlock within an Estate, the Head of the Estate was empowered to cast the deciding vote.[22]

The Estates asked that the Executive Committee in ordinary times should consist of eight members, two from each Estate, the Governor or in his absence the highest ranking Chief Officer of the Land presiding. In extraordinary times when a Reinforced Executive Committee was to be elected, each Estate should be represented by three additional members. This had been the case in 1790 and 1791. The term of office of the regular Executive Committee was to be six years, three members being elected every three years.

The Gubernium agreed to these proposals except as to who should be presiding officer in case the Governor were unable to preside. The Council believed that the "first" member of the Executive Committee and not the next ranking Chief Officer of the Land should preside. That was in keeping with the government's policy of excluding the old feudal officials from a share in the government, no matter how slight.

The attorney for the Commission on Desideria recommended that the Reinforced Executive Committee consist of fifteen instead of twenty members, and that the civil list of 1764 be accepted as the basis. Leopold II accepted this and ruled that the Estates should prepare a plan to show the activities, civil list, and instructions of the Executive Committee in 1764.

The remaining proposals of the Estates with regard to the Executive Committee had to do mainly with the internal workings and with the civil list of that institution. The

[22] See in turn the Second Desideria, the Protokoll der Konferenz, March 12, 1791, and the Court Decree of August 12, 1791, M I Archiv, Carton 517.

Estates declared that they would not formally propose the "Instructions" for the Committee until Leopold II had passed on the essentials of its constitution. They would do so later. They could not refrain, however, from making a few suggestions in that direction. The eight members of the Committee were to "refer," i.e. make reports, and the Estates wished to give it the right to correspond directly "not only with the public offices and the local administration of Bohemia, but also with the central offices in Vienna."

The Gubernium agreed that all members of the Committee should report, but refused to allow the direct correspondence which the Estates desired. Not only the Gubernium, but all the other offices of government refused to give the Executive Committee this right of correspondence which it had possessed before 1749. The Gubernium would allow only such correspondence as the Executive Committee had in 1764, namely "with the officials of the circle, the local subtreasuries, and the administration entrusted to the Diet. Baron Lamoth, the staunchest Josephinian in the Gubernium, remarked that this would only be more "scribbling" and would mean "more paper wasted."

The Estates announced that the accounts of the Treasury of the Estates had not yet been audited, and they were thus unable to discuss their budget and the civil list. They wished to postpone the question of salaries of the Committee and of the remaining officials of the administration under the control of the Estates, but it was quite evident they wished to increase both.

The Gubernium put in a good word for the equality of salaries for the Committee, because "all worked equally." Heretofore, stated the Council, the clergy and the nobility had been paid the most, the City Estate the least. The Josephinian Gubernium, if it could not destroy the Estates, wished at least to make the word "equality" mean something among them.

The Commission on the Desideria entered upon an examination of the civil list of the Bohemian Diet and began to slash it unmercifully. Among other things, the Estates had asked that in the future their administration be housed in a separate building, a "Land-Haus." Naturally the attorney for the Commission saw his chance. He assailed the Diet for extravagance. How, he exclaimed, could such a useless expenditure be thought of when the imperial finances were in such a deplorable condition!

Leopold II instructed the Estates to go ahead and make out the report they had promised, assuring them at the same time that they were to have an Executive Committee which should have the powers and activity of the one of 1764 at least.[24]

Here the matter lodged in the archives for a while. On September 7, 1792, and again in January, 1794, and for years thereafter, reports and conferences followed one another on the constitution of the Executive Committee. All this while the committee had existed *de facto,* but not *de jure;* it was still a mere favor of the monarch. The government refused to bring the matter to a settlement. It used several subterfuges; for example, the unsettled times brought on by the French Revolution, it said, allowed no constitutional changes. As a matter of fact, at the bottom of the quarrel was the refusal of the government to allow the Estates to extend their activity and their influence. The central government tried to check them by reducing the civil list and the salaries to a ridiculously small amount. After 1805 the Estates appear to have dropped the matter. The government had won.[25]

[24] Protokoll der Konferenz, March 12, 1791, *ibid.*
[25] For the history of the negotiations pertaining to the Executive Committee after the death of Leopold II see M I Archiv, Carton 690: 752 ex Julio 1794. Kalousek, *České státní právo,* 512 ff. has the best published account of the negotiations after the death of Leopold II. To get an idea of the small salaries allowed by the Estates under pressure by the government one may examine the Journal of the Diet of June 10, 1791, where it is recorded that the Governor was to receive 1200 florins for his work as presiding officer, the nobility and the clergy each 1000 florins, the knights each 800 florins, and the Estate of the Cities only 400 florins yearly.

III

THE CHIEF OFFICIALS OF THE LAND

Joseph II had either abolished or left vacant the great feudal offices of Bohemia. The Estates pointed out in the Second Desideria, dated September 4, 1790, that from the time of Vladislav (1471-1517)[26] there had existed certain "Chief Officials of the Land." These officials were accustomed to swear an oath of office to the king, to the knights and the nobles, and to the whole country. At a later date, by stipulation (A33), in the Land Ordinance of Maximilian (1564), the following officials were chosen from the nobility: (1) the Chief Count of Castle at Prague; (2) the Chief Court Chamberlain; (3) the Chief Marshall; (4) the Chief Treasurer; (5) the Chief Justice; (6) the Chief Chancellor; (7) the Chief Feudal Justice; (8) the President of the Appellate Court; (9) the President of the Treasury; and (10) the two Counts of the Castle of Karlův Týn (Karlstein). From among the knights came, according to the Estates, and it is a correct statement, the Chief Secretary of the Land, the Subtreasurers, and the Castle Count of Hradec Králové (Königgrätz). The importance of these officials, as the Estates in 1790 urged, was best seen in the Letter of Majesty of Vladislav (1508) when in absence of the king, the Chief Castle Count of Prague and the remaining Chief Officials carried on the government, forming thus a council of regency. The Diet of 1526 decided that the king could not deprive them of their positions, and that of 1547 passed a law to the effect that no official was to be appointed in the government without preliminary consultation with these Chief Officials. Even in matters with regard to the tariff and internal tolls they were consulted by the king. The Diet of 1606 gave them full power to secure help from neighboring Powers and to muster out the country's military forces. Moreover, they had considerable influence on justice and the judicial administration. Many documents, claimed

[26] Second Desideria, M I Archiv, Carton 517.

the Estates, confirmed the fact that only native Bohemians could hold these positions.[27]

By the Land Ordinance of Ferdinand II (1627) and by the royal Rescript of September 3, 1628, these officials became instead of "Chief Officials of the Land," "Chief Royal Officials of the Land" and were required to swear an oath to the king and not as heretofore to the Estates and to the country. The king henceforth appointed these Chief Officials from the inhabitants of Bohemia for a term of five years. Otherwise, these Chief Officials existed as before down to the time of Maria Theresa.[28]

Maria Theresa, however, curtailed their activity. The Estates pictured the beginning of the attack of the central government on the Chief Officials by the queen's abolition of the Statthalterei on May 7, 1749. The Statthalterei was the Council made up of the Chief Officials of the Land. Thereafter the Chief Officials were put into a committee (*concessus*) for public and judicial matters (*Publico judicalia*) under the presidency of the Chief Castle Count. In 1763 and 1764 the committee was united with the Gubernium, a bureaucratic council, which replaced the Directorium, the successor of the old Statthalterei. This union, between the Gubernium, a bureaucratic council, and the Judicial Committee of the Chief Officials, representing the Estates, lasted until 1771 when the Gubernium was divided into a political and judicial senate. The Chief Officials were separated from political affairs and put into the judicial senate. Thereafter, they were divorced from political affairs. Finally, in 1782, Joseph II suppressed the judicial senate of the Gubernium (*Gubernium in judicialibus*) and the Chief Officials were entirely separated from public affairs in Bohemia. Many changes followed very rapidly

[27] Second Desideria, M I Archiv, Carton 517, citing large parts of the Land Ordinance of Maximilian (1564). See Kalousek, *České státní právo*, appendix. There is a very instructive document on the origin and the development of the Chief Officials of the Land in the Series Allegatorum, 25, appended to the Second Desideria.
[28] *Ibid.* See Jireček, *Die Verneuerte Landesordnung*, 1627, A36 ff. and Series Allegatorum, 26.

one after another. The Greater Court of the Land, the old Treasury, and the Land Tables were deprived of much of their old significance. The Chief Chamberlain's office was united to that of the president of the new Appellate Court. The Chief Justice became the president of the reformed Court of the Land; the Chief Feudal Justice became its vice-president. By the Court Decree of September 25, 1783, all other Chief Officials were declared to be honorary. "The damage . . . is too important, too serious, to allow the faithful Estates to pass over [these changes] in silence," maintained the Desideria of 1790."

The Estates further argued that in the past these officials had been the "fathers of the country" and that they had an excellent knowledge of the State. Joseph II "had trampled upon the rights of a great part of the citizens of the state." All misfortunes which had come to the Habsburg monarch in Bohemia in the last years of the reign of Joseph II could be traced to "this ruthless disregard of the former power and the influence of the Chief Officials" and of the Estates which might have assisted in government and legislation and thus much trouble might have been avoided. Of course, the implication in these remarks was that these foreign bureaucrats had no knowledge of the country over which they came to rule and that they had supplanted men who had been born in Bohemia, men who formerly had been accustomed to ruling their own country.

The Bohemian Estates next proceeded to ask that all these officials be restored with their salaries and with their former sphere of activity in so far as this was possible. This meant a certain reorganization of the Gubernium and of the judicial system. In the case of the Gubernium, the Chief Officials were to be informed when matters pertaining to "a whole Estate"

---

²⁹ This is on the whole the best piece of historical introduction which the Bohemian Estates presented in 1790. See also for Maria Theresa M I Archiv, 3 in J. 1749 B III A 4 Einrichtung, 81 ex Junio 1763 L III A 4 Einrichtung, and 284 ex Aug. 1771 B III A 4 Einrichtung in the Archive of the Ministry of the Interior.

were to come up for discussion. They could then make use of their seat in the Council of the Gubernium as they had in the Statthalterei. In the judicial system, room was to be given to them in the senates of the Court of the Land and the Court of Appeals, although they were to sit only once on a case.

The Bohemian Estates also asked that Bohemia be provided with a Reporter—perhaps minister (*Landesreferat*) in the Court Chancellery, who was to be a native Bohemian. The Diet wished to keep a permanent deputy or ambassador at the Court at Vienna to take care of its business. The Chief Castle Count, or the Governor, was, according to the Estates, to be appointed for five years, and they wished to have the right to file complaints against him before the succeeding Chief Officer who would then call a Diet to hear the charges. The office of Chief Mint Minister, founded in 1536 and abolished in 1783, was to be reëstablished and his office and mint removed from Vienna. And finally, the chief officials in the local administration of Bohemia, the circle captains and the circle commissioners, were to be selected from the Estates of the nobility and of the knights.[30]

In general, the Gubernium agreed that the Chief Officials of the Land should be restored, although it narrated their past history in a somewhat different way. The Gubernium did not dispute the Estates' statement about them as they existed before the Land Ordinance of Ferdinand II. It was in favor of giving them some influence in the judicial organization of Bohemia or at least it hinted in that direction. The Gubernium contended, however, that under Ferdinand II the Statthalterei consisted of the king's "secret men and other judges and then of the Chief Officials." It argued that the Chief Officials from that time on were practically restricted to judicial affairs and only now and then were called upon "separately" to give advice in political matters. Hence it was quite natural for Maria Theresa to separate them from political

[30] Second Desideria, M I Archiv, Carton 517. Protokoll der Konferenz, 2. Julius, 1791. Carton 519.

affairs altogether and for Joseph II, after he had reformed his judicial system, to abolish practically all of them. The request of the Estates that the Chief Officials sit in the Council of the Gubernium roused its ire. The Gubernium declared that if they had formerly sat in the Council of the Statthalterei, they sat not as Chief Officials but as Councillors of the Statthalterei.[31]

The Commission on the Desideria, through its attorney, opposed the desire of the Estates to restore the Chief Officials on the ground that the new Constitution of the political and judicial administration as it existed in 1790 could not be changed so as to allow of their restoration.[32]

The Supreme Court, as head of the judicial system, fought hard to keep them out of its sphere, and one is inevitably drawn to the conclusion that both the Gubernium and the Supreme Court were willing to see the old officials restored, but not to their respective spheres of influence. And in 1790 there were only two departments of government, the political and the judicial.[33]

Leopold II decided that the vacant Chief Offices of the Land should be restored and filled, doubtless with a view to the approaching coronation, where their ceremonial nature would be of distinct service. He called them "honorary offices," but ordered an investigation to be made to see if the titles of the Chief Land Officials could not in some way be given to the heads of various officials of the new Josephinian Constitution. He suggested, for instance, that the title of Chief Chamberlain be appended to that of the President of the Appellate Court, of Chief Treasurer to the Vice-President of the Gubernium, of Chief Justice to the President of the Court of the Land, of Chief Feudal Justice to the Vice-President of the same court, and so forth. He instructed the Court Chancellery and the Supreme Court at Vienna to advise about this subject and report their opinions to him. In this, he was fol-

[31] Bericht des böhm. Landes-Guberniums, 18. Feb. 1791, M I Archiv, Carton 519.
[32] Protokoll des Konferenz, March 12, 1791, M I Archiv, Carton 517.
[33] See Chapter VI.

lowing and extending the example of Joseph II, and at the same time showing his ability to make satisfactory compromises.[34]

The Gubernium and the Commission on the Desideria opposed the appointment of a Bohemian minister in the Chancellery on the ground that the Chancellery was always a royal office and therefore under the complete power of the king. Both also opposed the keeping by the Bohemian Diet of an ambassador in Vienna and the appointment of only nobles and knights to be circle captains and circle commissioners. The ambassador was useless and expensive. Nobles and knights wishing to enter the service of the government could attain to the offices in the local administration only through examination and able service. Both, however, recommended the restoration of the Mint and of the Mint Master on the ground that it was a financial saving.

Leopold II decided to restore the Mint and the Mint Master. He refused to allow a Bohemian minister in the Court Chancellery. He would not let down the bureaucratic bars of the local administration to the upper Estates, nor permit the Estates to keep an ambassador at the Court. That might be a dangerous beginning. He was in favor of taking counsel with the Estates in case of future appointments to judicial and civil positions in Bohemia. But he would not restrict the term of office of the Governor to five years nor allow any other officer to call a Diet to hear charges against the Governor. The Estates, as well as individuals, would have the right to file charges against the Governor before Leopold II himself, in case they so desired.[35]

IV

THE TREASURY OF THE ESTATES

The Treasury of the Bohemian Estates, which in the course of the Eighteenth Century had acquired the name of "Domestic Fund," was abolished by Joseph II in everything but name.

[34] Decree of August 12, 1791.   [35] See fn. 30-34 inclusive.

Whether or not it should be restored was the real question before the Diet of 1790. We have seen in a previous chapter the
financial situation of Bohemia in the Eighteenth Century.
Here we shall consider the Treasury as part of the Constitution
of which it was one of the vital organs. The Estates found it
hard exactly to define their Treasury. In their introductory
words on this subject they maintained that that part of the
revenues raised in Bohemia and left there for purposes of
administration had belonged to their Treasury from 1569
down to 1748. Then came the Financial Agreement of 1749
and later the decennial agreements or recesses, of which more
in a later chapter. What was left to the Estates from the
income of the taxes after all expenses were paid was considered by them as belonging to their Treasury and as being at
their disposal. But in the course of a half century between
the accession of Maria Theresa and the death of Joseph II
(1740-1790) this income greatly diminished and at the end of
that period amounted yearly to about two or three hundred
thousand florins. In 1790 the royal government introduced a
new system by auditing the accounts of the Estates in spite of
protestations by the Diet. In 1782 Joseph II decreed that the
permission of the Court Chancellery should be requisite for
any payment to be made from the Treasury of the Estates in
the future. The Estates now asked that they be allowed to
make payments out of their Treasury without the permission
of the central government. They promised to submit reports
from time to time on the state of their finances and asked that
they be given full right to administer and dispose of all funds
in their care which the financial recesses of 1748 and those
which followed legally gave them.[**]

The Gubernium replied rather cynically by asking of what
treasury the Estates spoke and claimed that there never had
been such an institution but only a certain separation of revenues, some of which went to the support of the government
at Vienna, others to the support of that at Prague. It ad-

[**] See fn. 30-34 inclusive.

vanced once more the clever argument that there was a difference between "the Estates" and "the people," and the "Estates" were not "the people," according to the Gubernium. How then could the revenues be separated? There really were none which belonged to the "Estates," as all revenues came from "the people" whom the Estates did not represent. In consequence the funds were the king's to administer. Finally, the Gubernium contended that if there were a treasury, the Estates at best could be nothing more than its administrators. The Gubernium recommended that everything be left as it was and completely turned down the attempt of the Estates to regain control over revenues which were expressly theirs by the financial contracts. Under no conditions should the Estates be allowed to make payments without the permission of the Chancellery. The three dissenting councillors of the Gubernium declared that the financial agreements which the Estates had executed with the government contained no such limitation as the necessity of the government's permission to dispose of their funds.[37]

The Commission on Desideria was completely convinced by the argument of the Gubernium. The attorney declared that if there was a treasury (or domestic fund as they called it) it did not consist of the amount left over when all the contractual stipulations in the financial recesses were satisfied, but rather of the smaller amount left over when all expenses for the recesses, for the administration, and for interest on debts had been paid. He was pointing out a sum about one-tenth as large as that which the Estates wished to designate as their fund.

Leopold II sided with the Gubernium and the Commission and accepted the suggestion of the Governor to the effect that all the legislation of Maria Theresa and Joseph II on this matter should remain intact but that the Estates should be allowed to make unrestricted payments out of their fund up

[37] Bericht des böhm. Landes-Guberniums, 18. Feb. 1791, M I Archiv, Carton 519.

to a certain amount. This, as well as the attempt of the Estates to have the government keep its faith with them in the financial agreements, which we shall explain in a later chapter, ended in the complete triumph of the central government.[88] The fiscal policy of the Habsburgs in Bohemia in the Eighteenth Century was not of the kind which a statesman who had the welfare of Bohemia at heart, would have followed. In apology for Leopold II it may be urged that in these first years of the French Revolution the central government was on the verge of bankruptcy and that it was resorting to the highest law known to any state, namely self-preservation. But that is apology, not vindication.

Looking back at this period of the reconstruction of the Bohemian Constitution, we see several general tendencies in the current of events. The first was the tendency of the Estates to base all their arguments on the Constitution of Bohemia before the Battle of White Mountain, paying little attention to the newer constitutional and political ideas in Western Europe. The compact theory of Rousseau was the façade rather than the foundation of the half-absolute, half-medieval government which the Bohemian Estates proposed in 1790. And so, while they knew their Montesquieu and their Rousseau, they went rather into the history of Bohemia than into the realm of the newer political thinking, which led too briskly down the path of popular representation and economic and social emancipation of the lower classes.

The Bohemian Estates in 1790 were not modern, they were medieval in their political thinking. They recognized no political representatives for Bohemia but themselves. They thought of no real representation for Bohemia. The reaction which they represented was not violent, even though they went far back into the Sixteenth Century for its basis. They would have a new constitution which would recognize the old Estates, and which would accept the great central reforms of Maria Theresa. They wished to bind the sovereign to the Constitu-

[88] See the Decree of August 12, 1791 and Chapter VIII.

tion by an inviolable oath or pragmatical—they wished to make it unchangeable. In that way they would get around the absolute power of the monarch. The constitution which the Bohemian Estates proposed in 1790 was an attempt to fit the medieval stat᠈ into the semi-modern structure of Maria Theresa.

The government—i.e. the administration—was ridiculously careful of the rights of the sovereign. The Gubernium defended the Land Ordinance of 1627 whenever it was useful for argument and brushed it aside where Joseph II had trampled on it. The Chancellery and the Commission on Desideria generally followed along the same road. Leopold II, however, was able to free himself from their convenient logic once in a while and make a decision favorable to the Estates. But, on the whole, the Bohemian Estates received only the Constitution of 1764. It was not that of 1745, as Count Clary urged; nor that of 1600, as the Estates really desired; but also it was not that of 1789 as the Josephinian statesmen wished. Constitutionally Bohemia for fifty years after 1790 was based on the arrangements which Maria Theresa had carried through down to the end of the Seven Years' War. Bohemia had a constitution, but the government was almost wholly absolute, with here and there a constitutional feature.

Space forbids a comparison here between what Bohemia and the other parts of the Habsburg Monarchy obtained as redress for their Desideria on the Constitution.⁸⁹ It is certain that of the Bohemian and Austrian Lands, Bohemia asked for the most radical changes, but received no more than the others. Hungary secured its autonomy, a better provision for lawmaking,

⁸⁹ See Bidermann, "Die Verfassungs-Krisis in Steiermark zur Zeit der ersten französichen Revolution" (*MHV Steiermark,* 1873, XXI); Bibl, *Die Restauration der Nieder-Österr. Landesverfassung unter K. Leopold II;* Kosta, "Ein Beitrag zur Geschichte des Ständewesens in Krain" (*MHV Krain,* 1859, XIV, p. 29 ff.); Egger, *Geschichte Tirols von den ältesten Zeiten bis in die Neuzeit,* III Bd. The Moravian Constitutional Desideria are printed in d'Elvert, *Schriften der hist. statist. Sektion der k. k. Mähr.-Schles. Gesellschaft zur Beförderung des Ackerbaues, der Natur-und landeskunde,* XIV Bd. For Hungary see fn. pp. 84-5, 99-101, and Marczali, *Das ungarische Staatsrecht,* and his *Der ungarische Landtag im 1790 und 1791.*

and the assurance that the Statthalterei would exist permanently. Unlike the Hungarians, the Bohemian Estates were weak where they should have been strong. Their aim should have been likewise to secure independent statehood as distinguished from the Austrian provinces, to get back the Statthalterei, Chancellery, and Treasury—in other words, to secure the withdrawal of the great centralizing reforms of Maria Theresa. Instead, the Bohemian Estates, under Leopold II, missed a golden opportunity to stand up for the autonomy of Bohemia.

CHAPTER VI

THE JUDICIAL SYSTEM AND LAW

THE movement which led the Estates to ask for the restoration of the essentials of the old Bohemian Constitution was accompanied, though to a lesser degree, by a desire to restore some of the features of the old Bohemian judicial system and law. Necessarily, it was important for the Bohemian Estates to know how much of both they should ask to be restored to them and how far back into the old order of things they should go. The government, on the other hand, foresaw that the reaction was gaining speed and that prompt and decisive measures were necessary. That was why Leopold II called into a series of conferences the Court Chancellery and the Supreme Court, the two highest central organs of government, which in October and December of 1790 alone had his confidence. Here the principles were laid down on which the Desideria should be judged in matters pertaining to the judicial system and law.

It became clear from these conferences [1] that these two institutions agreed in some things, and disagreed in others. They agreed, for instance, that questions pertaining to law and its codification were to be handed over to the new Codification

[1] See **M I** Archiv, Carton 513, 30 Dec. 1790: M. I. Allerunterthänigste Vortrag der Obersten Justizstelle: "Die Grundsätze nach welcher die Desideria der Stände in den, das Justizfach betreffenden Gegenständen, so wohl in der Art der Behandlung als in der Beurtheilung aufzunehmen sind, betrefl." The Justices mentioned were Count Seilern, Baron Martini, Baron Karg, von Bregent, von Peck, von Nikowitz, von Ebenser. Keesz was attorney (referent). The document came under discussion in the State Council after the Court Chancellery had criticized it in H H S Archiv, Staatsrat Akten, 3380 in 1790: Vortrag der Obersten Justizstelle vom 26ten Oktober, 1790. Necessarily the first document is fuller and will be referred to as "Justizstelle Grundsätze," the latter as "State Council on Justizstelle Grundsätze."

Commission which Leopold II had appointed.[2] This commission had already set to work with the idea of continuing the labor of codification where Maria Theresa had left off. Later we shall see that, owing to the severe reaction which was taking place, its greater labors were interrupted long enough to forestall the Estates by a series of laws, thereby correcting the worst mistakes of Joseph II. But in other matters as well, the Supreme Court and the Court Chancellery disagreed.

The Supreme Court, among other things, maintained that the Desideria on the judicial system and law from all the provinces of the Bohemian, Austrian, and Galician Lands should be considered together at one and the same time. In the discussion of these Desideria before the Supreme Court and the Court Chancellery the matters were to be treated in full sessions of both, not in their separate senates, such as the Bohemian senate and the Austrian senate. The Supreme Court also maintained that it would be "superfluous" for the Estates to send delegates to Vienna to represent themselves before these organs of government or before the Commission on Desideria. Wherever the Estates pointed out the evils of the administration and of the legislation of Joseph II, these were to be "zealously examined." But otherwise, the Supreme Court was not inclined to depart from the existing order of things, because it was impossible for a "constitution [just] planted to grow and to bear fruit, if the seed were dug up before it had a chance to sprout." This cast no doubt on the leanings of this body toward Josephinism. If there were any doubts they were dispelled when the Estates heard from it that, so far as matters pertaining to law and the judicial system were concerned, the underlying principle on which the Desideria were to be judged, was that of uniformity. And on this point, the court avowed, they "would not permit themselves to pry into the secret plans which lie concealed in this

---

[2] The new Codification or Compilation Commission, among whom was Baron Francis Běšín, made its first report on August 21, 1790. Pfaff-Hofmann, *Excurse* I, 64, and Čelakovský, *O účastí právníkův a stavů ze zemí českých na kodifikaci občanského práva rakouského,* pp. 19-20.

fundamental principle for the Austrian monarchy, but that it gave a state strength and durability was very evident." [3]

The Supreme Court ventured to state clearly their position on detail, as well as on general principles. They argued that the Estates deserved all due regard and assistance in matters concerning the security and the possession of their real estate, concerning the maintenance of their credit, and even concerning the inner workings of their make-up as Estates. But under no circumstances would the court allow the Estates to treat themselves as if they were a "state within a state" or permit them to encroach upon the rights of the remaining populace, or to make themselves an exception from laws for the general welfare, or finally to allow them to elevate themselves at the cost of the city or peasant Estates. Justice in her "true and real understanding" was to be clearly and promptly administered, and "firm and proof against prejudice." Nor was any date or epoch to be set to which the future order of things was to be likened. The Supreme Court argued that all reigns had their good and their evil sides and that no past epoch could be picked out which would serve as a perfect model. All these and other arguments show conclusively the Josephinian leaning of the Supreme Court. It was a plea for the constitution of Joseph II, for uniformity and for the *status quo*. They were willing to protect the Estates as landowners, but not as politically superior classes. In their minds, there was no doubt that the Estates should forever be divorced from politics and shut up in an economic world which was hemmed in on all sides by thousands of decrees. [4]

[3] State Council on Justizstelle Grundsätze, H H S Archiv, Staatsrat Akten, 3380 in 1790. The passage is surely interesting enough to repeat here in the words of the text: "Hatten wailly . . . des Kaisers Majestät (Joseph II) den Grundsatz der Einformigkeit aufgestellet, die treugehorsamste Oberste Justizstelle darf sich nicht erlauben, in jene geheimen Absichten einzudringen, die in diesem Grundsatze für die Österreichische Monarchie verborgen liegen, dass aber dieser Grundsatz einem Staate Kraft und Festigkeit gebe, ist vielleuchtend. Daher erachtet man, diesen Grundsatz noch beizuhalten, und sich von selbem nur so weit zu entfernen, als es auffallend wäre dass ganz besonderen Verhältnisse für diese oder jene Provinz eine Ausnahme zur Notwendigkeit machen."

[4] See footnote 1.

On the contrary, the Court Chancellery maintained that the Desideria should be treated separately by provinces and at different times. In each case, the circumstances of the particular provinces were to be taken into account, and all the complaints and recommendations of the Estates were to be examined whether they referred to the old order of things or not.

The disagreement which existed between the Supreme Court and the Court Chancellery was carried into the State Council. Here Eger, Izdenczy, and Reichsach, in general, held the views of the Supreme Court, while Count Hatzfeld made a strong plea for the views of the Court Chancellery. Prince Kaunitz, for the most part, took neutral ground. Leopold II accepted Eger's suggestion that the rescript of instruction for the Codification Commission should be made less sweeping. The Codification Commission was not "to examine the laws and the institutions of the former reign," but merely to see how far they ought to be changed. In accepting this correction, Leopold II was already retracing his footsteps from the position which he had taken at the beginning of his reign. He saw six months later that he had gone too far in favor of the reaction. He ruled, also, that the Desideria of the different provinces were to be considered separately and at different times as the Chancellery urged, and that all complaints and demands were to be admitted and judged according to the circumstances existing in each province. He accepted Count Hatzfeld's long and animated opinion that a noble should be treated differently from common citizens in details of justice, such as imprisonment. This had been the argument of the Court Chancellery, Count Hatzfeld merely expanding it. And finally, in case the Supreme Court and the Court Chancellery disagreed in any matters concerning law and the judicial system, the question was to be immediately submitted to Leopold II for decision. This ruling of Leopold II, which became law for all the Bohemian, Austrian, and Polish Lands, was favorable to those who believed in the times of Maria Theresa, i.e. to the Court Chancellery and to Count Hatzfeld, and was a blow for the followers of Joseph II, the Supreme Court, and Eger and his colleagues in the State Council. The point of view with which the government approached questions in law and justice was Theresian and not Josephinian and this was largely due to Leopold II.[5]

I

THE JUDICIAL SYSTEM

It may be said without exaggeration that the Estates surprised the government when they declared in their Desideria that they would not ask to have the judicial system of Joseph II abolished. This does not mean that they were satisfied with it as it stood: on the contrary, they expressly declared that they desired to see the system entirely abolished. But they realized that this would upset too much the existing order and would present also many new difficulties.[6] But while not asking that the whole system be abolished, they had nevertheless definite proposals to make as to how the Josephinian organization might better suit their needs.

Joseph II, in the matter of judicial organization,[7] gave to the Habsburg Monarchy the very best that he had. On examination one perceives that in building up the system he carefully combined tradition and historical institutions with the prevailing theory of three instances and bureaucracy. This is quite in contrast to his procedure in other things. Generally tradition and history were forsaken for a flight into the realms of theory. But in this particular field Joseph II built solidly

[5] H H S Archiv, Staatsrat Akten, 3380 in 1790.
[6] See M I Archiv, Carton 519: An seine M., Bericht der treugehorsamsten böhmischen Stände mit den Vorstellungen über die im dritten Absatze des Reskripts von 1ten Mai . . . Gegenstände. Nov. 27, 1790. Hereafter to be cited Third Desideria. With regard to the complaints on the judicial system and law see the part entitled: "Über das den Höheren Ständen entzogene eigene Zivil- und Kriminal-Forum."
[7] The best monograph on the judicial reforms of Maria Theresa and of Joseph II is Adler, *Das adelige Landrecht in Nieder- und Ober-Österreich und die Gerichts-Reformen des XVIII. Jahrhunderts.*

on the past—of course, however, always in favor of absolutism. Those cognizant with the history of the judicial system of Bohemia will doubtless recall that the Greater Land Court became the Land Court of Bohemia, the first instance in civil matters for Bohemia. It was assisted by the magistracies of Prague and other cities, by the local manorial courts, and by the mining courts in the cities of Jáchymov (Joachimsthal), Příbram, Kutná Hora (Kuttenberg), and the like. This court had a proud history. It had been the supreme court of Bohemia down to the Battle of White Mountain. But the Land Ordinance of 1627 had made revision by the king possible, and its fortunes had fallen with those of the Bohemian Estates.[8] In 1790 it was a court of the first instance, consisting of the magistracies of Prague and fifteen other cities. Down to the middle of the Eighteenth Century the courts of 381 cities, market places, and manors had the right to sentence persons to death, i.e. they had the right of *jus gladii*. Maria Theresa by the famous criminal ordinance of 1765 reduced this number to thirty and thoroughly reorganized the official force which administered these courts both as to qualifications and as to salaries.[9] It was therefore on these two bases, namely the old Greater Court of the Land and the reformed criminal courts, that Joseph II built his courts of the first instance in Bohemia.

As the court of second instance in both civil and criminal cases, the Royal Appellate Court,[10] which traced its origin to 1548, was selected. It was the most recently established of the courts of Bohemia, and it had practically remained insignificant. But in contrast to the Greater Court of the Land, its fortunes grew with the king's increase in power. In 1790 it

[8] See Kapras, *Právní dějiny*, II and III, and Kalousek, *České státní právo*, 361, 363, 376-9, 446, 483-4. For a brief, but serviceable, German account of this court see Domin-Petrushevecz, *Neuere österreichische Rechtsgeschichte*, 3-32. For the changes in the Court by the Land Ordinance see Jireček, *Verneuerte Landesordnung*, 1627, A xxxii ff. and B.

[9] Maasburg, *Die Organisirung der böhm. Halsgerichte in Jahr 1765*, pp. 12 ff., 93 ff.

[10] Auersperg, *Geschichte des königlichen böhmischen Appellationsgerichtes*, I, 11 ff.

was really the supreme court in Bohemia, there being only one instance higher, namely the Supreme Court in Vienna, the court of third instance. The old Royal Appellate Court was originally established for the royal jurisdiction over, and protection of, the cities. The Land Court had represented the interests of the Estates, the Appellate Court, those of the king; the one the country, the other the cities. By 1690 the Royal Appellate Court was the Court of Appeal for 136 royal and subject cities, and by the middle of the Eighteenth Century it had absorbed much of the civil and criminal jurisdiction of other courts, using its right of administering justice in cases of treason or of denied justice, and insisting to good effect upon its right to hear appeals. Through historical evolution it had become the nucleus of royal justice in Bohemia and, under Joseph II, Bohemia's highest court.

The third instance was created as already mentioned by Maria Theresa in 1749. It had long before become evident to the monarch that the chancelleries of the Austrian and Bohemian Lands could not handle in due time the vast number of revisions which litigants had demanded of them in appealing from the lower courts. The Supreme Court [11] (*Die Oberste Justizstelle*) was therefore established in 1749 in Vienna. Its active work in 1790 was conducted in three senates, the Bohemian, the Austrian, and the Galician, and its councillors administered and served on the basis of seniority, i.e. bureaucracy, not birth. After a duel with the Bohemian-Austrian Court Chancellery (really the Directorium to 1763) it was agreed between these two central organs of government that matters pertaining to *Fidei Commisse* (land-trusts), guilds, and industrial ordinances which called for the grant and interpretation of special privileges should belong to the Chancellery, while the other legal matters should belong to the Supreme Court. Few can understand the vast significance of this central institution which Maria Theresa established, un-

---

[11] See the standard work, Maasburg, *Geschichte der Obersten Justizstelle in Wien*, 2d ed., 1-35.

less they bear in mind that henceforth from its offices injunctions and instructions issued in a steady stream to the smallest court in any of the Bohemian, Austrian, and Galician Lands, and that from it the labors of codification received their initiation and constant stimulus.[12] It was the "heating-iron" of centralization so far as the judicial system and law in the Habsburg Monarchy were concerned.

That Joseph II had created an excellent judicial system was voiced in the Bohemian Diet by Count Francis Sternberg,[13] to whom we owe the best private account of Bohemia's most important Diet since the Battle of White Mountain. He came out strongly for the three instances as they then existed. To his mind the old system of courts—the Greater and Lesser Land Court, the Royal Treasury Court, the Court of the Chief Castle Count, and others—was neither practical nor necessary for the good of the Estates. He pointed out that the former method of holding courts only a few times in the year (wherefore they received the name, *Judiciorum temporancorum*) was not at all to be compared with the new idea of a court permanently in session. Formerly, courts had held sessions but three or four times a year, they had no referent, and read all *acta* or cases *per extensum*. Under the new system the complaints and the cases were registered in the exhibitory protocol and the court was open every day throughout the entire year. After registering a case the referent got it the next day, and within a month the court sat upon it. Moreover, under the old system the law had been only an avocation, and a judge therefore not a particularly important person. As a result litigants had feared the courts because they gave no security. In all this, Count Sternberg favored the retention of the Josephinian system as it stood. He was, however, in favor of giving the criminal jurisdiction to the Court of the Land which had formerly enjoyed it and of restoring the *Praerogativa Proces-*

[12] Čelakovský, *O účastí právníkův a stavů ze zemí českých na kodifikaci*, pp. 5 ff.
[13] Count Sternberg Memoir: Gutachten über die vorzunehmende Organisirung einiger Gerichte. Č N M Archiv, Nachlasse Sternbergs.

sus Accusatori (certain prerogatives of various classes of litigants). So far as the clergy were concerned he favored their request that jurisdiction in cases touching the persons of the clergy (*in causis personalibus ecclesiasticis*) should be returned to them, but that an appeal or revision should go to the Appellate Court and finally to the Supreme Court at Vienna. According to him all the Chief Land Officials were to have the right to visit the Court of the Land and the Appellate Court, but they might vote on a case in one instance only. And finally, Count Sternberg advocated that in the Appellate Court a separate senate of nobles and knights be created to look after the interests of the Estates.

The similarity of these proposals to the actual recommendations and requests which the Bohemian Estates made in the Third Desideria will presently become very evident. In fact, it is very likely that Count Sternberg really persuaded the Estates to abandon the attack on the system as a system and to concentrate their efforts on the removal of those appendages and features of it which had shown themselves useless or offensive to the Estates. With unerring aim, therefore, the Estates leveled their artillery rather at forcing an entrance into the edifice than at tearing down the structure. They wished to incorporate themselves into the organization.

They argued [14] that from the Fifteenth Century down to the reign of Joseph II the high courts of Bohemia had always included a stipulated number of councillors from the Estates of the nobles and the knights. This right had been confirmed by many sovereigns. Up to the reign of Ferdinand II (1619-1637) the Courts of the Land and of the Treasury were made up of councillors chosen from among the nobles and the knights. The clergy had been accustomed to judgment in personal matters by ecclesiastical officials; in matters pertaining to property by the Court of the Land. By the Confirmation of Privileges which Ferdinand II had issued in 1627

[14] See in the M I Archiv, the Third Desideria (III 1, a 4). See also the Land Ordinance of Ferdinand I, A 6, A 10, 12, 13; the L. O. of Maximilian II, A 35-42 and that of Ferdinand II, B 4 ff., as well as A a and A 24.

every Estate was guaranteed its rights, its courts, and its law.[15] Moreover, the constitution and the seating of the Court of the Land, the Chief Land Officials, and the Councillors, had been determined by this same ordinance (B 2) and had remained in force down to 1783. By the Decree of April 4 and the Patent of April 14, 1783, they had been deprived of these rights; the clergy were handed over to the secular courts, and the courts of the nobles and the knights were filled, for the most part, with members of the Fourth Estate (the *Bourgeois*). Not only was the majority of the councillors at the Court of the Land composed of men who did not belong to the nobility, they were even foreigners, declared the Estates, and did not know Bohemian law. Furthermore, they had many other duties to perform, neglecting what they had to do. The nobles and the knights maintained that they were being treated worse than the bourgeois, for the latter were always judged by their equals. It was indeed true that though the Prague burghers had lost the *Processus Accusatori*, they still retained the *Processus Inquisitorii* in criminal matters. The other Estates, however, had been literally stripped of their rights. In all this it is evident that they were aiming at the learned bureaucrats who had ousted the less learned nobility from the hitherto lucrative positions of Bohemia.

The purpose of the Estates in this introduction was to demonstrate that by their past Constitution the courts had contained members from their Estates. From this they turned to concrete recommendations. It is a matter of the greatest surprise that they said nothing about the Supreme Court at Vienna, as though it were beyond their ken. This may have been due to government pressure or to the fact that certain members of this court, like Count Leopold Clary, played leading rôles in the Bohemian Diet and were able to muster enough votes to defeat any proposition planned as an attack upon the great judicial melting-pot. Like the Bohemian-

[15] Confirmation of Privileges, May 29, 1629: dass ein jeder Stand im landes-eignen Gerichte auch nach seinem eigenem Rechte behandelt und gerichtet werden solle. *Ibid.*, Third Desideria.

Austrian Court Chancellery, the court included high Bohemian nobility who were strong enough to overawe the Diet. Thus they were able to consider the system and themselves safe. It was infinitely safer for a man to be Chief Chancellor of all the Bohemian, Austrian, and Galician Lands or President of the Supreme Court than to be the Chancellor of the old Bohemian Chancellery or the President of the old Court of the Land. Here lay the chief blunder of the Bohemian Estates in the time of Leopold II. They did not go far enough in their demands to make up a clear and complete political program for the future.

They asked that the Royal Appellate Court, the court of second instance, be divided into two senates, one for cases pertaining to the higher Estates, and one for appeals in all other cases. According to their idea, it should be organized into three benches or Estates, the nobility, the knights, and the learned doctors, their number and rank, as well as seating, to be determined as customary where Estates existed. They asked that the Chief Land Officials, whom Joseph II had banished from participation in public business in 1782, should have the right to sit in the Appellate Court, voting once on a case only. They were agreed that the jurisdiction of this court should be left just as it was. In asking that members of their Estates be allowed to sit as councillors or judges in this court, they were demanding, at least so far as they were concerned, the right of judgment by their peers. At the price of not wrecking the system they wanted the security and the guaranty that their legal rights would be protected and their social position respected.

They demanded the same rights in the Court of the Land that they had asked for in the Court of Appeals. The presidency of the Court of the Land was to be in the hands of the Noble Estate, and the court itself was to consist of at least seven nobles and seven knights. The Estates agreed that the union of the Court of the Land and the Land Tables, which Joseph II had carried out, was satisfactory but they asked that the Chief Justice of that court have supervision over the

Land Tables and that the Chief Officials of the Land be allowed to sit and vote in it.

The lowest courts, the feeders for the Court of the Land and for the criminal courts, the Estates left alone, except in two cases. The lord of a subject city was to retain his control over the magistracy of that city. In courts on the manors, cases which arose as to reckonings between the officials of the manors and serfs, were to be treated under the Statute of 1734. This statute gave the lord the right to judge the case himself, making this the first instance, the Appellate Court the second, the Supreme Court the third. In addition the Estates demanded that the Chief Officials of the Land receive once more the salaries due them as officials. All the minor officials, such as the councillors at the Court of Appeals and the Court of the Land, were likewise to receive their salaries and emoluments. And all of them at all times were to sit and rank according to birth (estate) and not according to seniority.[16]

The propositions of the Bohemian Estates, so far as they referred to the judicial organization, were discussed in turn by the Bohemian Gubernium, by the Vienna Supreme Court, by the Court Chancellery, by the Commission on Desideria, and finally they came up through the State Council to Leopold II. The Bohemian Gubernium declared that it would give an opinion only on the political aspects of the propositions. Naturally, the opinion of the Supreme Court was the most important one.

The Bohemian Gubernium [17] was opposed to changes in the Appellate Court and advised the rejection of the idea of the separate chamber. To divide up the court into three benches was unnecessary. This would be making an exception for Bohemia alone and would force the administration to rehabilitate the inner organization of the entire system of justice. The councillors worked equally hard, therefore they

[16] See fn. 14.
[17] Bericht des böhmischen Landes-Guberniums . . . in Aussicht auf die Civil und Strafgesetze, . . . u. s. w. Prag, 18. Feb. 1791. M I Archiv, Carton 520.

should receive pay and rank according to service and age, and not according to birth. The Gubernium also opposed the idea that the Chief Officials of the Land should take seats and vote in the Appellate Court and in the Court of the Land. Nor did the Gubernium favor the restoration of the separate ecclesiastical court in personal matters. Only in one particular did they have no remarks to make and that was in the reference by the Estates to the Land Tables.

The Supreme Court next rendered its report. The attorney before this august body was Keesz, the most zealous Josephinian of them all. He out-Josephined the Josephinian Supreme Court and gave his reports with such a fiery and sarcastic point of view that that court, in order to avoid ridicule and censure, had to urge him to be less vehement. It may be of interest nevertheless to present Keesz's point of view on some of these questions before proceeding to the opinion of the Supreme Court. Keesz was not the only official who felt the way he wrote.

Keesz [18] viewed the demands of the Estates, and not only in Bohemia but everywhere in the Monarchy, as a gross injustice and an immoral attempt on the part of the lazy, ignorant, and degenerate nobility to take away from the learned doctors and trained loyal servants of the dynasty the positions which Joseph II had given them. He was violently opposed to giving the councillors rank and position according to their estate as against service and ability. In the future, he hoped, the sons of the nobility would receive such an education as would make them "by head and heart capable of fulfilling their duty toward their monarch in matters of justice." He wished to see them industrious, and, their overweening pride laid aside, bringing honor to their offices and taking pride in rendering real services so that the profession should not be made up of burghers only. He saw that the only just basis was in the equal right to compete, and not in the right which a man

[18] Referat des Hofraths von Keesz über die Desiderien der böhmischen Stände. M I Archiv, Carton 519.

acquired by birth. He wished to see real judges and not men who played the "rôle" only, while the real work was done for them by secretaries and lawyers.[19] Keesz declared that out of thirteen councillors in the Court of the Land, ten were men from the nobility and belonged to the Estates. But he did not state whether they had just been raised to the nobility or whether they were foreigners. Justice, he argued, was never a privilege but a two-sided obligation of both sovereign and people. The judges should come from all classes of people, so that justice might be properly rendered. And as for what the Court of the Land had really developed into in the course of the last two centuries, Keesz was positive that it had changed its feudal and "caste-like" aspect. It had broadened its scope of action. Questions about villages, about the subjects of the Ottoman Porte, about fiscal matters, about serfdom, about the military, about inheritance, and about the making of loans came before it. All these showed that it had lost its narrow character. Many classes in 1790 could complain against making it once more a court for the Estates alone, as it had been in the old days of feudalism. These and other opinions of Keesz show his point of view. It is needless to say that the Estates were not necessarily trying to make the system a "system for the Estates alone" but rather trying to incorporate themselves into it. Perhaps a statesman might have seen a way in which that could be possible, but to a man like Keesz, black was black and white was white. And he was logically correct.

The President of the Supreme Court [20] took especial pains to point out that he and the court did not agree with Referent Keesz on several very important points. He declared the latter's remarks on the question of the precedence, the seating, and the

[19] *Ibid.* A few lines from his report will serve to give local color: "Sonst wird man in die den Augen der ganzen Welt vorgelegenen Zeiten zurück treten, wo die Landräthe aus den Ständen nur den Namen und den Schein des Richteramts führten, das Amt selbst nicht verwalteten, sich ihr Voto von Sekretären, und Advokaten aufsetzen liessen, sich in diese oder jene Stimmen der Deklamatoren blindlings festeten und also nur die Rolle der Richter spielten. . . ."

[20] M I Archiv, Carton 518. Obersten Justizstelle Protokoll, May 25, 1791. 239 ex Aug. 1791.

salaries of the councillors took the form of a libel or lampoon
(*Schmähschrift*). Though lacking time to give all of Keesz's
remarks careful study, the President of the Court declared
that while some of the attorney's premises were good, his conclusions were incorrectly drawn. He, too, was satisfied that
the knights and the learned doctors had rendered great
services, but the nobles had done so likewise. The names of
Spork, Stürk, Herbertstein, Štampach, Blümegen, Wallis, and
others testified to this. Keesz, moreover, had shown too much
zeal for the Jews, and there were phrases in his report which
would, in general, "do honor to his pen, but not to his judgment." Nothing would be harder to prove than that the
knights or doctors had a better education and bringing-up
than the nobility. He ended by ordering the referent to
"smooth out all the hard and pricking expressions."

The Supreme Court thus showed that it was able to distinguish between Keesz's overheated hatred of the nobility
and a conservative appreciation of Joseph II's judicial system.
They opposed the separate court for the clergy and the idea of
having the Chief Land Officials sit in the Courts of the Land
and of Appeals. They declared the question at issue was
whether the courts should be kept as modern judicial offices,
where those learned and experienced in law should preside, or
whether there should be a return to the old haphazard system.
Saurau, another referent of the Supreme Court, declared that
the Bohemian Estates in asking for a separate senate in the
Court of Appeals, had gone farther than their old Constitution
and farther than other provinces of the Monarchy. The Supreme Court wanted genuine, active officials and not honorary,
inactive ornaments. On that basis, it rejected the request of
the Estates to give the Lesser Land Officials, such as the old
councillors of the courts used to be, their former salaries and
emoluments. There was no doubt at all where this court
stood on the question of government service. The judicial system, henceforth, was to be bureaucratic, and a person was to
rise to councillorship as the result of education and ability,

and not because he was a noble. In other words, without calling the Estates any names, the Supreme Court rejected everyone of their propositions firmly and politely. This was in marked contrast to the methods of Keesz.

The Court Chancellery held that in judicial matters more than in political, capability and service should open the way to the highest place. They observed that the separate senate idea did not stand in direct opposition to the general welfare or to the administration of justice, and that it was in no way bound up with them. However, the noble was now living in a different age, while the Estates were looking back to a bygone day. In all other points likewise, the Court Chancellery agreed with the Supreme Court, and the Commission on Desideria [21] and the State Council respected the agreement. In accordance with the decision of Leopold II late in 1790, that when the Court Chancellery and the Supreme Court agreed it was unnecessary further to discuss the matter, he therefore accepted the report just as it had been agreed upon by both of these institutions.

In this way, then, the attempt of the Bohemian Estates to incorporate themselves into the judicial structure which Joseph II had so nobly built, was foiled. There was only one way to enter it. That was through an examination based on education and through long and loyal service. On a question like this, the Supreme Court and the Court Chancellery, both of them filled only with such officials, could easily agree. Their own self-preservation was at stake. A statesman might have tried to combine the two, the system of bureaucracy and that of the Estates, so as to get, at one and the same time, satisfactory service and the respect and confidence of his heretofore most powerful subjects. Leopold II was too busy to

[21] There is a complete statement of the reports of the Supreme Court and the Court Chancellery in the Journal of the Commission on Desideria. Protokoll der Konferenz über die Beschwerden der böhm. Stände im politischen Justiz- und Kriminal-Fache welcher den 2. Julius 1791 gehalten ward. M I Archiv, Carton 519.

plan such a happy combination, although it is certain some
such idea was in his mind.

II

LAW

The attempt of the Estates to bring about changes in the
Josephinian codification of law was more successful than their
efforts as regards the judicial system which administered them.
At least two factors help to explain why this was true. In the
first place, there was the course which the labors of codification took and in the second place, the nature of the reaction,
which followed hard upon the promulgation of the various
codes, was of a very different sort from that which concerned
itself with the judicial system. Let us consider briefly these
two factors.

Few chapters of Bohemian history are as interesting as
those which deal with the codification of law in Bohemia.[22]
There were two sources for law in Bohemia, the German cities
and the Slavic countryside. The former looked to the law
of Magdeburg and Leipzig, the latter to ancient Slavic custom
law. Codifications of each of these at various times would
eventually have led to a complete amalgamation of the two.[23]
But the Battle of White Mountain interrupted this harmoni-
ous development and abruptly introduced a great deal of
Roman law.[24] The Land Ordinance of 1627, which must also
be looked upon as a partial codification of law, contained ele-

[22] For a select bibliography on this subject see Čelakovský, *O účasti
právníkův a stavů ze zemí českých na kodifikaci občanského práva rakouského*, pp. 3-4. Incidentally of considerable usefulness are Schmid von Bergenhold, *Geschichte der Privatrechts-Gesetzgebung und Gerichtsverfassung im
Königreiche Böhmen von den ältesten Zeiten bis zum 21. Sept. 1865*, 7 ff.;
Kapras, *Právní dějiny*, I; Kalousek, *České státní právo*, Chapters I and IV,
and Čelakovský, *Povšechné české dějiny právní*, 2d ed.
[23] As for instance the codification of Land Law in 1500 and City Law in
1536. Čelakovský, *Povšechné dějiny*, and Voigt, *Geist der böhmischen Gesetze*,
pp. 182-186.
[24] Ott, *Beiträge zur Receptionsgeschichte des röm-canon. Processes in den
böhm. Ländern*, 259 ff.

ments of Roman, Czech, and German law." On this basis law in Bohemia remained with slight alterations down to the time of Joseph II. That does not mean that there were no attempts to codify and to reform Bohemian law." In 1710 Joseph I called together a commission to advise him as to how the public and private law of Bohemia should be codified. The commission labored for over a decade without any concrete result, and Charles VI gave up the idea of codifying Bohemian law because foreign wars kept him too busy." It was only after the Supreme Court had been established in 1749 that the labors of codification received further attention from the Habsburg monarchs. The great centralizations which Maria Theresa carried out in the decade of peace, 1746-1756, led in 1753 " to the appointment of the Codification Commission whose duty it was to plan a code for all the Bohemian and Austrian Lands. Up to that time the men behind the codification had intended a code for Bohemia alone, or perhaps at most to include the other lands of the Bohemian Crown. The centralizing and unifying feature of the new policy as regards codification was of great importance. For over a quarter of a century a series of commissions worked on the new "universal" code. In the end, Maria Theresa rejected their labors. It may even be said that her reign ended with a reaction against one general code for so many differently developed provinces. Each had legal traditions of its own which would have to suffer in the making of this general code. However, certain fundamentals were firmly agreed upon as the bases on which the codification might be carried out. The work was divided into four books after the manner of the Justinian Code, and the

²⁵ Gindely, *Geschichte der Gegenreformation in Böhmen,* 484 ff.
²⁶ Among these must be mentioned the instructions issued to the Royal Appellate Court in 1644, the Novella or new additions to the Land Ordinance of 1627 promulgated in 1640, the debtors' law of 1644, and the savage criminal ordinance of July 16, 1707. See Auersperg, *Geschichte des k. böhm. Appellationsgerichts,* 28 ff. and Maasburg, *Die Organisirung der böhmischen Halsgerichte im J. 1765,* pp. 1-3.
²⁷ Čelakovský, *O účasti právníkův a stavů,* 1-6.
²⁸ Pfaff-Hoffmann, *Commentar zum österreichischen allgem. bürgerl. Gesetzbuche,* I, 8, 16.

bases on which the codification should rest were to be written law. Where there was any doubt as to what that written law was, the sovereign was to make a special decision by virtue of his right to make laws. Natural law was to be used only when necessary to "fill in" the places where written law, largely Roman, did not legislate. In this way, therefore, various parts of old Czech, German, and Roman law found their way into the Theresian code, which however was never proclaimed. The advocates of natural law, the law of nature, were not strong enough down to 1780 to secure the insertion of noticeable portions of it into the new code; their influence was theoretical, rather than practical. The Theresian code was accordingly aristocratic in tone. The higher classes were "kept up," and the social and political distinctions peculiar to the Estates remained. Thus, equal right of inheritance was not given to women of the higher Estates, illegitimate children were excluded from inheriting from father or mother, and the Church was maintained in its old power over marriage. Incidentally, the view of the Church on forced marriage was accepted, and illegitimate children could claim only paternal care and support.[29] The fact that the code was not promulgated is a good illustration of Maria Theresa's method of governing. During the last five years of her reign, the great lawyers and the learned compilers agreed that one general code for all of the Bohemian and Austrian Lands was then practically unachievable. To abolish at one stroke of the pen thousands of laws and ancient customs was not only to reach deep into the very structure of the political constitutions of the various provinces, but also sure to bring endless friction. They recommended rather a reform of such law as existed in each of the provinces. Keesz, of whom we have already heard, argued at that time in a purely Montesquian way that laws should answer the spirit

[29] Harras von Harrasowsky, *Geschichte der Codification des österreich. Civilrechtes,* 17 ff. See also Čelakovský, *O účasti,* 7-12; Wellspacher, "Das Naturrecht und das allgemeine bürgerliche Gesetzbuch" (*Festschrift zur Jahrhundertfeier des allg. bürgerl. Gesetzbuches*); Voltelini, "Der Codex Theresianus im österreichischen Staatsrat" (*ibid.,* I, 52).

of nations, their manner of thinking, their morals, and their political and geographical conditions. The two decades of labor on the codification could not have been a greater failure —but this was also the greatest tribute to the statesmanship of Maria Theresa. She deserved great credit not for compiling a universal code, but because she judged that under the existing circumstances it was an impossibility.[30]

Joseph II, however, refused to be led by the experiences of the preceding generation. He truly comprehended the need of a reformed system of courts, and this he carried out in such a manner as to earn the praises of both friends and enemies of his well-intentioned activity. The fact that he had such complete success with the system of courts goaded him on to give these new institutions new law in which to hand down their decisions. With Joseph II's efforts at codification came the triumph of the law of nature, and when it became evident that a universal code made up of this essential element was an impossibility in the short time which Joseph II had set down for its publication, he issued a series of smaller codes and laws which legislated on many questions in the new spirit of the law of nature. The idea of equality was carried to its logical extreme, and all citizens became equal before the law. The prerogatives of the Estates were swept away completely. Marriage became a civil contract and the religious courts were abolished. The Protestants became citizens and the serf was given a freer legal personality. These and many other provisions of Joseph II's copious legislation were in direct contrast to the intended code of Maria Theresa. She had maintained the Estates, he abolished them. She had allowed the Church its old power over marriage; he made it a civil contract. She had accepted the old views of Roman law on society, he displaced Roman law with natural law and proclaimed a new legal epoch.[31]

[30] Harras v. Harrasowsky, *Der Codex Theresianus und seine Umarbeitung*, I, 43, 144; and Čelakovský, *O účasti*, 15.

[31] Domin-Petrushewecz, *Neuere österr. Rechtsgeschichte*, 45-88. An excellent short account. See the patents in Joseph II Justizgesetzsammlung No. 9 ff.

The course which the labors of codification took was peculiar and the work of Joseph II was wholly unexpected as it was entirely against the teachings of past experience. Moreover, it was too sudden, too abrupt. His legislation practically made over the Habsburg Monarchy from feudalism to modernism in law. And these changes reached into every feature of life. Had they affected only the members of the higher Estates, perhaps the reaction would not have been so strong, but they affected everyone, whether cleric, noble, knight, burgher, or peasant. In the matter of the reorganization of the courts of justice only the higher Estates, the nobles and the knights, were concerned, but in these partial codifications everybody was affected from the highest to the lowest. Bearing in mind, therefore, these two factors, the course of the labor of codification and the universality of the reaction, we can explain why the Estates in Bohemia, as elsewhere, secured many important changes in law.

Naturally the greatest complaints of the Estates were directed against the part of the civil code that Joseph II had issued. It dealt with persons and their property, and many of the demands of the Estates involved questions of inheritance. One of the most important cases was that of the great land-trusts (*Fidei Commisse*) of Spanish or Roman origin, kept together for religious and family reasons. Joseph II did not go so far as his advisers, who desired to abolish them, but he allodialized them and allowed debts to one-third of their value. The Estates asked that these later changes be done away with; in other words, they wanted the *Fidei Commisse* to be put back where they were before 1780. They argued that these land-trusts had been created for the "glamor" and the welfare of the noble families and that allodialization and the

On January 16, 1783, the Patent on Marriage was published, May 11, 1786, the Patent on Inheritance, November 1, 1786, the first part of the Civil Code pertaining to persons, in April, 1787, the General Code for criminal offenses, June 17, 1788, the Criminal Court Ordinance. These were the great decrees which Joseph II published as law. To ease the work of the court he issued also the "General Court Ordinance," May 1, 1781, and the "General Bankruptcy Ordinance," at the same time.

privilege of going into debt on their security would soon prevent them from being "the planting ground" of such families. The Gubernium Council thought the question was a legal one and therefore not within its sphere. Nevertheless, they ventured a few observations on the subject. This "splendor" about which the Estates talked might be of doubtful value to a state. For a few to possess so many millions, meant that many millions of citizens were all the poorer. In states where this was not true the general welfare was secure. The law of April 3, 1787, allowed the holder of the trust to give four per cent of the income of one-third of the Estate yearly for the support of such children and for the support of the mother (not stepmother) as he desired. By this means, other children, even illegitimate children, were sure of support, whereas formerly all the income went to one person. The Gubernium could see in this no real diminution of property but an actual service. This Council also argued that to change a land-trust into a money-trust was not deteriorating it because the money was invested in the public fund and was thereby secured against all attacks. Not a change of the laws, but better economy on the part of the trustholders would do more good to the families under consideration.

Keesz, as referent before the Supreme Court, went into the subject with his characteristic zeal. He pointed out that the land-trusts had a tabular value of 24.6 millions, but that their real value was about 32 million florins. In addition to this there were fourteen Bohemian noble families which owned estates elsewhere valued at 13.8 millions. Thus 46 millions worth of property was in the hands of fifty-eight people. These families were "decaying instead of setting up live sprouts." The history of their presence at the coronations was proof enough! For such fifty-eight persons 46 millions of property were held perpetually, while hundreds of children were left out of a share in the wealth because the inheritance was indivisible. Keesz recommended strongly their dissolution, but the President of the Supreme Court did not agree with him as to

their uselessness, and both that institution and the Court
Chancellery agreed that the *Fidei Commisse* should be kept,
but that the legislation of Joseph II should likewise be preserved. The Chancellery made the point that the monarch
had the right to dissolve such trusts when their holders violated the regulations laid down when they were created. In
his Decree of October 21, 1791, Leopold II ruled that the land-
trusts should remain and that the other desires of the Estates
should be taken into careful consideration."

The question of the existence of, and the inheritance in,
Fidei Commisse involved the law of property and inheritance
of only their holders and those of the nobility directly concerned. The Estates next turned to the law of inheritance as
far as it concerned the rest of the nobility. They asked that
there should be no equality of inheritance as between males
and females in the same family." All of the legislation of
Joseph II had been in favor of breaking up primogeniture and
the position of the male as superior to the female. The Estates
argued that a son had to offer his services to the state, whereas
women often married out of the country and property and
money went with them. They fell back on their old laws
before the Patent of May 11, 1786, had changed them, and
asked that the old order of things be restored. But the Gubernium considered equality of inheritance a good thing for the
nobility. What the daughters took away the wife had already
brought in. Besides, the king was always sure to get his money
fee on departure (*Abfahrtsgelde*). And as for inheritance,
that, by the new law, went back to the sixth line, and only

<hr/>

[32] For the *Fidei Commisse* see M I Archiv, Carton 519. Third Desideria:
15th Beschwerde: Die allgemein gestattete Verkummerung des Drittheils und
Verwandlung der Reale in Pekunial Fidei Kommisei; Gubernium opinion,
Ibid.; Protokoll der Konferenz, 2 July 1791 in Carton 519 and the Court
Decree of October 28, 1791. Much of Keesz's argument is reprinted in the
footnotes of Čelakovský's *O účasti právníkův,* pp. 22 ff. The origin of the
Fidei Commisse is traced in the *Commentar zum österr. allgemeinen bürger-
lichen Gesetzbuche* (Pfaff und Hoffmann), II, 210 ff. See also J. Kapras,
Velkostatky a fideikomisy v českém státě, p. 10 ff. The Referat des Hofraths
v. Keesz is also in Carton 519.
[33] The Estates fell back on the Land Ordinance of Ferdinand II, O 32 and
Novella K K 7. See M I Archiv, Carton 519, Third Desideria.

when no other heirs were present, and that really did not mean "splitting up." The Supreme Court in its report declared that this matter had already come up before the new Codification Commission and that there was nothing to change about the matter. Leopold II in his Decree of October 28, 1791, decided to leave the law of inheritance for the higher Estate as it was until the new code was thoroughly discussed and agreed upon.

There were questions involving inheritance and trusteeship of the other Estates likewise. In trusteeship a noble who was a trustee had a right, down to the legislation of Joseph II, to enjoy a sixth of the revenue of the estate of his ward, whether noble or not, until the latter's twentieth year, and from then until his ward obtained full possession of the property, one-twelfth. The latter could not amount to more than 200,000 "shock" yearly. The Gubernium opposed this. It argued for a better economic management of the Estate because the wealth of the young ward would be diminished, and the trusteeship would be too oppressive. The Supreme Court and the Chancellery declared that the new code would legislate on this, hinting that the Josephinian legislation, which allowed much less than the old laws, should be kept. The Chancellery pointed out that in a mortgage valued at 120,000, 4,800 florins being the real income, the trustee would collect 800 yearly without the slightest trouble. This would lead to an extensive mortgage industry in which the trustees would seek large returns for little labor. Leopold II ruled that the law should remain until the new code removed all doubts on the question. He clearly inclined toward the Josephinian point of view.[34]

Next came the request of the Estates that the burghers be given prior right to buy the palaces and castles of the nobles. This right was taken away by the Decree of March 27, 1789. The Guberinum supported the request because it favored the

[34] M I Archiv, Carton 519, Third Desideria: Die Aufhebung des vormundschaftlichen Sechstels bei adelichen Vormundschaften . . . 17ten Beschwerde. Gubernium Opinion, Protokoll der Konferenz, 2. Juli, 1791, and Decree of Oct. 28, 1791.

Estate of the Cities. But both the Supreme Court and the Chancellery agreed that this right would be practically limited to Prague and that no prior right should be given to any one class of people—Bohemia could make no exception in this matter.

The Estates raised the question of the inheritance of curates. Before Joseph II's time the right to one-third of the inheritance left by the curate went to the patron, if the curate died in his patronship. The Estates asked that this right, as well as the right of religious foundations for fuller inheritance in the case of their deceased members, be restored to them. The Gubernium saw no objections to this, but the Supreme Court did, and it refused to depart from the new legislation which gave one-third to the poor, the remaining two-thirds going respectively to the State and to the family of the curate. Councillor Ebenfeld made a plea before the Court Chancellery for the patron asking that he receive some compensation for his services. But the Chancellery remained firm, and Leopold II accepted, without further legislation, the agreement of the Court Chancellery and the Supreme Court.

Not the least among the complaints of the Estates [55] was directed against giving illegitimate children the right to inherit. The Estates asked that the law be abolished. The Guberinum feared to say anything about it at all, and in the meanwhile the new Codification Commission had issued on February 22, 1791, a patent whereby the succession of illegitimate children was abolished, thus forestalling as much as possible this request of the Estates.

Joseph II had desired to place the fortunes of the landlord somewhat in the hands of his subjects when he legislated to the effect that when there was a pawn on the landlord's estate

[55] M I Archiv, Carton 519, Third Desideria: Über das dem Patrone entzogene Drittel der Intestat-Verlassenschaft seines Kuratgeistlichen, und über die den Stiften verschränkte Erbfolge in die Verlassenschaften ihrer Ordensglieder. By the Diet of 1564, the synod of Prague, 14 Jan. 1764 and Maria Theresa's Confirmation, one-third of the curate's wealth went to the church, one-third to his relatives, and one-third to his patron. By the decree of 1754 in case of members of orders, the inheritance went to the order. The Patent of December 12, 1788, eliminated the orders from inheritance.

it should be held to one-eighth of its value by the serfs. The Estates protested violently against this but had to wait for relief until the "new code should be finished." It is important to note that both the Gubernium and the Supreme Court agreed that the Josephinian legislation on this point should be abolished.[58]

The Estates finally took up the question of the property of the serf and of his legal personality. The Estates complained that the partial emancipation of the serfs by Joseph II had disrupted the political and social organism, which from top to bottom should have a definite relation. They hinted, in general terms, that some sort of closer bond between the landlord and the serf should be created. Their main concern in this matter was to prevent the officials of the circle (county) administration from stepping in between the two parties. They demanded that the Penal Patent of September 1, 1781, be abolished as it was obsolete and did not fit the new conditions. In Chapter IX on serfdom we shall discuss so much of this matter as concerns serfdom; here only the legal aspects of it are involved. The Gubernium rightly characterized the desire of the Estates for a "closer" bond as too general and too overdrawn. The Chancellery said that the Estates had not shown any proof why the new condition of things should not be upheld. The system of circle officials was recognized everywhere as good for the general welfare, and the Penal Patent of September 1, 1781, in spite of its brutality and harshness, had made the serf practically a new legal personality in criminal and civil law.

The Estates in the Third Desideria declared it to be "aimless and in part useless, because of the character of administration and execution." Josephinian legislation had aimed to free the serf from pecuniary fines because they really led to further enserfment, from severe corporal punishment meted out by circle officials, and from the ill effects which confiscation of the serf's land for criminal offenses or indebtedness had

[58] M I Archiv, Carton 519, Third Desideria: Über die der Obrigkeit durch das Patent vom 10. Julius 1789 angedrungene Verfändung des achten Theils ihrer Güter zu Händen der Unterthanen, etc.

not only upon the offender but on his whole family. The Estates recommended severer punishment "for the raw spirit of the Bohemian peasant"; they were in favor of irons, of whippings with the "karabač" or knout, of money fines against serfs who had property, and finally, of confiscation and banishment. In all cases, except the last, they advocated that the village judge and the sworn men execute the sentence immediately and allow the serf to complain afterwards, thus eliminating the official of the circle until after the punishment had been inflicted. Space forbids further detail here. Suffice it to say that these recommendations of the Bohemian Estates were the subject of discussion between them and the government for several years, and a compromise was finally reached. What is of importance to us is that these Estates, "the representatives" of the nation, not only wished to tighten the "bond" to secure "their property," but also to keep the serf below the legal level by diminishing his legal personality. This was throwing him back into the feudal pool from which Josephinian legislation had just fished him out.[37]

With the exception of a few minor details that was the substance of the negotiations as to law between the Estates and the government under Leopold II. But that was not all of the legislation under Leopold II pertaining to the judicial system and law. We have already mentioned the fact that the new Commission of Codification, which Leopold II had appointed, interrupted its labors long enough to issue the Patent of February 22, 1791.[38] By this law, equal inheritance of illegitimate children was abolished, process in divorce was done away with, oaths for trustees were made unnecessary,

[37] See Chapter IX.

[38] See Patent, February 22, 1791, in *K. k. Maj. Leopold des IIten politischen Gesetze und Verordnungen für die deutschen, böhmischen und gallizischen Erbländer*, II, 84-94: Nachtrag zu dem Allgemeinen bürgerlichen Gesetzbuche: 1) on "richterliche Urtheilen," 26 Absatz I was stricken out; 2) on cases pertaining to divorce, patents of 11 Oct. 1785; 12 Aug. and 15 Dec. 1788 as far as S S 105 to 108, thus preventing process in such cases: 3) on illegitimate children: 10-18 Absatz IV: i.e. 16 Feb., 7 March, 12 April, 12 July, 16 October, 1787 and 9 May, 1788 were suppressed, with new rules laid down: 1) the illegitimate child was not to suffer in honor thereby; 2) children were to be supported until able to take care of themselves; 3) the father, if known, must support them, otherwise the mother; 4) the child takes the name of the mother and inherits only after her.

the right of investment of money of wards in securities
other than state papers was allowed, and guardians were permitted for the care of spendthrifts. This law literally stole
thunder from the Estates. By another law, the Patent of
June 26, 1791, Leopold II ordered a new inheritance law for
peasant landholders so as better to secure the indivisibility of
their inheritances. By a series of regulations, Leopold II soft-
ened the brutal aspects of Josephinian legislation with regard
to imprisonment. Public punishment such as beating and
whipping, chaining and branding, was abolished, and the pris-
oners were given warm food, better care, and were kept employed. Judges were given the power to soften or to make
severe the prisoner's sentence according to behavior.[39]

After Leopold II died in March, 1792, the Codification Commission with a few interruptions kept at its work for a decade.
The great Austrian Code was promulgated in 1811. The triumph of anti-Josephinian reaction under Leopold II can be
seen in the clauses relating to illegitimate children, in mortgage limits under trusteeship, in inheritance of women in the
nobility, and in laws on usury. Josephinian legislation remained intact elsewhere as in the case of the *Fidei Commisse,*
of matters pertaining to marriage and religion, and of general
trusteeship.[40] The Code of 1811 was a compromise between
the legislation of Joseph II and the reaction which followed his
death—it was a restatement of the compromises which Leopold II had made with the Estates in Bohemia and elsewhere.

If we should sum up the history of the judicial system and
law under Leopold II in a few words, we should say that
Leopold II saved the judicial system of Joseph II and compromised on Josephinian law. Early in 1790, under the influence of Leopold II, seconded ably by the Court Chancellery
and Count Hatzfeld, the government assumed a very favorable attitude toward the Estates by its preliminary action on

[39] *Ibid.,* I, Patent of May 10, 1790, 33 ff. and II.
[40] See Čelakovský, *O účasti,* 44 ff. Offner, *Der Urentwurf und die
Berathungsprotokolle des österreichischen allg. bürgerl. Gesetzbuches,* I,
448 ff. and II, 53 ff.

the Desideria and by its instructions to the Codification Commission. Leopold II and some of his advisers were ready then for concessions. But the reaction gained such strength that it threatened to destroy all that Joseph II had done in this field. Leopold II therefore decided to keep the judicial system intact, i.e. just as bureaucratic as Joseph II had made it. It was, after all, a masterpiece of constructive political effort. Had Leopold II had time he might have combined his own and the Estates' desires in such a way as to give satisfaction to the Estates. It would have taken nothing less than the highest statesmanship to bring the Estates into the system of the courts—but Leopold II was not the man to balk at ordinary obstacles.

Having stood firm on the system of courts, Leopold II compromised on law. He forestalled the Estates and stole their thunder from them. It is clear, however, that he did not mean to give up the idea of the universal code, and it is more than likely that he meant to make up some of the ground he had lost in compromising over the Desideria. He died too soon to reconcile the Estates with the system of courts or to see the work of codification ended. Nevertheless, the Code of 1811, which was until 1918 the foundation of all law in the Lands of the Bohemian Crown and in Austria, contains some of the compromises which Leopold II made with the Estates. By way of contrast, in the lands of the Hungarian Crown, conditions reverted to the Theresian basis.

PART III
ECONOMIC

CHAPTER VII

COMMERCE AND INDUSTRY

To Bohemia the Thirty Years' War brought about the collapse of economic activity. It resulted in the immense confiscations in which nearly two-thirds of the manors of Bohemia changed masters;[1] it left the cities almost depopulated, for the overwhelming majority of the Protestant population had been urban; and it devastated and ruined the countryside. Before the war, Bohemia's population had been estimated at nearly three millions, after the war barely 900,000 souls were left.[2] Accompanying this great decrease in population came a great increase in the amount of revenue demanded by the Habsburgs from Bohemia, two facts that it is well to bear in mind when tracing the economic development of that country in the Seventeenth and Eighteenth Centuries. And to replace the Protestant Czech and German urban population, the Jews came in increasing numbers.[3]

Nor should it be forgotten, in dealing with the trend of economic forces in Bohemia during the two centuries which followed the Thirty Years' War, that these forces were themselves affected by manifestations which were general throughout Europe. Bohemia was not isolated. It was a part of Central Europe. But if it shared in the general tendencies of

[1] Bílek, *Dějiny konfiskaci v Čechách po r. 1618,* Introduction, I, i-cl. In connection with this see the analyses by Opočenský and Werštadt under the title of "Bílá Hora a česká historiografie" (*Pokrokovy Revue,* 1912, IX, 1913, X); Pekař, *Po Bílé Hoře,* pp. 3-25 and *passim;* and Jellinek, *Die Böhmen im Kampfe um ihre Selbständigkeit, 1618-1648,* vols. I and II.

[2] Pekař, "Český katastry" (*ČČH,* XVIII-XXII, 1912-15) and *Kniha o Kosti,* II, 161 ff. Slavík, "O popisu Čech po třicetileté válce" (*Zprávy Zemského Archivu Království Českého,* 1910, III). Tomek, *Sněmy české,* calculated it at 800,000.

[3] Alfred Příbram, "Zur Geschichte des böhmischen Handels und der böhmischen Industrie" (*MGDB,* XXXVI, 222).

Central Europe, it also had some currents, local in nature, within itself, and these must not be overlooked. Thus, because Bohemia was a part of the Austrian Monarchy, and because it lay at the crossroads of Central Europe, such movements as those which resulted in the political and economic centralization of other states in Europe also affected Bohemia. Political centralization, for the benefit of an absolute monarch, brought with it the destruction of the political feudal state and prepared the way for a policy of national legislation. It produced the bureaucracy and the flow of money to the capital of the state. Economic centralization dissolved the economic feudal state, prepared the way for mercantilism and for the transition from local economy, such as feudalism had called for, to national economy, such as the new modern state at the end of the Eighteenth Century demanded, and finally, it paved the way for the high protective tariff and ultimately for the industrial revolution. All these things can be traced in the history of almost any state in Europe; they were general tendencies.

During this time there was at least one manifestation which was peculiar to Bohemia alone. The wars over Silesia, waged between the Habsburgs and the Hohenzollerns in the middle of the Eighteenth Century, resulted in Austria's loss of Silesia and in the closing to it of the commerce on the Oder and the Elbe. Had Bohemia at that time belonged to some other house its economic history in the last half of the Eighteenth Century would have been different. But Bohemia remained a part of the Habsburg Monarchy. The closing up of these rivers to free navigation and the adoption of the policy of mercantilism by the states of Central Europe forced the Habsburg Monarchy, whose most important natural outlet had been these two streams, to seek another. It was found at Trieste. As has been noted, this meant practically a revolution in the trade routes of the Monarchy, and Bohemia which before 1763 had the most favorable position both for its own trade and for the transit trade, after that year found itself in the worst position;

it was farthest from the new commercial outlet of the Austrian Monarchy.

In the next three chapters, we shall discuss some of these tendencies, general and local, as they affected Bohemian commerce and industry, finances, taxation, and serfdom. The present chapter on commerce and industry, treated, as all the others are, with a view to conditions under Leopold II, will include a treatment of the general tariff policy, which culminated with the prohibitive tariff and the downfall of commerce in Bohemia. It will also include some remarks on the internal structure of commerce and industry, namely, the guilds, the city markets, and local feudal economics. The chapter on finance and taxation covers a brief survey of the public and royal revenues of Bohemia with a view to explaining the great resources and power of the king and the imbecility of the Estates, together with the remedies offered by the latter in the reign of Leopold II. Incidentally many other economic questions are briefly touched upon in this chapter. And finally, the chapter on serfdom, which by nature is necessarily social in its aspects but under Leopold II was made wholly political and economic, will treat the relations between landlord and serf, especially as regards the amount of labor the serf should render and how this might be changed into a money rental.

I

FACTORS IN THE COMMERCIAL AND INDUSTRIAL POLICY OF
THE HABSBURGS IN BOHEMIA IN THE
EIGHTEENTH CENTURY

In the century which followed the Thirty Years' War (roughly 1640 to 1740), Bohemia was hard put to recover from its effects. During all of this time the Habsburgs were interested elsewhere, mainly in chasing the phantoms of dynastic ambitions in Spain and in Italy, and their relations to Bohemia bore an extremely fiscal character. To them it was a matter of how much could be got out of Bohemia in revenue;

the prosperity of the country was not their principal object. On the other hand, the Bohemian Estates, on whose shoulders rested the task of obtaining the enormous sums demanded of Bohemia, were in this century, the promoters, the planners of reforms. The Estates were hampered by the lack of legislative initiative, taken away from them by the Land Ordinance of Ferdinand II (1627),[4] and at best could only appoint commissions and make reports. They petitioned and compiled Desideria, but generally in vain. The Monarchy "heard, but acted not," and their bulky memoirs gathered dust in the archives of Vienna.

A commission of the Estates, appointed to investigate economic conditions in Bohemia, reported in 1705 that the Bohemian and Austrian Lands should form one tariff unit and that the waterways should be improved. It was not until Charles VI (1711-1740) came to the throne that reform was begun. In 1724 the Royal Commerce College was created at Prague, but unfortunately with only the power to recommend and report. It had a task which can hardly be imagined. Roads were bad, insecure and overcrowded with pay-stations, there being some seven hundred of the latter in Bohemia. After much urging on the part of the Estates, the Commerce College in 1725 secured an increase in the number of yearly fairs (*Jahrmärkte*). The guilds, which had played so important a rôle in the past, were a hindrance politically and economically. They worked to bind tighter the economic forces which, in the last quarter of the Eighteenth Century, it was the task of Enlightened Despotism to free. They were the monopolists and the "trusts" of that day, while the Jews, who increased in numbers after the Thirty Years' War, became a real factor in Bohemia's business and financial life.[5]

Charles VI made two excursions into the realm of reform.

[4] See Chapters I, IV, and V.
[5] Alfred Přibram, "Zur Geschichte des böhmischen Handels und Industrie" (*MVGDB*, XXXVI, 226 ff.). See also Baldauf, *Beiträge zur Handels- und Zollpolitik Österreichs in der zweiten Hälfte des XVIII. Jahrhunderts insbesondere unter Joseph II*, pp. 24 ff.

In 1731 he took away from the Bohemian guilds their political autonomy, but left their economic basis unchanged.[6] In 1738 he gave Bohemia a tariff, which, while it contained no prohibitions on importation and few on exportation, was a start in the general direction of protection to Bohemian industry.[7]

By taking away political autonomy from the guilds, Charles VI prepared the way for the destruction of their economic monopoly under Joseph II in 1786. They represented an economic and social system united into a little world which evolved about a hierarchy of masters, helpers, and apprentices all differing from one another by a rigid set of regulations, in which social conditions such as marriage and death, and the practice of religion and coöperative economic assistance played a very important part. The guilds were adapted to a small territory within which they had a privileged monopoly. In the Eighteenth Century, the principles of mercantilism necessitated a larger field for industrial and commercial enterprise.

The tariff of 1658 had proved insufficient; its main object had been revenue, not protection, and Bohemia like other Habsburg Lands had for years been flooded with foreign wares. There had been conferences on the tariff question since 1658 and especially from 1718 to 1732, but nothing came of them. A report of the Commerce College in 1732 ended in a recommendation for the continuance of the liberal tariff policy. But six years later the tariff of 1738 showed the first faint beginnings of a policy to protect native industries.[8]

Down to 1740 the Habsburgs had practically neglected the internal administration of Bohemia and left it to the Estates

[6] Gindely, "Das Zunftwesen in Böhmen von 16. bis zum 18. Jhdt." (*Abh. KAW*, 1884).

[7] A. Přibram, "Zur Geschichte des böhmischen Handels und Industrie" (*ibid.*, XXXVI, 249 ff.).

[8] *Ibid.* On the whole Charles VI's reign is criticized by Přibram severely, p. 24a: "Der streng fiskalische Gesichtspunkt, der bei der Betrachtung der Industrie— und Handels-Fragen vorherrschte, und die irrige Anschauung der Wiener Regierung von den wahren Ursachen des Nationalenreichtums haben in gleicher Weise ein entsprechendes Empörblühen der böhmischen Industrie und des böhmischen Handels verhindert, deren Hebung das Commerzcollegium, wie aus dem angeführten zu ersehen ist, mit allem Eifer angestrebt hat." My archival studies agree with this conclusion.

with a much crippled legislative power. After 1740 and for a half century, thereafter, the monarch became the reforming agency. The causes for this were, first, the seizure of Silesia by Frederick II, and, second, the threatened decrease of the revenues from the land tax, together with the increase in the expenses of the Monarchy. The Monarchy, possessing full power of legislation and an army, planned, urged, and reformed. It ended by driving the Estates from their reforming attitude into one of sullen obstruction or at best indifference. Thus the Estates were radical and the government conservative in the first century after the Thirty Years' War. In the last half of the Eighteenth Century, the government was radical and the Estates conservative.

The seizure of Silesia and the acceptance in Europe of the principles of mercantilism led to a high protective tariff and the downfall of commerce in Bohemia. Were we to examine the economic situation in Bohemia at the time Frederick II seized Silesia (1740), we would discover that the Bohemian Crown Lands had formed one economic unit whose two natural outlets were the Elbe and the Oder. Silesia had been both a manufacturer of woolen goods, linen, yarn, and silk, and the middleman for Bohemia and Moravia, the other two Bohemian Crown Lands, as well as for the northern and eastern parts of Europe. Bohemia, because of its position on the Elbe and its connection with Hamburg, took care of the west and also of the south. It was customary for Silesia to take yarn and cheap linen cloth out of Bohemia and to spin the first in Silesia and to export the latter with Silesian products. Silesia's position was therefore a very important one, and with the loss of that province there was lost also the northern and eastern European market, at this time a lucrative one.[9] The Bohemian Crown Lands contained also the bulk of the industry of the Habsburg Monarchy. Following Frederick II's seizure

[9] See Fournier, "Maria Theresia und die Anfänge ihrer Industrie- und Handelspolitik" (AÖG, 1887, LXVII, 341 ff.); Carl Přibram, Geschichte der österr. Gewerbepolitik von 1740 zu 1860, I, pp. 23-24 and Srbik, Der staatliche Exporthandel Österreichs, 417 ff.

of Silesia, a bitter tariff war resulted with Prussia, which lasted throughout the remainder of the Eighteenth Century and brought momentous results. The economic problem of the Habsburg Monarchy was now a serious one. A market had to be found for Hungarian agricultural products. Bohemian glass and linen and other industrial products, Moravian cloth, and Styrian and Austrian iron wares, had to have protection and a field for export. So, in the decade of peace, 1746-1756, Maria Theresa laid down the principles of an economic policy which culminated in attempts to win markets in the east, in Poland and Russia, and in the south, in the Balkans and in Italy. During this time that part of trade which Bohemia had had with western Europe decayed and to all intents and purposes the Habsburg Monarchy was cut off, with a few exceptions, from the west. When it turned from German lands to the east and the south, it turned from Germanic Europe to Slavic Europe. The course of trade was encouraged to go south, to Trieste and down the Danube and not to the north as it had gone for centuries through Bohemia and Silesia down the Elbe and the Oder. In short, the second half of the Eighteenth Century brought with it an economic revolution.

We can trace here only a few of the larger features of this revolution. In the history of the tariff in Bohemia and in the Habsburg Monarchy in the second half of the Eighteenth Century, we can single out three stages in its development. The first, lasting from 1749 to the end of the Seven Years' War (1763), marked the beginning of the protective tariff and of the tariff war with Prussia. From that time on the principles of mercantilism were religiously applied. The second stage was that of the high protective tariff, but it was likewise a period of vacillation. One did not know whether to enter permanently upon extreme prohibitions or whether to go back to a partly protective and partly revenue-producing tariff. This period lasted approximately from the close of the Seven Years' War to the promulgation of the prohibitive tariff of 1784. The third stage in the history of the tariff began in

1784 and continued into the reign of Leopold II. It was the period of the excessively prohibitive tariff. We shall take up briefly the story of the tariff during this period and then explain the attitude of the neighbors of the Austrian Monarchy toward it.

The tariff of 1738, as is true of all the tariffs of that period in the Habsburg Monarchy, was provincial; it concerned only Bohemia. But with the centralizations carried out in the central government in 1748 and 1749 the desire for one tariff for the entire Monarchy grew. Thus in 1751 a tariff was arranged embracing all three of the Bohemian Crown Lands, Bohemia, Moravia, and Silesia, and it was also the first protective tariff there. In 1753 the average of the tariff was about 30 per cent and its main object was to "destroy Prussian Silesia economically" on the basis that Bohemia was necessary to Silesia in order that the latter might exist. In 1754 Frederick II replied with a duty of 30 per cent on Austrian paper, iron wares, and tallow. Reprisals followed on both sides and the tariff war between Prussia and Austria—one of the causes of the Seven Years' War—was on.[10]

During the decade of peace, 1746-1756, various attempts were made to revive industry at the expense of commerce. Francis I, who came from Lorraine, introduced his ideas into industrial undertakings in Bohemia. In 1753 the Bureau of Manufactures (*Manufacturant*) was created, the Commerce College was abolished, and industrial ventures of all kinds were subsidized by the government.[11] But the Seven Years' War ended with the Prussians still in Silesia and the new industry in Bohemia almost wrecked. Moreover, it became more

[10] Fournier, "Maria Theresia und die Anfänge ihr. Industrie- und Handelspolitik" (*AÖG*, LXIX, 350 ff.). See also Fechner, *Die handelspolitischen Beziehungen Preussens zu Österreich während der provinziellen Selbständigkeit Schlesiens, 1741-1806*, for the Prussian point of view. Beer (*AÖG*, LXXIX, 445-533) states that such articles as fine and dyed yarn and other kinds of yarn had a higher duty than 30%; colonial wares from Hamburg over Breslau (Silesia) bore 30%; spices 10%; fish 40%; but other things such as Silesian raw products which were needed for Bohemian and Austrian industry came in for a lower duty: wool for 9%; flax for 10%; "Fäherrothe" for 7%.

[11] Schreyer, *Kommerz, Fabriken, und Manufacturen des Königreichs Böhmen*, Prague and Leipzig, 1792: I, 31 ff. See also, Fournier (*AÖG*, LXIX, 354 ff.).

and more evident that Bohemian commerce was rapidly disappearing, but this we shall consider presently.[12]

The second stage, in the history of the tariff, began with the high tariff of 1764 which mollified Saxony but made no impression on Prussia. By this time not even the rich traders in Bohemia objected to the high tariff, because, along with the nobles who, on the encouragement of the government, had embarked in industrial enterprises, they too were helped and assisted into the field. Both noble and rich trader saw a golden future in the economic isolation to which the protective policy of the Habsburgs was leading. In 1775 the movement for making one tariff unit out of the Bohemian and Austrian Lands was successful. We have noted that in 1738 there was a tariff for Bohemia alone, in 1753 one for Bohemia, Moravia and Silesia, in 1775, one for all the Bohemian and Austrian Lands. There remained the Lands of the Hungarian Crown and Galicia. The tariff of that year contained a reduction in the number of prohibitions, and showed clearly that the government was wavering between a prohibitive tariff and a return to a more liberal policy.[13]

Joseph II inaugurated the third stage by rudely brushing aside free-traders like Zinzendorf and by promulgating in 1784 a tariff with an average of 60 per cent and prohibitions for many articles.[14] The plan for one tariff unit between Austria and Hungary at this time came to naught because the

[12] See M I Archiv, Carton 518, Vorschlag zur Errichtung einer Leihbank für die Hochlöbl. böhmischn Landesstände. July 3, 1790. No. 239 ex Aug. 1791. Also Protokolum commissiones habita den 17. Sept. 1771: Über den Hofkriegsräthe: Vortrag die in dem K. Boheim vollendete Seelen- und Zugviehs-Conscription. M I Archiv, Carton 449; 218, or Bartenstein, Denkschrift über die innere Verfassung Böhmens, 1759, H H S Archiv, 29. See the chapter on Finances (VIII) for Bohemia's financial rôle in the Seven Years' War.

[13] See Beer, "Die Zollpolitik und die Schaffung eines einheitlichen Zollgebietes unter Maria Theresia" (MIÖG, XIV, 237 ff.) and his "Die handelspolitischen Beziehungen" (AÖG, LXXIX, 542 ff.); and "Handelspolitik unter Maria Theresia und Joseph II" (AÖG, LXXXVI, 25, 74-76). Galicia was included in the Austrian unit in 1718, but under Maria Theresa, Transylvania, Noaquisita, and the Banat of Temesvar were not a part of the Hungarian customs unit.

[14] Hock, Österr. Staatsrath, 549 ff. Among the prohibitions were Stockfische Häringe, Zwiebelen, Getrockeneten Wemberren, Zuckerwerk, Linsenbondern, Wollwaren, Spitzen, Borten, Leder (Juchten ausgenommen). Bijouterien, Uhren, Schmucksachen, Stahl-Arbeiten, Porzellan-Fayence, Tabak-Fabrikate.

Josephinian statesmen feared that Hungarian wines and agricultural products, especially their cheap grains, would ruin the Bohemian and Austrian peasant, whereas Hungary could not furnish a sufficient field for Bohemian and Austrian industry. The dream of those who believed in making the Habsburg Monarchy self-subsistent, i.e. of those who believed in mercantilism, was dashed to pieces on these fears. Yet it was a beautiful dream—to have the Bohemian and Austrian provinces supply the industrial needs of the Monarchy, the Hungarian the agricultural.[15]

The new tariff of 1784 was practically the acme of prohibition—its object was to create modern industry in the Habsburg Monarchy—and we shall see later its results in Bohemia under Leopold II. Personally, Joseph II derived much satisfaction from the statistical tables of 1787 which showed that only 7,250,000 florins worth of goods were imported in excess of the amount exported.[16]

The attitude of neighboring powers was, however, a factor also to be taken into account. With Prussia the tariff war had been going on without alleviation since the middle of the Eighteenth Century. This situation and the seizure of Silesia had destroyed the trade down the Oder. The Seven Years' War and the tariff of 1764 had brought on a similar tariff war with Saxony and had closed the Elbe to trade.[17] In a way, it is easy to over-estimate these two facts, for the principles of mercantilism would also have led ultimately to these results. Already in 1733 the states on the Elbe had closed that river against free navigation for the Emperor's metal fleets.[18] But the extreme policy of the Habsburgs prevented the making of treaties with these powers. Thus, for instance, of all the states

---

[15] Hock, 549 ff. and Fournier (*AÖG*, LXIX, 339-40). Marczali, *Hungary in the Eighteenth Century*, Chapter I.

[16] Hock, *Österr. Staatsrath*, 558. This led Joseph II to order more prohibitions: Baumwollwaren, gestreiften und geblünten Mousseline, Battiste und Linons.

[17] Beer, "Die handelspolitischen Beziehungen" (*AÖG*, LXXIX, 542 ff.) and Wieske, *Der Elbhandel und die Elbhandelspolitik bis zum Beginn des 19. Jahrhunderts*, pp. 25 ff.

[18] Srbik, *Der staatliche Exporthandel Österreichs von Leopold I bis zu Maria Theresia*, 399-407.

in the west, Bavaria alone made a commercial treaty with Austria in 1777, but this was of special significance for Tyrol and Voralberg alone.[19]

Mercantilism had led France in 1781 to a prohibitive tariff thus shutting the doors opened in 1756 to Bohemian linen and Hungarian wines. It was impossible to come to terms with England, because Austria wanted commercial independence, and England, taking advantage of Austria's loss of Silesia, offered it only economic dependence. Bohemian glass, far-famed for centuries, had long been exported to Spain and to Portugal and to their colonies, to the Scandinavian countries, and to the Levant. But in the seventies of the Eighteenth Century, it began to feel the competition of factories erected in these countries. In Spain glass factories were set up at San Ildefonso. The war of the American Revolution also had done much to ruin the Bohemian glass trade, for English privateers swooped down on vessels bearing the commodity to the French, Spanish, and Dutch colonies. The trade never recovered from the blow. The lucrative Bohemian linen trade likewise decayed owing to competition in foreign countries.[20]

In such ways the markets of the western and northern parts of Europe had been closed to the Habsburg Monarchy. Its statesmen, who now began to call even Germans in the empire "foreigners," thereupon turned to the east and the south. In 1775 the Austrian Monarchy secured a commercial treaty with Poland through Russian assistance and in 1783 a treaty with that state itself. In the Balkan Peninsula the Treaty of Passarowitz (1718) still served as a good basis, and the Habsburg possessions in Italy—Lombardy and Tuscany—also offered some markets. Thus the energies of the Habsburg Monarchy instead of following the Elbe and the Oder north and west turned southward to the Adriatic and down the Danube. Trieste was first encouraged in 1733 and by 1751 its harbor rivaled that of Venice. In 1777 Fiume became the

[19] Beer, "Die handelspolitischen Beziehungen" (AÖG, LXXIX, 560 ff.).
[20] See Salz, Geschichte der böhmischen Industrie in der Neuzeit, pp. 269 and Beer, "Handelspolitik unter Maria Theresia und Joseph II" (AÖG, LXXXVI, 25, 74-76).

outlet of Hungary and seven years later the first ship left
Vienna to sail down the Danube to the Black Sea.[21] The
economic revolution was completed.

This great state—the new Austrian Monarchy, immediately
following this reversal of trade routes that so radically changed
the external aspects of its economic policy—underwent also,
striking internal changes. In 1781 the "Leibeigenschaft"—let
us say serfdom for the time being—was abolished and the serf
received the right to carry on whatsoever trade or learn whatsoever profession, he desired. He was also free to emigrate
anywhere. The Patent of Toleration of 1781 freed both Protestants and Jews from religious persecution, and in 1786
Joseph II abolished all guilds and monopolies.[22] These were
the reforms which Joseph II had carried out in order to make
possible the modern economic state in which industrial and
commercial enterprise were to be free from feudal trammels.

And what were the results? If we trust Josephinian tables,
we would say that in 1788 there were twice as many masters in Bohemia as in 1781 and that the number of factory
undertakings had increased 150 per cent in that time. This
was doubtless due to the reforms in serfdom and to the abolition of the guilds. The number of industrial enterprises had
increased and so also the quantity of articles which they
produced. Bohemia was said to have something like 400,000
people engaged in industry and to have twice as much industry as the rest of the Bohemian-Austrian Lands put together.
Already protectionists were exclaiming that Bohemia produced
in one year over five million florins more in factory products
than in agricultural commodities.[23] These were the high lights
of the picture. What were its shadows? If the products of the

[21] See Neumann, *Recueil des Traités et Conventions conclus par l'Autriche
avec les Puissances Étrangères depuis 1763 jusqu'à nos Jours*, I (to 1800),
1, 9, 30, 206, 380, etc. See also Baldauf, *Beiträge zur Handels- und Zollpolitik
Österreichs*, 35 ff.

[22] Gindely, *Das Zunftwesen in Böhmen von 16. bis ins 18. Jhdt.*, 11 ff. and
Carl Příbram, *Geschichte der österr. Gewerbepolitik*, I, 9 ff.; 359-60 ff.

[23] Schreyer, *Kommerz, Fabriken, und Manufakturen*, introduction to part I,
tables in appendix; Salz, *Geschichte der böhmischen Industrie in der Neuzeit*,
tables in appendix; *Schematismus für das Königreich Böhmen*, 1789, 1790,
1791. See also Riegger, *Skizze einer statistischen Landeskunde Böhmens*, I, 97.

new industry were numerous, they were poor in quality. If industry had been encouraged, commerce had been destroyed and business was largely at a standstill. The extreme prohibitive policy of the Habsburgs had alienated their neighbors, and the enmity to Prussia had prevented an understanding which would have been to the best interests of Bohemia and Silesia. The course of events had closed up the Elbe and the Oder, and the Turkish War had closed the Danube (1787-1791). Trieste in 1790 remained the only free outlet of the Monarchy with the exception of that sanctioned by the commercial treaty with Bavaria which concerned Tyrol especially.

We shall leave it to the Estates to picture the economic condition of Bohemia in 1790.

II

The Attitude of the Estates and the Government on Commerce and Industry under Leopold II

The Bohemian Estates in 1790 treated questions relating to commerce and industry under two headings; the one dealt with the tariff, and the other had to do with internal local conditions.

The complaint of the Estates on the tariff took the form of a plea for the "opening up of commerce." They put forth their plea in two ways. They asked directly that the tariff be revised so as to allow the importation of certain commodities, and indirectly, by means of two memoirs, they advocated a betterment of local conditions through the creation of a national bank, the making of treaties with neighboring powers, and a program of industrial education. What were some of the principles that they urged upon Leopold II?

In their direct plea against the excessively prohibitive tariff of Joseph II, the Estates complained against its many absolute prohibitions.[24] They declared that the citizens of Prague and of Trutnov (Trautenau) did not cease demonstrating to

[24] See M I Archiv, Carton 518, the Third Desideria: "Mit den Vorstellungen über die im dritten Absatze des Reskripts von 1ten Mai . . . Gegenstände. November 27, 1790. II E—25ten Wunsch: Wegen Eröffnung des Kommerzes.

public officials that the prohibitions were harmful. They maintained that, "Bohemia had practically lost its trade with the neighboring lands, and in its place smuggling flourished." Many of the people, according to the Estates in the Third Desideria, were idle, and even those engaged in agriculture had much spare time on their hands. The Estates assured Leopold II that they would gladly furnish proof to show how harmful the prohibitive tariff was to Bohemia, but because of the lack of accurate government statistics on detailed branches of the imports and exports, they could not go into detail with regard to this matter. The Bohemian Diet, however, was opposed to many of the prohibitions and asked especially that the prohibitions on the importation of various kinds of fish be removed.[25]

The Gubernium[26] very properly declared that the Estates were too indefinite in their treatment of the tariff and suggested that perhaps the Decree of December 16, 1790, which we shall later consider, and which was issued after the Estates had written their complaints, would doubtless answer their plea. In this case, both the Diet and the Gubernium were in the right. The Diet could make no assertions because it lacked the information, and the Gubernium did not consider it a part of its duty to offer either information or a solution.

By means of two memoirs, the Estates indirectly argued much more. The one, mainly advocating the erection of a national bank at Prague, was written by Count John Buquoy and Count Francis Anton Kolovrat. It is very suggestive on contemporary economic conditions in Bohemia and positive in its recommendations. The title of the memoir is, "The Plan for the Establishment of a Loan Bank for the Honorable Bohemian Estates."[27] The other memoir, dealing primarily with

[25] "Stockfische und Häringe," etc.
[26] Bericht des böhmischen Landes-Guberniums die von den Ständen anher übergebenen Beschwerden und Wünsche in Rücksicht so wohl in Aufsicht auf die Civil- und Strafgesetze als in Beziehung auf die politischen und kammeral Verfügungen werden, Gutachten begleitet. Feb. 18, 1791. M I Archiv, Carton 520, IV H 2. Hereafter cited as Gubernium Opinion.
[27] Entwurf des Vorschlags zur Errichtung einer Leihbank für die Hochlöbl. Böhmischen Landesstände. July 3, 1790 in M I Archiv, Carton 518:239 ex

questions of commerce and industry, is by Bishop Schulstein, formerly Ferdinand Kindermann, the organizer of the German public school system in Bohemia and the head of the school system at that time. His memoir bears the title: "Humble Reflections on the Lack of Industry and Commerce in the Kingdom of Bohemia and some Means to help out the Same."[28] Both of these memoirs were sent to Vienna as supplements of the Third Desideria of 1790 and they represent the opinion of many of the members of the Estates and indirectly that of the Bohemian Diet.

In their advocacy of a national bank for Bohemia, the two noblemen argued that Bohemia was economically in ruins. They described the poverty of the landed classes and the "nation" in general, and showed that the commercial and industrial classes lacked capital with which to operate. As a result of a series of measures, beginning with the Urbarial Patent (Serf Labor Patent) of 1775 and ending with the introduction of the new system of taxation in 1789, the credit of all classes of people in Bohemia had been ruined outside and within Bohemia. Capitalists in foreign countries refused any longer to lend money to landed interests and to business undertakings where things were so insecure and where landed interests were subject to such constant attacks and encroachments by the Monarchy. And within Bohemia, the usurer, freed by the abolition of the laws against usury, practiced his black art openly. These two causes, together with the wars, had driven the rate of interest from 4 per cent to 20, 30 and even 40 per cent.[29] As a result, capital for commercial and industrial undertakings was wholly lacking.

Aug. 1791. For other papers on this question see "Kurzer Begriff einer Ständischen Leihbank," and Rieger's article in the *Osvěta* (1887), as well as Chapter VIII on Finances.

[28] "Unmassgebige Gedanken über die Mängel der Industrie und des Kommerzes im Königreiche Böhmen und einige Mittel demselben abzuhelfen." Lit. G. No. 278:22 November, 1790. M I Archiv, Carton 516: III Partie 207 ex Julio 1791-IV H 2b.

[29] Entwurf . . . einer Leihbank. For instance in a contemporary account, *Beobachtungen in und über Prag* (Prague, 1787), p. 99, one reads: "Wenn man ihnen [the Jews] von 12 Prozenten sagt, da lachen sie. . . ."

In addition to the two causes just mentioned, the memoir asserted that the influx of gold from Bohemia's foreign trade had been much diminished, while Vienna's demands on Bohemia's revenues increased each year and threatened to drain every "grosch" out of that country. The barrier set up by mercantilism, the wars, the prohibitions of Joseph II, all had helped to check the flow of money into Bohemia. Since the Seven Years' War the wheat trade of Bohemia could no longer go down the Elbe River through Saxony to Hamburg and be exchanged for commodities and manufactured products of Saxony and Hamburg. The memoir also argued that out of the twelve million florins contributed by Bohemia to the royal coffers, only five remained in that country to pay for the administration and for the army. Fully seven and a half millions were drawn out of the country by the central administration at Vienna and also by "absentee" foreigners who owned land and commercial and industrial establishments in it.[30]

To balance this, after the "drying-out" of the above-mentioned Elbe grain trade, Bohemia could report from all other exports only a yearly balance of seven and a half million florins, thus barely equalizing the outflow of money to Vienna and to foreign lands. A state in such a situation would soon be brought to the very brink of ruin, for it needed, according to these two noblemen, a surplus of three or four millions yearly to keep up a healthy credit.[31] They recommended, therefore, that a national bank be established at Prague,

[30] *Ibid.* Two and a half millions annually were drawn out by those foreigners who owned lands in Bohemia; but some of this revenue came from tobacco rentals and the lottery business. It is interesting to note that the Bohemian Estates complained of the export of gold and gave practically the same reasons in 1740: "Zu den bisherigen Verfall dieses Konigreiches dass der grösste Theil des mit grosser Mühe und besonder Industrie der hierlandes benöthigten Wirtschaftsorth zusammenbringen, den baren Geldes, durch allerley Praestationes, Cammeral-Gaaben, und das so hohe Contributionale eines Theils—andertens auch durch die bey den Kay. Hof in Specie zu Wien stabilirte, und anderwärts in fremden Ländern sich aufhaltende, hierlands begütterte Innwohner ausser Landes hinausgezohen, mithin auss der innerlichen Circulation gebracht." M I Archiv, Carton 513, 18 von Jahre 1740.

[31] This is well stated in the "Kurzer Begriff einer Leihbank." See Chapter VIII.

which would keep the money centered in Bohemia, furnish capital to commerce and industry, and put credit upon a safe basis by helping out the landed interests [32] with loans at a low rate of interest. It cannot be denied that this was a scheme worthy of consideration, and it is to the credit of Leopold II that over the opposition and indifference of his councillors he approved of it in principle and ordered an investigation as to its possible working out in practice.[33] He was interested in the project.

Bishop Schulstein in his travels about Bohemia, in the capacity of Superintendent of Schools, had noticed much that was important for an understanding of the conditions of commerce, industry, and agriculture. Moreover, if Counts Buquoy and Kolovrat in their memoir on the national bank, were inclined to be hostile to the government, Bishop Schulstein was not. He was an appointee of the central government and owed everything to it. It is therefore well to get his point of view in contrast to that of the two gentlemen.

The Bishop began his memoir by saying that it might seem outside his sphere of activity to discuss commerce and industry. But he pointed out that these fields of human activity had a direct effect upon his flock, and at any rate, his hobby had always been "interest in the earning of one's daily bread." He thought that idleness had been brought about by the downfall of commerce in Bohemia and that this lowered the morals and the manners of the people. His flock instead of "engaging in honorable business and trade gave itself up to illegal smuggling." The people fell into poverty because of lack of employment and "into frivolity which in turn lowered still more their morals." In putting his ideas on paper, he said he was not making up a plan, but merely suggesting the first principles on which such a plan should be drawn up. He also stated that he had not consulted his colleagues or any

[32] *Beobachtungen in und über Prag* (1787) makes the statement that one-third of the landed wealth of the nobility of Bohemia was in the hands of usurers.

[33] See the Court Decree of October 28, 1791 and Chapter VIII.

books with which to correct his thoughts, but expressed them just as they came to him from his many years of experience in traveling about Bohemia.

Fundamental to all plans [54] for the betterment of commercial and industrial conditions in Bohemia was the fact that "the political and natural situation of the country must be taken into account." Bohemia did not possess the most favorable position for commerce, the state did not border on a sea, nor was it marked out otherwise for a wholly commercial state. "Bohemia," he wrote, "will never become the first trading state; and heaven be thanked that we have other resources." [55]

But if commerce was not destined to be the chief occupation of the people of Bohemia, the country could gain great advantages from better commercial establishments and more efficient industrial organization; in truth, commerce within and without could be promoted. The population of Bohemia had increased by leaps and bounds. The increased cost of living and the improved taste of the people appeared to favor the promotion of commerce. He then asked the question: "Why has our foreign commerce, in spite of the increasing population and its needs, fallen instead of risen? And how did this come about?" The first dominant fact, according to Bishop Schulstein, was that Bohemia had too little to offer in return for purchases abroad. The country consumed nearly all that it produced, and for products of Bohemian industries, except for glass and linen, there was little demand. This led to another question: "How did it come that in Bohemia there was so little surplus of that which the country produced? Such as, for instance, was the case with grain and cattle." [56] Both the population of Bohemia and the military forces sta-

[54] I have taken all that follows from his Unmassgebige Gedanken, M I Archiv, Carton 516.

[55] Ibid., Böhmen wird vermüthlich nie der erste Handels-Staat werden; und dem Himmel sey Dank, dass wir andern Resoursen haben."

[56] For some excellent suggestions on the cattle and meat question in Bohemia at this time see M I Archiv, Carton 518, Third Desideria: Wunsch 30: Wegen Wiedereinführung der Viktual Taxe and the Gubernium Opinion on this question.

tioned therein had greatly increased. Further, the neighbors of Bohemia in Lusatia, Thüringia, Saxony, Bavaria, and Silesia had improved their agriculture more rapidly than the inhabitants of Bohemia had improved theirs so that, on Bohemia's very frontiers they were able to support their own dense populations. And finally, more attention was paid in the latter country to the cultivation of fields rather than fodder and less attention given to the raising of cattle. Nor had the farmer in Bohemia succeeded in increasing the amount of grain produced. Hence there was a surplus neither in grain nor in cattle. A country like Bohemia which depended so much upon her agricultural products alone for her support and had little or none left over as a commodity of commerce was likely to be stricken by famines in the first bad harvest or in a disastrous war. This, Bishop Schulstein pointed out, was the case in 1771, 1772, and 1790.[17] Had Bohemia produced some grain for trade in addition to what was produced for home consumption, a prohibition on its export during such years would be an automatic remedy.

This led to a second direct and fundamental question: "Then, why cannot Bohemia have a sufficient surplus to offset this from her output in arts, from her factories, and from her industries?" The Bishop went at once to the very core of the subject, and he answered directly: "the common people lack open minds and skilled hands, the country good navigable rivers and public highways." [18] Bishop Schulstein thought in particular that the chief obstacle to the restoration of trade and commerce was the ignorance of the common man. The average native knew too little how to improve his product, whether agricultural or industrial, and when he traveled abroad his insight into things was not intelligent enough to perceive and to make use of the advantages of foreign industrial progress. Therefore the enlightenment of the whole

[17] See also Entwurf . . . einer Leihbank.
[18] "Es mangelte dem gemeinen Volke an offenen Köpfen und geschickten Händen, allein an offenen Flüssen und Strassen." Unmassgebige Gedanken, M I Archiv, Carton 516.

nation in order to make possible further expansion of industry was a necessity to the improvement of conditions.

For that reason Bishop Schulstein advocated industrial, commercial, and business schools where these essential things were to be instilled in the minds of the young.[39] The youth should first be accustomed to finer, more scientific and artistic industrial work, before the man could turn out a superior article. A class of tradesmen who could command capital and who should be daring enough to take risks must be created. Commerce and industry should be made honorable, progressive callings and the nobility urged to engage in them so that the common man might see that they were honorable. Industry should be subsidized, and established on a national, not merely local plane. Prizes should be given and industry put on a basis strong enough to support it in competition with the neighbors of Bohemia. The increase in the cost of living made it impossible for the Bohemian manufacturer with his crude products to compete with the better products of his neighbors. The result was that the country lost not only because it could not capture trade, but also because much money went out of Bohemia for the purchase of foreign wares. Another reason why the Bohemian manufacturer could not compete with foreigners was the fact that he could not secure suitable capital for his enterprise.

"What, then, was the remedy for this situation?" War had impoverished the treasury of the government and closed it to appeals for help for commerce and industry. The neighbors of Bohemia were for the most part not in alliance with the

[39] Bishop Schulstein was a champion of industrial education in Bohemia. See especially Weiss, *Geschichte der Thersianischen Schulreform in Böhmen*, and the essay: "Kurze Beschreibung des Probsten v. Schulstein von der Entstehungs- und Verbreitungs-Art der Industrialklassen in den Volkschulen des Königreichs Böhmen" printed in Riegger, *Archiv für Geschichte und Statistik insbesondere von Böhmen*. In the same work see also Schulsteins: "Nachricht an die Vorsteher böhmischer Ortschaften im flachen Lande, die Frage: Wie man in Böhmen die Industrie des deutschen Gebirgsbauers auf dem böhmischen Landmann am besten verbreiten, oder ins flache Land übertragen könne." See in this connection also Šafránek, "Pravda o školách v království českém za vrchní zpravy Kindermannovy" (*Osvěta*, 1907, I) and Adler, *Die Unterrichtsverfassung Kaiser Leopolds II und die financielle Fundierung der österreichischen Universitäten nach Anträgen Martinis*, 1-50.

Habsburg Monarchy. While the Austrian prohibitions were in effect, they had been constantly improving their products, so that they no longer needed Bohemia's exports. Moreover, because of the prohibitions, they retaliated with reprisals in a mood which would not readily disappear. And within the Habsburg Monarchy, the population with its twenty-four millions was ever on the increase, and the "lot of the government had been more population, but not more land!" The increased population could not support itself unless production was increased, while the articles produced must be better than those of the "foreigners"—that meant even Germans.⁴⁰ For this reason, Bishop Schulstein recommended that teachers in commercial studies be added to the staff of the normal schools after the manner of the commercial school at Hamburg. Already the Realschule of Vienna had such courses. This would help native business, revive commerce, and give it honor as an occupation. In general, the Bishop was opposed to inviting immigrants to Bohemia, because they increased the population, especially the consuming part of it, and did not much benefit industry.

Industry brought in returns of from seven to ten florins to a strip of land, urged Bishop Schulstein, while agriculture could produce only two florins. Taking the example of cotton, he pointed out that it passed through Bohemia to Saxony to be finished, and returned to be sold in Bohemia either refined or as cloth. Bohemian weavers should learn how to weave it as well as or better than the Saxons. Bee culture should be more widely spread, not only for the honey, but for the wax, which could be used for religious and commercial purposes. Cattle should be raised more carefully so that not so much money should go to Poland, Hungary, and Bavaria. On the other hand, sugar should come in for a small tax. Improving the quality of the articles of production would take time, and

⁴⁰ Unmassgebige Gedanken, M I Archiv, Carton 516. It is interesting to see Bishop Schulstein, a German Austrian, call the Germans in Saxony and Bavaria "foreigners." This shows the influence of ideas of mercantilism in the Eighteenth Century.

foreign countries had put millions into building up factories, which the treasury in the Habsburg Monarchy could not afford to do. Bishop Schulstein urged finally that a plan for improving these conditions be worked out by the Estates in coöperation with the central government "wholly for Bohemia alone," [41] that is, he was reacting against the "all-empire" idea prevalent under Maria Theresa and Joseph II. He recommended that the sovereign seek to open up the Danube, closed because of the Turkish war then in progress, and the Elbe, as they were thirty years before, and to promote the Hamburg-to-Trieste canal. The Bohemian Estates were to coöperate with the central government through the creation of industrial schools, and by means of investigations carried on in circles whose object would be to ascertain what were the best articles to manufacture locally and what should be grown in the fields, in order to determine more scientifically the policy to be followed. In closing his memoir, he pointed to the city of Liberec (Reichenberg), which, in 1782 a subject (serf) city with no property of its own, had become in 1790 an industrial center and counted a population of 12,000, while the royal city of Böhmisch Brod, which possessed all the rights pertaining to property-owning, had a population of 800.

Another memoir, whose authorship is unknown, is to be found in the State Archive. It probably belongs to the last two or three years of the reign of Joseph II or to the year 1790. Although it is not so important as the two memoirs we have just described, it contains a few suggestions of interest to us. This memoir entitled, "On the Development of Bohemian Industry" [42] tells in military metaphor of there being such a thing as every state's "having its own strategy"—and that Bohemia had its strategy. From 1785 the balance of trade in its favor had been three million florins yearly. The unknown writer laid much stress on the increase of population and the necessity of keeping it engaged in industry. He

[41] *Ibid.* "Bloss für Böhmen."
[42] Hebung der böhmischen Industrie, 17xx H H S Archiv.

agreed with Bishop Schulstein that heretofore Bohemia had
given too much attention to agriculture. The consequence
was that outside of Pilsen there was not a growing trading
city of any size. Bohemia lacked men who were educated to
take active part in commerce and industry, for neither the
nobility nor the officials were competent in this respect. The
author recommended the growing of flax and the encouragement of wool culture and its manufacture, and, in general,
made a plea for the protection of industry.

The three memoirs agree in so many ways and are so clear
and to the point that it is unnecessary to comment on them.
The policy of Maria Theresa and Joseph II had destroyed
commerce in Bohemia. In spite of its increase, industry was
of a very poor quality and not extensive enough to keep the
fast increasing population busy. Agriculture could not support
the large population permanently, and cattle-raising was far
below what it should be. The remedies advocated by these
memoirs were a bank and usury laws, commercial and industrial education, and commercial treaties with neighboring
states with the object of opening up the three great outlets of
the Habsburg Monarchy, the Elbe, the Oder, and the Danube.

The Council of the Gubernium [13] considered the memoir of
Bishop Schulstein as especially worthy of notice, and it was
in turn also praised by the Court Chancellery and the State
Council. All of them saw much that was good in it although
the "unsettled times demanded that the serious consideration
of it be postponed until things had cleared up." The State
flatly refused to help Bohemia in industrial education, even
though Vienna had schools like those which Prague wanted.
The teachers of "salesmanship" urged by Bishop Schulstein
were declared to be "of no special use" and further than what
he was doing himself in the establishment of lower industrial

[13] See in turn Gubernium Opinion on Third Desideria, the Protokoll der
Studien-Hof-Commission, Protokoll der Konferenz, 2. Julius 1791 in M I
Archiv, Carton 519 and the Court Decree of October 28, 1791, Carton 515 ad
936 ex Oktober 1791. The Gubernium in all seriousness declared that these
teachers "von keinem sonderlichen Nutzen seyn." Three hundred florins for
such a person would be wasted in Prague.

220 BOHEMIA IN THE EIGHTEENTH CENTURY

schools in the country and in the small cities nothing could
be attempted because of a "lack of funds." Thus another
worthy plan was stifled because of the "fiscal proclivities" of
administration at Vienna, which swallowed millions yearly
but refused to give back a few thousands for so good a cause.

As early as the fall of 1790 the State Council[44] in Vienna
considered a general plan of lowering the tariff and of removing some, if not all, of the prohibitions for the Habsburg
Monarchy. Various elements in the Monarchy desired that
the duties on meat, salt, tobacco, and liquors be revised down-
ward. Cities like Vienna and Prague, and business men in
general, complained against the prohibitions of the tariff. Public opinion on the whole was opposed to keeping up the general
prohibitions, even if a few special prohibitions should be kept
on certain foreign wares. But when the Court Auditing Treasury (*Hofrechnungskammer*) proposed that these general prohibitions should be removed by May 1, 1791, the Court Chancellery and the State Council opposed it.

They argued that it would be a violation of a public promise
once made to keep the prohibitions. The industrial classes,
which then amounted to about seven or eight hundred thousand in the entire Monarchy, would be injured by such action.
Style, the Court Chancellery argued, was only frivolity. It
was pointed out that, since the prohibitions went into effect,
the amount of gold in the Monarchy had increased in spite of
the war and in spite of the higher cost of living, and that it
would be of more importance to watch the increase of population than of the "traders' profession." Finally, the State
Council decided to investigate the working of the tariff by
means of a special commission.

In addition, many other complaints came up before the
Council as to the conditions in Bohemia. It is certain that in
spite of Joseph II's efforts to improve roads and transportation there, much was still to be desired in that direction. For
instance, one memoir complained against the poor roads, the

[44] Staatsrat Akten 1580 and 2117 in 1790, H H S Archiv.

high and numerous tolls, the illegitimate and ignorant trades-people, the monopoly of the Jews, and the lack of good schools. All this was put into a paper explaining the difficulties of making good linen in Bohemia.[45]

Leopold II was willing, in actual practice, to go farther than his councillors. He sought for better commercial, as well as diplomatic, relations with Prussia. Both Bohemia and Silesia were suffering as a result of their separation one from the other. Prussia, on the other hand, was continually being urged by the Silesians to negotiate a commercial treaty.[46] Leopold II agreed to it in principle, but the State Council, which hated Prussia, was very slow in getting around to it, and eventually postponed the negotiations because of "unsettled times." Leopold II died before anything was done in this direction.

As far as the tariff itself was concerned, Leopold II, in his Decree of October 28, 1791,[47] declared to the Bohemian Estates that he was willing to take into consideration the removal of the prohibition of "one or more of the foreign wares" and to give attention to worthy proposals submitted by the Estates. He had already issued various ordinances whereby the duties on the importation of certain kinds of fish (stockfish and herrings) were abolished and the ban on foreign refined sugar taken off. In 1791 the natives of Bohemia were allowed to export horned cattle to the Palatinate, to Bavaria, and to Saxony. But he would not allow soap and candles to be put on the free list. The export of soap was forbidden, and after October 1, 1791, because of a good harvest, grain was no longer allowed to be imported free of duty but was made subject to a duty equal to that placed on Hungarian grain.[48]

[45] Especially Staatsrat Akten, 2117 in 1790, H H S Archiv.
[46] See Fechner, *Die handelspolitischen Beziehungen Preussens zu Österreich während der provinziellen Selbständigkeit Schlesiens, 1741-1806*, p. 520 ff.
[47] Hof Dekret, Oct. 28, 1791 ad 936 ex Okt. 1791 in M I Archiv, Carton 515. See also Slokar, *Geschichte der österreichischen Industrie und ihrer Forderung unter Kaiser Franz I*, 5 ff.
[48] Kropatschek, *Leopold des Zweyten, politische Gesetze und Verordnungen*, II, 170, 173; III, 238, 239.

In general, then, Leopold II left the structure of the prohibitive tariff standing, but here and there in articles and commodities which affected the common man's cost of living some alleviation was allowed. That does not prove that Leopold II approved entirely of the system of extreme prohibition which the Habsburgs had introduced into their domains, but it does show that he had the wisdom to allow changes and encouraged a hope of more in the future.

At the beginning of this section it was stated that the Bohemian Estates treated first questions of tariff and then questions relating to internal local conditions. The second of these two subjects will be considered next.

Among other things, the Bohemian Estates requested that the government should make some sort of reparation or give damages to those who owned dams and mill sites on rivers made navigable by the government since 1776. They also asked that those who owned private tariff zones which had been suppressed by the Decree of November 2, 1782, should be reimbursed.[49]

The Gubernium considered that the subject of private tariff zones fell properly under that of regalia, i.e. rights belonging to the king. As to the other, the government had performed a duty for the benefit of the State. Those who had built bridges and roads on commercial highways had received something annually out of the Road Fund. The Gubernium admitted, however, that the Estates and individual members thereof were not properly recompensed for the repairs which they were accustomed to make, but pointed out that it had already called the attention of the government to that fact. The Gubernium considered it impossible to expect damages for all of the confiscations which Joseph II had carried out against long established rights, but suggested that individu-

[49] M I Archiv, Carton 518, Third Desideria: 5ten Beschwerde: Über das die durch das Hofdekret von 14. Junius 1776 veranlasste Abreissung der Wehren auf den Flüssen und über die vermöge des Hofdekrets von 2. November 1782 erfolgte Aufhebung der Privatmäuthe. See also Kropatschek, *Joseph II Gesetze*, III, 260-268.

ally, i.e. not as Estates assembled in the Bohemian Diet, some might find relief by petitioning the sovereign. This was but pushing off the solution of the real question. It was an implied admission on the part of the government that the confiscations and regulations of Joseph II had not been all that was just and fair.[50]

The citizens of Prague petitioned that the road tolls into Prague be lowered or that the first pay stations be placed some distance from the city so as to allow the inhabitants of the city to walk out, whether to till the fields, or after business hours for recreation, without having to pay the government toll. The Gubernium recommended that the people of Prague be allowed the condition that prevailed before Joseph II published his Decree of August 28, 1788. By the legislation which existed prior to that date, only those who used the highways for commercial purposes paid the tolls. This was agreed to by the central government at Vienna.[51]

In the question of the restoration of guilds, the Estates criticized very sharply the situation brought about by the greater ease of securing the right of mastership in a trade as a result of Joseph II's abolition of the guilds. In asking that the guilds be restored the Bohemian Diet [52] promised that such as were restored would not have a "limited" ("closed") number and that the abuses hitherto prevalent among them would be done away with promptly upon their being discovered by government officials. The Gubernium declared that Leopold II had already restored certain guilds, and that the right of mastership had been curtailed so that masters might live properly on good wages. The same held good for the commercial guilds (grocers, etc.) composed mostly of women; such guilds also would be allowed to exist. In this action Leopold II anticipated the Estates in their demands.

[50] Gubernium Opinion on Third Desideria, Art. 5, M I Archiv, Carton 518.
[51] Third Desideria, ibid., 31ten Wunsch: Der Prager Einwohner in der Wegmautentrichtung eine billige Erleichterung angedeihen zu lassen. Gubernium Opinion, ibid.
[52] Third Desideria, ibid., 29th Wunsch: Wegen Wiederherstellung der aufgehobenen Zünfte. Gubernium Opinion, ibid.

The next subject treated by the Estates was that of the markets in Bohemian cities. They desired that all taxes, that is imports on market goods in cities, be restored. They argued that competition instead of lowering prices had resulted in just the opposite. The public became a prey to the merciless petty merchants. All dealers understood each other perfectly, even though there were more of them, and they used the abolition of the taxes to their advantage by a general advance in prices. Hence the prices should be regulated, the Estates argued, by a complete tax ordinance because they were only partly regulated by the one of April 26, 1790, which Leopold II had issued after convincing himself that the conditions produced by Joseph II's legislation on markets had become unbearable.

The Gubernium opposed the plea of the Estates and brought up the report of the investigation committee appointed by the Council, which had found that the magistrates in Prague were decidedly in favor of free grain and free meat from Hungary and Poland in order to force prices down. The Gubernium argued that the price of beer and wood had risen recently because of the severity of the last two winters and the lack of competition. They agreed, however, only with the magistrates, while the burghers clamored as consumers that they be protected by legislation, i.e. by taxes against high prices.[53]

Leopold II, on the advice of the Court Chancellery, ruled October 28, 1791, that since the Ordinance of April 2, 1790, was promulgated the situation had changed radically. In the spring of 1790 he had been in favor of helping out only partly, but in 1791 he resolved to put into force a complete tax ordinance for city markets. In this matter, therefore, the royal decision was completely in favor of the Estates.[54]

Although they put their demands forth very feebly, the

[53] Third Desideria and Gubernium Opinion on 30th Wunsch: Wegen Wiedereinführung der Viktual Taxe. M I Archiv, Carton 518.
[54] Decree, Oct. 28, 1791 ad 936 ex Okt. 1791 in M I Archiv, Carton 515.

Estates were in favor of a more liberal tariff in 1790. One can see this unmistakably in their desire to have commerce "reopened." They wished to free the Elbe, the Oder, and the Danube for Bohemian and Austrian commerce. They advocated commercial treaties with neighboring states. And finally, they asked that certain prohibitions, doubtless more were to follow later, be suppressed in the tariff. So far as internal economic conditions were concerned they asked for a restoration of the guilds. The reforms of Joseph II in freeing the economic energies within the State and in abolishing too rapidly the feudal barriers to a policy of national economy, according to them, had failed. So too had the market policy of Joseph II. Instead of free competition, the Estates were in favor of regulated monopoly in both cases.

The government was by theory and attitude protectionist. To reverse the economic policy was not easy, especially as the enmity of Prussia always stood in the way. Leopold II personally did much to dissolve that enmity, but his councillors were too much filled with it to carry out his idea that Austria should be friendly to Prussia. Leopold II was also in favor of alleviations in matters pertaining to the tariff, and it seems was willing to meet the Estates halfway. But in regard both to Prussia and the Estates, the State Council assumed a hostile attitude, which ended in fatal delay and in the failure to do what had been unmistakably pointed out by the Estates in their memoirs. Joseph II had hoped to speed up the economic evolution of his empire by a generation. He ended by setting it back by two. Leopold II, in his short reign, could trim off only some of the ragged edges of Joseph II's well intentioned, but overzealous, activity in matters pertaining to commerce and industry.

CHAPTER VIII

FINANCE AND TAXATION

BOHEMIA was the richest and most permanent source of revenue which the Habsburg dynasty possessed in the Sixteenth, Seventeenth, and Eighteenth Centuries. The history of its finances and of its system of taxation leads us directly into the great financial problems which confronted the Austrian Monarchy. In this chapter we shall briefly review some of the high-lights in the financial history of both Bohemia and the Monarchy as a whole with a view to understanding why the resources of the monarch were so great and why the Monarchy was able to reduce the Estates to the condition of imbecility in financial matters in which they found themselves in the reign of Leopold II.

From the reign of Ferdinand I (1526-1564) to that of Leopold II (1790-1792) the finances of the House of Habsburg fell into three divisions. There was first, the revenue of the monarch—his private revenue as landowner; there was second, the revenue of the monarchy or dynasty which he represented as a public person; this we shall call "royal"; and there was finally, the revenue which the states of his Monarchy collected and which may be termed "provincial." In the latter we include such states as Bohemia, Hungary, etc. Thus all three revenues were to be found in each state under the Habsburgs.

The king of Bohemia was the owner of estates in that country as he was in other states under his rule. He owned these lands as a private person and paid taxes for them like any one else. In early times, he had a large income from the royal domain—i.e. these private lands—which up to 1620 amounted

to one-ninth of the total area of Bohemia. After the Battle
of White Mountain (1620) Ferdinand II gave about half of
the royal domain away to the warriors and priests who had
helped him regain Bohemia.[1] This aspect of the finances
does not concern us; it is private and though it was not insignificant, with it the Estates had absolutely nothing to do.

The royal revenue was derived from regal rights, such as
customs and tolls, mines, the salt and tobacco monopolies,
liquors, and even at times, provisions. The royal cities were
regular contributors to the coffers of the king. They paid a
regular "interest" from their estates, and after 1547 and 1620
they were subject to certain penal taxes for attempted upris-
ings. In addition to this there was the income from the Jews
and from escheats. Even before the Battle of White Mountain, attempts had been made to estimate the private and
royal revenue of the king of Bohemia. The annual total was
estimated at one million florins, and Stransky, the noted
Czech publicist of the Seventeenth Century, had heard on
good authority that four-fifths of this was all that was necessary to support both the court and the state administration.
Whence comes the startling conclusion that the king could
well have lived on his own. And in medieval days in Bohemia,
this was the prevailing theory.[2]

The provincial revenue consisted in what the Estates voted
in taxes. In early times the land tax was levied almost exclusively, but in the Sixteenth Century a number of other
taxes, such as those on persons (*capitation*), buildings, chimneys and mills, distilleries and breweries, and provisions and
foodstuffs were also collected, for fear lest the landowners
might be ruined. In the Sixteenth Century, there developed
the custom of the royal postulata. When the Diet met, the
king wrote out his demands for taxes in the royal postulata

---

[1] Gindely, "Geschichte der böhmischen Finanzen vom 1526 bis 1618"
(*Phil. Hist. Kl. KAW*, 1868, pp. 18-24). For Sixteenth-Century finances of
the Habsburgs see: Oberleitner, "Finanzen und Kriegswesen unter Ferdinand
I (1526-1564)" (*AKÖG*, 1860, XXII, 5-233) and Plachta, *České daně, 1517-
1652*, 12 ff.

[2] Kalousek, *České státní právo*, 280-287.

and after receiving the Diet's confirmation of them gave it a receipt (called *Revers*).[3]

These were then the three great sources of the income of the king in his triple capacity: of private landowner, public ruler, and sovereign working in coöperation with the Diet. The Estates had absolutely nothing to do with the first; in theory they had nothing to do with the second; and their power could most forcibly be used, if at all, in the third. One may say that the royal revenue was derived from indirect taxation, the provincial from direct. In the course of the Eighteenth Century these two classes of revenues received respectively the names of *cameral état* and *military état*.[4] These distinctions should be kept in mind.

In reality, down to 1806 legally only these three classes of revenue were so subdivided. But even with Ferdinand I we have the beginning of a fictitious central state, as yet unnamed, in the creation of three ministries, the Secret Council, the Council of War, and the Court Treasury. The centralizations of Maria Theresa strengthened the fictitious state, and while it did not legally exist (as the Estates in 1790 claimed it did not) it was nevertheless a *de facto* state.[5] The monarch, as head of this state, as well as head of the other states, which soon were in practice degraded to the title of provinces, bargained with the Lands of the Bohemian and Austrian Crowns and later even with those of the Hungarian Crown, in order to arrive at an interstate proportion whereby a quota could be determined which each "province was to contribute to the *common* government." Of course, the states combated the theory, but the "central state" steadily became more and more a practical reality, first in the unit composed of the Bohemian and Austrian Crown Lands, later in a unit that

[3] *Ibid.*, 317 ff.; Gindely, *Ges. der böhm. Finanzen,* 17 ff. and Bachmann, *Österr. Reichsgeschichte,* 253. See also M I Archiv, Carton 537 ff. Landtag Postulata in specie zu 1549. The postulata originated in the Sixteenth, developed in the Seventeenth, and became a pure formality in the Eighteenth Century.

[4] Mensi, *Die Finanzen Österreichs von 1701 bis 1740,* 1-5.

[5] For an exposition of the theory of the fictitious state see Baxa, *K dějinam veřejného práva,* p. 8 ff., and Kapras, *Právní dějiny,* III, *passim.*

included even the Hungarian Lands. Thus, in 1542, an interstate financial agreement was consummated between the Lands of the Bohemian Crown and the Austrian Lands. In 1682 and 1748 other agreements followed. By these agreements two things were generally determined; first, the number of tax units, or farmers, which should be accepted by each state, and second, the amount of the quota in actual money, i.e. the amount per unit, per quota. The quota or contribution for each state having been determined a financial contract or "Recess" was entered into between the king and the Estates, especially after 1748, in which the details of the provincial revenue were concretely established. This "Recess" may therefore be defined as an interstate financial contract carried out by the "central" government or the king on one hand, and the separate states on the other, and it involved later a further contract within the state as between the king and the Estates.

In discussing the financial policy of the Habsburgs in the Eighteenth Century down to the reign of Leopold II we shall take up first, the interstate financial contracts, next, the development and growth of the royal revenue, and finally, the history of the provincial revenue.

I

The Financial Policy of the Habsburgs in Bohemia in the Eighteenth Century

The policy of the Habsburgs in interstate financial contracts was to get as much as possible from the Bohemian Lands and to be lenient to the Austrian and the Hungarian Lands. Thus in 1541 a financial agreement was carried through whereby the representatives of various provinces came together and assured a land tax to the dynasty. The Hungarian Lands were not included in this; their contributions at this time, at any rate, were insignificant compared to those of Bohemia.[6] The

---

[6] *Böhmische Landtagsverhandlungen—Český sněmy*, I, 532 ff. For a secondary account of this see Huber-Dopsch, *Österr. Reichsgeschichte*, 211-212.

Bohemian Lands, Bohemia, Moravia, Silesia, and the Lusatias, bound themselves to take over 67 per cent or 770,000 florins, of which Bohemia's portion was 32.8 per cent of the total for all Lands. In other words, the proportion stood at a little over two-thirds for the Bohemian Lands to one-third for the Austrian, or to put it another way, with the divisor 18, the former took 12, the latter 6.[7]

The Thirty Years' War resulted in the loss of the Lusatias. In 1682[8] another interstate financial agreement was therefore consummated whereby, owing to the loss of the Lusatias, the share of the Bohemian Lands stood at 11¾ while the Austrian took 6¼, or 282 to 150. Of the quota for the Bohemian Lands, Bohemia assumed one-half, Moravia one-sixth, Silesia one-third. This was the quota as between the Bohemian and Austrian Lands down to 1748. In the century after the Thirty Years' War, Bohemia, even though it was the heaviest sufferer from that war, was contributing the largest quota 32.6 per cent—almost as much as all the Austrian Lands put together.

If we should compare the respective amounts received from Bohemia and Hungary during this period, we should at once see the vast importance of Bohemia in Austrian finances. Hungary was not included in the financial agreement of 1682 and, in general throughout the Eighteenth Century, paid only the costs of its own internal civil administration but contributed an annual amount to the "central" treasury for the military. Bohemia during this time retained about five per cent of its own revenues for its administrative expenses and contributed ninety-five per cent of those revenues, together with the quota for the military, to the "central" treasury. Thus, in 1722, Hungary gave 2,138,000 florins; from 1728 on 2,500,000 annually, and at this figure the quota stood for a

---

[7] Steuer-Fusses, M I Archiv, Fasc. 576, 71 ex Januario 1748. Mensi, Österr. Finanzgesch., 13-14.
[8] Steuer-Fusses, M I Archiv, Fasc. 575, 5 vom Jahre 1691 Böhmen and Fasc. 576, 71 ex Jan. 1748. For remarks in print on this see Toman, Das böhmische Staatsrecht, 96 ff. Bidermann, II, 92; D'Elvert, Finanzgeschichte, XXV, 222 f.

long time.[9] During the same period Bohemia gave for the
same purpose, the military, 2,666,660 florins in 1716, 2,425,000
in 1730, 3,152,000 in 1735, and 3,132,800 in 1739, besides
ninety-five per cent of its provincial revenues, which must
have amounted to an almost equal sum.[10] Italy, Tyrol,
and later the Netherlands enjoyed privileges similar to those
of Hungary. Few investigators know that in the years between
1716 and 1739 the Bohemian Lands contributed 75.8 per cent
of the quota for military expenses; that is, more than three-
fourths of the total collected from all of the Bohemian,
Austrian, and Hungarian Lands. It is indeed not an exaggeration to say that for the period between 1648 and 1748,
the Bohemian Lands contributed twice as much to the treasury of the Habsburgs, for military matters alone, as all the
Hungarian Lands. Furthermore, it was in this period that
Hungary was forever saved from the Turks and the advance
into the Balkans was begun.[11]

After the loss of Silesia the Habsburg Monarchy had to
"brace up." Along with centralization in political and economic matters came centralization in finances. The Directorium, created on the ruins of the Bohemian Chancellery
and Treasury and of similar offices in the Austrian Lands,
became in 1749 the Central Chancellery and Treasury for all
of the Bohemian and Austrian Lands. In 1761 the Treasury
was separated from the Chancellery, but later, in 1782, again
combined with the Chancellery.[12] Leopold II once more separated them. And by this means the Bohemian Treasury was

[9] Huber-Dopsch, Österr. Reichsgesch. 211-212.
[10] See M I Archiv, Fasc. 576, 71 ex. Jan. 1748 and H K Archiv, A. B. 218
D. 1760-1763, Nos. 105-127. Compare with the memoirs, cited later in this
chapter, written in 1790, and with Staatsrat Akten, 2510 in 1790, H H S Archiv.
[11] H K Archiv, A. B. 218 D. 1763; Österreichischer Erbfolge-Krieg, 1740-
1748. Nach den Feld-Akten und anderen authentischen Quellen bearbeitet
in der kriegsgeschichtlichen Abtheilung des k. und k. Kriegs-archivs, I, 294-
295. Out of the total of 165.9 millions, Bohemia gave 62.9. See also Pekař,
"Český katastry, 1654-1789" (ČČH, 1913, XIX).
[12] See the scholarly monograph, Beer, "Die Finanzverwaltung Oesterreichs,
1749-1816" (MIÖG, 1894, XV, 237-366, especially, 238-300). D'Elvert, Zur
österr. Verwaltungsgeschichte mit besonderer Rücksicht auf die böhmischen
Länder and his Zur österr. Finanzgeschichte are worth consulting and contain a valuable bibliography.

made to disappear while the "central" treasury remained
de facto.

Count Haugwitz, the "iron chancellor," was the person who
carried through the interstate financial agreement of 1748
whereby the new departure of making a detailed Recess after
the conclusion of the interstate agreement was entered upon.
We shall, however, limit ourselves here to the interstate agreement, leaving the Recess to the next section of this chapter,
where it rightly belongs. Haugwitz wanted a standing army
of 108,000 men and a revenue for the military from all of the
Bohemian, Austrian, and Hungarian Lands of 14 million
florins annually.[13] Furthermore, he wished to get rid of a
stack of debts contracted by the "central" treasury during the
first two Silesian wars. The practical problem was, first, to
make up the loss of Silesia's revenue and, second, to get the
Estates to assume these quotas under a ten-year contract.

The loss of Silesia was equivalent in concrete figures to
fourteen-fifteenths of its former self, 31.8 per cent of the
entire interstate quota of the Bohemian Lands, and in military
revenue a sum that, during the last few years before its seizure,
had amounted to between 3.2 to 3.6 million florins.[14] The
quota between the Austrian and Bohemian Lands was fixed
at 44.2 per cent to 55.7 per cent respectively with Bohemia
alone paying 40.16 per cent. Thereby Bohemia bound itself
to contribute 5,270,488 florins yearly into the "central" treasury, of which amount 4,200,000 florins were to go for the
military alone and the rest for the central civil administration
and for the payment of debts contracted by the central government, and to assume as well a debt of 8,575,231 florins.[15]
By comparison with all the other lands, it will be seen that the
general increase everywhere amounted to about 10 per cent

[13] Arneth, *Geschichte Maria Theresias,* IV, 1-36; see also Prokeš, "Boj o
Haugvicovo 'Directorium in publicis et cameralibus' r. 1761" (*VKSN,* 1926-27).
[14] See M I Archiv, Fasc. 575, Steuer-Fusses—Memoir entitled: Wenn also
das gesambte . . . etc.; 6 von 1747 Böhm. Also Fasc. 576, 71 ex Januario 1748
and Hof Kammer, A. B. 218 D. 1760-1763.
[15] M I Archiv, Fasc. 576, 18 ex Augusto 1748, Landtagsschlüsse, 1747
(xvi-xvii) and Beer, "Die Staatschulden und die Ordnung des Staatshau-
shaltes unter Maria Theresia" (*AÖG,* 1895, LXXXII, 1-137 and appendix).

of the loss represented by Silesia, and that Bohemia had assumed 35 per cent of this loss herself.[16] In 1790 the Estates pointed out that Bohemia had been overburdened by this extra 670,000 florins annually which, in the forty-three years for which she paid the amount, had reached over twenty-eight million florins.[17] It was not until 1791 that Hungary paid a military contribution equal to Bohemia's, yet all that while it retained control of all its income save the small sum contributed to the military. In Bohemia itself we shall see presently how this was managed. The interstate contract entered into in 1748 lasted for a century.

One further consideration will serve to show the position of Bohemia's revenues in central financial history. Thus far we have considered only the ordinary military contribution. If its rôle was the most important one in the ordinary military contribution, it was doubly so in the extraordinary. Bohemia had suffered most by the first two Silesian wars, yet in 1748 it assumed the greatest financial burdens of the Monarchy. Its devastation in the Seven Years' War was most severe, yet the records show that it paid the greatest part of the ordinary and extraordinary military expenses.

A few examples will serve to make this clear. Besides the regular amounts called for by the interstate contract of 1748, the states were called on for voluntary extra contributions. From each of the Hungarian Lands and from the Holy Roman Empire came the sum of 7.8 millions. Hungary itself contributed 4.4 millions in cash, 3 millions in civil administration credit, and 92,000 florins in serf contributions—7.5 millions in seven years. The Bohemian Lands contributed over 46 million florins, of which Bohemia alone contributed over 32 millions (17.5 in cash and 14.6 in kind). The Austrian Lands contributed about 39.6 millions. Thus all of the Bohemian and Austrian Lands contributed 14.7 times as much as the Hungarian Lands. Bohemia alone paid in voluntarily four times

[16] Calculate from statistics in documents cited in fn. 3 and 4.
[17] See Ständische Ausweis, M I Archiv, Carton 518, 239 ex Augusto 1791.

as much as Hungary. It may therefore be truthfully said that in addition to carrying 32 per cent of the ordinary military contribution for all the Bohemian, Austrian, and Hungarian Lands, besides turning over 95 per cent of its provincial revenue, Bohemia paid in extras one-third of all the extraordinary revenue of the entire Monarchy, that was collected to pay the cost of the Seven Years' War. Netherlands helped with a sum of 53.4 millions, of which 49 millions (or 7 millions annually) was its quota to the military, for that province, like Hungary, took care of its own civil administration. Should the extra and the ordinary grants of Bohemia be added, we should come to a total of about 69 millions and this does not include the royal income of between 15 and 25 millions.[18] It is certainly justifiable to conclude that Bohemia was the richest and steadiest source of revenue of the Habsburgs during the Sixteenth, Seventeenth, and Eighteenth Centuries.

In discussing the second question, the development and growth of the royal revenue, we shall bear in mind one fact. It was the policy of the monarch to increase his revenues which were derived from indirect taxation, at the expense of the Estates. The increasing population naturally consumed more and more of taxable commodities. It was also a part of the king's policy to take away from the Estates—to make *cameral*, as they called it in the Eighteenth Century—all the indirect taxes the Estates had in their charge. Having absorbed nearly all of these, Joseph II in 1789, by his new system of taxation, grasped after the direct taxes of the Diet. Had not the reaction succeeded in preventing this from remaining a law, the power of taxation of the provincial diets would have disappeared entirely.

[18] This is based on H K Archiv, A. B. 218 D. Staats Inventory. Haupt Billanze, 1760-1763, No. 105-127. Tabella Was zu Bestreitung des Extraordinarii Beym letzen Krieg für gratis Beyträge auch freywillig und angesonnene Anticipationen mit baaren Gelde, Naturalien, und ausgesteltere Papieren auch weme geleistet worden. Verfaszet mit Ende May Anno, 1763. See also M I Archiv, Carton 518, 239 ex Augusto 1791, Ausweis, and H K Archiv, V, A 4, Book No. 13 D. 1750. Out of the total of 16,441,377 florins brought in from all the Bohemian, Austrian and Hungarian Lands, Bohemia paid in 5,270,488 florins, Hungary, 2,147,772.

As we have said before, the royal revenue was collected from the regal rights, i.e. indirect taxes for the most part: customs and tolls, salt and tobacco, and mines; from the royal cities, and from the Jews and escheats. To increase the number and income of his revenues the king, by means of bargains with the Estates or by merely using his autocratic legislative power, made royal or *cameral,* the beer tax in 1657, the tobacco tax in 1691, the capitation tax in 1692, and the property or income tax in 1700.[19] These he kept and took good care of. Profits from some of these sources of revenue were immense. Thus salt alone in 1739 brought in 1,100,000 florins, and beer 700,000 florins.[20] During the Eighteenth Century the royal income from Bohemia down to 1748 was about one-third of the provincial revenue of that country.[21] When Joseph II died (1790), the relation of royal to provincial revenue was as three is to four, not counting the new arrangement as to the land tax. Salt in 1763 brought in 1.6 millions; in 1791, 1.9 millions. Tobacco in 1763 yielded 169,520 florins; in 1791, 1 million florins. Liquors in 1763 yielded 396,554; in 1791, 2 million florins.[22] These figures give one an idea of the king's immense resources, and over these, in theory, the Diet had no power at all. Along with those taxes which the king made royal before 1745, came new taxes grasped from the Estates, who, in order to avoid increasing their already unjust quota, surrendered them without a murmur. In this way, in 1750 part of the salt tax became royal—that part of it which had been under the care of the Estates alone. In 1763 further taxes on tobacco, stamps, and capital amounting to 346,362 florins yearly were made royal; thus in 1789, besides the land tax, which was that year completely changed, the Estates had remaining an income of only some 300,000 florins from insig-

[19] M I Archiv, Carton 518, 239 ex Augusto 1791. See also Kalousek, *České státní právo,* 467.
[20] Pekař, "České katastry, 1654-1789" (*ČČH,* 1913, XIX, 188 ff.).
[21] See fn. 19.
[22] H K Archiv, Book, 1763-1784, 227 D. Schriften über die Finanzen der Monarchie überhaupt; Book 1763-1791, Finanzen 229/A/D Erforderniss und Bedeckung Aufsatz der gesamten Staats Einkünfte und Ausgaben für das Militärjahr, 1791, and Finanz Gegenstände, 1791.

nificant supplementary taxes.[23] The facts presented in this section must be borne in mind when one wishes to make an estimate of the justice of the central government's attitude toward the Estates in 1790, when they asked to be relieved of the extra burden heaped up on them as a result of the war with Prussia and the loss of Silesia.

The third and last phase of Bohemian finances in the Eighteenth Century is the history of the provincial revenues which were a matter of direct concern to both the king and the Estates. The great bulk of the provincial revenues came from the direct land tax, the rest from supplementary direct and indirect taxes. Down to 1789, all of these taxes were raised and distributed and collected by the Diet and its officials. Even the Land Ordinance of 1627 did not deprive the Diet of the right to legislate on these taxes, although as early as 1748, when the Estates were still able to bargain, the royal Postulata had become formal. After 1748 the Decennial Recesses codified the Postulata and reduced the granting of taxes by the Diet almost to a ceremony, taking place formally each year and contractually every decade.

In the first century of the rule of the Habsburgs (1526-1627), the amount raised by the Diet's taxation was quadrupled.[24] And less than five per cent of that amount remained in Bohemia. Ferdinand II began in 1627 the custom of asking for a stated amount and not for separate taxes. He would leave it to the Estates to determine which taxes to levy so long as he got his quota. He began with the "unheard-of" sum of 800,000 florins; by the end of the Seventeenth Century the sum had reached a total of over a million, and by the middle of the next the amount asked for was over four millions.[25] During the period down to 1748, three-fourths of the provincial revenue was derived from the land tax, one-fourth from the supplementary taxes. And the land tax at that time made

[23] Compare Domestikal Einkünfte und Ausgaben for 1749 in M I Archiv, Carton 518, 239 ex Augusto 1791. The figure 346,362 florins is the average of the income over fourteen years. Kalousek, *České státní právo*, 469, is correct.

[24] Gindely, *Gesch. der böhm. Finanzen*, p. 17.

[25] Tomek, *Sněmy české dle obnoveného zřízení Ferd. II*, pp. 16-80.

up about fifty to fifty-five per cent of the total royal and provincial revenue of Bohemia.[26]

In 1748, as we have already stated, came the Decennial Recess. It was a bargain—a poor one for the Estates—whereby the Estates bound themselves to an annual quota of 5,270,000 florins and a debt of 8,575,231 florins. The Estates [27] pointed out that they had long been paying 1,620,000 florins proportionately more than Lower Austria, but that complaint was of no avail; they had to obey or suffer Maria Theresa's wrath for swearing homage to the Duke of Bavaria in 1742. The contract was signed between the monarch and the Estates —this point is of importance in 1790—"without prejudice to their well-founded rights." [28] The sovereign bound herself to the following clause, often later violated: "No other postulatum either for the civil or for the military administration, whether dona gratuita, property, Turk, head (*capitation*) or auxiliary, itinerary, fortification or marriage gifts or taxes were to be asked under whatever pretext, whether in peace or war." [29] Secondly, the Estates surrendered their care of the military forces. Henceforth, quartering, remounting, and supplying was to be done by the government. In order to soothe the Estates, a part of the liquor tax and the tax on music were given to them. The king took all the other taxes except the meat penny and the insignificant tobacco auxiliary tax.[30] The details of the debts assumed by the Estates will be discussed in the section treating of finances under Leopold II.

At intervals of ten years there followed the Recesses of 1757, 1766-7, 1775, and 1785.[31] Except for details as to the land tax the two Recesses of 1757 and 1766-67 altered nothing in the annual quota, and the last-named Recess confirmed a debt of over 15 million florins. The Recess of 1775 lowered

[26] See fn. 19.
[27] Landtagsschlüsse, 1747 (xvi-xvii) and M I Archiv, Fasc. 576, 18 ex Augusto 1748.
[28] Landtagsschlüsse, 1748 (xviii): ihren besitzenden Privilegien/ Freyheiten/ Begnadigungen/ wohl-hergebrachten Gewohnheiten/ und den freyn Verwilligungen in keinen Dingen praejudiciren.
[29] Ibid., xxxiv-xxxv.
[30] Ibid., xlviii ff.
[31] Ibid. for years, 1757, 1766-67, 1775, 1785-86.

the annual quota to 4.7 millions and it remained at that figure until 1789.[32] In that year the relation of royal to provincial revenue had already changed to the ratio of three to four, and the land tax, owing to the manner in which the king made royal the supplementary taxes belonging to the Estates, instead of being 76 per cent as it was after 1748, was 87 per cent of the provincial revenue.[33]

By this means we are able to determine that, even if the Estates had been the ablest of financiers and the boldest of politicians, the monarch could easily have overawed them with his vast resources. The revenues of the king, based as they were on indirect taxes, grew proportionately as the population, let us say about 40 per cent in the half century (1740 to 1790), while the revenues of the province, based on direct taxation for the most part, remained after 1748 for almost thirty years at a standstill and then decreased. One may truthfully say that in 1789 the king received a royal revenue, if we include his private income, which practically equaled what the Estates raised by the land tax. All of this revenue was beyond the control of the Diet.

But if this makes evident the great power of the king in finances and his vast independent resources and shows up the imbecility of the Estates, the new system of taxation which Joseph II promulgated in 1789 really aimed to make royal even the land tax. Had Joseph II succeeded in this great reform there would have been no provincial revenue—it would have been all royal. We shall take up briefly some of the main tendencies in land taxation in Bohemia with a view to explaining what this reform of Joseph II meant and why the Estates took the attitude they assumed in 1790.

II

THE LAND TAX IN BOHEMIA IN THE EIGHTEENTH CENTURY

It is not our intention here to enter into the details of the

[32] See also M I Archiv, Carton 545, Recess, 1776-1785.
[33] Ausweis, 1749-1790, M I Archiv, Carton 518, 239 ex Augusto 1791.

system of land taxation in Bohemia. The part which interests us—and it interested the Estates in 1790—is what the landlord and the serf paid in relation to each other and why.

We know that, in contrast to the lords of Poland and Hungary, before the Battle of White Mountain (1627) the Bohemian Estates paid the annual tax from their land together with the serf. The victory of the Counter Reformation brought the spirit of Roman law into the relations of master and serf. Thereafter the lord refused to pay the land tax regularly and soon the custom arose for the lord to pay extras now and then, until in the Eighteenth Century, it was a recognized theory that the serf paid the regular land tax, but that the lord assisted, when necessary, with an extraordinary land tax. In 1748 Maria Theresa persuaded the Estates to give up this theory in practice and to pay an annual tax on their land, though on a different basis of valuation. The serf had paid his land tax out of the land survey called "rustical"; the landlord, after the survey of 1757, paid it out of the "dominical." And from that time down to 1789, when Joseph II inaugurated his new system, both serf and landlord paid a regular land tax, but on unequal evaluations and at a percentage distinctly favorable to the landlord.[34]

The unit of taxation in Bohemia was "the farmer" (*Usedlý-Angesessen*). This "farmer" held an amount of land which was assessed at a certain rate. This may have differed with the epoch and with the location of the land. Thus after 1683 [35] a person who held about 67 strips or 7/10 of an average fief (*lán-leno*) and paid a tax of 19 florins 2 kreuzer yearly from it, was a farmer. In 1736 the tax had risen to 60 florins for the same area. In 1638, there were 58,585 such farmers in Bohemia. A recent investigation has shown that in one of the most typical manors in Bohemia—one cannot claim that it is

[34] Pekař, *Kniha o Kosti*, II, ch. VIII. The same is affirmed by Tomek, *České sněmy dle zemské zřízení Ferdinanda II*, 12 ff. and by Falk, *Die Grundsteuer Verfassung von Böhmen von den ältesten Zeiten bis auf die gegenwärtige Zeit*, 1-12. The latter work on the period down to 1748 is antiquated.
[35] Pekař, "Český katastry" (*ČČH*, 1913, XIX, 51 ff.) and his *Kniha o Kosti*, II, 188 ff. See also Carton 575, 28 vom Jahre 1713.

representative for all of Bohemia—the State took 54 to 56
per cent, the landlord 40 to 42 per cent and the Church 2 to 5
per cent of the total revenues of a serf from a "farm." Beginning with 1681 and concluding in 1700, it was shown that
the robot had remained the same, but the land tax had increased 29 per cent and the tithe by 33-1/3 per cent. In general, the investigator concluded that about 73 per cent of the
total revenues of a farm went to the State, landlord, and
Church, and about 26.4 per cent was left to the farmer.[36]

In 1725 a new basis of evaluating the farm was made. Of
the rough produce of the given unit, 180 florins was called its
yield; one-third went for the cost of cultivation, one-third for
maintenance of the cultivator, and one-third or 60 florins for
the land tax. But the government had little success with it.
Wars diminished the land under cultivation and the landlords
concealed much of it without the knowledge of the government. In 1757, as we have already said, the Estates first discovered that the amount or quota of 5,720,000 florins yearly
could not be produced by the 41,850 farmers they were able
to apportion it to. The central government gave them no
help, and so the 11,200 fictitious farmers were called into existence. The serf instead of paying 60 florins out of 180, paid 60
out of 142 and the landlord 29 instead of 25 out of 100 per
cent.[37]

This meant that both the Estates and the serfs since 1748
were paying the land taxes of other states in the Habsburg
Monarchy. From the two new land surveys which Maria Theresa had carried to a successful conclusion, the serf land survey
in 1748 and the landlord's in 1757, certain interesting compari-
sons can be made. The dominical (landlord's) land, in area,
was about 77 per cent of the rustical (the serf's). It was
actually valued at 87 per cent of the rustical, and paid 36 per
cent of the amount of taxes which the serf land had to pay.
The farm of the serf from 1749 to 1751 paid 60 florins out of

[36] *Ibid.*, "Český katastry," 21-35; *Kniha o Kosti*, II, 195.
[37] Falk, *Die Grundsteuerverfassung*, 40 ff.

142; from 1751 to 1756, 60.5 florins; from 1756 to 1763, 60 florins; from 1763 to 1772, 66 florins out of 142—doubtless owing to the ravages of the Seven Years' War and the poverty of the country. In 1773 and 1774 the tax was lowered to 57 florins, owing to the famines of 1771 and 1772; and from 1775 to 1789 the ratio stood at 60 out of 142 florins. In other words, a farm which in 1683 paid 19 florins 2 kreuzer land tax, in 1775 was paying 60 florins.[38]

When Joseph II ascended the throne in 1780 all his subjects —whether they belonged to the Estates or to the serfs—paid taxes and, if they owned land, the land tax. But the Estates as we have pointed out paid the tax on an evaluation and a percentage very favorable to themselves. Joseph II was an ardent champion of the theories of the physiocrats and by means of a new system of taxation and serfdom, he resolved to put the finances of his State on a more profitable basis, to do justice to the serf by making all taxpayers pay an equal percentage on an equal basis of evaluation, and to discover the concealed lands.

To go into the details of this complicated system is not our purpose here, nor would it be profitable, even if space allowed. We shall point out some of its larger features. In the first place, it took the administration of taxation out of the hands of the Estates and gave it to 184 tax collectors at a total cost of over 300,000 florins yearly. Manorial distinctions, whenever possible, were erased and tax districts mapped out. Then the land was measured "by engineers and sworn men"—the Estates later said "by bureaucrats and peasants"—and all income-bearing land was sought out, measured, evaluated, and its "grain product" (*Körnererträgnis*) estimated on the basis of the produce of the land for the last ten years. Some account was taken also of distance of location from the mar-

[38] See Ständische Ausweis, M I Archiv, Carton 518, 239 ex Augusto 1791. The calculations with regard to the dominical and the rustical land can be found by comparing this document with the patents promulgating the land-surveys. The patents are to be found very much abbreviated in Falk, *Die Grundsteuer Verfassung*, 20-73 ff.

ket or city. All, by principle, were supposed to be treated alike—and a landlord was to pay the same for his arable land, for his meadow, for his woods, as the serf whether he had brought it under cultivation or not. Finally a hard and fast rule was laid down that 70 out of every 100 florins of produce were to be declared free to the serf. There remained 30 florins for the land tax and the satisfaction of the money dues resulting from the abolition of robot. The State was to take 12 florins 13-1/2 kreuzer for its share, the landlord, 17 florins 36-2/3 kreuzer as a settlement for all the obligations of the serf. The tithe was abolished. And so when the law went into effect in 1789 (October) there was only one grand land survey. In theory, all taxation had been made equal and just in the Josephinian land survey. Distinctions such as dominical and rustical disappeared so far as taxation was concerned.[89] And what was of supreme importance, it was definitely pointed out that Bohemia had been unjustly overburdened with the fictitious 11,200 farmers.

To pass judgment on the system would be audacious. Suffice it to say that the Commission discovered about 2.7 million "joch"—about one-third of the total surface measured—of concealed lands. The system meant a revolution in the economic life of the subjects of Joseph II. We have already said that at the beginning of the century about 73 per cent of the serf's income went to the State, landlord, and the Church. Joseph II, by the new system, planned to leave 70 per cent to the serf. To-day, 77 per cent goes to the farmer and 22 per cent to the State. Calm critics will perhaps say that in theory the system was just, but because it was so rapidly introduced, it became unjust in practice. One could not change suddenly a dilettante farmer-landlord, who lived off the robot and the dues of his serf, into a real farmer, who, if the 17 florins 46-2/3 kreuzer from every 100 florins of the serf's income did not suffice, would find it necessary to hire labor and cultivate his own lands. Nor, too, could one make, overnight, a re-

[89] Riegger, *Archiv von Böhmen*, II: Kataster Bestand in Böhmen 1789 and Rieger, *Zřizeni krajské*, II, 251 ff.

spectable tiller of the soil who paid his debts regularly, out of a serf who hitherto had often been dependent on his lord and to whom such independence might still mean a license for idleness? Revolutions, such as Joseph II planned, require decades, not years, even if technically they are perfect.

In the next two sections of this chapter we shall take up first, questions dealing with finance, and then, those dealing with taxation, bearing in mind always the great financial sacrifices Bohemia had made for the Habsburg Monarchy.

III

The Financial Policy of the Estates and the Government under Leopold II

In order to understand fully the financial burdens which the government had to assume under Leopold II, we shall examine first the state of finances of the Habsburg Monarchy and of Bohemia, and then the financial problems peculiar to Bohemia alone.

A memoir composed by Mallowent, one of the officials of the Court Auditing Treasury, on July 16, 1790,[40] gives us a clear insight into the financial conditions which Leopold II had to meet during the first six months of his reign. The War Council had demanded an additional sum for the expenses of the war. This the Treasury could not give, for the following reasons. The Netherlands, "where in former wars a great part of the costs of war was covered" was not a contributor to the royal coffers because it was in a state of revolution. The revolt in the Netherlands had stopped the making of loans in Holland, "which among all foreign countries most easily raised the sums." "Except from payments in kind (*in natura*), which in this year (1790) had been refused, Hungary had not given anything for the support of the (Turkish) war." "The war tax just written out for 1790 would bring in very little revenue owing to the fact that the German provinces, such as Inner Austria and Galicia, had evaded it, giving internal

[40] Staatsrat Akten, 2510 in 1790, H H S Archiv.

unrest as the excuse, while in other provinces the guilds and the unions (Innungen) had sworn to smaller incomes." The costs of the Turkish War (1787-1791) had increased every year, while the finances were not even ready, or had not in 1790 as yet adjusted themselves, to the first year's extraordinary demand for money. Credit had to be resorted to. The army formed in Luxemburg against the Netherlands had caused much extra expense which the War Council had not calculated as war costs. The military expenses, in the three years since the Turkish War had begun, had already reached the enormous figure of two hundred million florins; such a tremendous outlay in less than three full years "must make necessary the entire exhaustion of the finances." In addition to this the imperial election was about to take place and that would swallow much more than the election of Francis I, because he paid part of the three millions himself, the Hungarian magnates and the provinces helping out with the rest. Nor was the thought of a loan very satisfying. There were only three places where one could be secured, Amsterdam, Genoa, and Frankfurt. The last-named place could scarcely take care of the money needed for the army in Luxemburg. The other two places, even if Vienna could place loans there, would very likely cover only a part of what was desired, because in 1790 there was an unusual demand for money in Europe. The Mallowent memoir, therefore, "took the liberty to represent to his majesty, Leopold II, the extremely serious condition of the finances and the fearful results which might follow." [41] On July 16, 1790, the Habsburgs had a reserve of only 6 million florins on hand.

A year later, Count Zinzendorf,[42] the president of the same institution, tendered another report which described financial

[41] *Ibid.* "So habe ich mir die ehrerbietigste Freiheit genommen, E. M. die äusserst bedenkliche Lage der Finanzen, und die schrecklichen Folgen allergehorsamst vorzustellen. . . ."

[42] Staatsrat Akten, 5743 in 1791, H H S Archiv, Vortrag des Hof-Rechenkammer Präsidenten Grafen von Zinzendorf, 25. O'bris 1791, mittels welchen die von der Hof-Rechenkammer zu Stände gebrachten praeporatorischen Ausarbeitungen zur Gründung eines Haushalterischen Finanzsystems vorgelegt werden.

conditions for the entire year, 1790. Debts had increased to 418 million florins and the interest on them mounted to over 16 millions annually. The calculated ordinary expenses for that year (1790-1791) were over a million and a half higher than the income of the entire Monarchy. Meanwhile in the last twenty years the ordinary expenses for military affairs had risen from sixteen to twenty-seven millions annually. Another report a little later in the same year showed that there would be a deficit of seven millions in the ordinary expenses instead of a million and a half. The army of the Netherlands itself took almost fourteen millions, that stationed in Hungary five. Thus adding together the deficit in the ordinary expenses and that in the Netherlands and Hungary, which may be termed extraordinary, the total deficit for 1791 amounted to twenty-six millions.[43]

This same report showed the net income from various lands belonging to the Habsburg Monarchy. Bohemia produced the largest net income, three and a half million florins, all of the Austrian Lands except Upper and Lower Austria produced a clear profit of two and two-tenths millions; Italy, two millions; Hungary, two; and Galicia, six-tenths of a million. The Netherlands showed a deficit of one and eight-tenths millions and Upper and Lower Austria, into whose budget were unjustly heaped many general payments in this case, showed a deficit of fifteen and three-tenths millions. Thus in the critical year of 1791 Bohemia once more vindicated its position: it was the steadiest and richest permanent source of income which the Habsburgs had. And that was at a time when a French memoir on the state of finances of the Habsburg Monarchy declared that it enjoyed about six-sevenths of the revenues of France. Belgium, Lombardy, Hungary, and Tyrol held exceptional positions "and were oppressed with fewer taxes, than really appeared desirable to the government. Lower Austria became richer every year because Vienna was

[43] H K Archiv, Book 1763-1791. Finanzen 229 A/D. Finanz-Gegenstände, 1791.

the residence city of the emperor and because of its situation on the Danube. Inner Austria had lucrative mines. Upper Austria enjoyed a large transit trade and the provinces on the Adriatic Sea got a share in the coast trade. "Only in the Slavic provinces, in Bohemia, Moravia, and Galicia were taxes too high altogether." [44]

The general finances of the Habsburg Monarchy under Leopold II were, therefore, in a very critical condition. One province after another refused to assist the Central Treasury, and bankruptcy really stared the government in the face. Leopold II could do little else except guard carefully against the too free use of paper money and hope to win back his former sources of revenue, the revolting or recalcitrant provinces. [45] In 1791 he carried through an administrative reform whereby he separated the political administration from the financial, i.e. the Court Chancellery from the Treasury and its supplementary financial department, which had existed as one office since 1782. He hoped thereby to speed up financial transactions. [46]

Turning from central finances to provincial finances, we come upon many interesting facts in the financial history of Bohemia under Leopold II. In Chapter VII on Commerce and Industry in Bohemia so much of the memoir of Count Buquoy and Count Kolovrat on the need of a national bank was discussed as related to the economic condition of the country. Here the financial side of the matter concerns us particularly.

The Buquoy and Kolovrat memoir of July 3, 1790, [47] clearly

---

[44] Cited in Mitrofanv, *Joseph II*, II, 461-462. The document is P. A. v. 42 Autriche 1757-1789: Mémoires sur les Finances et Revenues d'Autriche, considerée comme Puissance, 1786.

[45] Beer, *Die Finanzen Österreichs in XIX. Jahrhundert*, and his "Finanzgeschichtliche Studien" (*Sitzungs-Berichte, KAW*, 1903, 10-72).

[46] Staatsrat Akten, 292 in 1791, H H S Archiv.

[47] The original is in M I Archiv, Carton 518, 239 ex Augusto 1791. Entwurf des Vorschlags zur Errichtung einer Leihbank für die Hochlöbl. Böhmischen Landesstände, July 3, 1790; Nachlasse Kaspar Sternbergs in the Č N M Archiv, have Promemoria einiger Mitglieder der böhm. Stände und des böhmischen Landtags bezüglich einer Creditbank für Böhmen; the Lobkovic Library, Prague, has Kurzer Begriff einer Ständischen Leihbank für das

exposed financial conditions in Bohemia and gave a brief, but caustic, review of the financial policy of the Habsburgs from the Seven Years' War down to 1790. According to the memoir, the story of Bohemia had been "misery, debt, and poverty" since that time." The landlords, in the security of whose property rested the financial credit of Bohemia, had really helped the serf on many occasions and especially in the famines of 1770 and 1771. They had been confirmed in their property rights for over a century by the sovereigns of Bohemia, and it was on the basis of these rights that they had contracted financial obligations. The legislation on serf matters of 1775 brought not only great losses to the landlord in property, because by it the landlord was deprived of a certain amount of the labor of the serf (robot) to which he had accustomed himself for over a century, but also the greatest damage possible in credit. Forthwith the value of what had belonged to the landlord was made insecure and diminished. The legislation of Joseph II "whose desires in all undertakings nobody misunderstood" brought with it the abolition of "Leibeigenschaft"—serfdom. "The foreign creditor who knew only the external picture of this serfdom consequently came to the conclusion that the landlords had lost much in their incomes, calculated on the value of property, as if it had really been lowered thereby, and became suspicious toward his debtor and more averse to making loans." Thus, at a time when there was very little money in the country anyway, the foreign creditor was less and less willing to lend it."

Then, suddenly, in 1786 came the ordinance, which required all church, benevolent, and orphan capital to be made public and to be deposited in the public fund instead of being invested in private undertakings, thereby diminishing the rate

Königreich Böhmen und der Ursachen wegen welcher sie notwendig ist. See a summary of the main point of the first document in Rieger, "Navrh české zemské banky r. 1790 (Osvěta, 1887, pp. 193-198).

48 Entwurf: "Elend, Schulden und Mangel. . . ."
49 Entwurf . . . einer Leihbank, M I Archiv, Carton 518: . . . und so stockte der Einfluss des Geldes von aussen zu einer Zeit zu welcher in dem Lande selbst wenig baares Geld war.

of per cent, but adding to its security.[50] The rush for that capital almost created a panic. The new system of taxation (1789), which without the consent of the Estates legislated away more of the property rights of the landlord, was not designed to make the creditor more lenient nor to increase the amount of money in the country. The creditor was thereafter wholly unable to calculate the losses which each manor had to sustain, as a result of the finding of concealed lands and a higher tax rate for landlords' property than they were accustomed to before, and this ended in a further lowering of the value of landed property in Bohemia and in an increased rate of interest. The insecurity which the numberless ordinances of the monarch had produced, tended to lower values still further. In addition to this, the government began to sell the lands which had belonged to the religious orders suppressed by Joseph II and permitted the great land trusts, the *Fidei Commisse,* to be mortgaged to a third of their value. The State made loans during the war against Turkey at five per cent, and finally, "without preparation" published the Patent of January 29, 1787, whereby the penalty for usury was abolished as well as all regulations against usury. "To the complete destruction of all property owners whose mortgages were held by foreigners,—and how many were there whose estates were entirely free from debt?—there was lacking just this step."[51] The usurer, who up to this time had worked his "black art in secrecy," could because of this legislation stand on the street corner.

The total result of Joseph II's financial legislation was a great lack of money and an excessively high rate of interest, which in many cases ran up to 40 per cent. Industry and commerce, which needed capital, could not secure it so as to make investment profitable, and old families with landed

[50] That is, the holders of this kind of money had to surrender their mortgages and seek others.
[51] Entwurf . . . zur Vollendung des gänzlichen Verderbens aller Güter-Besitzer auf deren Eigenthum fremde Gelder haften,—und wie viele gibt es derer welche ihre Güter von allen Schulden ganz rein besitzen?—fehlte nur noch dieser Schritt.

property were ruined outright. All prize essays on usury, and there were many written in the Habsburg Monarchy in the years between 1782 and 1785, had not suggested a practical remedy.[52] In the opinion of the Bohemian Estates there were two ways to mend the situation; by the creation of a bank for the Estates and by the abolition of much of Joseph II's financial legislation, returning thereby to legislation against usury.[53] The bank would keep money centered in Bohemia and help to hold up, in that country's favor, the fine balance between the inflow and outflow of money. Legislation against usury would run down the rate of interest and punish those who undermined the prosperity of the State.

The national bank which the Bohemian Estates planned, was, among other things, to have a twofold function. It was to issue a kind of paper money at the rate of about two million florins annually up to a third of the value of property registered in the Land Tables. It was also to undertake all the other functions of a bank, such as making loans to property owners who had property registered in the Land Tables, and borrowing money itself from abroad or elsewhere in the Habsburg Monarchy. The issue of paper money by the bank was to receive the sanction of the monarch, and the money itself was to circulate as legal tender in sums of from five to one hundred florins. One-third of the land tax the first year, a half of the land tax the second year, all wills and foundations which amounted to more than one hundred florins, all deposits in mortgages, all purchases of houses, were to be paid for in this paper money. Loans were to be made by the bank at 4 per cent interest up to one-third of the value of the debtor's landed property. Questions arising as to the circulation of the paper money were not easy to settle.

In the first place, a loan of twenty million florins had to be secured in order to put the bank on a solid foundation and ready for work. The Estates were in favor of raising this in

[52] Staatsrat Akten, 1042 in 1790 and 266 in 1791, H H S Archiv.
[53] Third Desideria, M I Archiv, Carton 518.

some foreign land, but if this were not allowed, then in Bohemia. Three or four branch banks were to be established in the sixteen circles, and the paper money of the bank was to be accepted as legal tender in all the local royal sub-treasuries. Naturally the paper money issued by the new Bank of Bohemia and the paper money of the quasi-public Vienna City Bank (*Wiener Stadt Bank*) would be circulating in Bohemia at the same time. The Estates estimated that of the twenty millions of paper money which the Vienna City Bank had in circulation about four millions could be found in Bohemia. If the new bank issued seven millions there would then be about eleven million florins of paper notes in circulation in that country. To the assertion that the two kinds of paper money would be confusing and cause much trouble, the memoir added the question, "What connection has the Vienna City Bank with the kingdom of Bohemia anyway?" They implied that their constitutional law did not recognize a half-public, half-private city bank which helped to carry on the central finances. "Will that bank save the Bohemian land-owner from the hands of the usurer and lend him money at 4 per cent?" Their object was to remedy the lack of money and here they were offering a local remedy—their own paper money based on one-third of their property. Nor did they propose, the memoir declared, to issue the seven or eight millions of paper money in one year, but to spread their issue over a series of years and then only in answer to the real financial need of Bohemia. Thereby commercial and industrial promoters would be able to secure capital, and the rate of interest, because of this competition, would necessarily fall. And finally, the Estates urged that the Habsburg Monarchy should not fall behind the Prussians in this matter. The Prussians had already established a system of provincial banks, such as the one in Silesia, and the Estates offered that as an example of what they themselves desired.[54]

The Diet sent the memoir on the creation of a national

[54] See the memoirs on the bank cited in fn. 27, 28, and 47 in this section.

bank to Vienna and in the Third Desideria briefly demanded the restoration of laws against usury. In the opinion of the Bohemian Estates the abolition of laws against usury by Joseph II had been carried out "because of the sophism of a class of skeptics of our age, who either out of private desire or out of fashion had cast doubt on the existence and then on the possibility of punishing usury." They argued that they would not abuse the patience of Leopold II by stopping to answer: "What is usury?" a question so frequently on the lips of the opponents of the reaction and on which so many prize essays had already been written. They knew it existed in practice, even if theorists could not determine what it was. That it was harmful to Bohemia they also knew, and they were looking about for a remedy. The national bank was one way of relieving conditions, the restoration of the laws against usury was another.[55]

We shall pass from the Estates to the government. The Council of the Gubernium[56] favored in a general way the establishment of a bank, but opposed laws against usury, although it admitted that "usury had then risen to its highest point." In regard to the bank, the Gubernium declared that only such landowners should be allowed to secure loans who could give ample security, i.e. notarial (or pragmatical) security as it was then called. The money loaned was to be secured by landed property which was properly registered in the Land Tables, and regulations were to be drawn up whereby the money which the bank loaned could not be made use of by professional usurers. The Gubernium thought that the loan of twenty millions, proposed as the capital of the bank, was too large, especially if only pragmatical securities were to be used to back up paper money. Then, as to usury, the Gubernium was absolutely sure that all the laws of Maria

[55] Third Desideria, M I Archiv, Carton 518, 6ten Beschwerde. Wucher Gesetze. Durch die Scheingründe einer Klasse von Szeptiken unsers Zeitalters verleitet worden zu seyn, die entwder aus Privat-Absichten oder aus Mode das Daseyn die Strafbarkeit des Wuchers in Zweifel gezogen hatten.

[56] Bericht des böhmischen Landes-Guberniums, Feb. 18, 1791, M I Archiv, Carton 520.

Theresa against the practice had proved failures. The Patent of April 26, 1751, which had fixed the rate of interest at 5 per cent, brought forth so many complaints that in 1766 the maximum rate of interest was set at 4 per cent. Even then there had been no cessation of complaints—in fact the legislation was publicly recognized as unworkable. Accordingly Joseph II, by the Patent of January 29, 1787, suppressed the laws against usury and the maximum rate of interest, although before the courts no rates of interest except 4, 5, and 6 per cent were to be recognized. The Gubernium also made the following generalizations. No one needs to borrow; the law does not force him to borrow! Money, like wares, is controlled by laws of supply and demand, security, and the economic conditions which determine each situation. Money-lending is a business and should be as unhampered by restrictions as possible. But here all the philosophizing and advice stopped. In the next paragraph the Gubernium concluded that Bohemia suffered greatly from the usurer and that a solution of the question should be thought out.

The Court Chancellery [57] thought that the Patent of February 25, 1791, partly met the situation with regard to usury. The lack of money had already been taken care of in a series of ordinances issued by Leopold II, allowing the loaning of church, benevolent, and orphan money on good security to private persons. The Chancellery predicted that the coming peace with Turkey would end loan making on the part of the government and would bring better financial times. The Chancellery was in favor of raising money for the bank within the Habsburg Monarchy and not in foreign lands, because the interest would go out of the Monarchy and later, the capital also. The issue of paper money did not meet with its approval, and the plan as a whole lacked detail. Both the Court Chancellery and the Commission on Desideria decided that a bank should not be allowed just then, although the plan could be worked out for some future time. If after a time, the lack of

[57] Protokoll der Konferenz, 2. Julius 1791, M I Archiv, Carton 519.

money continued to be acute, the Estates could take up the matter once more.

Leopold II, in the Decree of October 28, 1791, urged the Estates to try the legislation then in force against usury and to await his further decision as to when and how a bank should be established. A few months later, he decided that a bank should be established on the model of the one in Silesia and by a person who was thoroughly acquainted with Bohemian law.[58]

The matter was debated later, and plans were drawn up but in vain; no result was obtained, and the bank never came into being in the Eighteenth Century. But it will be readily seen from the negotiations that the plan was worthy of consideration and was so recognized by Leopold II. He was not ready to return to the severe legislation of Maria Theresa against the usurers, even though all the government officials had to admit the presence of flagrant usury.

By means of laws against usury and by means of the bank the Estates planned directly to overcome the great lack of money in Bohemia. They planned to do the same indirectly in another way and that was by asking the central government to pay off the debts which they, as Estates, had contracted to be liquidated by means of their financial recesses. The Estates were asking nothing else than that the government should pay the debts which they had assumed, with the money which they annually turned into the Treasury for that purpose. On January 29, 1791, in a memoir on Finances,[59] the Estates prepared for Leopold II their humble proposals "on the serious condition of the royal credit business under their guaranty."

In this document the Bohemian Estates recognized no central government, only the king of Bohemia, who as sovereign of the country had contracted the debts. They maintained the

[58] Decree, Oct. 28, 1791. M I Archiv, Carton 515, 936 ex Okt. 1791.
[59] An E. M. unterthänigste Vorstellungen der böhmischen Stände, über die bedenkliche Lage des unter ihrer Garanzie bestehenden Aerarial-Kredit-geschäftes, 29. Jan. 1791. M I Archiv, Carton 517.

thesis that these debts did not make a real credit or public
fund for the whole Monarchy but a guaranteed sinking fund
agreement entered into between the Estates and the king. To
them the state was Bohemia, and not the Austrian Monarchy
(*Die Österreichische Monarchie*) which was fictitious and did
not exist."" We must bear in mind that at this time the Holy
Roman Empire still existed, the Austrian Empire not being
proclaimed until 1806.

The Estates explained ⁶¹ that they had the care of providing
taxes and of taking into account the needs of the land. When
war came on and sudden and great demands were made upon
the country, loans had to be resorted to. Some of these loans
were contracted between the sovereign and the Estates in
behalf of Bohemia, and these were called the aerarial—recess
debts or the contracted Treasury debts. Other loans or debts
were contracted by the Estates themselves in behalf of the
country, and these were called domestic debts. The central
government wished to sink the former class of debts into a
general-all-empire credit operation. Thus a debt contracted
by the king and Bohemia would be included in the general
debt for the entire Monarchy. The Bohemian Estates had no
desire to be caught in such a financial game; they would soon
be paying the debts of Hungary and other provinces as they
had long been paying their taxes. On the other hand, the
Bohemian Estates could point out that such debts as they had
contracted under their guaranty retained that guaranty only
so long as they were not settled by a sinking fund. In other
words, the Estates claimed that the relation between Bohemia
and the rest of the Lands belonging to the Habsburgs financially was a personal, not a real one, and that being so, they
were not called upon to share all the financial obligations of
the dynasty, but only such as they themselves guaranteed and
accepted in the name of Bohemia. That is why in their
memoir on Finances of January 29, 1791, they asked the sov-

⁶⁰ For an exposition of the constitutional law here involved see Baxa,
K dějinám veřejného práva v zemích koruny české, I, 82 ff.
⁶¹ See fn. 59.

ereign to keep his word in the financial agreements and pay off the debts with the money which both had agreed should be set aside for such purposes and which the Estates had really supplied.

The Estates then proceeded to explain the Financial Recesses or Agreements of 1748 and of 1766 and 1767 so far as they pertained to debts. By the Financial Recess of 1748 the Estates had assumed 6,552,731 florins of debts under their guaranty. Along with this they had promised yearly to supply the king with 5,270,000 florins as their quota for the Habsburg dynasty. Out of this last-named sum 327,636 florins were to be set aside to pay the interest of five per cent on the debt of six and a half millions, and 65,527 florins were to be put into the sinking fund each year. The Seven Years' War prevented the government from living up to the agreement, i.e. paying off the interest with money which the Estates set aside, and it added many new debts.

In April, 1767, a new financial agreement was carried through between Maria Theresa and the Bohemian Estates. The total amount of debts which the Bohemian Estates assumed in 1767 was over fifteen million florins. Out of the quota which Bohemia yearly paid into the coffers of the Habsburg dynasty 655,715 florins were to be set aside to pay the interest (6, 4, and 3 per cent) on this huge debt. As a sinking fund, 150,326 florins additional were to be set aside, thus making the interest fund and the sinking fund, yearly, 806,041 florins. This sum was paid over in the quota of 5,270,000 florins which Bohemia raised annually. The sovereign was bound by this contract in the most solemn way to use the 806,041 florins for that purpose only. And this the Bohemian Estates declared to be a closed contract which was not fulfilled until both had obeyed its provisions.[63]

The Estates next pointed out that if the sovereign had obeyed the provisions of the contract and paid off the interest

[63] The Estates are accurate in their figures here. Verify in the Diet Conclusions of 1748, 1767.

and the sinking fund in 1790, only a debt of something over two millions would have been left. Instead of that something entirely different happened. Out of the enormous sum of 21,777,597 florins collected for the purpose of paying off the debt in twenty-three years, only 8,638,034 florins had been actually paid, while over thirteen millions were diverted by the government into other channels. In addition to that, the "Credit-Fund" of the Estates, which till then had been a closed credit fund of the Estates under their guaranty alone, was transformed into a general fund for Bohemia where all the mortgages of churches, of benevolent foundations, and of orphans had been put and the name changed to "Public Credit Fund." In other words, from a treasury which distinctly belonged to the Estates alone, the government turned it into a public treasury, under the control of the central government.

Then came the order of the sovereign that 167,000 florins which the Estates planned to set aside for the payment of their own—the domestic—debts should instead be used to pay the debts of the entire Monarchy, i.e. the money should be put into the "Universal State Debt Treasury." Thus all the money which the Estates in 1767 had planned and the sovereign had duly contracted should go to the payment of the debts which Bohemia had assumed from the sovereign, went to pay other debts which that country had not contracted at all. In 1790 the Bohemian Estates calculated that they therefore had a debt of 18,275,424 florins still on their hands although they had already paid over fourteen millions into the "Universal State Debt Treasury."

The Estates asked that all interest and sinking fund dues be regularly paid off henceforth. They desired to discontinue paying into the "Universal State Treasury" and wanted the sovereign to live up to the terms of the Financial Recess of 1767. However, that money which the Bohemian Estates had already paid into the "Universal State Treasury" was to be deducted from the debt they had contracted in 1767. And finally, all of the mortgages of churches, foundations, and orphans were to be separated from their fund which was henceforth to be what it was before, the credit fund of the Estates, and not the public fund.[63]

The Gubernium[64] did not question the figures which the Estates had brought up, but merely the argument as to what the money was to be used for. That Council knew nothing about any changes which the sovereign had carried out in the terms of the financial contracts. It contented itself with remarking that the status of the active and passive, debit and credit, funds was not such as to warrant the fears of the Estates. Finally, if the credit of the Estates should become so bad as to reach a danger point, the Gubernium was sure that the "Universal State Treasury" would step in and help Bohemia out.

That was exactly what the Bohemian Estates did not want. They had a solvent and rich country and could easily pay off their own debts. They were, by means of the memoir on finances, trying to push off the bankruptcy which the nearly insolvent central government—which by the way they did not recognize—was busy saddling upon the country. They did not desire to become bankrupt, and then have the magnanimous central government play the rôle of savior. And it is to their credit that they understood the game at this point.

The matter came up next before the Imperial and Royal Court Treasury Chamber and Commercial Court Offices, March 16, 1791.[65] It was the opinion of that Council that "the financial operations which were carried on by the Estates of all of the 'Hereditary Provinces' made up a part of the credit of the state as a whole, and that therefore one province could not be separated from its connection with the rest in

[63] See fn. 59.
[64] An eine hochlöbliche k. k. böhm.-öst. Hofkanzlei, Bericht des böhmischen Landes-Guberniums der von den Ständen anher mitgetheilte Bericht an seine Majestät über die Lage des unter der Ständischen Garanzie bestehenden Aerarial Kreditsgeschäfts wird gutächtlich einbegleitet, 22. Feb. 1791, M I Archiv, Carton 517.
[65] Protokollsauszug: K. u. k. Hofkammer, Ministerial Banko-Deputation und Kommerz-Hofstelle vom 16. März, 1791. M I Archiv, Carton 516. III Partie 207 ex Julio 1791.

the matter of public credit." "" Should it really become necessary or advisable to change the credit operations at all, then
a "more peaceful time" would have to be found. War was
still a fact and revolution still smoldered in various parts of
the Monarchy. "It was only the war which had just broken
out [i.e. Turkish War, 1787-1791], which interrupted the
credit operations and broke off the payments into the sinking
fund." "" "But," added the Council, "it was better to hold
back such money than to levy more from the country in another way." In short, by contrast to the Gubernium which
pleaded ignorance, the government at Vienna admitted that
besides the enormous sums which it had taken from Bohemia
by means of the financial contracts, it had diverted thirteen
millions illegally. However, beyond admitting the fact, the
central government did nothing; it did not even promise to
live up to the contracts in the future. Indeed, when one keeps
in mind the state of finances described in the first part of this
section it is difficult to see how the central government could
have lived up to its promises.

IV

QUESTIONS PERTAINING TO TAXATION

Questions with regard to taxation under Leopold II naturally fell under two heads. There was the discussion with
regard to the greatest of all taxes, the land tax, and there was
a consideration of several other minor taxes, such as the tax
or monopoly on salt and on beer, the inheritance tax, and
some other impositions. Keeping in mind this division, we
shall discuss first, the land tax, and then the other taxes.

"" *Ibid.* Die Finanz-Vorkehrungen, welche in dem Creditsfache der Stände
in den gesamten erbländischen Provinzen getroffen worden sind, machen einen
Theil des Staatskredits in seinem Ganzen aus, daher lässt sich eine Provinz
von dem Zusammenhange der übrigen in Angelegenheiten des öffentlichen
Credits nicht trennen.
"" *Ibid.* Nur die ausgebrochenen Kriege und die damit verbundene aus-
erordentliche Staatsbestreitungen haben die Ausführung der abgesehenen
Creditsoperation, oder eigentlich zu sagen, des Rückzahlungs-Geschäfts unter-
brochen.

The land tax naturally was one of the most important matters under discussion in the reign of Leopold II. After Joseph II had promulgated his new system of taxation, it was the object of the Estates everywhere in the Habsburg Monarchy, including Bohemia, to bring about its abolition. In Chapter III, we have already discussed the series of negotiations which led to the suppression of the new system of taxation by Leopold II on May 9, 1790. At first the Estates thought that the calling of the Little Diet in the spring of 1790 would be the only opportunity to treat on the question of taxation. And so, besides bringing forth arguments why Joseph II's system should be abolished, they also made concrete proposals for a new system. But when they discovered that Leopold II was inclined to abolish the new system and to call Diets for a thorough discussion of the ills of the Monarchy, the Estates concluded a temporary bargain and prepared for a general overhauling of the entire Bohemian Constitution. It was in this way, then, that the Bohemian Estates agreed to go back to the old system of taxation whose basis was that used in the time of Maria Theresa. Whereas the system of taxation of Joseph II had shown that many of the Estates had concealed lands from taxation and that they were paying too small a ratio in proportion to the serf who, on the return to the old system, had to pay more, the Bohemian Diet agreed to assume provisionally for 1790, 244,000 florins of the taxation which the serf would have paid under the old system, in order to make it easy for him to return to the old state of affairs.** This was a temporary measure.

When the Diet of the summer of 1790 assembled there really was only one great question with regard to land taxation before it and that was, "What shall be the new basis of the future land tax of Bohemia?" But the discussion lasted so long that the provisional basis agreed on in the spring of

** *Sammlung einiger Schriften von den königl. böhmischen Ständen über das neue Steuer- und Urbarial-System veranlasst worden* (1790). Beylage I, II, XIII, XXVI, LXII; *Leopold II, Politische Gesetze*, I, 2-3; the Patent of May 9, 1790, is printed in full in Grünberg, *Bauernbefreiung*, II, 458-462.

1790 had to be extended. In these two matters, therefore, the provisional basis and the future basis—the negotiations with regard to the land tax centered during the entire reign of Leopold II. Incidentally both of these questions involved another. Would Bohemia be forced to pay taxes for the 11,200 fictitious farmers which it had assumed in 1748 and 1757 and which the calculations of the new system of Joseph II had shown were unjustly overburdening that country in comparison to the other provinces?

We shall take up first the discussions which arose over the determination of a provisional basis of land taxation until such time as the new basis to be agreed on between Leopold II and the Estates should be accepted. The debates in the Bohemian Diet on July 12, 1790, and on the days following,[69] culminating in the first memoir of the Diet on the question of land taxation, dated September 4, 1790,[70] showed that the Estates did not desire to assume provisionally for the next year 1791, as much as they had assumed for 1790. Count Buquoy was in favor of assuming 153,000 florins and of asking the serfs to make up the 91,000 florins. The Governor, however, urged that Leopold II "had set his heart" on helping the serf out and that the Bohemian Estates should assume the entire 244,000 florins. Finally, the Diet agreed to do so but on the condition that this should be considered "a free gift" and not written into the regular royal demands, "Royal Postulata," submitted to the Diet. Thereby an important question was settled. The discussion on the future basis of taxation had a year's grace in which to arrive at concrete results.

In the same memoir of September 4, 1790, the Bohemian Estates asked to be relieved of the 11,200 fictitious farmers assumed in 1748. They pointed out that from 1748 to 1790, i.e. forty-three years of land taxation, they had paid over twenty-eight million florins at the rate of 672,000 florins yearly for the fictitious farmers, declared by the new system of Joseph

---

[69] S Archiv, Journal of the Diet, July 12, 1790; Sternberg Diary, *ibid.*, Č N M Archiv, and for the days following down to September 4, 1790.
[70] M I Archiv, Carton 514: 207 ex Julio 1791.

II to be unjust to Bohemia.[71] The Bohemian Diet was giving the central government advance information that it would not pay the taxes of other provinces from 1791 on, that is, that its future quota should contain 540,000 florins less than the old one down to 1789.[72]

The Council of the Gubernium in the spring of 1791, reported on this part of the demands of the Estates.[73] They agreed with the Estates that in comparison to other provinces Bohemia was decidedly overtaxed. "The proof of this is documentary, and there is not the slightest doubt about it." [74] But they also pointed out, in order to show the Estates that they were not so magnanimous as they posed, that the actual increase of taxation in going from the Josephinian basis to the old Theresian basis was 792,826 florins, not 672,000 florins, and that the 244,000 florins which the Estates offered to assume was less than a third of it. The Gubernium declared that the greatest burden of going back to the old system would fall on the serf and how loaded down the serf was the central government was very well informed by the evidence piling up in its archives. The Gubernium recommended that Bohemia be relieved of the 11,200 fictitious farmers or at least of the 540,000 florins yearly for which the Diet asked. The Council also recommended that a reasonable agreement be made by the central government with the other Bohemian and Austrian Lands with a view to removing this unjust burden from the Bohemian serf.

On February 9, 1791, in the meanwhile, the Commission on

[71] See *ibid.*, and Buquoy, Erinnerungen über die vom Grafen v. Lažanský Ex. den versammelten h. Ständen vorgelegten Bedenklichkeiten. *Ibid.*, Carton 515.

[72] The Estates declared they had a right to ask to be relieved of the entire 672,000 florins annually, but were willing to assume 90,000 florins of that amount themselves. M I Archiv, Carton 514. 207 ex Julio 1791.

[73] See M I Archiv, Carton 514, 207 in Julio, 1791. See the reports of November 23, 1790 and Bericht des böhmischen Landes-Guberniums, mittels dessen die von den Ständen in Abschrift übergebenen Vorschläge zur Berichtigung und Konsolidierung des Steuersystems gutächtlich begleitet werden, April 8, 1791.

[74] *Ibid.*: "Dass das Königreich Böhmen gegen andere Erbländer an der Steuer merklich übersetzt ist, wird . . . erwiesen . . ." Dieser Beweis ist aktenmässig und kann keinem Zweifel unterliegen. . . ."

the Desideria,["] consisting of the heir to the throne, the Archduke Francis, Chief Chancellor Count Kolovrat, Chancellor Baron Kressel, Chief Chamberlain Ugarte, and others held a meeting to consider the questions, how much the landlords of Bohemia should take over and how Bohemia should be treated in the matter of the unfair quota. The Commission agreed that the Estates were right in stating that the country was overtaxed. The "relief demanded by the Estates could not be more timely." The Commission advised that the Estates enter into negotiations with the Treasury to see if the latter could take over about 400,000 florins or negotiate a loan for that purpose.

The Commission on Desideria held another meeting a month later [°] which was attended by the new Governor of Bohemia, Count Rottenhan, and four deputies of the Bohemian Estates, Bishop Krieger, Count Leopold Clary, Knight von Hennet, and Mayor Steiner of Prague. Here all the previous reports and opinions rendered in the matter were threshed out once more. The government took the stand— it was a new one—that before taking steps to relieve Bohemia of overtaxation it would have to negotiate with all the other provinces. The time was too critical just then, and the central government feared a general parliament of all the provinces. But relief was urgently necessary. Count Chotek advised the central government to pay the 500,000 florins itself, but that would plunge it so much farther down the road of deficit and bankruptcy. Then it was suggested that a loan be made in Holland with the provision that the landlords carry its burdens for three or four years. At this suggestion the deputies of the Estates balked. They could at best take that suggestion "ad referendum." Chief Chancellor Kolovrat advised against such a foreign credit operation and urged that

[°] M I Archiv, Carton 514. 207 in Julio 1792. Protokoll der Konsertazion welche über die Beschwerden der böhmischen Stände gehalten ward den 9. hornung, 1791.
[°] M I Archiv, Carton 514. 207 in Julio 1791. Protokoll über die Konsertazion, welche über die Beschwerden der böhmischen Stände abgehalten ward, den 12ten März, 1791, mit Zuziehung der ständischen Deputierten.

the matter be settled between the Treasury and the Estates in the nature of a loan which the Estates should guarantee. Thus the central government cleverly threw the burden—which it frankly recognized to be unjust—back on Bohemia.

The State Council [77] dallied with the matter and came to no other result than had the Commission on Desideria. Councillor Eger as usual had the first vote. After making a very eloquent appeal on the sacrifices which the preparation of the Josephinian system of taxation had demanded from him and his assistants, as the men who had executed this gigantic labor, he said it was at least satisfaction to see that it had accomplished some good. Seven million units (*metz*) of "concealed" land had been uncovered in Bohemia, and it was proved that Bohemia was overtaxed by half a million florins yearly. In this all the other councillors, Izdenczy, Reichsach, Hatzfeld, and Kaunitz agreed. In another opinion,[78] Eger argued that the Estates wished to take this load off the shoulders of the serf and put it on the Treasury. "If the Estates were really in earnest to lighten the burden of taxation of the serf, why had they not done so long ago? Why did they remain inactive so long, until Joseph II went down from the height of his throne into the hut of the yearning serf, put an end to his misery, and saw all with his own eyes." "Not out of his autocratic power or domination, but out of the conviction of his duty did Joseph II decide to introduce the new system." "The State should not demand from the serf what it does not use; but what it needs it cannot overlook without running the danger of threatening the general welfare." Count Hatzfeld, who more than anyone else in the State Council sympathized with the Estates and their legitimate aspirations, characterized Eger's attempt to throw the burdens of overtaxation from the serf and the government upon the landowners as "unreasonable."

[77] H H S Archiv, Staatsrat Akten, 1792 in 1791. Zwei Hofkonferenz Protokolle vom 9. Feb. und 12. März, 1791. Über die Beschwerde und Desiderien der böhmischen Stände.
[78] *Ibid.*, Staatsrat Akten, 3529 in 1791.

Finally on July 22, 1791,[79] Leopold II gave his decision on the two questions we have thus far considered, the provisional basis of taxation and the fate of the 11,200 fictitious farmers. He wrote to the Governor of Bohemia that, since it was impossible to come to a definite agreement on the future permanent basis of land taxation, he would accept the 244,000 florins willingly assumed by the Estates from the serf's obligations for the year 1791. But this, as the Estates expressly desired, was to be regarded as a free gift and not a part of the postulated land tax, i.e. it was only provisional and not inserted into the Postulata made out by the government each year and submitted to the Diet. He hoped that the exact details of the future land tax would make it possible to collect the tax of 1792 on the new basis. But should this matter be unsettled then he thought it would be necessary for the Bohemian Estates to take over the 244,000 florins for 1792 also. The finances of the central government, wrote Leopold II, were not in a condition to stand a loss of 500,000 florins yearly and as the suggestion of making a foreign loan was not very inviting, the creation of a sinking fund guaranteed by the Estates was perhaps the best way out of the situation. Leopold II, following the argument of Eger, advised the Estates to take over the half-million florins until a "fund was found, which would supply the money necessary to cover this amount." In other words, neither the State nor the serf was to bear the unjust burden, but the landowners, until relief came from another direction.

But the Governor of Bohemia was unable to move the Estates to such a "patriotic action," as he called the assumption of these added burdens. On October 28, 1791, Leopold II officially sanctioned the deduction of the 11,200 fictitious farmers (amounting to 570,000 florins yearly) from the quota to be got from the land tax. The matter was to be settled by a loan, and in the meanwhile Bohemia was to carry the bur-

[79] M I Archiv, Carton 516, 207 ex Julio 1791. Leopold II to Count Rottenhan, Governor of Bohemia.

den for three years more. The steadfastness with which the Estates refused to assume the burden and the hopeless financial situation of the central government led ultimately to the easiest solution. In 1790, when it was as yet not known whether the Bohemian peasant would rise up in revolt, the weight of the burden which he had carried for forty-three years was tossed first from the Estates to the government and then back to the Estates. Late in 1791 and early in 1792 it became evident that the serf would not revolt—even though he wished to attend the Diet—and so both the government and the Estates relieved themselves by placing the burden back where it was before 1789, on the serf.

In the Patent for the Land Tax, dated June 30, 1792, the sum of 570,000 florins was to be assumed for three years more dating from November 1 of the military or fiscal year of 1792 and the Estates were to contract a loan which was to be paid in twelve yearly installments. "The payments as well as the interest were to be paid by the serf to whose benefit alone the granted reduction of 570,000 florins operated." [80]

The basis and the details of the future land tax of Bohemia came up for serious discussion in 1791 and 1792. In their memoir [81] of January 26, 1791, the Bohemian Estates first gave their completed program for the new system as they wished it to be. They made several fundamental rules by which they thought a just basis could be secured. In the first place, they would accept the old basis of Maria Theresa's land surveys of 1748 and 1757, but include therein the "concealed lands" which Joseph II's Commission on Taxation had discovered. Under no circumstances would they accept the Josephinian basis of land measurements and the newly created "gross product estimate" (*Brutto-Ertrag*). In their minds, the

[80] *Ibid.* See also Falk, *Das Grundsteuer in Böhmen,* pp. 63 ff.
[81] Bericht. Die treugehorsamsten böhmischen Stände schlagen die Modalitäten vor, nach welchen ihres Erachtens die Fehler des alten böhmischen Steuer-Katasters verbessert, die bei der neuen Ausmessung mehr gefundenen Gründe in die Belegung gezogen, und die Steuer sowohl zwischen den Obrigkeiten und Unterthanen, als zwischen Obrigkeit gegen Obrigkeit und Unterthan gegen Unterthan auf die billigste Art eingeglichen werden könnte. January 26, 1791. M I Archiv, Carton 514: 207 in Julio 1791.

Josephinian system of taxation was carried out by peasants and unreliable officials and the results showed a false evaluation of property or unreliable estimates of the gross product. The system had been shown unreasonable by the Estates throughout all the Bohemian and Austrian provinces. In the second place, Leopold II had, by the Patent of May 9, 1790, abolished the system of taxation of Joseph II, because it was generally recognized that "the gross product estimate was estimated too high for the landlords and too low for the serf." In the third place, both the land, as measured and recorded in the old land surveys of 1748 and 1757, and the new lands uncovered by Joseph II, were to be subjected to a tax whose percentage for the landlord as for the serf was to be the same. By this proposition, the Bohemian Estates declared they were merely proposing what had already been done in Moravia.

The Gubernium [82] was quick to see the point of the Estates' discussion as to equal percentage of taxation on the old Theresian basis. Count Lažanský, one of the ablest members of the Bohemian Diet, had already very aptly pointed this out in his "Reflections." [83] He saw the difference between that proposal and the Josephinian system, which had an equal percentage for serf and landlord upon one valuation for all. He was entirely in favor of the Josephinian system. The Estates proposed in their plan to have an equal percentage of taxation for serf and landlord but on the old Theresian basis of evaluation, which favored the landlord. Thus one had an equal basis of incidence but an unequal result owing to two very different bases of evaluation. Count Buquoy in his "Recollections" or "Remarks" [84] argued in favor of the Bohemian Estates, because they had other expenses on their manors which the serf did not have. They had to pay for the officials of the govern-

[82] Bericht des böhmischen Landes-Guberniums mittels dessen die von den Ständen in Abschrift übergebenen Vorschläge zur Berichtigung und Konsolidirung des Steuersystems gutachtlich begleitet werden. April 8, 1791. M I Archiv, Carton 514: 207 in Julio, 1791.

[83] Bedenklichkeiten des Obristen Landrechts Grafen von Lažanský, Carton 515.

[84] Erinnerungen über die vom Grafen v. Lažanský, Ex. den versammelten h. Ständen vorgelegten Bedenklichkeiten. M I Archiv, Carton 515.

ment and of the manor and they had been accustomed to use their land differently from the serf. The serf had been a real farmer, the landlord was really a capitalist "rental" landlord who lived off his rents and the robot of his serfs and whose own land was not subjected to the same rigors of cultivation to which the serf subjected his. Count Buquoy had a really good argument in the fact that the old taxation system of Maria Theresa cost very little to operate because every lord collected the land tax for his own manor or manors, while the Josephinian system was exceedingly complicated and cost hundreds of thousands of florins yearly and employed a horde of officials. The Gubernium followed largely the arguments of Count Lažanský. It argued concretely by taking the exact case at hand. The serf paid 60 florins out of every 180 florins of his revenues from land. The landlord paid 33 1/3 florins out of 100 florins, or 33 1/3 per cent. The percentage of the incidence of the tax was equal, but how about the evaluations on which the percentage fell? And in this everybody, even the Estates, agreed that the evaluations contained in the land surveys of Maria Theresa were favorable to the landlord.

But it is to be noticed here that what the Estates proposed in 1791 was more advantageous to the serf than what he had to pay in 1757. Thus 60 florins out of 180 was better than 60 out of 142, i.e. 33 1/3 per cent was better than 42 per cent, which the serf had actually paid over a period of forty years. On the other hand, in offering to pay 33 1/3 per cent from their own Theresian evaluations, the landlords were offering 4 1/3 per cent more than they had ever paid before. This was surely a compromise between the old basis of Maria Theresa and that of Joseph II and it does not appear to have been an unjust one.

The Gubernium further claimed that the Estates had not proved their point about the "gross product estimate" of the Josephinian system, but in the next paragraph admitted that "complaints against it had showed it was not serviceable." In a detailed discussion of the old land surveys of 1748 and 1757 the Council showed why it considered them "favorable to the land-owner and oppressive to the serf." It declared these surveys were "not calculated to bring general satisfaction and welfare to the country." And finally, it ended in a memoir written by Count P. Clary [85] which suggested a new survey to be carried out in Bohemia. The novel feature of this survey was that it should be written up from the cities outward, because the cities had their land values recorded in "landbooks" and sales of land had everywhere taken place in their neighborhood.

The Commission on the Desideria [86] held a series of meetings on July 2, 4, and 25, 1791, to discuss the future land tax of Bohemia. At the first and the last of these sessions the deputies of the Bohemian Estates were present. The Commission accepted the offer of the Estates of an equal percentage on the old evaluation basis of Maria Theresa. The idea that the tax should once more be collected by the manors and not by the government was also agreeable to that Commission.

Leopold II accepted the principle of the suggestions of the Estates in his Decree of October 21, 1791, and, after further negotiation as to detail, the whole was incorporated in the Patent on the Land Tax of February 22, 1792. Four months later the great Patent of the Land Tax of June 30, 1792, issued by Leopold II's successor, Francis II, summed up in its six provisions all that had resulted from the two years of negotiation on this subject. [87] Thus the land tax which existed in Bohemia from 1792 to 1867 was really a compromise between the old unfair basis of 1749-1757 and the well-meant but radical basis of 1789. On the whole, the serf was a little better off, but not so well off as he would have been under the Josephinian system of taxation.

We shall now turn to the other taxes considered by the

[85] Votum über das Steuer-System. Graf. Filip v. Clary. August 10, 1790. Lobkovic Library, Prague.

[86] Protokoll der Konferenzen, 2, 4, 25 Julius, 1791, M I Archiv, Carton 515.

[87] H H S Archiv, Staatsrat Akten, 3529 in 1791; 3404 in 1792, and Falk, *Grundsteuer*, pp. 63-65.

Bohemian Estates, namely the salt tax or monopoly, the penal
beer tax, and the inheritance tax.

In the question of the salt monopoly, which in a certain
way must be called a tax, the Bohemian Estates asked in the
Third Desideria that the price of salt (and therefore the tax)
be lowered in order that the culture of cattle might be promoted. Salt was one of the monopolies which the Habsburg
kings had acquired in Bohemia. The salt profits of the Bohemian kings were immense. In 1739 [88] the king received annually 1,700,000 florins from this source; in 1763,[89] 1,653,031
florins; in 1791 [90] 1,905,000 florins. By the Financial Recess
of 1748 the Estates agreed with the sovereign that Bohemia
would sell 240,000 measures (*centner*) of salt yearly at the
price of five florins 39 kreuzer each. In 1769 [91] the contract
had been renewed at seven florins per centner and the landlords were allowed to sell it to their serfs at seven florins 40
kreuzer. In the Bohemian Diet Count Francis Anton Kolovrat proposed a plan whereby the salt which was sold above
the contracted amount was to be reduced to two florins 30
kreuzer.[92] Baron Henniger presented a paper to the Diet
wherein he argued that the Estates should take the contracted
amount but at five florins, the difference in the amount of
money being made up by purchasing 96,000 centner more at
that price.[93] The Diet decided, however, to ask that the price
of salt be lowered without specifying just how, suggesting
that the amount of revenues would doubtless be the same, if
not greater, and that the cattle of the kingdom would greatly
benefit thereby.[94]

The Gubernium saw no good reason why the price of salt

[88] Pekař, *Kniha o Kosti*, II, 162 ff. and "České katastry" (*ČČH*, XIX-XXII, 1912-15).
[89] H K Archiv, D. 227, 1763 and Book 1763-1791 Finanzen 229 A/D.
[90] Landtagsschlüsse, 1747, 1748, and fn. 2.
[91] *Ibid.* 1769 and Henniger: Über den Salzhandel, October 30, 1790, Stern-berg Nachlasse, Č N M Archiv.
[92] S Archiv, Journal of the Diet, November 3, 1790, Sternberg Diary, same data, Č N M Archiv, and especially Kurze Anmerkungen.
[93] See fn. 91.
[94] Third Desideria, 24ten Wunsch. M I Archiv, Carton 519.

should not be reduced, but the Central Court Treasury did. It took the stand that the lowering of the price of salt could not be carried out in a single province or in all of them without great loss to the Treasury. Until the matter was taken up with all of the provinces, the price would have to stay as it was.

Leopold II in the Court Decree [95] of October 28, 1791, decided that all due effort should be made to lower the price of salt. Before a new system could be worked out, however, Bohemia, Moravia, and Upper Austria would have to guarantee the amount of salt to be purchased based on the averages of the last six years, if they wished to lower it at once. Salt in Bohemia was a smuggled article, and the price of a centner of it was doubtless of great importance to every housewife as well as to every landowner. It is to the credit of the Estates that they asked that its price be lowered, although the fact that they limited the argument of its usefulness to cattle alone does not exonerate them from another charge.

Another complaint which hit the royal or private income of the king was that which the Bohemian Estates made against the penal beer tax. This tax traced its origin to the days of White Mountain. The penal tax was levied against beer brewed in the cities which had revolted against Ferdinand II in 1618. By the Land Ordinance article A 34 one florin was collected from each barrel of beer brewed in all royal cities except Pilsen and Budweis, which had remained loyal to the monarch. In 1790 the Estates asked that the tax be suppressed on the ground that the reason for it had long disappeared.

The Gubernium favored the proposal, especially since, by the Financial Agreement of 1775, the universal beer tax of three florins per barrel had been introduced and the price of wood and brewing accessories had risen considerably after that. "That was the reason why it was almost impossible to brew good beer in the Bohemian cities."

The Court Treasury did not deny the value of these obser-

[95] Decree, Oct. 28, 1791. *Ibid.*, Carton 519.

vations, but 148,585 florins annual revenue to an almost insolvent monarch meant much. It felt that this revenue must not be lost without an equivalent, and it offered to find some substitute but could not. Leopold II decided by the Decree of October 28, 1791, that the tax would have to continue at least three years longer in the hope that a substitute source of revenue could be found in that time."

The price of salt and the penal beer tax were matters which dealt with the royal revenue of the sovereign; in the next complaint, that on the inheritance tax, the Estates dealt with a tax which they collected themselves. It was one of the last remnants of the income of the Estates. In 1789 it yielded 50,000 florins. The Estates asked that its rate of percentage, which struck only the rich, be lowered. But Leopold II ruled that no change would be made in the inheritance tax although the rate on fees due at the death of a person, involving changes in the registrations at the Land Tables (Mortuarium) might be lowered."

All other complaints of the Estates in matters on taxation and finance were refused redress by the government. The Church could not recover its former control over what was originally called the treasury for matters of faith, "the Cassae Salis," and what later became the "Religious Fund for Bohemia." The action of the government on the complaints of the cities, which declared they had to pay all the charges of justice and criminal care-taking, was postponed indefinitely. The Estates failed to secure a definite pension law for public officials, because the government had diverted the fees "into other channels." And several other complaints against usury, which called for a restoration of the laws against the practice, were likewise brushed aside."

We have been able to bring to light the vast importance

"" M I Archiv, Carton 519, Third Desideria, 11te Beschwerde, Bericht des böhm. Guberniums. Feb. 18, 1791, Carton 520, Protokoll der Konferenz, 2. Julius, 1791, Carton 519; Protokolls Auszug: K. k. Hof Kammer, 22. April 1791, Carton 516; and finally Decree, Oct. 28, 1791. Carton 519.
"" Ibid.
"" See Third Desideria, M I Archiv, Carton 519, especially, 16te Beschwerde and the 33te Wunsch. Beschwerde, 7, 8, 9, 10, 11 are also among those which might be cited here.

of Bohemia in the finances of the Habsburg Monarchy. The sacrifices which that country made for the Monarchy in the Seventeenth and Eighteenth Centuries were immense. But they were not sufficient to prevent the government at Vienna from acquiring a chronic deficit under Joseph II or to banish fears of insolvency under Leopold II. In 1790 it was a clear and indisputable fact that Bohemia had been for almost half a century paying taxes for other provinces and since 1767 likewise paying their debts. Yet the central government was not able to help Bohemia out, either by obtaining a juster interstate agreement or by assuming the unjust burden itself.

The bank, which the Estates urged and to which Leopold II agreed, was postponed until discarded by the government. Usury laws remained, in general, abolished as Joseph II had done away with them. The charge of the Estates that the central government had diverted millions of their money from the payment of debts for other purposes was frankly admitted to be true, but the situation was left unremedied. And finally, the unjust burden of taxation, the 11,200 fictitious farmers, was thrown back upon the Bohemian serf, "who had paid it before." The new system of taxation, which the Estates proposed and which the government accepted, represented a compromise between the old Theresian basis and the new Josephinian basis. Its fundamental principle was equal percentage of taxation on two distinct bases of evaluation. Nevertheless, the serf did gain by this compromise, and the landlord was paying a little more in 1792 than he had been accustomed to pay before 1789. In this respect there was a slight progress. But on the whole, in the matter of finances the central government did not appear to advantage as against the Estates. The Estates had "indestructible proof on their side."

CHAPTER IX

SERFDOM

I

The Introduction

HISTORICAL research has made it clear that the Lands of the Bohemian Crown, namely, Bohemia, Moravia, and Silesia, in agrarian history at least, had essentially the same type of serfdom as all the lands of the Hohenzollerns to the north and of the Habsburgs to the south. These regions were situated east of the river Elbe and the Bohemian Forest and they had, as the corner stone of their agrarian constitution, the institution of "hereditary subjection" (*Erbunterthänigkeit*) as distinguished from "Leibeigenschaft" which in a legal sense was slavery.[1] No such institution as the latter existed in Bohemia in the Seventeenth and Eighteenth Centuries.[2] German and Czech historians also agree that the population was not enserfed suddenly in the reign of Vladislav II (1471-1516). The most

[1] Knapp, "Leibeigenschaft in Österreich" (*Beilage zur Allgemeinen Zeitung*, no. 203, July 23, 1892). This is merely a popular statement of the results of the work of his many pupils on the problems relating to serfdom.

[2] For "Leibeigenschaft" in Bohemia in early medieval times see Lippert, *Die Knechtschaft in Böhmen*, for one view, Peiskar, same title, for the other. Milkowic (Lemberg), in reviewing the two opposing theses (*MIÖG*, 1894, XV) asserts Lippert had gone too far to charge that the Bohemians were knaves or slaves, while Peisker went too far to make out that they lived under a form of light serfdom. Perhaps, suggests Milkowic, Palacký was right when he wrote that the institution of "Leibeigenschaft" could not take root in Bohemia and disappeared very rapidly. See also Grünberg, *Die Bauernbefreiung und die Auflösung des gutsherrlich-bauerlichen Verhältnisses in Böhmen, Mähren, und Schlesien*. He points out that the word "Leibeigenschaft" is foreign to Bohemian legislation—appearing only three times before Joseph II used it. It is to be found in the parentheses of the Rescript of June 23, 1651 (*Weingartner Codex*, 281, 12 note one), in the Gesundordnung of January 25, 1765 (Title II F 10) and in the Patent of December 2, 1773— all of these laws were published after the Land Ordinance of 1627 which did not contain the word and which was the legal basis of serfdom down to 1781.

recent authorities on the subject hold that the process was a gradual one controlled by the economic development of Central Europe and that it took place in the Fifteenth and Sixteenth Centuries.[3] The ownership of the land was long a disputed question between the Estates and the serfs.[4] The Estates claimed that it belonged to the lord and that the serf had a right to perpetual rental on satisfaction of the obligation. The serf, urged on by the bureaucracy and encouraged by the humanitarian movement, argued that the land was his, but that it carried certain obligations to the lord. The dispute ended in a victory for the lords. The State and the serf in 1848 made payment for the land to the lords of the manors.

Bohemia had between nine hundred and fifty and a thousand manors. As elsewhere in western Europe, the manor came down into the Eighteenth Century as a small constitutional, institutional, administrative, and agrarian state, a little self-sufficient economic world. The lord of the manor was military commander, judge, and tax collector. He alone was a citizen of the Bohemian state; the serfs were merely "his subjects." Once out of his manor, they were on "foreign" territory where they had no rights at all. Serfdom in Bohemia was hereditary, but it was connected with the soil and not with the person of the serf. He performed robot (Czech word for "work") because he held the land, not because he was what he was personally. After the beginning of the Sixteenth Century he was not allowed to migrate at will. Further, the lord somehow acquired, though rather late in the development of the institution, the right to determine the occupation of his serf and to arrange for his marriage. These three rights, which the lord acquired over the serf, were the outcome of that miniature state, the manor, into which the medieval

[3] See Pekař, *Kniha o Kosti*, II, 110, the standard work on the agrarian history of Bohemia at present. The old view was held by Palacký whom Kalousek and Grünberg followed.

[4] See the clearest statement of the attitude taken by the landowners in Puteani, *Ueber das Eigenthumsrecht der böhmischen Obrigkeiten auf dem Grunde ihrer Unterthanen und über die Gerechtigkeit der hieraus entstehenden Frohn- oder Robotschuldigkeit* (2nd ed. Prague, 1790). It is to be found in the library of the Bohemian Museum.

world locked itself up. Thereby the lord tried to regulate the supply and character of the labor needed for his manor and the question of marriages between manors. These three rights Joseph II, in 1781, returned to the Bohemian serf. But Joseph II took away from the serf his local political autonomy by the law of 1785, in which he introduced the justice of the peace. What remained of serfdom was swept away in the Revolution of 1848.[*]

The State took its contribution, the Church its tithe, and the lord his obligations from the serf. Land, as pointed out in the preceding chapter, was of two kinds, that which belonged to the lord outright, called *dominical*, which he used himself but sometimes rented in part to serfs, and that which he had of yore "rented" to the serf, called *rustical*. On the former, the serf had only those rights which he received from the land by means of written contracts. On the latter, he was distinctly an hereditary tenant by tradition and could never be ousted save through failure to fulfill his obligations. Originally, the serf had to give the lord either a rental in money, or a payment in kind, or both, twice a year. In the course of time robot (or *corvée*) was added to this. But the manual and team labor, robot, differed in quantity and quality with the time and place.[*]

So much for placing and defining our subject. We shall now turn to the historical development of serfdom in Bohemia in the Seventeenth and Eighteenth Centuries with a view to understanding the relations of master and serf in regard to robot.

The Battle of White Mountain (1620) and the Land Ordinance of 1627 ushered in a new epoch in the history of serfdom in Bohemia. Before that time the Bohemian serf was treated by his Czech masters in a patriarchal way; after it, he became the victim of the full force of Roman law, which his new German masters introduced more and more, because

---

[*] See general remarks in Grünberg, *Bauernbefreiung*, I, first three chapters and in Pekař, *Kniha o Kosti*, II, in the first and last chapters.

[*] Grünberg, *Bauernbefreiung*, I, 75-130, Pekař, *Kniha o Kosti*, II, 89 ff.

they were representatives of the Counter Reformation. New masters came with the huge confiscations of manors; accurate statistics indicate that about two-thirds of the manors were confiscated outright or in part. They were masters who had no sympathy with, or understanding of the institutions they found in Bohemia; and least of all, the institution of serf-dom.[7] The robot was increased by the victors at such an alarming rate that in 1680 the peasants rose up in revolt, but were quickly overcome by the military. In the course of the negotiations with the rebel serfs, Leopold I on March 22 and June 28, 1680,[8] issued two patents whose importance was decisive in determining the development of Bohemian serfdom. The first was issued while yet negotiations might have succeeded in securing peace without the use of military force. But, even in this first patent Leopold I declared in no uncertain terms "that (they could not fall back) on any privileges of their serf communities nor could the serfs in this our hereditary kingdom of Bohemia make reflection on any (privileges), which they had or enjoyed before the time of the wretched (abscheulichen) rebellion, but that these are to be regarded as forever done away with, abolished and cashiered," and only those rights which they had obtained from their lords or in any other way after the rebellion were to be given legal value. Those communities or serfs who, without first seeking redress of the circle officials, turned directly to the king with their complaints, "against these same" would he cause action to be taken with due penalty. And the military forces were sent out to restore peace.

Having "simplified" the task both for himself and the new

[7] Grünberg, *Bauernbefreiung*, I, 106-108. "Das erklärt es auch, weshalb der Staat, trotzdem durch die Schlacht am weisen Berge (1620) die bis dahin fast unbeschränkte politische Macht der Stände gebrochen und der königliche Absolutismus begründet worden war, die ungünstige Entwickelung der gutsherrlich—bäuerlichen Verhältnisse Anfangs gar nicht aufzuhalten versucht hat." See also Pekař, *Kniha o Kosti*, II, 112-114 and Rieger *Zřízení krajské*, I, 270-282.

[8] See the patents in Grünberg, *Bauernbefreiung*, II, 3-10. Documents and his exposition of the law, I, 130-131. One should read also the interesting remarks of Pekař, *Kniha o Kosti*, II, 169 ff., and Šimák, "Zpravy o selské bouři r. 1680 z říšského válečního archivu" (*VČA*, XXII).

lords by the Patent of March 22, the First Robot Patent of June 28, 1680, was issued by Leopold I as a final adjustment of the situation. The serfs were to render robot at most three days a week; in addition in certain cases they were to render also "extraordinary robot," and in other cases—"in special ones"—to assist even outside of the manor. The indefinite character of this is clear. Nevertheless, robot was forbidden on Sundays and holidays; the serfs were to receive some consideration for long hauls; the rents were not to be raised voluntarily; the serfs were not to be subjected to excessive and gruesome punishment; and they were not to be forced to buy their provisions from the landlord, unless it was so stated in their contracts. But no penalty was prescribed against the lords, and the clearest proof that the Patent was a dead letter for even the few doubtful rights it guaranteed to the serf is that up to the year 1736 not one case was brought by the government against oppression or a violation by a lord. What it did without a doubt was to take away the rights of the serfs. Which serfs and what rebellion (1678 or 1680) were meant, were left unspecified. And so the dominant opinion took it that the rights of the serfs before the Thirty Years' War were abolished. Naturally, all serfs were meant, even those who had not rebelled. In this fashion the State, as represented by the Habsburg dynasty, began to look after the welfare of its serfs in Bohemia.

The Second Robot Patent of 1717 and the Third Robot Patent of 1738 helped little. Both failed because the local administration was in the hands of the Estates, the landlords, and a serf could get little or no redress against his lord. The second, declares an authority, was "a very important step backward." The first two patents, those of 1680 and 1717, had made indefinite generalizations on law; that of 1738, by specifically naming many of the cases in which the lord had a right to the robot, prevented an interpretation favorable to the serfs. The law of 1738 codified about all that the lord could desire. In the meanwhile robot had increased by leaps and bounds toward the middle of the century, thanks to the beneficent influence of the unfortunate legislation of the Habsburgs.[9]

Maria Theresa began the reform of the condition of serfdom in Bohemia in three ways. In 1748 and 1751 the local administration of Bohemia became bureaucratic and thereafter efficient, so far as the protection of the serf was concerned.[10] The empress promulgated the Fourth Robot Patent of 1775, which remained the basis of Bohemian serfdom down to 1848, with the exception of a few years under Joseph II. And she began on her own estates the system of private abolition of robot, which Joseph II had wished to make public and uniform, but which the reaction under Leopold II had prevented. The principle of private abolition of serfdom was accepted at least in theory by the Bohemian Estates, codified in law in 1798, and thereafter carried out slowly until the Revolution of 1848 terminated the entire matter. This indicates the importance of the reign of Maria Theresa so far as serfdom is concerned.

The Report of the War Council [11] in 1771 determined beyond a doubt the exact state of serfdom in Bohemia. In many circles "a bad growth of manhood" was reported. Child labor was very common in Bohemia at this time; disease, idleness, and drunkenness were just as common. In addition, the famines of 1771 and 1772 had caused about fourteen per cent of the population to disappear. Maria Theresa, urged by Joseph, now emperor, determined to reform these conditions. Negotiations were entered into with the Bohemian Estates for the

[9] For the patents see Grünberg, *Bauernbefreiung*, II, 13-38, discussion I, 134-141.
[10] Rieger, *Zřízení krajské*, II, 5-8. This is the standard work on the local government of Bohemia and of great importance for the entire Austrian Monarchy.
[11] M I Archiv, Carton 449: IV A 8 Volkszählung, Böhmen, 219: Vortrag die in dem K. Boheim vollendete Seelen- und Zugviehs-Conscription betreff. 11. Sept. 1771. For other reports see Grünberg, II, 55-175. See also Adamek, "Království české v r. 1771" (*Památky Archaeologických a Místopisných*, XXV); Roubik, "Relace císaře Josefa II o jeho cestě do Čech, Moravy, a Slezka r. 1771" (*Časopis pro Dějiny Venkova s přílohou Selský Archiv*, 1926, XIII); and Prokeš, "Memorialy o hospodářskem stavu Čech před selskou bouři z r. 1775" (*ibid.*, 1924, XI, 1925, XII).

issue of a patent similar to the one of 1771 in Silesia. Unfortunately these led to a victory of the Estates, who, by delay and negotiation and even obstruction, refused eventually to disturb the *status quo*. In the meanwhile, the Bohemian serf lost patience and rose up in revolt. Strong as were his complaints against economic oppression, the religious factor was also to be found among his grievances. Hussite songs were sung, and churches were sacked and burned along with the castles of the landlords.[12]

In order to quiet this situation the Fourth Robot Patent of 1775 was issued, this time by the monarch and without consultation with the Estates. It did not wholly set aside the law of 1738, but it legislated more precisely in doubtful places. The Habsburg Monarchy, which had done so much to secure "the well earned rights" of the lord, now took some away and limited others. A standard day of robot, as well as its value in money, was set for the three classes of serfs, the "innleute" or lesser serfs who worked thirteen days, the serfs who owned a house and who worked twenty-six days, and the serfs who owned teams and who worked out respectively three one-horse, three two-horse, and three three-horse, "hauling-days in a normal year, such as 1773." Extraordinary robot was abolished for all classes of serfs, except the "two or more-horsed peasant." The Gordian knot had been cut. The Fourth Robot Patent opened a new era in the history of Bohemian serfdom.[13]

The system of private abolition of robot was planned by Francis von Raab. Its fundamental principle was to change manual and team robot into a money rental whereby the serf could devote his entire time to his own fields. Maria Theresa began it on her private estates in 1775.[14]

Maria Theresa had concerned herself merely with the eco-

[12] Grünberg, I, 155-222 gives much important information on the course of events. See also Adamek, *Příspěvky k dějinam selského lidu z okoli Hlinska v XVIII. věku*, pp. 1-20; Svatek, *Kulturhistorische Bildungen*, 188-205.
[13] Grünberg, *Bauernbefreiung*, I, 222-230 for discussion and II, 257-267 for the patent.
[14] *Ibid.*, I, 277 ff.

nomic aspect of serfdom. Joseph II determined to carry out legislative reforms on the social aspects of serfdom as well. In April, 1781,[15] he asked the Bohemian Estates how the kind of "Leibeigenschaft" in Bohemia could be changed into the form of serfdom then existing in the Austrian provinces. The Bohemian Estates did not dare oppose his all-powerful will, so they declared that they had no objections to the change if the existing economic obligations remained as they had been determined by law. When they got beyond making general statements and down to specific facts, however, Joseph II discovered that they were merely changing names on the statute books and not real social conditions. In fact, they[16] were willing to allow only such serfs to migrate as were actually contributors to the land tax, and this only if the lord could find a substitute for them.

By this time Joseph II was contemplating a patent for all the Bohemian and Austrian Lands. On November 1, 1781,[17] by a stroke of the pen, he emancipated the serfs in all these Lands in respect to conditions of marriage and of choice of work. It was no longer necessary for the serf to seek the landlord's consent in order to marry, and he might devote himself "to handiworking, arts, and sciences"; i.e. he could choose his vocation without securing the consent of his lord. And, finally, he could migrate from place to place in Bohemia.

By means of the Patent of September 1, 1781—a law which we shall discuss in the section on Leopold II—a penal code for the serf was drawn up for the guidance of the landlord and the officials of the local government in giving justice to the serf in his future environment. A labor ordinance published in September, 1782,[18] was designed, for the benefit of the landlord, so as to hold the agricultural laborers under certain limitations. In 1785 the justices of the peace were instituted

[15] Grünberg, I, 278-283.
[16] *Ibid.*, II, 373-374. Landesausschuss Äusserung, 11. Mai, 1781.
[17] *Ibid.*, II, 360-381. See the arguments of the Estates, II, 375-378.
[18] Roth-Blasek, *Auszug aller im Königreiche Böhmen bestehender Gesetze und Verordnungen*, O. XL, 290-297; Rieger, *Zřizení krajské*, II, 483 ff.; 526-528. See also *Handbuch der Verordnungen und Gesetze unter Joseph II*, I, 65-79.

by Joseph II, and while they abolished the political autonomy of many serf communities and represented the ever-more penetrating arm of the central government, they were likewise an assistance to the serf in his conflict with the landlords.[19]

In the second half of his reign, Joseph II turned from social legislation on serfdom to take account of its economic aspects. To all outward and inward appearances the Raab system of the abolition of serfdom had worked well on the government estates. Joseph II after 1785 planned to carry out the abolition of robot by changing these obligations to a money rental. He wished to apply it all over Bohemia and in the other Bohemian and Austrian Lands. Fortunately or unfortunately, he decided that the reform of the land tax, which we have already considered (Chapter VIII) and the abolition of robot should be combined in one masterpiece of economic legislation. As already explained, out of the gross produce of the land (*Grundbruttoertrag*) seventy per cent was to remain to the serf and his family and thirty per cent was to go to the State and the landlord, the former taking 12-2/9 per cent as a settlement for the land tax, the landlord, 17-2/9 per cent for all the obligations of the serf: team or manual robot, money or grain rents, fees, and any other obligations. This new system applied only to such peasants as were living on *rustical* land, as distinguished from their less fortunate brothers who lived on the *dominical* land, and further, it applied only to rustical serfs who paid a land tax of two or more florins a year. It excluded from the benefits of the abolition of robot all dominical serfs and all rustical serfs whose annual land tax amounted to less than two florins.[20] Just what the relation was between the numbers included in the benefits and those excluded from them is not known. It is known that in 1790 there were about 122,000 peasants who paid two florins or more for the land tax and that there were about 442,000 who were either sons of peasants, or their helpers who paid less than two florins. It is safe to conclude that the number of those excluded was

[19] See Chapter VI.   [20] Grünberg, I, 314-326.

great. Their attitude toward this reform was, therefore, important.

These two great reforms, the Emancipation Patent of 1781 and the new system of Taxation and Serfdom of 1789, practically revolutionized agrarian labor conditions in Bohemia. One authority has estimated that the price of labor rose after 1781 so that by the end of the reign of Joseph II, there was hardly a manor that had not suffered a loss of at least one-fourth of the income it had received from robot, while some had suffered a loss of as much as two-thirds. Joseph II had carried out these great reforms without offering any compensatory damages whatsoever and without the coöperation of the Estates.[21]

Besides the obstinate resistance which Joseph II met on the part of the landlords, who cried out that he was attacking their property and who were able to gather their strength together because, unable to bring the war with Turkey to a conclusion, he had been forced to yield to Hungary, he also had to meet the hostile attitude of the serfs. Could anyone imagine that the dominical serfs and those rustical serfs who had been excluded from the benefits of the reform, were going to remain silent while their more fortunate brothers who happened to be rustical serfs paying two florins of land tax, were allowed henceforth to pay their robot in money? As for the rustical serf who was to profit by the reform, he became so impatient that he could not wait the dawn of his freedom from robot. When news came in September, 1790, that the inauguration of the new system was to be postponed, many of these rustical serfs refused to render robot. Thus there were set in motion two currents of unrest among the serfs.

In the last six months of his reign Joseph II saw the need of stricter legislation against impatient and obstinate serfs. A patent was promulgated in September, 1789, by which such serfs were to be forced to work in irons, and their sentence sharpened by being put on a bread and water diet. In addi-

[21] Grünberg, I, 327-331.

tion, if their debts increased too much, they were to be expelled from their holdings. In November, 1789, Joseph II authorized the use of the military forces; these were to be resorted to, however, only when whole villages refused to render robot. It was evident that Joseph II had stirred up an unrest among the serfs which it would not be easy to calm. In vain he wrote in one of his last decisions in regard to Bohemian serfdom, "Nothing can be more reasonable, and no one can complain if the landlord is given the right, in case the serf does not wish to render or pay his last obligations, to proceed to law, which stands open to every creditor against his debtor and which will be properly observed by all courts of justice." [11] To his successor, Leopold II, Joseph II left pending momentous unsolved problems concerning serfdom in Bohemia. The landlord worked for the repeal of as much of Joseph II's legislation as possible. The serf excluded from its benefits wished to share in it. The serf, who had been benefited by the legislation after its promulgation in October, 1789, rejoiced and buried "King Robot with all due ceremony."

If the reform were abolished, the Estates and the serf who was excluded from its benefits, would be satisfied. What would be the effect upon the serf who had tasted the benefits of the legislation?

II

SERFDOM UNDER LEOPOLD II

The outstanding problems that confronted Leopold II, so far as serfdom was concerned, were three in number. The first of these was, would the rustical Bohemian serf rise in revolt as a result of the abolition of the Josephinian system of taxation and serfdom? The second question—which particularly irritated the Bohemian Estates—was, how should a serf be treated if he refused to render his robot, and how should the entire problem of serf unrest be handled? The third problem was the determination of a policy whereby

[11] See M I Archiv, Carton 2492, 44 ex Aprili 1790, 136 ex Nov. 1789 and Grünberg, II, 450 ff.

robot could be changed into a money payment—a policy which would be just both to the landlord and to the serf. Each of these questions will be discussed in turn in this section.

Both the Estates and the government realized that there was great dissatisfaction among the Bohemian serfs in 1790. We have seen that the Little Diet ended its activity after having assured itself that the new system of taxation and serfdom would be abolished. But it had offered no solution to the problems which confronted the government immediately thereafter, and not the least of these was whether the serf would revolt. No plan of changing robot into a money payment or a money rental had been brought up in the Diet. On the contrary, many of the Estates had hoped for the restoration of the days before 1775, and as a whole the Estates were clamoring for stricter laws against the serf, their deputation having asked for military assistance in Vienna.[23] The government was slow to grant this, although it had a large army in Bohemia watching the Prussians across the frontier. The spring of 1790 ended with the new system of taxation and serfdom abolished and the right of free bargaining with regard to robot and to money rentals sanctioned by the Patent of May 9, 1790.[24]

Vavak,[25] the country justice of the peace, who gives in his diary some of the best descriptions of economic conditions in Bohemia in the last half of the Eighteenth Century, wrote that the abolition of the new system of taxation and serfdom produced untold hardships among the peasants. When news came in 1789 that they would no longer have to render robot,

[23] See *Sammlung einiger Schriften welche von den königl. böhmischen Ständen über das neue Steuer- und Urbarial-System veranlasst worden* (1790) Beylage, I, II, III, IV, pp. xxii-xxxvi, lii-lxii, ff. See Grünberg, *Bauernbefreiung*, I, 350 ff. and II, 450 ff.
[24] Grünberg, *Bauernbefreiung*, II, 451-463. The Patent is printed there in full. The passage about free bargaining is important, it ran as follows: "wo es die obrigkeitliche Wirtschaftsbetreibung, an welcher dem Staate selbst vieles gelegen sei, zulasse, und es dem Unterthane an Nebenverdienst nicht fehle, zu einem billigen Einverständnisse auf eine bestimmte Anzahl von Jahren . . . durch freiwillige Herbeilassung von Seiten der Grundobrigkeiten und der Unterthanen unserem besonderen Wohlgefallen gereichen."
[25] Č N M Archiv, *Vavak Memoirs*, 1790 (May), pp. 134 ff.

they had sold their horses and cattle and kept quite generally
only two head apiece. The recent hard times resulting from
bad harvests had piled up many new debts. To buy new
draught animals with which to render robot because of the
abolition of the Josephinian system of taxation and serfdom
was not easy under the conditions created by the war with
Turkey and in view of the rise in prices. And so the Bohemian serf, upon the restoration of robot by the Patent of May
9, 1790, "was like the drowning man who was pulled out of the
Elbe and then thrown in again."

III
REVOLT OR PASSIVE RESISTANCE?

Even in the most critical days of 1790, the serf in general
had not been rebellious. He was openly restless only in certain localities. But though not rebellious, he nevertheless
quietly and firmly refused to render robot or to return to the
old system of taxation without some diminution of his former
burdens. In other words, he, too, wished to gain by the
change.[26] In trying to understand the course of serf unrest in
Bohemia for about a half year after the abolition of the Josephinian reforms, we must keep in mind several fundamental
facts. Before the abolition of the reforms the Estates pre-
tended to foresee no rebellion; that attitude was necessary in
order to secure the repeal of the new system. But after the
abolition of the reforms, they became very much afraid of a
revolt. We shall see presently whether this was pretense or
not, and whether it was designed to secure for many years to
come such a commanding position as to guarantee them what
they wished. The Gubernium, however, foresaw a revolt, if
the Josephinian system were abolished, largely because it
wished to frighten the Estates out of the idea. After the reforms were abolished, it urged that the Bohemian serf, except
in a very few localities, was not maliciously rebellious or de-

[26] *Ibid.*, 139, 140, 141, 145.

structive and that no extraordinary military measures were necessary. The Gubernium feared that the reaction in favor of the Estates might go so far as to produce very unfavorable legislation for the serf,[27] even military rule.

Immediately after the promulgation of the Patent on May 9, 1790, the Bohemian serf stubbornly refused to render robot. He wanted the Josephinian reforms or at least better terms than those under which he had rendered robot before the reforms went into effect (October, 1789). At first the serf quietly refused to render robot and the officials of the circle tried to frighten him by sending picked "refusers" to Prague to be packed off to the army or somewhere else. In Sojšicky and at Čáslav, after several serfs had been separated from their environment in this way, the serfs made a "run" on the castle and caused the director of the manor and his henchmen to flee, hastily scattering a report that the population had risen in revolt. The rumor flew fast over Bohemia, and the officials of many of the manors decamped with more haste than decorum. Meanwhile, dragoons and hussars were sent to quiet the people, who had only struggled to get in touch with those with whom they might bargain for better terms. This was a sad commentary on the consciences of the manorial officials. As Vavak remarked, the serf had nothing against the monarch or the landlord, and desired only to arrange for a more moderate form of robot or money rental. "We do not wish to start a revolt or to break the sacred peace, only moderation, patience we ask." According to Vavak, those who were most to blame for putting a false light on the whole situation were a few "hare-brained" military officers, "who would have liked to see the serf back in the days before 1775," and the faint-hearted manorial officials.[28] Had he heard the debates of the Bohemian Diet, he would doubtless have added the majority of the Bohemian Estates to this select company.

[27] Compare documents in M I Archiv, Carton 2492 and others cited previously bearing the date before February, 1790 and after June, 1790.
[28] Č N M Archiv, *Vavak Memoirs*, 1790: p. 140.

It is true that on some manors things went beyond passive disobedience and threat. In the circles of Klatovy (Klattau), Chrudim, Eger, Bydžow (Bidschow), and Rakovník (Rakonitz), the serf complained bitterly of the return to the old system, although in the circle of Čáslav there was one justice of the peace who, together with several peasant deputies, had previously petitioned for the old system. The serfs of the circle of Prachim appeared satisfied, while in the circle of Boleslav (Bunzlau), deeds of violence and loss of life were reported on the manors of Liberec (Reichenberg) and of Č. Lípa (Böhmischer Aicha). The peasants there intimidated the manorial officials and forced them to settle payments on the basis of the Josephinian system. They also held meetings in the woods and threatened to plunder and to murder.[39]

In the meanwhile, the Bohemian Estates on May 26, 1790, had reported to the Gubernium on the state of serf unrest and on June 17, 1790, they received the authorization that the rebellious serf could be handled by the landlords under the terms of the Penal Code of September 1, 1781, and in pressing cases "could be lodged in confinement with ten blows from wood." The Estates, if they wished, might submit to the Gubernium a plan of an "Execution Ordinance," that is, a new ordinance of execution, to strengthen the Penal Code in its control of the new situation caused by the return to the old system.[40] The Governor of Bohemia, Count Ludwig Cavriani, announced in a report dated June 24, 1790, that he had ceased sending offenders off to the army, and had given orders to separate the guilty and the more obstinate from the rest and to punish them in the regular civil way. Reports that came in from the country confirm Vavak's statements. Be-

[39] Grünberg, *Bauernbefreiung*, I, 352 ff. and Carton 2469. From all of this it is clear that in some places there had been a great difference between the old system and the new Josephinian system, in other places this was less true. At any rate, the difference was not so universal nor the abuses so great as to cause a general revolt.

[40] M I Archiv, Carton 2467: 187 ex Junio 1790. See also Grünberg, *Bauernbefreiung*, II, 463-464.

sides this, the reports also stated that many of the field hands
of the serfs had been recruited for the war against Turkey
and that the smaller peasant landowners were without sufficient help. This, together with the lack of draught animals,
revealed countless practical difficulties when the landlord came
to demand his robot, even if the serf were not rebellious.[31]

IV
CIVIL OR MILITARY RULE FOR THE SERFS?

On the very next day after the Big Bohemian Diet opened,
namely, on the thirteenth of July, 1790, the question of serfdom came up in a very concrete form.[32] Many of the nobles
complained that their serfs were "insolent and went unpun-
ished" and refused to render robot or pay its equivalent in
money, and also agriculture had been neglected and famine
and misery threatened the country. After some debate the
Diet concluded to write a communication to the Gubernium
exposing the critical situation and suggesting that doubtful
parts of the Patent of May 9, 1790, be made clear. By this
they meant that doubtful passages should be interpreted in
favor of the landlord. The letter which was sent to the Gubernium is an imperishable argument against the Bohemian
Estates in questions relating to serfdom.

The communication,[33] dated July 14, 1790, asserted that
complaints from all circles showed how impudent and un-
punished the serf was, and how he had refused to render
robot or to pay its equivalent in money. All these things
showed the "raw spirit of the Bohemian serf and the pro-
fundity of his stubbornness and his rebellious desires which
had spread among the people for some years past with as
much result as zeal." [34] Property owners had loudly appealed

[31] M I Archiv, Carton 2469: 35 ex Julio 1790. Governor Cavriani to the
Court Chancellery.
    [32] S Archiv, Journal of the Diet; Č N M Archiv, Sternberg Diary; and
S V Archiv, Kurze Anmerkungen for July 13, 1790. The Sternberg Diary
is especially good for matters pertaining to serfdom.
    [33] The document may be found in the S Archiv, Abt. 1786-1795, Fasc.
Diaet, No. 2. subn. 159.
    [34] Ibid.

for help, but in vain. The Penal Code of September 1, 1781, and the Patent of May 30, 1786, the Diet pointed out, authorized arrest, penal work, beatings, military service, and finally expulsion. The Estates considered that the serf was misled by dubious passages in the Patent of May 7, 1790. He was doubtless befuddled by the labored Czech translations which the officials of the circles published, and was urged on by evil-minded men and officials. The government officials, maintained the Diet, lacked the courage to enforce the legal penalties against the serf. Such help as the circle officials gave the manors was too weak, and their own dealings with the serfs showed woeful timidity. Then the Diet inserted its interpretation of the Patent of May 9, 1790, namely, the abolition of robot or the transformation of robot into a money rental was to be carried out "only" by the good will (or favor) of the landlord. The Estates further advised the use of the severest means of compulsion on the serf and advocated the prohibition of the sale of powder to him.[35] And finally, in order to prevent future misinterpretations, the Diet offered to help the Gubernium in translating the Patent into Czech "so that the serf could understand it."

The Gubernium seems to have taken this as a request for a new statement of the law of May 9, 1790. On July 25, 1790, the Council restated the law but did not insert the interpretation of the Diet. Nor was that Council frightened into thinking that the serf intended to revolt. All the evidence which came into the central office at Prague and which was transmitted to the Court Chancellery at Vienna showed that everywhere the unrest was calming down. Here and there sporadic disagreements bobbed up, but these generally occurred in places where the return to the old system often meant an increase in taxation, or robot, or both, by fifty per cent.[36] It was becoming more and more clear to the govern-

---

[35] *Ibid.* . . . welche in eine andere zu verwandeln *nur* von der Gnade der Obrigkeit abhängt, die Leistung der natural Frohnen sey—und dass die Unterthanen *nur* durch ein bereitwilliges Beuchnen nur durch billige Revizions Anträge und durch Unterwürfigkeit dieser Gnade sich würdig machen können. . . .

[36] H H S Archiv, Staatsrat Akten, 2290 in 1790.

ment that much of the unrest among the serfs was due to the
fact that robot had been reintroduced so suddenly and at a
time when the serf was in the midst of his own field work.
By the end of July the serfs at Liberec (Reichenberg) and
at Münchengrätz had returned to obedience, and several weeks
later the Gubernium was able to report that the return to
the old system of taxation and serfdom had been accomplished in Bohemia "without a revolution" and that there
was no longer any need of sending serfs off to the army, but
that the civil authorities on the spot could take care of all
situations. The Court Chancellery, in receiving this reassuring statement in the middle of August, 1790, stated that it
had expected the greatest difficulties as a result of the return
to the old system everywhere, "even in Bohemia."(!) It gave
orders immediately that the serfs who were obstinate or
rebellious should no longer be sent off to the army.[87]

But this did not satisfy the Bohemian Estates. They composed another communication, this time to Leopold II, and
entrusted Count Harrach with its presentation. In the meanwhile, a committee of the Estates visited the Gubernium and
wished to see the originals of the Court Decree of July 12,
which they declared was contrary to the Patents of May 9,
1790, and July 21, 1790, as the Gubernium promulgated
them.[88] The Gubernium fell back on its authority, and refused to show the original document, declaring that there had
never before been an instance of such distrust. It would show
the committee of the Estates merely a copy of the decree in
question and so much of the decree of August 20, 1790, as
concerned the Estates. The Court Chancellery stood behind
the Gubernium in its refusal to show the original document
and the Estates were blocked completely in this direction.[89]

Meanwhile, Count Harrach presented his Promemoria on

[87] H H S Archiv, Staatsrat Akten, 2380 in 1790 and M I Archiv, Carton
2469, 244 ex Augusto 1790 containing the report of Governor Cavriani to
the Court Chancellery, August 11, 1790.
[88] S Archiv, Journal of the Diet, August 16, 1790. Č N M Archiv, Nachlasse Sternbergs, August 21, 1790.
[89] M I Archiv, Carton 2469, 12 ex 7 ber 1780. Court Chancellery to
Gubernium, September 3, 1790. S Archiv, Journal of the Diet, August
21, 1790.

serf unrest in Bohemia at Vienna on September 12, 1790. It stated tersely the desire of the Estates that upon the application of the landlords the compulsory means of execution should be resorted to by the officials of the circle, and urged that the Estates and the Gubernium should enter into each other's confidence and coöperate to hold the serf down. The Estates also desired to be allowed to turn to the Court at Vienna directly and in pressing cases to lay them immediately before the monarch. Count Harrach saw that Leopold II wished to avoid answering the Promemoria, and on November 23, 1790, rewrote it and sent it to him again. But it never came up for consideration and the matter was soon forgotten in the avalanche of Desideria which fell upon Vienna from every part of the Monarchy. One thing is sure, Leopold II was firmly and resolutely on the side of the serf and stood by the government in handling the question. He had repealed the Josephinian system of taxation and serfdom, not because he wished to do so, but because the reaction had compelled him to take that step.[40]

With Leopold II's refusal to reverse the Gubernium's policy of treating the serf by means of the civil weapons it had at hand, for the military and penal policy which the Estates proposed, all signs of acute unrest soon disappeared. The Estates addressed themselves to a review of the laws which Joseph II had made for the punishment of the serf in order to see if by this means there was a possibility of taming the ever-assertive spirit of the Bohemian serf. Naturally all suggestions on this question centered in a revision of the Penal Code of 1781 which Joseph II had issued at the time of the emancipation of the serfs.

V

THE PENAL CODE

In the debates [41] of the Bohemian Diet on this subject

[40] Č N M Archiv, Nachlasse Sternbergs, September 12, 1790 and Sternberg Diary, Nov. 1790.
[41] S Archiv, Journal of the Diet, August 18 and November 8, 1790 and Č N M Archiv, Sternberg Diary, ibid.

there were many nobles who expressed a desire to use the penalty of banishment and confiscation oftener than the Code of 1781 allowed. Count Adolph Černín advocated the use of expulsion only in the most serious offenses and spoke against pecuniary fines. He openly deprecated the language of the communications of the Estates as well as their attempts at this point to write a savage ordinance against the serfs into the statute books. Count Francis Sternberg[42] remarked that it did not seem fitting to insert in a document which was to be sent to the king "in the name of a nation, language which insulted a part of that nation or a class of its people." The Estates had characterized the Bohemian peasant as vulgar and given over to idleness. He declared these assertions "not only overdrawn and in part false, but insulting. They should have been directed only against those who had been guilty of the charges enumerated." In general, the *Czech* nobility defended the serf from charges which naturally would reflect back upon them because of their common nationality.

The Estates inserted in the nineteenth grievance of the Third Desideria[43] the change they desired in the Penal Code of September 1, 1781, which they declared "aimless, inapplicable, and, owing to the manner of its execution, ineffective." Arrest, the first punishment enumerated in the code, was aimless because the "vulgar spirit of the Bohemian peasant was not affected by any injured feeling of honor" and there were no landlords' jails, the health officials having closed them. Work, the second punishment, was not easy to adjudge and to carry out in practice. They saw in the third punishment—the sharpening of the penalty with irons—"something that could be felt." To them the fourth punishment—expulsion and confiscation—was "the most efficient, perhaps the only applicable, penalty because it was the severest of all and easiest to execute." The circle officials made the administration of justice in such matters doubly worse.

---

[42] Sternberg Diary, November 8, 1790.
[43] M I Archiv, Carton 519:936 Oct. 1791.

The Estates therefore asked that the revised penal code
should contain certain fundamental rules. No manorial official
was to punish a serf personally or to imprison him. Serfs
guilty of disobedience or obstinacy were to be called up before
the village justice and two witnesses, and the penalty inflicted
upon him was to be inscribed in a protocol or book. The
guilty serf was thereupon to be forced to carry out the terms
of the sentence according to the seriousness of the offense, the
punishments including strapping in irons or, according to the
character of the person, ten to twenty blows with the knout
(*karabač*). Against peasants owning property proportionate
money fines were to be levied, the fines to go to the benefit of
the poor of the village in which the offender lived. Finally,
serious offenses were to be punished by expulsion and confiscation. All of these punishments except the last were to be
dealt out immediately on the spot without preliminary notice
to officials of the circle, and the serf was to have no right of
appeal. After the serf had been punished (!), if he thought
the punishment were undeserved, he might bring a complaint
before the officials of the circle, and if these officials found
that the serf had been punished undeservedly, the officials of
the manor were to be fined two florins, for each blow which
the unfortunate serf had received, one florin going to the serf,
the other to the poor. If the offense of the manorial official in
question were very serious, he might be arrested and even
deprived of his office. The family of the expelled serf was
not to be allowed to put in a claim on his property. It is to
the credit of Count Hartmann,[44] who got up a minority
opinion supported strongly by Count Buquoy, Count O'Kelley,
and Baron Běšín, that he opposed the last provision and held
that the offense of the father should not affect the family.

The Gubernium,[45] to its own credit, refused to accept the

[44] *Ibid.*, Carton 518:239 ex Augusto 1791. Votum Separatum of Hartmann:
Zur Einbegleitung an S. M. betreffend der als eine Strafe fürgeschlagene
und pr. Majora concludirte Abstiftung der stutzigen Unterthanen von ihren
eingekauften Wirtschaften.
[45] Bericht des böhmischen Landes-Guberniums, February 18, 1791. M I
Archiv, Carton 519.

definition of a Bohemian serf as given by the Estates. "The Bohemian peasant to his and to the government's honor, is not what they make him out to be. . . ." The new school system and the emancipation of serfdom had already had a powerful influence for the better on his character. Arrest no longer was "aimless," because the peasant now worked for himself; if arrested he lost the freedom for which he had so much yearned. In the reign of Joseph II, however, only that form of arrest was abolished which had clearly been destructive to the health of the arrested. The Gubernium showed itself opposed to corporal punishment; at most only the ten blows should be given which the Patent of June 17, 1790, allowed. Pecuniary fines were also to be avoided; they tended to bring the serf back to bondage. And under no circumstances should punishment take place without the cognizance of the circle official. A minority of the Gubernium Council, consisting of Count James Cavriani (not the Governor) and Barons MacNeven and Rosenthal, argued that all the reforms of Joseph II, and especially that of the school system, would bear fruit in the next generation. The present generation, however, needed stricter laws. But Councillors Lamoth and Grohmann refused to depart one whit from the Code of September 1, 1781, and staunchly stood up against corporal punishment in any form whatever.

The Court Chancellery [44] also rushed to the defense of the Bohemian serf. He was "not so insensible to the feeling of honor that he would disrespect the penalties of the law with regard to corporal punishment or irons." "Experience had shown this to be false, and even if his education had not reached the status which one had expected from the new school system, nevertheless his sense of honor would not be silenced now if he should be subjected to blows and to expulsion." According to the Court Chancellery there was not the slightest reason for departing from the Code of September

---

[44] Protokolle der Konferenzen . . . 4. und 23. Julius 1791 bei der böhm.-österr. Hofkanzlei gehalten wurden. H K Archiv, IV H 2 B.

1, 1781. If blows were necessary, they should be administered only by the officials of the circle. Further, the plea of Count Hartmann and his colleagues was worth careful consideration. Surely, the offender's wealth should go to the family, otherwise not only he, but several others, would be turned loose in the country, homeless and penniless.

Leopold II ruled in the Decree of October 28, 1791,[47] that the Code of 1781 should be maintained. The landlords were ordered to refrain from dealing out corporal punishment, and, if corporal punishment were found necessary, the protocol was to be sent to the officials of the circle, who were to decide whether the serf should be punished or not. In the case of expulsion of serfs, the family was to receive what was left of the wealth of the offender after the penalty had been satisfied. In every case of punishment of a serf the due knowledge of the officials was necessary to give validity to the penalty. Pamphleteers who stirred up the serfs were to be punished where caught, and no petition was to be accepted from the serfs which did not contain the signature of the writer.

By this means the government saved the Josephinian Code for the punishment of the Bohemian serf. But if it was satisfied that the law was sound, it realized that the manner of executing the Code was not effective enough to meet the new conditions. And this the central government planned to rectify by proposing that the Estates give their opinion on a new "Execution Ordinance on Obligations of Serfdom." As early as June 25, 1790, Leopold II had urged the Bohemian Estates to draft such an ordinance, but at that time they thought they could persuade the monarch to change the law— not the manner of execution, which they thought would follow of itself. Their report was not handed in, therefore, until April 14, 1791. It was considered by the Court Chancellery on July 4 and 23, 1791,[48] and a patent was actually drafted a few months later. But Leopold II died before it received the final consent of the Estates, and it never became a law.

[47] M I Archiv, Carton 519:936 Oct. 1791.   [48] See fn. 10.

The negotiations with regard to this "Execution Ordinance" are of lesser importance to us. Some of its most outstanding features, however, deserve notice. It dealt almost entirely with rentals in kind and with the fees which the serf had to give to his landlord. Matters pertaining to robot were left just as they were treated in the Penal Code of 1781. And it was the policy of the government to treat all matters coming under the Execution Ordinance as belonging to the sphere of activity of the political department, not of the judicial, in order to avoid swamping the courts, and to give to officials of the circle full authority in such matters. When the Estates argued strongly for expulsion or sequestration, the Court Chancellery remarked that what was true in Bohemia a generation ago was not true in 1791. "The time was past, when the State put the Estates in her lap and gave them power equal to her own and begged them to hold the peasant in the degrading condition of knavery and ignorance which one at that time considered necessary out of mistaken grounds for the interest of a single class of people. Serfdom (Leibeigenschaft) was abolished and the greater number of services lessened, and through the control of the officials of the circle a powerful dam set up against oppression." It was the aim of the Execution Ordinance to do justice to both sides; to free the serf from the oppression of the manorial officials, "many of whom likewise had a poor education"; and to hold the serf to his legal obligations.[49]

Leopold II was inclined to stand by the general principles of the government's policy in regard to serfdom. In every case, the official of the circle by his cognizance or by his presence was to give validity to each penalty. The landlords were to help out in case of fire or weather damages to the serfs and were not to ruin the serfs by demanding the payment of debts at such times. The property of the serfs was not to be allowed to fall into the hands of the landlord, but was to be sold publicly. In cases where the serf had refused to pay a just debt,

[49] See fn. 10.

the officials of the circle were to be notified immediately. They were to investigate the charge, and if found just, they were to proceed with the execution according to the manner prescribed in the Ordinance. That is as far as this piece of legislation got in the reign of Leopold II, and there is no evidence that it was taken up after his death. It is, however, a good commentary on the attitude of the Estates and the government, and clears up our confusion as to where each of them stood on the matter of serf unrest in those critical years after Joseph II had died. The Bohemian serf had had no real desire to revolt in 1790, nor was he as black as the Estates painted him, and it is to the praise of the central government that it refused to be misled by the Estates in this matter.[50]

VI

WAS ROBOT TO BE ABOLISHED?

The third problem in regard to serfdom, in which the Bohemian Estates and the government interested themselves in the reign of Leopold II, was the determination of a policy whereby personal robot could be changed into a money payment. Should the abolition of robot take place by means of a contract between landlord and serf? How and in what manner should the contract be made? Would the officials of the circles act as umpires and judges in the making of the contract, and would the government at Vienna lay down the rules of bargaining? These were the main questions which the statesmen of that day had to answer.

On August 11, 1790, the Executive Committee reported in the Diet that the monarch desired that robot be abolished and a rental in money substituted.[51] Robot was to remain only where local conditions made a change to the money rental impossible. The Diet in a half-hearted way accepted the report, but refused to make out a list of those who had abol-

[50] H H S Archiv, Staatsratakten 3526 in 1791. M I Archiv, Carton 2492, 244 in Februario, 1792.
[51] S Archiv, Journal of the Diet, August 11, 1790.

ished robot on their estates, "because only a few landlords had made such contracts." In the First Desideria[52] of September 4, 1790, the Estates argued against the idea of a uniform plan for the abolition of robot; in fact, against its abolition in any way whatsoever. The Estates declared that the serf had too much time on his hands. He had little opportunity to profit by odd jobs, and in physically working off his robot, he would be doing something of real value to himself. The Estates asserted that since 1775 "when the very moderate (!) robot ceased," the serf was lost to mankind, to the State, and to himself. He put his time into holidays given over to idleness and frivolity. His debts were sure to remain unpaid in the future, and the number of his cattle would diminish. Misery moreover was sure to come upon him and his class.

The Bohemian Estates, in this Desideria of September 4, 1790, pointed out that the Patents of May 9, and of May 21, 1790, allowed free bargaining between landlord and serf. It was really their intention not to oppress the serf but to come to an understanding with him. Where the terms of abolition offered by the landlord did not suit the serf, he could stay by his robot! In other words, that was exactly what the Estates wanted. In this clever way, the Bohemian Estates had interpreted the two Patents completely in their own favor.

The Gubernium[53] rejected the argument about the serf's idleness and declared that his fields and the introduction of industry were keeping him busier than the Estates admitted, and in the future would keep him still busier. The Council admitted that it was not easy to arrive at a uniform system for the abolition of serfdom. Yet such great landowners as Prince Adam Auersperg, Prince Kinský, and Chief Chancellor Leopold Kolovrat had successfully abolished robot at

[52] Äusserung der böhmischen Stände über den ersten Absatz des höchsten Reskripts von 1ten Mai, 1790. Die Eingleichung der Steuer und Ablösung der unterthänigen Frohnen betreffend. M I Archiv, Carton 514, 207 in Julio 1791.
[53] Bericht des böhmischen Landes-Guberniums . . . November 23, 1790. M I Archiv, Carton 514, 207 in Julio 1791.

the Josephinian ratio, 17 florins 46⅔ kreuzer. The government estates, where robot was abolished, likewise worked well.

A minority report of the Council of the Gubernium combated these views of the majority. The two members, Count Sweerts and Count James Cavriani, declared that the government lands could not serve as an example, because the value of the robot there had not been taken into account in the making out of the contracts. They stated that the decrease in cattle was a great disadvantage to the State, for the landlords had a superior grade of cattle and draught animals, and no account was taken of this in the government demand for transport. They concluded that any law on the abolition of robot would necessarily be an attack on property.[54]

The Governor of Bohemia, in a letter accompanying the views of the Estates and of the Gubernium, was of the opinion that the provision of free bargaining in the Patents of May 9 and July 21, 1790, should be lived up to. The officials of the circle should interfere only when the serf made a complaint. The Commission on Desideria in its session of March 12, 1791, also advocated this point of view. But Eger of the State Council declared he would be a "doubting Thomas" along with the Gubernium as to whether the abolition of robot by free bargaining would ever come to pass in a way satisfactory to both parties without the intervention of the officials of the government. In another conference Eger urged vehemently that the government take direct charge of the making of contracts, because "if it does not likewise give matters pertaining to serfdom a solid legal basis, they will be of little or no permanent good, and they are matters which alone give security to the throne, solidity to the State, and restore and maintain lasting peace and satisfaction within between citizen and citizen." [55]

[54] *Ibid.*
[55] See Protokoll der Konzertazion welche über die Beschwerden der böhmischen Stände gehalten ward den 9. Hornung 1791. M I Archiv, Carton 514, 207 in Julio 1792. H H S Archiv, Staatsrat Akten 1791 in 1792, and 3529 in 1791.

On July 29, 1791, Leopold II once more advised the Estates to address themselves to a plan for the abolition of robot modified to fit local conditions and following out some of the suggestions of the Gubernium.[56] The matter was then to come up once more for discussion.

If there were any doubts as to the attitude of the Bohemian Estates on the question of the abolition of robot, they were dispelled in the session of October 27, 1790.[57] The serfs of Reichenberg, who had been turbulent in the early summer, demanded through the Gubernium that they be given the Josephinian basis as regards serfdom, i.e. 17 florins 46⅔ kreuzer out of 100 florins. The debate waxed warm. Count Chotek remarked that the serfs should have announced their desires first to Count Gallas, their lord, and that he would have been willing to meet them halfway. Count Hartmann, the friend of the serfs, stood up manfully for a plan of abolition, "but his opinion had no votes." Count O'Kelley ended the debate by warning "the Estates against all vain efforts at equality, and pictured the promoters of equality as the originators of the greatest evil of the last and of the preceding reigns."

This debate, and the negotiations which we have just given, accurately describe the situation. The government desired the abolition of robot and was willing to help the Estates make a plan for its accomplishment. The Estates opposed any uniform plan on the ground that this was practically impossible. The patents gave them what they wanted—free bargaining. If the serf did not like the offer of the landlord, he could go on rendering robot. In other words: if there were to be any abolition of robot it was by individual landlords, unhampered by the government, where they could be free to name their own terms. And so the negotiations dragged on wearily for almost two years. During this time the question of taxation and of finances in general so absorbed the government that

[56] Hof Kanzlei Sitzung vom 8. Julius 1791 containing Leopold II's decision of July 29, 1791 on the last few pages. M I Archiv, Carton 517, 207 ex Julio 1791.

[57] Č N M Archiv, Sternberg Diary, October 27, 1790.

the Estates thought the question of the abolition of robot would be forgotten.

But fortunately, and to the great honor of the government, it did not forget the matter. During the last few months of Leopold II's reign the Estates were interrogated by that monarch as to whether they had a plan ready for submission, and finally they were given four weeks in which to prepare one, or the government would do so itself. To such a low ebb had that dear right to legislate sunk in two years—the right for which they were execrating Joseph II in 1789 and 1790! After much hemming and hawing the Bohemian Diet began its debate on the abolition of robot on April 27, 1792, two months after Leopold II had died.

One diarist [58] wrote, "Count Francis Anton Kolovrat, *subterraneus,* came forth with a breast full of papers, and assured us that he had taken the trouble to exhaust the subject entirely." He "spoke with heated words to the presiding officer and otherwise bored the assembly." Nevertheless, he spoke the mind of the assembly. He expatiated [59] at great length on the Patents of May 9, and August 13, 1790, of course interpreting the phrase "free bargaining" in its broadest sense, declared property should no longer be attacked, and took a fling at "the wicked pamphleteers and scribblers who had won the hearts, not only of the obstinate serfs, but of the officials also." Beyond this he added nothing new to the arguments which the Estates had already presented. He compared conditions in Bohemia with those in Silesia and bewailed the fact that the Estates of Bohemia "could not obtain from their righteous king a like protection."

The Diet, [60] after declaring that it had never promised to draw up a plan for the abolition of robot, restated carefully

[58] Č N M Archiv, Sternberg Nachlasse, April 23-27, 1790. But these few pages were not written by the author of the extended diary, Francis Count Sternberg.

[59] Votum des Grafen Anton von Kolovrat, welches im Landtage vorgelegt wurde, von der Urbarial- oder Robotschuldigkeit nicht absugehen. Lobkovic Library and Z Archiv, Prague.

[60] Zuschrift der böhmischen Stände an K. Leopold (i.e. Franz) in der Frage der Frohnen-Reluirung betreffend. Prague Dom, S V Archiv, M. S. 87 copia.

its old arguments and its claim that the Patent of 1775 really contained the basis of their conception of the future condition of things. Robot could not be abolished without great losses to the landlord. Thus even by 1792, the Estates had not suggested a plan for its abolition.

By this time the government of Francis II, while in many respects influenced by Josephinian tendencies, was affected by the course of events in France. The government lost interest, and the Estates by persisting in their course won out in the end. How little the landlords wished individually to abolish robot is seen when one considers that in 1794, out of nearly a thousand manors, 351 had abolished it wholly, 108 partly; but of this number 117 had belonged to the state in which the Raab and Hoyer system had long been introduced: in other words, only a little over a third had done so. But more striking still is the statement that 103 of these manors had abolished robot without contracts, so averse were they to making them out.[61] When finally, on September 1, 1798, the law for the abolition of robot was promulgated, it sanctioned the complete victory of the Bohemian Estates. Free bargaining was expressly proclaimed, "but in only such a case would the contract be valid, when it was approved by an official of the circle." That did not necessarily mean that the official acted as judge; on the contrary, his confirmation might come after the bargain had been concluded. An historian of Bohemian serfdom rightly concluded: "The Patent of September 1, 1798, closed the epoch of social and political legislation in (Bohemian) agrarian history for almost half a century."[62] Not till the foundations of the Austrian Monarchy were once

---

[61] Grünberg, *Bauernbefreiung*, II, 476, citing the Übersichtstabelle, 133 ex Aprili 1794, M I Archiv, Carton 2492.

[62] *Ibid.* The Patent of September 1, 1798 is printed in Grünberg, I, 478-479. See especially F I. "Jeder Vertrag, wodurch ein Gutsbesitzer seinen Unterthanen die Entrichtung der üblichen Personal- und Natural-Giebigkeiten, gegen Ertrag eines Geldbetrages, auf immwährende Zeit erlässt oder wodurch sämmtliche Grundstücke, ein Mayerhof oder andere beträchtliche Bestandtheile der Herrschaft, an die Unterthanen vertheilt werden, hat zwar von dem Tage seiner Errichtung, jedoch nur in dem Falle seine gültige Wirkung wenn er von dem Kreisamte bestättigt wird."

more shaken, this time by the revolution of 1848, were the bonds of serfdom dissolved.

VII
THE SERF AND THE BOHEMIAN DIET

One more episode illustrates the spirit of the times and shows that in 1792 the Habsburg Monarchy stood on the threshold of a new era. And that was the attempt of the Bohemian peasants [88] to enter the Diet as an Estate early in 1792. The question of the future basis of taxation and of serfdom was still before the Diet and no conclusion had been reached. The serf's patience was worn out. When it was announced that the first session of the Diet in the new year would be held on January 9, 1792, the peasant population hit upon the idea of sending a deputy from each district (*Gemeinde*) to take part in the discussions of the Diet, for these two matters concerned them especially. In the circle of Klatovy (Klattau) Jacob Kubsch (commonly called Freek), a justice of the peace, was said to be scattering the report that the sovereign had ordered the districts to send deputies to the Diet in Prague. He himself had set out for that city. The circle captain immediately notified the government to watch the gates of Prague for the arrival of peasant deputies and to arrest Kubsch.

The Governor, Count Rottenhan, hastily called together his councillors, and precautions were taken to catch the deputies as they arrived before Prague. The report that the peasant had been called to take part in the discussions of the Diet spread like wildfire throughout Bohemia and especially in the west. The police were everywhere warned, and the military were cautioned to be ready. Presently, the central police

[88] M I Archiv, Carton 2492. Böhmen-Unterthanleistungen in genere, 1784-1810, 59 in Feb. 1792. See Bericht des böhmischen Landes-Praesidiums: Über die verbreitete irrige Meinung, dass auch die Bauern zum Landtage einberufen seyn; allerunterthänigster Vortrag der Hofkanzlei, 21. Januar, 1792; Sitzung, 3. Feb. 1792. See also Roubík, "Sedlaci na zemský sněm do Prahy v lednu 1792" (*Časopis pro Dějiny Venkova s přilohou Selský Archiv, 1925*, XII).

office at Prague received word that "suspicious" peasants were betaking themselves to Prague from the circles of Rakovník (Rakonitz), Žatec (Saatz), and even from Eger under pretense of visiting the financial offices there (*Fiskal-Amt*). It was soon discovered that they had little or nothing to do with those offices. The deputies from the circles of Žatec (Saatz) and Rakovník (Rakonitz) actually arrived in Prague to attend the Diet. But many of the others were met on the road and either turned back or placed under arrest. Meanwhile, the military forces moved into the circle of Klatovy, where it was feared an outbreak might take place. Finally, on February 10, 1792, Kubsch was located and immediately arrested.

The report of the Governor about this episode was sent posthaste to the Court Chancellery and to Leopold II. The Court Chancellery was not inclined to see in this the beginning of a revolt as yet, but urged that the circle captain who first reported the matter be rewarded for his zeal and promptness. Accordingly, Leopold II decorated Count Vratislav, the captain of the circle of Klatovy, with a gold medal of extra large size. "The results were too important for one to let such service go unrewarded." In 1848, these peasants became parliamentarians.

We have seen, therefore, that it was the Habsburg dynasty itself which almost ruined the Bohemian serf with a series of robot patents extending over a century from 1680 to 1773. During this time, as the Chancellery rightly put it, the government took the Estates into its lap, gave them power and strength to hold the serf in slavery, and oppressed the serf in countless ways. The alliance between the government and the Estates to keep the serf down dissolved in 1775. One of the factors in this dissolution was doubtless the fact that the revenue of the state from the land tax was threatened. In 1775 the absolute state under Maria Theresa entered upon a campaign of reform which did not cease until robot had been

abolished and the serf made free to migrate, to marry, and to
learn whatever trade or profession he desired. Had the epoch
of reform continued a generation beyond 1790, it would have
led doubtless to a dissolution of the entire structure of serfdom and with it the disappearance of the last traces of feudalism in Bohemia.

But mistakes had been made. Where property rights are
legislated upon by the mere stroke of the pen, reaction is
mightiest. Nothing was more tenacious than the right of
property, confirmed as it had been by a century of Habsburg
Patents. Joseph II had only followed Maria Theresa's legislation; his was the logical result of hers. In matters pertaining to serfdom, as in all other matters except perhaps in his
reform of the courts, Joseph II blundered more by his haste
than by principle or even policy; more by his tactlessness
than by his directness. The Estates found a weak link in the
chain of reforms in the "gross grain product" of the taxation
question and in the general argument that a uniform law of
abolition was impossible, for conditions were not uniform.
They tore this weak link open and thereby weakened the
entire chain of reforms.

On going back to the old basis established by Maria Theresa
in 1775 it was feared that a revolt would take place in Bohemia. The serf did not rise in revolt—he was restless only
here and there—although a great number of serfs all over
Bohemia refused passively to render robot. Perhaps one
reason why a revolution did not take place was the fact that
not all serfs had been benefited by the abolition of robot. The
serf who refused to render his robot did not in general deny
the right of the landlord to the robot, but sought to make a
better bargain. Having failed in their efforts to persuade the
government that the serf was in rebellion, and to secure martial law instead of civil rule, the Estates tried next to fashion
the code by which the serf was to be punished. But even here
the government blocked them and rebuked them severely for
their attitude toward the Bohemian serf. The government

declared it would allow no change in the law, but rather in the manner of executing it. However, the death of Leopold II definitely prevented the enactment of an Execution Ordinance into law.

The French Revolution took from the government all desire to push the abolition of robot. The Estates from the very first adopted an indifferent and then an obstructive attitude toward the reform. The uniform public legislation under Joseph II was abandoned. It became the policy of the government to push it as a uniform plan for the landlords individually. But the Estates would listen to no uniform plan of abolition. If robot were to be abolished, it should be abolished only by the landlords as individuals and on their own terms, free bargaining. Leopold II, in the Patent of May 9, 1790, had given in temporarily to the principle of free bargaining. By the end of his reign he saw that he would have to give in permanently. Slowly but surely, the alliance, which lasted down to 1775, was resurrected after 1792 and cemented in 1798 by the new law, establishing the abolition of robot by free bargaining. The Bohemian Estates had won, not because of their own cleverness, but because the trend of the French Revolution had shown the need of an old-time friendship. But if the government did not "take the Estates into its lap" this time, at least it took them into partnership once more and resolved not to harm them.

Nevertheless, the serf, though not so well off as in 1789, was better off than in 1775, and the days of 1775 were as day compared to the night which had preceded them.

PART IV
SOCIAL

CHAPTER X

RELIGION

I

THE DOMINATION OF THE JESUITS, 1620-1774

FEW countries have been so unfortunate in their religious history as Bohemia. In few have more radical changes taken place in the religious and intellectual life of a people. From Slavic paganism to Latin Christianity, from Catholicism to Czech Hussitism and toleration, from toleration to the intolerance of the Jesuits, and then finally to Josephinian toleration and sectarianism, there is a series of transitions, some abrupt, others barely noticeable, unrivaled in the history of any other land.[1]

In the modern history of Europe, Bohemia on three occasions assisted in the great struggles which were fought for the freedom of religious belief and of the intellect. In the Fifteenth Century, after the burning of Hus, the embattled Hussites defended communion in both kinds against the Catholic crusaders of Europe. At the beginning of the Seventeenth Century in an effort to preserve the religious toleration which had existed in Bohemia for nearly two centuries, the Bohemian Estates became involved in a conflict which brought the whole of Europe into the great Thirty Years' War. And finally, after a century of oblivion, the educational writings of Comenius, the great Czech scholar, became the basis in the Eighteenth Century of the new schools of enlightenment of Europe. These were some of the high lights of Bohemia's interesting history.

[1] See Chapter I, pp. 1-10, for the course of Church history in Bohemia to 1620.

But there were also shadows. Such struggles demand not only stout hearts and keen minds and the sinews of large physical resources, but also that deep and penetrating culture which gives unflinching courage. The promising intellectual movements which Bohemia started were too gigantic for so small a country and for so insignificant a population. Hence the self-reliance and the rich resources which must accompany great intellectual conceptions, were lacking. The Hussite movement was followed by a species of religious toleration which eventually resulted in the moral weakening of the Czech nation. The struggle for toleration in the Seventeenth Century ended in the great catastrophe of the Battle of White Mountain, which delivered the most tolerant country of Europe into the hands of its most intolerant enemies, the Jesuits and the friends of Rome and of Spain. Her most capable citizens fled and became the Protestant émigrés of the Seventeenth Century. The Treaty of Westphalia in 1648 condemned them to eternal exile. When the dawn of the Eighteenth Century reddened the horizon of the Lands of the Habsburg Monarchy, the spirit of enlightenment adopted the ideas of Comenius, but instead of offering the fruits of his labor in the native language, Enlightened Despotism began the process of Germanization through the very instrument which a Czech of the Seventeenth Century had created.

It is an undeniable fact that Ferdinand II and his allies took vengeance upon the Czechs after the Battle of White Mountain (1620) not because they were Czechs (although that fact did not help them at all with a German master) but because Ferdinand II was a Catholic and the Czechs were Protestants who wished to deprive him of his crown. All Protestants were forced either to flee or to allow themselves to be converted. The owners of manors became Catholics and the Catholic Church by 1714 had acquired land equal to one-sixteenth of the area of Bohemia. The University and the gymnasia were handed over to the Jesuits, and the elementary schools to the Piarists. The Land Ordinance of 1627 codified this state of affairs, declared the Roman Catholic Church "the only dominating faith," called for an oath "on the Mother of God and all Holies" to be taken by all public officials, and canceled all and any privileges the Protestant Estates may have enjoyed at any earlier time.[2]

Then began a period of active "reconversion" of the population by the new Estates, by the Commissions on Religion appointed by the Diet, by the Jesuits and the Piarists, and by the Church of Rome at large. The champions of Roman law sympathized little with the population, and the process of "reconversion" went on with a bustle hardly imaginable, although more than revengeful force and the burning of the vast Czech literature by the Jesuits was necessary to win back eastern Bohemia, the home of the Bohemian Brethren. However, fate turned against those who resisted. In 1648 the Treaty of Westphalia offered the Protestants in Bohemia no hope and sealed the fortunes of those who had emigrated. Thereafter, those who remained in the country as secret Protestants looked to Sweden and later to Prussia for possible assistance. The Protestants in Silesia by the Dresden Accord of 1622 secured a sort of toleration, which was confirmed in the Treaty of Altranstadt (1707), whereby they received political equality, and 121 churches were given into their care, through the protection of Charles XII of Sweden.[3]

During this same period, the Bishoprics of Litoměřice (Leitmeritz), Budějovice (Budweis), and Hradec Králové (Königgrätz) were established and the last of the loyal Protestant nobles became converted. Leopold I (1657-1705) held to a milder policy toward the Protestants and during his

[2] See Czerwenka, *Geschichte der Evangelischen Kirche in Böhmen*, II, 576-622, 631, 640 ff. See also M I Archiv, Steuer-Fusses Fasc. 576, and Jireček, *Obnovené právo a zřízení zemské dědičného království českého—Verneuerte Landes-Ordnung des Erb-Königreichs Böhmen, 1627*, A XXIII, pp. 33-35, and 13. Gindely, *Geschichte der Gegenreformation in Böhmen, passim*.
[3] Rezek, *Dějiny prostonárodního hnutí náboženského v Čechách od vydání tolerančního Patentu až na naše časy*, I, 18-60 and ff. See also Bílek, *Reformace katolická neboli obnovené náboženství katolického v království českem po bitvě Bělohorské*, pp. 176 ff.; and Tomek, *Böhmische Geschichte*, last two chapters.

reign there was a lull in religious persecution, but his three successors, Joseph I (1705-1711), Charles VI (1711-1740), and even Maria Theresa (1740-1780) persecuted, often with a Spanish fervor unknown even in the time of Ferdinand II.

The religious persecution of Charles VI was worse than that of Ferdinand II because it was more systematic. The analogy between a Protestant England crushing a Catholic Ireland and a Catholic Austria destroying a Protestant Bohemia is very striking. As a result of Charles VI's labors in behalf of religious unity, Prussia and Saxony received Bohemia's best brains and its best talent. A series of decrees culminated in 1733 by a law whereby a change of faith on the part of a Catholic was declared a state crime (*crimem contra statum*). The inquisition was a reality, even if it had little legal basis and no machinery except the organization of the Jesuits. Finally, in 1735, the Bohemian Protestants appealed to Frederick William I of Prussia to stop the persecution. The Prussian Ambassador at Vienna handed Charles VI a rescript of the Prussian King about to be issued to the Imperial Diet publicly declaring that he stood on the side of the Bohemian Protestants. In that year, the persecution was abandoned. It had proved futile.[4]

Under Maria Theresa religious questions began to assume another aspect. The sectarians and secret Protestants increased after the victorious war of the Prussians. One could distinguish the Abrahamites (or Israelites), the Deists, Hussites, religious nihilists, and other groups or sects. Besides this, there were Lutherans and Calvinists and Jews. In 1742 the latter had assisted in bringing the French and Bavarians into Prague, and they were therefore banished from Bohemia. It was not until 1748 that they were allowed to return, and then on an increased tribute. Maria Theresa unmistakably continued the legislation and persecution against the Protestants. An instance of the extreme nature of some of the legisla-

[4] Rezek, *Dějiny prostonárodního hnutí náboženského,* 62 ff.; Gindely, "Die Processirung der Häretiker in Böhmen unter Kaiser Karl VI" (*Abh. BGW,* VII, Folge, 2bd.) contains much that is to the point here.

tion may be found in the Decree of November 29, 1752, whereby it was declared a capital offense to announce one's self to be a Protestant. The offense was named alongside of treason and rebellion, as one of the worst of political crimes. One thing made up for all persecution and that was the fact that warfare occupied Maria Theresa for over a third of her long reign of forty years. In 1773 the State Council advocated milder treatment and put the categorical question to the monarch: "What would happen if all the secret non-Catholics were punished?" In this way it hinted that there were many of them and that they were hard to get at. Lutheran preachers traveled through Bohemia in disguise, and there was more than one indication that the Jesuits, who had converted Bohemia, had ended their days of usefulness.[5]

Meanwhile it had become the cardinal principle of the absolute monarchy that it should be supreme within its own confines. The abolition of the order of the Jesuits in the Habsburg Monarchy thereupon became inevitable. In 1767 no bulls of the Church of Rome could have validity in the Monarchy's possessions without the permission (*placet*) of the monarch. In the next year no excommunication in private heresy could be launched by the Pope without a similar permission. In 1773 the clergy of the Lands of the Habsburgs was forbidden to correspond directly with Rome. And in the next year, 1774, the Jesuits were suppressed.

With the suppression of the Jesuits and the revolt of the peasants in 1775 a new epoch was ushered in. Religious persecution was completely abandoned[6] and as one journal an-

---

[5] Rezek, 105 ff.; Czerwenka, *Gesch. der Evangelischen Kirche in Böhmen*, II, last two chapters and 648-649; Friedberg, *Die Gränzen zwischen Staat und Kirche und die Garantien gegen deren Verletzung*, 137 ff.; Hock, *Der österr. Staatsrath*, 35, 58, 59 and Adamek, *Listiny k dějinam lidového náboženského na českem východě v XVIII. a XIX. věku*, I, 1750-1782. These are documents on the question, with especial reference to the eastern part of Bohemia. In 1760 (No. 24, p. 23). The Prague Consistory wrote in its correspondence: ". . . constante rumore increbres homines quosdam lingua et origine Slavos ex Hungaria in Bohemia saepius in anno penetrare . . . libros haereticos in utraque vernacula tum Bohemica tum Germanica recentibus typis editos in Regnum inferre. . . ."

[6] Frank, *Das Toleranz-Patent Kaiser Josephs II*, pp. 1-19 and Rezek, *Dějiny náb. hnutí*, 131-133. The peasants in 1775 got up a petition to Fred-

nounced "the Eighteenth Century had begun in Bohemia."
Of this there was no doubt whatsoever.

II
THE DAWN OF TOLERATION

Every age has its shibboleths and its heroes; each epoch its
high lights and its shadows. The Counter Reformation had
done much for Catholic Europe. It had sent surging into its
decaying arteries the fresh blood of Jesuitical enterprise. It
had ended with the Treaty of Westphalia in 1648, by a division
of Europe into two intolerant halves, exhausted after a generation of barbarous warfare. In the course of a century the
intolerance of both the Roman Catholic and the Protestant
groups declined. A new spirit came to guide the men of the
Eighteenth Century, the spirit of modern liberalism. And its
shibboleths were religious toleration, the freedom of scientific
investigation, humanitarianism, and finally, civic equality.
In Bohemia, this spirit made itself felt most strongly under
Joseph II. In England it was called Deism, in France, Ency-
clopaedism, in Germany, Rationalism. As it proceeded east-
ward it weakened in force and lost somewhat in content. The
Jesuits had been the champions of the Counter Reformation,
the Freemasons were the warriors who fought for the new
liberalism. Their weapons were neither fairer nor more brutal
than those of the Jesuits. If the forces of the Counter Reformation were moored steadfast in historical tradition, the
new energies of liberalism broke loose from the past and strove
to build a new world on the ruins of the old, not by patient
adjustment of traditions to fit newer conditions, but by sheer
revolution in all directions. The forces of the Counter Reformation had worked through the agency of the Church and its
religious resources; the new liberalism brushed the Church

erick the Great of Prussia. See also Č N M Archiv, *Vavak Memoirs* for 1775
and Hájková, "Vavak a jeho pojetí českých dějin" (*ČČH*, 1919, XXXV,
nos. 2, 3).

aside as only a secondary factor and operated directly through the new absolute State. In such an atmosphere, religion became no more important in the public life of the State than public sanitation or the welfare of the serf. In the reign of Joseph II the conflict between the Church, representing the Counter Reformation, and the State, representing the new liberalism, ended in a triumph of the State, and brought with it a revolution in matters pertaining to religion.[7]

The seeds of the new spirit were planted in Bohemia early in the Eighteenth Century by the Freemasons. Comenius, whose writings the Jesuits, after 1620, had consigned to the flames in Bohemia, had met with favor in England, Sweden, and Protestant Germany. Even Harvard College in the United States had heard of him and, it is said, offered him the presidency of that institution. He was personally active in the learned societies of Western Europe. In 1667 he outlined in his *Panegersia* the idea which later ripened into Freemasonry. The first lodge of Freemasons was established in England in 1717 under the title of St. John the Baptist. Nine years later the first lodge of Freemasons was created in Prague, although as early as 1719, two years after the foundation of the English lodge, Count Francis Anton Spork was accused of Protestantism by the Jesuits. The Bohemian lodge was the first lodge in all the Central European possessions of the Habsburgs, and it restored once more that tendency to intellectual union between England and Bohemia which had become so notable since the days of Wycliffe and Hus. From that time down to 1785 the lodges grew in number, there being about five in the countryside and two in Prague.[8] Some of the Freemasons of Bohemia worked for Germanization, others for a revival of

[7] For some suggestions see Vlček, "Z doby Josefinské" (*ČČH*, 1900, VI, 15, 97, 313 ff.).
[8] Svatek, *Obrazy z kulturních dějin českých*, Chapter II, "The Freemasons in Bohemia in the Eighteenth Century," 260 ff.; Kalousek, *Děje král. české společnosti nauk*, 9 ff.; Lewis, *Geschichte der Freimaurerei in Österreich*, pp. 17 ff. and Brunner, *Die Mysterien der Aufklärung in Österreich, 1700-1800*, especially the appendix.

the Czech language, but all worked together for a dissolution of the order of the Jesuits and for the destruction of feudal Bohemia.[9]

Jansenism within the Catholic Church, as Pietism in the Protestant, may be overestimated, but in the course of events it was a factor of considerable influence. It is to the credit of the Catholic clergy that there were some in its ranks who openly thought and planned for educational and social reform within the Church.[10] But this new counter reformation was very weak.

To state the political, economic, and social reasons why Joseph II granted religious toleration would lead us too far afield. Suffice it to say that Joseph II aimed to make the Protestant—whether German, Czech, or Hungarian—and the Jew loyal subjects of the House of Habsburg in its struggle against Prussia. For the sake of their advanced economic ideas Joseph II wished to invite Protestants to his territories. And finally, by subjecting the Church to the new all-powerful State, he sought to revive, to purify, and to extend the natural religious forces of the Roman Catholic Church.

The Josephinian Patent of Toleration, which was issued on October 30, 1781, granted toleration to three religions, the

[9] The origin of the Czech revival is a disputed one. For the most recent bibliographical notice of it see Novotný, *České dějiny*, I, I. 28 ff. Goll (*ČČH*, IV) in an article on Palacký declared that the Czech revival was carried out in the "spirit of the times." Hanuš and Kraus are at present carrying on a polemic as to its immediate origin, the former views the subject from his knowledge of Czech literature, the latter from his knowledge of German literature. The former considered the society of scholars, the founders of the First Scientific Society of Bohemia in 1775, the heating iron of the Czech revival, the latter argues that they were not. It has not been determined as yet whether this society was opposed to the "official enlightenment" which came from Vienna. Whichever it may have been, it is certain that these origins were (and remained for over a decade) very weak and uncertain. Hanuš has written: "Počátký král. české společností nauk" (*ČČH*, XIV, 141-152), "Dodatek k počatkum král. české společností nauk" (*ČČH*, XV, 277, 425), "Mikuláš Audaukt Voigt" (*Rozpravy, ČA*, 1910, III, no. 32). To the first, Kraus wrote a reply: *Pražské časopisy, 1770-1774 a české probuzení* (*Rozpravy, ČA*, 1910, III, no. 31).

[10] See the comments and bibliographical details in Mitrofanov, *Joseph II*, Chapter VIII, 666 ff. and Küntziger, *Fébronius et le Fébronianisme. Étude historique sur le mouvement réformateur provoqué dans l'église Catholique au XVIII° siècle par Fébronius et l'origine des réformes ecclésiastiques de Joseph II*.

Lutheran, the Calvinist, and the Ununited Greek Orthodox. The Roman Catholic Church was expressly designated as dominant and was alone allowed the right of conducting divine worship publicly. The three tolerated religions were allowed the right of private worship. Many minor provisions covered the details of the exact relations of the tolerated non-Catholics in their social, economic, and political relations to the State. Some of these will come up later, and we shall consider them more fully then. Schools and public offices were thrown open to them, and they were given the right to own landed property. The same rights were extended to the Jews who, in all the time during which the Protestants had been persecuted, had enjoyed limited toleration. Count Rottenhan, a member of the Council of the Gubernium in Bohemia, warned Joseph II that the introduction of religious toleration would be a precarious procedure in Bohemia. Count Hatzfeld predicted that a fourth of the people there would declare themselves non-Catholics, and non-Catholics were never well disposed to a sovereign who himself was not a non-Catholic. But Joseph II remained unmoved and the Patent was ordered to be promulgated.[11]

Clumsiness on the part of some of the officials of the local government in promulgating the Patent caused some trouble, although this was only temporary.[12] Much to the surprise of the central government those who declared themselves were neither Lutherans, Calvinists, or Ununited Greek Orthodox, but Deists, Israelites (Abrahamites), Taborites, Hussites, etc., namely, sectarians not included in the list of the tolerated![13]

[11] Frank, *Das Toleranz-Patent Kaiser Josephs II*, pp. 1-20, 37 ff. This is the most scholarly presentation of the question of Josephinian toleration from a Protestant point of view. See also, Brunner, *Die theologische Dienerschaft am Hofe Josephs II*, and also Z Archiv, Votum des Grafen Rottenhan über das Toleranz-Patent, 1781 copia.

[12] Adamek, *Listiny k dějinam lidového náboženského hnutí na českem východě v XVIII. a XIX. věku*, I, 1750-1782, pp. 145 ff. Hock, *Der österreichische Staatsrath*, 343-344.

[13] Hock, *ibid*. Kressel of the Court Chancellery on one occasion wrote: "es sei notorisch, dass in Böhmen weit mehr Hussiten als Protestanten des Augsburg. und Helvet. Bekenntnisses vorhanden wären." See also Czerwenka, *Gesch. d. Evang. Kirche in Böhmen*, II, 662.

After many foolish blunders, in which Joseph II also shared, a halfway solution was found for this difficulty. In general, the Hussites and Taborites were classed as Protestants and encouraged to become Lutherans. The Israelites were classed as Jews if circumcised; if not, they were persecuted as were the Deists. The dervishes were sent to madhouses. Count Kressel, of the Council of State, in the discussions as to what each sect really was, put the difficulty correctly when he asked about the true principles of faith: "Who has them? The Catholic people? Or the Circle Captain, who understands nothing of the three tolerated religions?" [14] If one should generalize, one would say that Joseph II tolerated the three religions and persecuted the sects as such.

In the next eight years of his reign, Joseph II both extended and curtailed the rights he had given to the tolerated religions. Some of these we shall consider later. In October, 1782, 21,580 people in Bohemia claimed toleration and over 70,000 declared themselves in all the Bohemian, Austrian, and Galician Lands. In 1788, in all these countries there were 156,865 non-Catholics, with 142 pastors, and 154 houses of prayer. One might estimate almost 50,000 non-Catholics in Bohemia in 1790. The policy of the government in regard to the Protestant Churches, their schools and their membership, was that of neutrality. It would not assist, nor would it interfere. Meanwhile, only the Catholic Church received the support of the State. [15]

The promulgation of toleration was one of the great achievements of Joseph II. It was one of his few lasting contributions to the Austrian State. Hand in hand with this went the suppression of monasteries and the further subserviency of the Church to the State. The suppression of monasteries began in the reign of Maria Theresa in Lombardy where their wealth was given to a Commission (*Regio Economato*) to

---

[14] Hock, *ibid.*, 368.
[15] Frank, *Das Toleranz-Patent*, 61-79; G. Wolf, *Josefinna*, pp. 85 ff. See the next section of this chapter. I believe the Estates exaggerated the numbers somewhat. Hock, *ibid.*, 351.

administer.[16] In the spring of 1781 the axe fell in the Habsburg Lands proper. Joseph II had long ago convinced himself that the monasteries "were useless and could not be pleasing to God." [17] They were neither schools, nor hospitals, nor anything else practical and useful; and those were the qualifications necessary in Joseph II's government. In vain, Count Hatzfeld tried to stem the tide. In the course of his reign, Joseph II suppressed 39 monasteries outright, scheduled 14 for reduction, reduced 31, and left 67 in Bohemia.[18] A year later, in 1782, Joseph II created the Central Commission on Religion, on the pattern of the one at Milan, and this body had charge of the branch commissions in the provinces. In general, the wealth these commissions had to administer turned out to be less productive than was expected. Coincident with the suppression of monasteries, the power of Rome was weakened within the Lands of the Habsburgs in another way. In 1775, 157 foreign monasteries exercised either active or formal legal rights over those within the Austrian Monarchy and 24 foreign monasteries had direct influence over the native orders. By the decree of December 22, 1781, Joseph II cut short the delegation and appeal of cases to Rome, and the Pope's visit in the next year failed.[19] In the last years of the reign of Joseph II the Roman Catholic Church sank ever more rapidly because of the lack of priests and the character of those who remained in the clergy.

III

THE QUESTION OF RELIGIOUS TOLERATION IN BOHEMIA BEFORE THE DIET AND THE GOVERNMENT UNDER LEOPOLD II

The central struggle in Bohemia, in questions pertaining to religion under Leopold II, was over the preservation of the

[16] Wolf, *Die Aufhebung der Klöster in Inner Österr., 1782-1790, passim.*
[17] Hock, *ibid.,* 394-409. ". . . ganz und gar nicht nützig sind, nicht Gott gefällig sein können. . . ."
[18] M I Archiv, Carton 513: 104 ex Aprili 1791.
[19] Hock, *ibid.,* 409-486 ff.; Schlitter, *Die Reise des Papstes Pius VI nach Wien und sein Aufenthalt daselbst.* See especially the introduction.

toleration which Joseph II had granted to the non-Catholics. Leopold II was a disciple of Montesquieu and a Jansenist. As such he had agreed with the religious policy of Joseph II in its substance, but not in the manner of its execution. Joseph II was fired with "fanaticism for the welfare of the State" and went to work like a political crusader armed to the teeth. Leopold II, with a calmness unruffled, always coldly polite, took each practical situation as it came up, and solved it with even greater firmness and decision than Joseph II. In some respects Leopold II did not agree with the tendencies of Joseph II's policy. He was opposed to the suppression of the seminaries and the establishment of certain general State seminaries, and he was in favor of giving the bishops greater power as over and against Rome.[10] It was because of these ideas, because of his generally fair attitude even toward his enemies, and because of the leeway that he gave to the reaction, that the Estate of the Clergy hoped for better times under Leopold II, possibly even for the withdrawal of Josephinian toleration.

Vavak, in his memoirs, blamed the sad condition of the Bohemian Catholic Church on work of the Illuminati and the Freemasons.[11] A certain monk, who called himself Josephus Locatelli, wrote a satire on Joseph II's religious policy, which is a classic. In Locatelli's *Babylon Bohemiae ab anno 1780 usque ad annum 1790* and in his *Memorabilia,* which he continued down into the reign of Francis II, are set forth the clergy's view of the reforms of Joseph II and the policy of his successors.[12] It is clear from these writings that, however the young clergy educated by Joseph II may have felt about many of his other reforms, both the young and the old clergy united at least on one question, namely, Josephinian toleration. All of them favored its limitation, if not its suppression.

[10] Huber, *Die Politik Kaiser Josephs II beurtheilt von seinem Bruder, Leopold von Toscana.* See also Reumont, *Geschichte Toscanas,* II, 79-186.
[11] Č N M Archiv, *Vavak Memoirs,* 1790-1791, pp. 79 ff.
[12] Podlaha, *Josephus Locatelli I, Babylon Bohemiae ab anno 1780 usque ad annum 1790.* Editiones archivii etc. Bibliothecas S. F. Metropolitani Capituli Praguensis. The *Memorabilia* is also published in this series.

In the reign of Leopold II there were two movements whose purpose was the restriction of Josephinian toleration. There was an attempt on the part of the bishops of all the Bohemian, Polish, and Austrian Lands, made through a collective plea early in 1790. Later, there were the attempts by the clergy in the various provinces—after the collective failure—to secure at least partial, if not total, withdrawal of toleration on the ground that it was justified by local conditions. In this section the demands of the bishops in their collective plea and of the Bohemian clergy with especial reference to Bohemia will be discussed.

On April 9, 1790, Leopold II allowed the bishops in all the Bohemian, Polish, and Austrian Lands to present their complaints against the Josephinian reforms.[23] The bishops of Hungary worked through the Hungarian Diet; those of Belgium were not in communication with the government, in fact, they were rebels at that time; while those of Lombardy acted separately. The bishops were not united in their desires and showed, by the multitude and character of their complaints, that, although there was much to be remedied, they really had no good ground for the withdrawal of Josephinian toleration. Some of their complaints called for the suppression of the decrees which put their former lands under the Religious Fund (which had been increased by the suppression of the monasteries); others called for the restoration of the right of papal dispensation, for the abolition of the Josephinian code of law on marriage, for the exclusion of the State from matters pertaining to the Church, and finally, for the abolition of the Court Commission and its auxiliary provincial branch commissions on Religion.

Leopold II, however, instead of abolishing the last-named institution, turned over to it the complaints of the bishops. On December 29, 1790, this Commission laid down two principles which were thereafter adhered to in the Austrian

[23] Friedberg, *Die Gränzen zwischen Staat und Kirche und die Garantien gegen deren Verletzung*, 176 ff.

Monarchy: first, that the Catholic Church, its clergy and its wealth, was under the superintendence of the State, i.e. subordinated to it; and second, that the office of the clergy was purely that of pastoral duty, of the celebration of the service of God, and of the administration of the sacraments. In other words, the Commission was Josephinian to the core. The bishops in their complaints had overstepped the boundaries of their rights and of their Estate. According to the Commission, they wished to deprive the sovereign of his rights—few really desired to improve the "true theological education or the pastorate." Some of the bishops, however, were Gallican enough to oppose the taking up of the direct relationship to Rome and to foreign monasteries. Only five, those from Gall, Brixen, Gradisca, the Levant, and Vienna boldly opposed the suppression of the monasteries.

The royal resolution was published on March 17, 1791. Josephinian toleration remained intact: the service of the Catholic Church, as Joseph II had made it, was to stand. The bishops were instructed to agree upon and recommend remedies for various details such as festal days, prayers, and songs. The monasteries would henceforth remain dissolved, but there was to be no further suppression or reduction. The courts were to remain as they were, having jurisdiction in all matters, even those pertaining to clergymen, but the clergy were to be protected from the officials of the local government and of the manors. The Church was warned that if it did not reform its abuses and maintain the good behavior of its officials, the State would take such matters in hand and deal with them vigorously. The tithe, abolished by Joseph II, was restored to the clergy. And finally, the general seminaries were to be abolished.[24]

Having failed in the general attempt to secure the withdrawal of Josephinian reforms, the Estates in the provinces addressed themselves to special attempts to attain their aim locally, arguing that special conditions necessitated extraordi-

[24] See Beidtel-Huber, *Österr. Staats-Verwaltung*, pp. 429-439. The documents may be found in Chmel, "Aktenstücke zur Geschichte des Böhmischen Katholischen Kirchenwesens unter Leopold II" (*AÖG*, 1850, I).

nary measures. In this and also in the next section we shall
trace the most important tendencies of this reaction in Bohemia. In discussing the attitude of the Diet, we shall take up
the manner in which it arrived at its conclusion. The opinion
of the government and the decision of Leopold II will follow
immediately thereafter.

In the first part of our task—to expose the attitude of the
Bohemian Estates on the question of toleration—it will be
necessary to examine the desires of the Estate of the Clergy
and how the Diet acted upon them.

In a memoir [25] which the Estate of the Clergy prepared on
the three headings of the Rescript of May 1, 1790, namely,
taxation and serfdom, the Constitution, and all other complaints, it showed an attitude of conciliation toward the other
Estates, except in questions of religion. The clergy were
willing to leave to the other Estates matters pertaining to the
land tax and to robot. On constitutional questions they took
the stand that the king should be crowned at Prague, that the
Land Ordinance should be reaffirmed because it contained the
essential rights of the Roman Catholic religion, and finally
that a host of minor laws which Joseph II had made on religious questions should be abolished. The substance of this
was repeated in a later, but more important, memoir which
we shall presently discuss.

Although there had been rumblings [26] of a conflict in the
Diet over religious questions, the battle royal of the forces of
intoleration against those of toleration did not begin until
November 20, 1790. Count Henniger, a staunch Catholic,
finally gained the floor and produced a memoir on religion,
which thereafter received the name of the Henniger memoir.[27]
This caused much debate in the Diet and resulted in the com-

[25] Prague, Dom Kapitel, S V Archiv, M. S. 87:1780, Gutachten des geistlichen Standes, Rescript Mai 1, 1790.

[26] See S Archiv, Journal of the Diet, November 6, 8, 13, 17, 1790. See
Č N M Archiv, Sternberg Diary and S V Archiv, Kurze Anmerkungen,
ibid.

[27] Votum des Wenzel Freihern von Henniger im böhm. Landtage dass die
Katholische Religion in jeder Hinsicht die Massgebende sein solle. November 20, 1780. M I Archiv, Carton 513:917 ex Okt. 1791. It was signed by all
the members of the clergy and eleven other members of the Diet.

position by the clergy of a memoir which fully stated their position on all the questions pertaining to religion before the Diet. The assembly pulled itself together by ordering the Executive Committee, after a careful examination of its former report on religious questions, of the Henniger memoir, and of the memoir of the clergy, to report on the basis of a policy. This report was handed in to the Diet on January 19, 1791, and was considered on that day and on January 22, 1791, when the conclusion of the Diet was finally formed.

The Henniger memoir discussed the principles on the basis of which toleration should be restricted. The clergy, however, went into a discussion of the constitutional rights of the Catholic religion, which Josephinian toleration had unconstitutionally changed. The tendency of Henniger's memoir can best be brought out by quoting a few of its most pungent sentences. "Why should Bohemia tolerate the Protestants, when they do not tolerate the Catholics in their countries?" "One thought that the Protestants and the adherents of the Reformed Church would be invited to purchase estates in large number in Bohemia, but none came. On the other hand native children had fallen . . . off from the church . . . therefore toleration in Bohemia had accomplished nothing else but apostasy." Hence, in Bohemia the Catholics should do as the Protestants do where their religion is the dominant one. If not, then "the times of trouble would return, times which one remembers with a shudder here."

The Executive Committee on January 19, 1791,[28] began to report on the memoirs. Taking up first the Henniger memoir, the committee admitted "without the slightest doubt" that the Roman Catholic religion was the "only dominant" religion in Bohemia. But it pointed out that the question really before the Diet was whether in the future one would wish to retain the fundamental principle. It maintained that by the Land Ordinance of 1627 and by the Treaties of Münster and

[28] Č N M Archiv, Sternberg Diary and S V Archiv, Kurze Anmerkungen, January 19, 1791.

Westphalia (1648), the Bohemian monarch had the right to reform (*jus reformandi*) without limitation and thus to change the rights of the Catholic religion at will. The committee was therefore of the opinion that one should no longer discuss what religion had been in the past, "but rather fix his gaze upon the essential conceptions of religion, of the freedom of conscience, and on the contemporary political condition of Bohemia."

The Executive Committee [29] proceeded next to treat the subject from two points of view, in its relation to the individual and in its relation to the State. Under the first, it declared that the faith of the individual was the result of his conviction of his duty toward God. This conviction was not dependent upon the will of others, and therefore could not be subject to any force or compulsion. "Freedom in thinking is one of the earliest [most original] rights of mankind." "Every citizen has, therefore, as his own possession the most holy claim to freedom of thinking, and he must have this freedom all the more where inner conviction alone guides him." Any prohibition, any limitation, on this freedom must cramp his morals. Therefore, "since every citizen has the right to think freely, he must also have the right to fashion his own religious principles, in other words, he must have freedom in faith." Every man who has the freedom to believe should also hâve the right to practice his faith so long as this practice is not harmful to the State or the general welfare. Any compulsion used on his conscience is a cramping of his morals and should not be resorted to. Hence no one should be compelled to believe in a religion against his conviction, and no one should be prevented from being instructed in the principles of the faith of his choice.

As for the relation of religion and its toleration to the State, that was too well known to comment upon. Yet, since the unity and the harmony of all the members of a State

<hr/>

[29] The Report of the Executive Committee can be found under: ex. Deputatione D. D. Statuum Regni Bohemiae, 1790. 22. Dec. Prague, Dom Kapitel, S V Archiv, M. S. 87. Copy in the Z Archiv at Prague.

make the first foundation stone of its strength, there is no source more productive of dissension than religion. So, too, argued the Executive Committee, if security for persons and their property be considered the second foundation stone of the State, it did not really exist if the great mass of its citizens lacked morals. Morals were determined by religion and its principles. Thus everything which injured the character and the sanctity of religion weakened also the morality of the citizens. Too much equality and too much condescension on the part of the State toward all kinds of religions must in the end lower religion in the eyes of those less enlightened, and that would mean a loss of morals.

"That was why," continued the Executive Committee, "the wise government sought to declare one religion dominant among all the others, in order to convince its citizens that religion was one of the most important matters which engaged the attention of the government and to lead them on to unity of faith." And finally, declared the Executive Committee, "The Roman Catholic religion had been declared the dominant one in Bohemia in the past and as such it must be favored. To other religions no such right should be given as would endanger the harmony of the citizens and the unity of the body politic." These were the principles which the Executive Committee declared guided it in its examination of the memoir of the clergy.[30]

The Committee then proceeded to expound this memoir,[31] which went back in Church history to 950 A.D. The clergy declared that from that time down to Ferdinand II (1618-1627) the religion of Bohemia had been Catholic except during the troubles caused by the Hussites. From the time of Ferdinand II it was the only religion allowed by the Constitution, and this a great many diplomas confirmed down to 1749. The enemies of the Catholic religion surrounded Bohemia on all sides. Prussia, the clergy wrote, "is still our enemy, and by

[30] See fn. 29.
[31] Geistliches Votum, M I Archiv, Carton 513:917 ex Oktober 1791.

position and by faith will remain so." Saxony was likewise
and Lusatia followed the example of Saxony. Bayreuth followed Prussia in faith, and all their population was Protestant. The Prussian king had instructed his watch on the Bohemian border in Silesia to look after the Protestants in case
of an outbreak of war. "The toleration which had been introduced into Hungary, Austria, and Poland was not applicable
to Bohemia and Moravia." These countries could not be
brought over to Catholicism, and so toleration existed there.
But Bohemia and Moravia "had accepted Roman Catholicism." The clergy further tried to emphasize two fundamental facts, first, that all the documents, even the Patent of
Toleration, called the Roman Catholic Church "the dominant
religion," and that since the days of Ferdinand II it had not
ceased to be dominant, and second, that the Roman Catholic
religion had remained a part of the Constitution of Bohemia.

Not all of this was correct historically, and at this point the
reading of the memoir of the clergy was interrupted by a
debate. The Executive Committee frankly declared that it
did not wish to abolish toleration, but desired rather to see it
somewhat restricted. "Bishop Krieger rose up and made
many indignant remarks," and asserted that all that the
Executive Committee had said was full of sophistry. He
thought that as every member had a right to express his own
opinion on the report, the Estate of the Clergy should not
neglect to prepare one. Count Nostic remarked that the
"peace" in Bohemia before the Patent of Toleration was
issued, was "a peace regulated by inquisition." "Tyranny and
sacrilege were the results of the compulsion used against the
Protestants." [32] Before anyone in the Diet realized it, the
assembly faced its most critical decision in questions on religion. The Diet sided with the Executive Committee on the
question whether the monarch had the right to reform the
Constitution and therefore the religion. Count Buquoy,
Baron MacNeven, and Count Štampach took especial pains to

[32] Č N M Archiv, Sternberg Diary, January 19, 1791.

point out to Count Adolph Kaunitz that the Treaty of Westphalia had expressly reserved the *jus reformandi* to the House
of Austria in its hereditary Lands. The Diet thereupon voted
on the great question as to whether the Roman Catholic religion should be the "one and only religion in Bohemia" as in
the time of Charles IV and of Ferdinand II. The result was
in the negative. The Patent of Toleration was saved so far
as the Diet was concerned. "Short Comments" (*Kurze
Anmerkungen*), a diary kept during the sessions of the Bohemian Diet, expressly states that the Diet voted against the
abolition of the Patent of Toleration for a very important
reason. "It was defeated by all the three secular Estates,
because they feared a revolution in Bohemia if the Patent
of Toleration were abolished."[33] Nevertheless, the Diet accepted the statement that the Roman Catholic religion should
be the dominant religion.

The forces of toleration and intolerance fought next over the
manner in which toleration was to be limited. The questions
were divided into two parts. In the first part, were considered
questions relating (1) to the cemeteries; (2) to the oath;
(3) to the censorship; (4) to the baptism of Jewish children
under eighteen years of age; and (5) to the conversion of the
children of non-Catholics. It will be seen that the rights were
those which pertained to religion in its relation to the individual. The second part pertained to the relation of the religion
of the non-Catholics to the State. There was (1) the *inkolat*
or right of citizenship; (2) the right of owning property; (3)
admission to public office; and (4) attendance in the universities and the public schools.[34] Thus part one dealt with the
individual, part two, more with the State; part one was social,
part two, political. We shall now discuss each one of the
proposed limitations on Josephinian toleration.

[33] S V Archiv, Kurze Anmerkungen, January 19, 1791 . . . "wurde durch
die Mehrheit der Stimmen, ja von allen drei weltlichen Ständen verworfen,
weilen eine erwiderte Revolution in Lande, falls das Toleranz-Gesetz aufgehoben sein sollte. zu befürchten ist."

[34] Z Archiv, Ex Deputatione. December 22, 1790.

In the first part, the kernel of the question with regard to the cemeteries was whether the Catholics would permit the non-Catholics to be buried in the same cemetery with Catholics. The Executive Committee favored no change in the Josephinian law which allowed common burial places. Bishop Krieger was for "absolute segregation at death, if they could not be separated in life." The Prelate Herites remarked that common burial grounds awakened religious animosity. Archdeacon von Bubna indulged in dogma to prove that a heretic should not be permitted to share in the sanctified cemeteries. The Abbott of Osseck advised the segregation, "not as a clergyman, but as a Catholic and a citizen." Count Nostic asked if a dead heretic should be denied a place in the cemetery seeing that while alive his admission to the Church had never been closed to him. Count Buquoy, one of the warmest friends of toleration, thought that segregation of cemeteries stretched "the domination of the Catholic religion" too far. Thereupon Bishop Krieger arose and declared that they would have to make new canon law. "All the better," was the reply from all sides. Count Kolovrat Libsteinský pointed to the example of Bishop Hay, of Königgrätz, whose tolerant behavior united all the opinions of his diocese and even brought back into the fold those who had wandered from the path of the faith. The Diet agreed with the Executive Committee that Josephinian legislation on this point was satisfactory. Protestants and Catholics might bury their dead in the same cemeteries if they chose.[35]

On the second question—that of the oath—the Executive Committee recommended that the old Catholic oath be restored for the Catholics, but advised against an oath which it would be impossible for the non-Catholics to take. The Diet accepted this also.

On the third question—that of the censorship of books— the Executive Committee took the stand that it was better to

[35] See Č N M Archiv, Sternberg Diary, January 19, 1791; Z Archiv, Ex Deputatione, Dec. 22, 1790.

have non-Catholic books printed in Bohemia rather than elsewhere. It would prevent a great deal of smuggling and the
country would not lose money to foreign countries through
their purchase. The name of the author was to be inserted
on the title page and due protection from unjust attacks was
to be given the Catholic religion. On this point, the Committee and the Diet accepted many of the clergy's propositions.

On the fourth and the fifth questions—the conversion of
non-Catholic children—a lively debate ensued. The clergy
considered it insulting to the Roman Catholic Church to
allow non-Catholics to perform the rites of christening and
burial of their children. The Executive Committee rejected
the memoir of the clergy here. The Diet stood by the Executive Committee, but allowed the Catholic Church to have
the right to judge when a Jewish child was old enough to be
baptized.[36]

Just as the memoir of the clergy on this first part was
being read, Count Taaffe interrupted the reader as he was
quoting from the Land Ordinance of Ferdinand II, A23. The
memoir misquoted the article in favor of its argument. The
actual text of the article was read before the Diet, and no
word could be found there on toleration. Count Taaffe then
asked "what could one expect from people who were not
ashamed to make use of such means." Baron MacNeven was
willing to forgive them—they had mixed up their comments
with their citations. After various altercations, it was decided
to correct the memoir of the clergy. Count Francis Anton
Kolovrat called for unity—not for words—and urged the
members of the Diet to strive for the common welfare, to
seek for harmony. "And to speak the truth," added Count
Taaffe.[37] When Counts Sweerts and Lanjus interrogated the
Executive Committee on how it could have passed over this
and other blunders in the memoir of the clergy, Baron Mac-
Neven, as spokesman for the Executive Committee, remarked

[36] Fn. 35. See also S V Archiv, Kurze Anmerkungen, Jan. 19, 1791.
[37] Č N M Archiv, Sternberg, Diary, Jan. 19, 1791.

that they had been of the opinion of departing entirely from the memoir and of making no use of it at all. Count O'Kelley ventured to remark that all heresies originated from false citations and that this incident was a most blameworthy one. And so the majority of the Diet was in favor of disregarding the memoir—neither to support, nor to oppose it—on questions coming under the first part.

Then came the discussion on the second part of the questions relating to toleration, namely, those which pertained to the State. The first question was that of the citizenship of non-Catholics in Bohemia. The memoir of the clergy asked that non-Catholics be excluded from the rights of citizenship (the *inkolat*), which had been opened to them by the legislation of October 13, 1781, and August 11, 1783. They advised that non-Catholics be given only the right of "transient guests." The Executive Committee, following the principles it had laid down at the start, accepted the opinion of the clergy. In this, many of those who had opposed the memoir of the Clergy, now supported it. Count Nostic stood by the Executive Committee, "because for one artisan who would come into Bohemia, one hundred useless beings would enter at the same time." Count Francis Kolovrat appealed to the assembly to be unified—"out of love for harmony"—although he knew that it was distasteful to manufacturers. If a fourth of the population of Bohemia, he argued, were non-Catholic, then he would speak differently, but non-Catholics were still small in numbers and uniformity could easily be maintained. Counts Taaffe and Hartmann declared themselves for the rights of the non-Catholics. They wished to see them enjoy full rights of citizenship.[38]

The Diet agreed with the Executive Committee and therefore the clergy won completely on this point. Count Buquoy and Baron MacNeven secured a minority vote in which they opposed the decision of the Diet.[39] To give non-Catholics only

[38] M I Archiv, Carton 513, 917 ex Oktober 1791.
[39] Separates Gutachten der Ausschussbesitzer, Grafen von Buquoy und Freiherrn MacNeven. Prague, Dom Kapitel, S V Archiv, M. S. 87.

the right of transit was to bring insecurity into their daily lives, to weaken their duty and fidelity to the State, and finally to set up a state within a state. The conclusion of the Diet was hostile to any immigration into Bohemia which might benefit Bohemian commerce and industry.

The second question in part two—the right of non-Catholics to own real estate—was likewise a thorny one. The clergy wished to declare the non-Catholics incapable of acquiring property in land. The Executive Committee, excepting Count Buquoy and Baron MacNeven, agreed in principle with the clergy, but wished to allow non-Catholics to hold real mortgages and to buy estates in Prague, subject to the condition that they later sell them back. Buquoy and MacNeven declared that such a conclusion would decrease the amount of money in the State. It would be a real danger, also, because foreign money would then control estates without the holders of the mortgage having the right to become members of the Estates. Baron Henniger wondered that "one defended the non-Catholics so zealously." Count Kolovrat Libsteinský assured him that he, meaning himself, "defended the rights of man . . . as for him, he thought it was just as little to be feared that toleration would turn Bohemia into a Protestant country as that toleration would make the Catholic religion dominant in Prussia." The Diet accepted the opinion of the Executive Committee and therefore of the Estate of the Clergy, while Count Buquoy and several others reserved the right to hand in a dissenting opinion.[40]

The third question—that of the eligibility of non-Catholics to public office—was taken up next. The clergy did not wish to tolerate non-Catholics in public office and demanded that the oath required by Maria Theresa be restored. This would automatically make it impossible for non-Catholics to attain to public office. The Executive Committee agreed with the clergy and even Count Buquoy and Baron MacNeven did likewise. Only Count Hochenrein did not want to see the

[40] Č N M Archiv, Sternberg Diary, Jan. 17, 1791. Z Archiv, Ex Deputatione, December 22, 1791; M I Archiv, Carton 513, 917 ex Oktober 1791. Geistliches Votum.

non-Catholics treated worse than the Jews, who could be lawyers and "lawyers had public influence."

And finally, the discussion came to the fifth and last question in part two—the relation of the non-Catholics to the school system. The clergy wished to exclude non-Catholics from teaching in any schools whatsoever, from the University, the gymnasia, the academies, and the elementary schools. They desired also to prevent non-Catholics from matriculating at the University of Prague and to deprive them of access to stipends. The clergy were especially indignant over this question. Bishop Krieger declared that one should not give the non-Catholics influence. A professor had great influence. Prelate Herites remarked that one's whole life depended "on the way in which his soul was led in youthful years." The Abbot of Osseck was inclined to look at the professor as a holder of a public office. Count Nostic remarked that jurisprudence, medicine, and philosophy each had their own field and nothing in common with religion. According to Count Francis Kolovrat the University of Prague never had "a lack of good Catholic heads." [41]

Count Henniger bewailed the fate of the seven-century-old University. But Count Kolovrat Libsteinský brought forth examples showing that there had been Protestant professors at Prague University and Catholic professors at Protestant universities. This silenced Count Henniger. Baron MacNeven in commenting upon the influence of the professor remarked that it was less than that of a village justice. He cited the case of Professor Meidner. "Catholics and non-Catholics," he continued, "can only have a moral philosophy, a teaching. Luther and St. Thomas alike understood Cicero." Count O'Kelley hoped that the Estates would not make themselves ridiculous by changing a conclusion they had already taken in another part of their Desideria. [42] The Diet stood by the Executive Committee and allowed the plea of the clergy only in the case of professors of theology.

Having been unwilling to give the non-Catholics the right

[41] *Ibid.,* January 22; rest same as fn. 40. [42] *Ibid.*

of citizenship, of landowning, and of holding public office, the Diet naturally refused to give them the right to sit and vote in that assembly. Count Buquoy handed in his dissenting vote on this question also.

When the question of what should be done with the Jews came up, the clergy presented a whole string of limitations which, if accepted, would have restored the relations of the Jews to the rest of the community and to the State as in the days of Maria Theresa. To the clergy the Jews were the "Treasury Knaves" (*Kameralknechte*). They had always been under the protection of the monarch through the payment of certain fees into the royal coffers and they were subjects of his special protection. The clergy argued that the Jews were in Bohemia "only on grace." In 1745 Maria Theresa had expelled them, but in 1748 she had received them back (*jure placitum*), and since that time they had again become "knaves." But Joseph II, in a series of decrees beginning with October 19, 1781, had changed their legal position. All the schools were opened to them. The stipends were allowed to the Jews. Their special dress was discarded and they were given permission to live outside the Jewish quarter. The Bohemian Diet, whose hatred of the Jews was strong, pointed to their increased numbers and their moral behavior. Concretely, the Diet asked that the sale of the houses of Christians and of other real property should remain forbidden to the Jews "because they would in a very short while drive the Christians out of all property owning." [43]

Unsatisfied with this harvest the Bohemian clergy took to writing further memoirs. Bishop Schulstein in his memoir entitled "A Supplement to show that the Edict of Toleration of June 30 and October 31, 1781, has not accomplished its true Aim," [44] took the ground that Joseph II's reason for granting toleration was to invite Protestant mechanics, handiworkers, and business men to Bohemia to improve industry.

[43] M I Archiv, Carton 513, 917 ex Oktober 1791. Geistliches Votum.
[44] Beilage zum Beweise dass das Toleranz-Gesetz vom 30ten Juny und 31ten Oktober 1781 in Böhmen seine wahre Absicht nicht erreicht habe. M I Archiv, Carton 513, 917 ex Okt. 1791.

He had not accomplished his aim, contended Bishop Schulstein. Instead of making one religion out of three or four,
Joseph II had been obliged to use the knout (*karabač*) on the
sectarians. There were, according to the bishop, 60,000 avowed
non-Catholics and 10,000 more under suspicion. The children
of good Catholics were abandoning the faith of their fathers.
And finally, the nine years of toleration, instead of bringing
factories and money into Bohemia, "had brought loads of
pamphlets on religion to mislead the faithful."

The Archdeacon von Bubna[45] in a memoir entitled, "Promemoria for the Catholic Religion in the Kingdom of Bohemia," took much the same ground. "How happy was the
State," he wrote, "where Church and State were one, where
all was unity? Could the slight advantages from commerce
and industry to be derived from the Protestants offset religious unity?" For about a half-million florins yearly—the estimated gain from the Protestant colonists—law and property
were made insecure and one was forced to listen to "French
or even English zealots preaching on their respective constitutions." He then asked, "when was Bohemia happiest? Under the intolerant, but great Emperor Charles VI or under
Václav II (Wenzel-James) and his successors down to Ferdinand II?" Already 6 out of every 300 were Protestants in
Bohemia. Why should 294 suffer for the sake of 6? There
was no doubt where either Schulstein or Bubna stood on
the question of toleration, yet they were of different nationalities and bred in different atmospheres. Schulstein was
a German, young in comparison with the other bishops, and,
so to speak, trained by Joseph II. Bubna was a Czech,
grown old in his profession. He had risen slowly and had all
the conservative ideas of his Estate. Yet both agreed perfectly on the question of toleration. In reality they wished to
see toleration withdrawn, although openly they said they
wished to see it limited only.

We see therefore that the clergy wished to take away all

---

[45] Von Bubna: Pro Memoria für die Katholische Religion im K. Böhmen.
Prague, Dom Kapitel, S V Archiv, M. S. 87.

the political and all the public rights of the non-Catholics. They wished to allow them only the right of transient guests. By such devices they would have made the Patent on Toleration only a dead letter on the statute books. The Bohemian Diet on the other hand, was willing to allow non-Catholics to retain many of the private rights which Joseph II had given them, but none of the political rights. Some men in the Diet, however, were willing to give them all the rights which Joseph II had given them—men like Count Buquoy and Baron MacNeven. Both the clergy and the Diet were opposed to further Protestant colonization.[46]

We shall now discuss the attitude of the government on these questions of toleration.

The Gubernium[47] declared it was of no use to enter into so far fetched or extended a discussion on the general principles of toleration as the Estates had done in their memoirs. The gist of the matter was: "whether the toleration of religion as it has been introduced, should remain so, or if not, how should it be restricted?" The Gubernium asserted that the demands of the Estates did not harmonize with the aims of Christianity. The Christian religion taught the greatest possible toleration and "is entirely without any spirit of domination." On the behest of the Gubernium, Joseph Anton Riegger, the best scholar in the Council, wrote a paper to show the character of the Christian religion. He pointed out that the life of Christ was one of forbearance, of patience, and of teaching. He was tolerant to Jews, Samaritans, to heathen, to all living men with whom he came in contact. "Blessed are the peace-loving [the tolerant], for they shall be called the children of God," was one of His most famous sayings. "The whole Christian religion is the most complete system of love

[46] Stände an den König. 22 Jan. 1791. M I Archiv, Carton 513.
[47] Gubernium Opinion: Bericht des böhmischen Landes-Guberniums der von den Ständen umher übergebene Bericht an S. M. wegen Bestimmung engerer Gränzen bei der hierlands bestehenden Toleranz, wird gutächtlich einbegleitet. Beilage A. Abgesonderte Meinung Gub. Räthe MacNeven und Wenzel Cavriani; B. Riegger: Religion. M I Archiv, Carton 513.

of mankind, of unlimited toleration." The Gubernium remarked further that, thanks to Joseph II, who knew the true
foundation of Christianity, intolerance, the inquisition of
heretics, and the spirit of persecution and "brotherly hatred"
were banished. If Joseph II had done nothing else than this,
that would have been enough. In answer to the Diet's plea
for unity, the Gubernium declared that experience had taught
that in Bohemia, when unmolested, the non-Catholics were
as obedient as other citizens.

The Commission on Desideria, in its sessions on July 2 and
23, 1791, defended toleration. "To reverse it would not be
practicable" it was argued.[48] The State Council raised no
voice against toleration. On October 21, 1791, Leopold II
wrote out his decision to the Gubernium. Any abrupt change
in toleration during the critical times in which they lived, ran
the opinion, was not practicable in the least, especially since
it was against the known "voice" of the people. As in all
other provinces, so in Bohemia, toleration would remain as
it was. This decision settled the matter of toleration for
Bohemia and saved one of Joseph II's chief labors. The
other decisions followed in quick order.

In the first question—on the oath—the Gubernium defended the Josephinian formula because it called upon "God
alone" and did not savor of "paganism," as did the other. In
pagan times, "one swore not by God, but by gods" they
argued. The Gubernium decided against the plea of the
Estates for the restoration of the old oath of Maria Theresa,
and the Commission on Desideria agreed with it. Leopold II
staunchly stood by the Gubernium and would not allow a
change to take place.

The Gubernium opposed the Estates flatly on the question
of censorship of books. To give the Ordinariate the right to
examine books on theology and dogma would increase the

[48] Zur Sitzung vom 21. Oktober 1791. M I Archiv, Carton 513, 917 in Okt.
1791. See also H H S Archiv, Staatsrat Akten, 3522 and 3523 in 1791.

friction between them and the theological faculty. The Court Chancellery advised that the Ordinariate be consulted, but that the government reserve the final decision to itself. Leopold II decided to call upon that body to present to the king its reasons why any certain book should not be published.

The Commission on Desideria thought that Jewish children under eighteen years of age might be converted in Bohemia. Leopold II ruled that he would allow political officials of the province to give dispensations in the case of such Jewish children over fourteen years of age, where there were important reasons for so doing. All other cases would come under the eighteen-year rule or would go to him directly.

Next came the political aspects of toleration. The Gubernium declared that, when the Diet refused to give non-Catholics the right of citizenship (the *inkolat*), or to allow them to hold land, or to attain to public office, or to sit and vote in the Diet, it left only "the empty name of toleration." Non-Catholics would, on such terms, always be strangers in the State. "They would remain wanderers, and never have the love of a fatherland in their hearts." The times of the "unhappy hatred" of Ferdinand II were past. "They would never return so long as enlightenment and toleration dominated." The Gubernium took the stand that non-Catholics should be allowed to become full citizens, to own property, to hold public office, to sit and vote in the Diet, and to become teachers. It was not enough to cease persecuting them. They were to be given the means to become peaceful, faithful, and patriotic inhabitants just like the Catholics. The Jews were to be included in the number of citizens and to have all the rights of the others.

In turn the Commission on Desideria, the Chancellery, and the State Council backed up the position of the Gubernium, using the identical arguments. Leopold II stood by the offices of the government and thus saved the work of toleration. The Bohemian clergy had desired to destroy it wholly; the Diet would destroy it so far as it referred to political matters. But the government declared for its complete retention in the form in which Joseph II had left it.[49]

IV

OTHER RELIGIOUS QUESTIONS

Besides toleration, there were other questions pertaining to religion, directly or indirectly.[50] Practically all of these come under the head of matters pertaining to the clergy as an Estate, such as, for instance, the suppression of the monasteries, the decrease in the number of clergy in the Diet owing to this suppression, acceptance into the orders, the administration of their capital, etc.

The first of these questions—that of the suppression of the monasteries and the consequent decrease in the Estate of the Clergy brought out detail which would only confuse us here. The Diet asked for the restoration of eight monasteries and four convents which formerly had seats in the Bohemian Diet.

The Gubernium[51] in discussing the restoration of these monasteries questioned whether the restoration would give the Estate of the Clergy any advantage. Only superfluous monasteries had been reduced. True, out of 154 monasteries and convents belonging to 25 orders over one-fourth had been suppressed and another fourth either reduced or designated for reduction. The Dominicans had lost 15, the Capuchins 19, the Piarists 13. But should they be restored—and the Gubernium staunchly opposed it—the Estate of the Clergy, even with its increased number, would derive no advantage from it. Just at that time—contended the Gubernium with much truth—the voting in the Diet was by individuals (*vota*

[49] See in turn Gubernium Opinion, M I Archiv, Carton 513; 917 in Okt. 1791 *ibid.*; and H H S Archiv, Staatsrat Akten, 3522 and 3523 in 1791. In some of these the Protokoll der Konferenz, 2, 23, Julius, 1791, M I Archiv, Carton 519 will be of use.

[50] Third Desideria: An seine M. Bericht d. geh. böhm. Stände mit den Vorstellungen über die im dritten Absatze des Reskripts vom 1ten Mai . . . Gegenstände. Nov. 27, 1790, M I Archiv, Carton 519:936 ex Okt. 1791.

[51] Gubernium Bericht, Feb. 18, 1791. M I Archiv, Carton 520.

viritim), and not by Estates (*vota curiata*). The nobles were always far more numerous. It was therefore of no consequence whether the clergy were seven or seventeen strong when it came to balloting. And when voting was by colleges, then it did not matter if the clergy had one representative or twenty or thirty. The Gubernium also pointed out that if the Estate of the Clergy were increased, then that of the knights should also be increased. Nor could that Council give the Estate of the Clergy its assurance that in the future no more suppressions or reductions would take place.

The Commission on Desideria in its sessions of July 23 and 26, 1791, suggested that the number of the clergy in the Diet could be increased by allowing to enter the Diet those deans who owned landed property.[52]

Leopold II, in the Decree of October 28, 1791,[53] frankly declared against the restoration of those monasteries which had been suppressed. Such monasteries, however, as had not been designated for reduction were to be assured permanence. He agreed also that the Estate of the Clergy might hope for an increase in its membership through the admittance of landowning deans or priors.

In another complaint, the Estate of the Clergy charged the government with putting obstructions in the way of those who wished to become members of the orders.[54] The clergy complained that they lost too many candidates because, by the regulations of March 30 and October 24, 1783, Joseph II had decreed that no one should be accepted into the orders who had not completed his studies and also the practice required of a priest in the general seminaries. By further decrees the numbers in certain monasteries had been limited. The Estate of the Clergy asked that the orders be allowed to accept secular candidates before the completion of their theological studies

[52] Protokoll der Konferenz, 23-26 July 1791, M I Archiv, Carton 519.
[53] Decree, October 28, 1791, M I Archiv, Carton 519 ad 936 ex Okt. 1791.
[54] Third Desideria, M I Archiv, Carton 519; 936 ex Okt. 1791: Die bestehenden Hindernisse in Aufnahme der Ordenskandidaten zu mendiren die Gnade haben. Beschwerde X.

and to permit them to continue their studies in the monasteries. It was a plea to save the fast diminishing numbers of the clergy and the monks.

The Gubernium remarked that the abolition of the general seminaries by Leopold II, as a result of the petition of the bishops, covered what the Estate of the Clergy really wanted here. The Court Commission on Religion would agree to allow the student candidates to enter the monasteries if these institutions were equipped with suitable teachers. Leopold II accepted this qualification.

In another grievance the Estate of the Clergy complained that many of their estates had been taken out of their hands to be administered by the government. The same was true of the woods belonging to many of the monasteries. The Gubernium could not agree with this, and the Court Commission on Religion hinted that the government had taken over the management of some estates because the clergy had mismanaged them. Leopold II ruled that in such cases the government should properly turn over the income of the lands. The Estate of the Clergy, however, might not claim any properties which had belonged to the suppressed monasteries and which were being administered for the benefit of the religious fund. In the case of the woods, the king ruled that they be returned to the clergy.

Two other questions remained. The first was the government's use of monastery and church funds at the low rates of 3 1/2 and 4 per cent interest. The Estate of the Clergy, as well as all the other Estates, complained against this. The funds had been drawn into the public treasury and deprived of the opportunity to get a higher rate of interest as well as chances for better investment. The Gubernium proposed that such capital should be allowed freedom of investment in mortgages on private property where covered by twice the value of unencumbered property. Leopold II ruled that this provision should be introduced into all the provinces, not in Bohemia alone. And second, the Estate of the Clergy asked that the right of patronate be established as it was in the time of Maria Theresa. The government refused to allow this, holding that the Ordinariate might suggest the candidates after they had passed their examinations but that the patron could always choose from among them the candidate whom he thought best.[55]

That religious toleration was saved from the clerical reaction in Bohemia was due to the firm stand of Leopold II. The Bohemian clergy wished to destroy Josephinian toleration. They might have condescended to leave a provision stating that non-Catholics who had already declared themselves, should be tolerated as transients. All others were to be regarded as Catholics and prevented from becoming non-Catholics. The Diet, by a majority consisting of the three Estates: the nobility, the knights, and the city Estate, "in fear of a revolution," voted to keep religious toleration so far as it had to do with the individual. But it wished, for the sake of political unity, and in order to prevent dissension, to take away the political rights which Joseph II had given to non-Catholics. The government refused to give way to these demands. It preserved Josephinian toleration just as that unhappy monarch had left it. Only here and there in its more crying innovations and actual mistakes was it repaired.

In all this we see the strange contradictions that dominate the history of Bohemia. The Habsburg dynasty in the Thirty Years' War had almost destroyed that country in order to convert it to the most extreme type of Catholicism. At that time the Bohemian Estates had upheld religious toleration. In the Eighteenth Century their respective positions were reversed. In 1790 the Estates attacked toleration and the government defended it. The Habsburg Monarchy, too late, was trying to atone for what it had done in the days of White Mountain.

And yet the clergy, the Estates, and the government were

[55] See fn. 52-54 and Gubernium Bericht, Feb. 18, 1791. M I Archiv, Carton 520.

on much better terms in 1792 than they had been at any time since the accession of Joseph II. Leopold II had proved to the clergy that they had nothing to fear from Josephinian toleration so long as they represented the true interests of the dominant religion and remained subservient to the State.

CHAPTER XI

THE SCHOOL SYSTEM, GERMANIZATION, AND THE CZECH REVIVAL

I

THE SYSTEM OF EDUCATION AND THE PROGRESS OF GERMANIZATION

IT was a great misfortune for the Czechs that the entire system of education should have been reformed at a time when their language and culture was weakest and the Eighteenth-Century spirit of political centralization and of Germanization strongest.

It is not our purpose here to go into the details of the system of education, nor to trace minutely its development. Our purpose is rather to point out the main tendencies of the new reforming spirit of the absolute monarchy in the Eighteenth Century and to describe the reaction under Leopold II. Incidentally, we shall touch very briefly upon the creation of the schools of the Counter Reformation after the Battle of White Mountain (1620), upon the decline of the Czech language and culture, upon the new educational system of Maria Theresa and Joseph II and their efforts to Germanize, and upon the beginnings of the Czech revival and of the reaction under Leopold II.

In education, as in all other activities of life, the loss of the Battle of White Mountain in 1620 by the Estates produced profound results. Under Charles IV (1346-1378) and Václav IV (Wenzel IV-James IV) (1378-1419) a well-developed system of education patterned mostly on the French ideas of the Luxemburgs had been created. The Rector of the

University of Prague was the superintendent of the entire school system. The Hussite Wars interrupted this splendid development, and it was not until the time of Rudolph II (1576-1612) that the system attained its former standards. The University at that time looked after 101 smaller and larger schools in Bohemia and 5 in Moravia. But the Catholics and the Bohemian Brethren refused to obey the Hussite University.[1] After the Battle of White Mountain (1620), the entire school system was turned over to the Catholic Church and put into the hands of the Jesuits and the Piarists. The Jesuits took care of the University and of the secondary schools, the Piarists for the most part confined their attention to the elementary schools. In place of toleration, came intoleration; in place of the free French spirit, the cold Roman spirit of the Counter Reformation.[2] In the upper schools instruction was in Latin, in the lower schools in Czech, for the most part; there was no effort at Germanization until the great reforms of the Eighteenth Century.

During the century and a half in which the Jesuits controlled the system of education in Bohemia two aims were never lost from view. They aimed to educate the young man for the priesthood and to teach good morals. This teaching was accompanied by the religious persecution explained in the preceding chapter. At the end of that period the spirit of the Counter Reformation had greatly degenerated.[3]

The Habsburg universities were falling behind the universities of Western Europe, a fact which scholars and government officials alike recognized. "The sciences were in the hands of the Jesuits; in theology, scholasticism and casuistry dominated; and in philosophy, the peripatetic philosophy was

[1] Tomek, "Paměti o školách českých z rektorských let m. Martina Bachačka, 1598-1612" (ČMČ, 1845, 370-97, 604-40); Helfert, Die Gründung der österreichischen Volksschule durch Maria Theresia, pp. 49-50; and Egger, Die Reform der österreichischen Volksschule unter Maria Theresia, 5 ff.

[2] Helfert, Volksschule, 41 ff.; Denis, La Bohême depuis la Montagne Blanche, I, 500 ff.; Kroess, Geschichte der böhmischen Provinz der Gesellschaft Jesu, II, 1, pp. 10 ff.; ibid., (Hist. Jahrbuch, XXXIV, I, p. 2 ff.) and the works of Snopek, Borovička, and Schlenz cited in the bibliography.

[3] Ibid.

about one hundred years behind the times." "Higher mathematics was regarded as a monopoly; medicine and law had been reduced to 'bread-making' professions; critical history, natural sciences and history, as well as all sciences, which were calculated to make enlightenment general and to combat prejudice were neglected or wholly unknown; and to perpetuate the despotism over the intellect, there existed a censorship which surpassed that of Rome, and which closed up the entrance to all the sources of better knowledge and forbade every work of good calling to everyone without distinction."[4] This contemporary analysis was doubtless overdrawn, but it is illuminating. Such was the atmosphere of the upper schools.

In the lower schools, young and old children mingled together. The teaching was mechanical. Religious instruction became pure memory work in which a few stock questions were asked. The average of scholarship was extremely low, and there was no compulsory education—in fact, the whole system of the Jesuits and the Piarists had degenerated. And what was worse, in addition to a decayed system of education, there was the decline of the Czech language and culture and the increasing burdens of robot which were heaped upon the Bohemian serf after the Battle of White Mountain. The Jesuits had destroyed the rich Hussite literature by consigning it to flames. But they themselves produced no Catholic Czech literature that was worth while. Unable to take care of the increased demands of the lord for robot, the Bohemian peasant was forced to send his child into the fields in order to render the robot. And so the course of events tended to make the Hussites, who had surprised Europe by their prowess and independence, knaves and cripples, physically, intellectually, and morally.[5]

[4] Wolf, *Das Unterrichtswesen in Österreich unter Kaiser Joseph II* (Report of Joseph V. Sonnenfels of 1785), pp. 5-6.
[5] M I Archiv, Carton 449: IV A 8: 219: Protokollen commissiones habita die 17. Sept. 1771; Über den Hofkriegsräthe: Vortrag über die in dem K. Böheim vollendeter Seelen- und Zugviehs-Conscription.

Naturally little could be done with such a system until the Order of the Jesuits had been dissolved. Gerhard Van Swieten, who had been called to Vienna from the Austrian Netherlands in 1745 and who really became the founder of the new system of higher education, i.e. the universities, died a year before the Order of the Jesuits was dissolved in 1773. He had rehabilitated the Austrian universities.[6] After the dissolution of the Order of the Jesuits the entire school system consisting of the universities, the gymnasia, and the elementary schools was reorganized and given the new program of enlightened despotism.

Space forbids our entering into the details of this reorganization. The idea of Van Swieten, that the schools should be separated from the Church and be made scientific and useful to the State, was carried out conscientiously. Specialists were called to lecture in the universities, and under Joseph II tuition fees were introduced in order to cut down the number of students. In 1774-1776 the gymnasia were reformed after a plan formulated by the Piarist, Max Gratian. Latin and Greek, Algebra and Geometry, General and National History, and the Natural Sciences were included in this plan, which was improved under Joseph II. Under that sovereign a tuition of 12 florins yearly was introduced for students in the gymnasia.[7] To Maria Theresa belongs the honor of founding the Austrian public school. When she came to introduce it in Bohemia she made use of a native movement for the reform of the lower schools, initiated by Joseph Sembdera at Friedland and by Ferdinand Kindermann at Kaplice (Kaplitz) at the very beginning of the seventies of the Eighteenth Century. The former had been sent by Father Scholz to inquire into the Felbiger art of instruction at the Sagan schools in Prussian Silesia, the latter had come in personal contact with

---

[6] Kink, *Geschichte der kaiserlichen Universität zu Wien*, I, 432 ff. Volume II contains documents which are of considerable value for the history of higher education in the Lands of the Habsburgs. For Bohemia see Tomek, *Geschichte der Prager Universität* (Also in Czech), but it is a less useful work.
[7] See fn. 4 and 6.

Felbiger, Benedict-Strauch, and Joseph Kautschke, all noted teachers of the Eighteenth Century. Soon this movement was taken up independently everywhere in Bohemia, even without the encouragement of the State, which did not come until 1775.[8] After that, it was guided by the Commission for Schools created by Maria Theresa. In 1775 the Prague Normal School was opened as a model school for the elementary institutions of Bohemia, and a school fund was created.

Cities and villages, noblemen and peasants, the clergy and the military, all vied with one another to aid schools for the masses.[9] Ferdinand Kindermann, later Bishop Schulstein of Litoměřice (Leitmeritz) and superintendent of the schools of Bohemia, became interested in the introduction of industrial and trades schools, after the example of Professor Sextroh of Göttingen and Joachim Henry Camp of Hamburg.[10] The outcome of the situation was that Bohemian schools became superior even to those in Austria and far ahead of those in Hungary. The government recognized this and employed Czech teachers to instruct the Slavic population in Galicia and in the military border lands in the south.[11]

The results obtained by this reforming activity were remarkable. It was the aim of Joseph II to increase the attendance in the lower schools and to decrease the attendance in the higher schools. In 1781, out of 776,000 children of school age in the Bohemian and Austrian Lands, 208,580 were attending school. Upon the introduction of school tuition there was a marked

[8] Kindermann, *Nachricht von der Landschule zu Kaplitz in Böhmen.* Unter dem Schutze Sr. Excellenz des Herrn Grafen von Buquoi. (2nd ed. 1774); Šafránek, "O Josefinském popise škol v království českém" (*VČSN,* 1902) and *ibid.,* "Pravda o školách v království českém za vrchní zpravy Kindermannovy" (*Osvěta,* 1907, I); Helfert, *Volkschule,* 179 ff.

[9] Helfert, *Volkschule,* 175 ff.; 413-415. See also Weiss, *Geschichte der Theresianischen Schulreform in Böhmen,* I, ix-xix.

[10] Riegger, *Archiv für Geschichte und Statistik insbesondere von Böhmen,* contains: "Kurze Beschreibung des Probsten v. Schulsteins, von der Entstehung und Verbreitungs-Art der Industrialklassen in den Volksschulen des Königreichs Böhmen." His memoir (1790) contains many hints on the value he put on industrial education: Unmassgebige Gedanken über den Mangel der Industrie und des Kommerzes im Königreiche Böhmen und einige Mittel demselben abzuhelfen. M I Archiv, Carton 516: 208. See also Chapter VII.

[11] Helfert, *Volksschule,* 459-468.

decrease in the number of those who attended the gymnasia. In 1785-1786 the number of such students fell off 25 per cent. In 1787 there were only 6,530 students in the gymnasia of the Bohemian and Austrian Lands as against 9,377 in 1781. In 1786, we know that there were 2,219 common schools in Bohemia and that they had a total attendance of 142,145 pupils out of 239,424 children of school age. In the summer course of 1790, 174,744 pupils were registered. On the whole this was appreciable progress.[12]

The Josephinian system of education was practical and simple, but in general too mechanical. Criticisms were leveled both at its chief in Vienna, Gottfried Van Swieten, the son of Gerhard Van Swieten, and at the system itself. Gottfried Van Swieten was accused of being a tyrant and of having established a despotism. An Austrian like Martini fought against it, and Schlösser, the noted German publicist of the Eighteenth Century, called Van Swieten in his *Staatsanzeigen,* "The University Pasha."

The system itself lacked spirit and creative energy. The doctors produced almost nothing in the entire decade. The standing of teachers fell into disrespect, while close application to the textbooks produced stagnation in the minds of teachers as well as of students. Above all, moral and religious conditions deteriorated appreciably owing to Joseph II's regulation on the relation between the schools and the teaching of religion. Bureaucrats, who did not have the slightest idea of school requirements or of pedagogical training, decided offhand the most difficult of pedagogical problems.

Joseph II, on February 9, 1790, admitted that he had been disappointed in his system. "Morals and Religion," he wrote to the Chancellor, "have given place to frivolous lightheartedness; science has sunk to pure memory work; yes, so far has it come that wise parents regard it as a duty to withdraw their sons from public instruction." Orders were given that a

[12] For these statistics see Hock, *Österr. Staatsrat,* 520-30; Weiss: *Theresianische Schulreform,* Part VII, p. 107. See also Šafránek, "O Josefinském popise škol v království českém, 1790-1792" (*VČSN,* 1902).

plan of changes should be drawn up but the disappointed monarch died before he had righted that wherein he knew he had gone wrong.[13]

In his legislation on the schools as an educational system, Joseph II had stirred up his citizens as individuals, parents of school children. In his legislation on the schools by which he furthered Germanization, he awakened not individuals, but nations—Czechs, Hungarians, and Poles. It is to this later phase of his activity that we shall now turn before we take up the development of these two currents, a reform in the school system and Germanization, under Leopold II.

Few questions are more interesting than the actual status of the two languages, Czech and German, in government service and in the schools of Bohemia in the Eighteenth Century. By the Land Ordinance of 1627, the German language was given equal rights with the Czech language in the public offices of the country.[14] All laws and the Conclusions of the Diet were published thereafter in both languages. Down to 1749, or as long as the Bohemian Court Chancellery and Staathalterei existed at Prague, the Czech language was not banished from the central provincial offices.[15] However, the fact that the Jesuits had destroyed the Hussite literature, and had failed to produce another in its place allowed German to advance steadily.

After 1749—when the Chancellery and Statthalterei were abolished and when the central offices were moved to Vienna —the Czech language lost ground rapidly. Every new centralization was accompanied by an increase in the bureaucracy, which almost exclusively spoke German, and especially in the higher offices. The political centralization of 1749, the economic centralization completed in 1775 by the tariff for the Bohemian and Austrian Lands, and the dissolution of the Jesuits at that time led naturally to attempts to make the

[13] Kink, *Geschichte der kais. Universität zu Wien,* I, 580-588. See vol. II for the documents.
[14] See Jireček, *Das Verneuerte Landeseordnung,* B12, C2, C3.
[15] Rieger, *Zřízení krajské v Čechách,* II, 43.

schools uniform not only in system, but likewise in the language of instruction.

It may be said that so far as Germanization was concerned it proceeded voluntarily down to 1774. At times before this it was both helped and retarded by the monarchs of the House of Habsburg. At best one can call their policy, up to that time, one of vaccillation.[16] But after 1774 and down to 1790 their policy was unmistakably one of Germanization backed by all the forces of government in the schoolroom and in public office. In 1774, German was made the language of instruction in the public elementary schools of Bohemia. Two years later, Maria Theresa proclaimed it as the language of instruction in the gymnasia. The new normal school at Prague became the "heating-iron" of Germanization of Czech cities, and the landed estates belonging to the king and to the government were made centers for Germanization in the country.[17]

There were men in Bohemia who thought that Joseph II would stop this onrush of Germanization, but they were mistaken. Joseph II continued the labor and nominally completed it. He found, however, that he could not make Germans out of Czechs overnight. Beginning with 1780 Czech was no longer tolerated in the gymnasia and after 1788, in order to gain entrance to these schools, the pupils had to know German. Already, under Maria Theresa some of the lecture courses were given in German at the University of Prague.[18] In 1784, Joseph II ruled that all lectures should be delivered in German, with the exception of those on theology and law which were still taught in Latin. And finally, in order to complete the nominal Germanization of Bohemia, Joseph II, in 1788, ordered that henceforth ordinances should be printed in German only.[19] On paper, at least, the process

[16] Rieger, "Z Germanisačního úsili 18. věku" (Osvěta, 1887, 385, 497).
[17] Ibid., II, 389-391. Šafránek, "Pravda o školách v královstí českém za vrchní spravy Kindermannovy" (Osvěta, 1907; I, 205 ff.).
[18] Rieger, "Z Germanisačního úsili," 497 ff. In 1776 the Czech language was allowed in only four of the sixteen gymnasia.
[19] Denis, La Bohême depuis la Montagne Blanche, I, 597 ff.

of Germanization was completed—as it had been completed
in Hungary, in Galicia, and in the Slavic and Italian Lands
to the south.

And yet some slight, but important, memories of the Czech
language and of its former ascendancy had been left. In
1775 a chair of the Czech language had been created at the
University of Vienna and at the Neustadt Military School.
Two years later a chair of Bohemian Theology was established
at the University of Prague. The Bohemian Diet still issued
its patents in large letters in Czech [20] and in smaller letters
in German, and Czech was still heard in its ceremonies, as we
have seen in a preceding chapter, and was spoken very audibly
in its antechambers. Also in spite of the nominal Germanization of Joseph II, when the officials of the local government
desired to make themselves understood by two-thirds of the
population of Bohemia, they published the local announce-
ments in Czech.

We are now ready to trace the two subjects, the development of the system of education and the retardation of Germanization under Leopold II.

II

THE ATTITUDE OF THE DIET AND OF THE GOVERNMENT ON THE
QUESTION OF SCHOOLS AND GERMANIZATION UNDER
LEOPOLD II

The Bohemian Diet [21] in the Third Desideria asked for the
abolition of the School Commissioners whom Joseph II had
established. The Estates demanded the restoration of the
Czech language in certain gymnasia and in the common
schools. They advocated the use of Latin and Czech in the
Bohemian theological schools. They urged the restoration of

[20] M I Archiv, Carton 545. Examine the patents throughout the Eighteenth Century.
[21] S Archiv, Journal of the Diet, July 17, Bills 47-56, Nov. 20, 1790. See
also Č N M Archiv, Sternberg Diary, *ibid.*, and Adler, *Die Unterrichtsverfassung Kaiser Leopolds II und die finanzielle Fundierung der österreichischen Universitäten nach Anträgen Martinis*, pp. 10 ff.

the gymnasia and seminaries which Joseph II had suppressed and demanded the restoration to themselves of the administration of the Straka Academy for young noblemen. And finally, they proposed the establishment of an academy for the children of the members of the Estates. We shall consider each of these in turn.[22]

The question of the retention or abolition of the school commissioners was a vital one.[23] By the Decree of August 29, 1787, Joseph II, declared the Estates, had created many school commissioners whose object it was "to bring the school system into uniformity, . . . to examine teachers, . . . and to look after the management of buildings and grounds." At the same time, in order to pay their salaries, Joseph II took 12,000 florins yearly from the treasury of the Estates. He did this without consulting them, thereby violating the Constitution. But the question was at bottom neither a haggle over the 12,000 florins, nor a battle over a great constitutional principle. The question at core was whether the government with its school commissioners or the Church and the Estates with their vicars and patrons would henceforth control the common school system. Down to 1775 the Church and the Estates had charge of the school system through the vicars and the patrons, but after the abolition of the Jesuits, the State took direct control. Once the school commissioners were eliminated from the common school system, the control by the State was weakened, and as experience had shown, the Church and the Estates through their representatives would exercise much power. The Estates therefore asked that the commissioners should be abolished.

The Gubernium [24] understood this very well. The Council declared that the Land Ordinance of Ferdinand II gave Joseph II the power to make use of the 12,000 florins yearly

[22] M I Archiv, Carton 518, Third Desideria: An Seine M., Bericht d. geh. böhm. Stände mit den Vorstellungen über die im dritten Absatze des Reskripts von 1ten Mai . . . Gegenstände, Nov. 27, 1790. No. 936 ex Okt. 1791.

[23] *Ibid.:* 1. Beschwerde: Die Belastung des ständischen Domestikalfonds mit dem Beitrag zur Besoldung der Schulkommissäre.

[24] Gubernium Bericht, Prag, 18. Feb. 1791, M I Archiv, Carton 520.

without inserting them into the Postulata. However, its logic on this was very strained. It argued further that the charge that the school commissioners had not accomplished the work for which they had been appointed, was not sustained. It admitted that there were "some" among the school commissioners who did not speak Czech. The commissioners had a great task to perform. There were 2,300 schools for the sixteen commissioners to visit. Hence each had 143 schools to look after. If he did his duty properly there was little time left for other things besides travel. The Gubernium also thought that the expense of transportation which the peasants had to cover and which the Estates guaranteed in the 12,000 florins was not oppressive.

In a minority report, Barons Cavriani, MacNeven, and Rosenthal, of the Gubernium Council, sided with the Estates and advised that the sum be left to "cover the expenses of charitable institutions." Together with the Bohemian Diet, they declared the commissioners "not of the least use." On the other hand, Baron Lamoth, also a Councillor, came out strongly in favor of retaining the commissioners as "an integral part of a system which was the wonder of foreigners." Councillors Riegger and Boulles were in favor of retaining them, the former at least for a few years longer, until the system had attained a lasting uniformity.

The Study and Censorship Commission to whom the Desideria on educational matters was handed for an opinion declared that Leopold II had already decided on the retention of the school commissioners at a meeting of the State Council, which we shall soon discuss. The Study Commission defended the results which the common school system had secured. It admitted that some of the clergy were excellent instructors, but these were rather the exceptions than the rule. In many of the theological seminaries in Bohemia, the young clergy had received instruction which lagged considerably behind that of the German schools. "One does not want to exclude the clergy from this activity, but rather to spur it on, to make it serviceable to mankind, to the State, and to the Church."

The Court Chancellery accepted the arguments of the Gubernium and of the Commission and added that the clergy had not really been excluded from the schools. The bishops, at canonical visitations, were allowed to visit the schools "so as to inform themselves as to their status." The Court Chancellery considered that the quarrels which arose between the school commissioners and the priests and patrons arose out of the latter's prejudice. The latter had misled the teachers and the commissioners. The government could not afford to take the burden of the 12,000 florins, but the Chancellery suggested that henceforth the amount be inserted in the royal Postulata in order to make the transaction constitutional.[25]

Leopold II decided that the school commissioners should be retained. The 12,000 florins were to be inscribed in the royal Postulata. By this decision the Estates gained only the constitutional point that the monarch could not legally take the money without inscribing it in the Postulata. They had to pay the 12,000 florins yearly in the future as well as forswear control of the entire common school system.[26]

The Bohemian Estates also demanded that the school tuition, which Joseph II had established in the gymnasia and in the common school system, be abolished except in the case of the three-year schools, where it would have to continue until another fund was found to cover the loss to the treasury. Their chief argument was that the poor could not get the education to which they were entitled if they were forced to pay tuition.

The Gubernium viewed tuition as a "healthy institution"—for a rather queer reason—because the stipends paid out of the money collected from this source "helped many poor students." It also stimulated the industry and the zeal of

[25] Protokoll der Konferenz über die Beschwerden der böhm. Stände im Politischen, Justiz- und Kriminal-Fache welche den 2. Julius 1791 gehalten ward. M I Archiv, Carton 519.
[26] Decree, 936 ex Okt. 1791, M I Archiv, Carton 515: Okt. 28, 1791.

those who were studying. The Gubernium, however, was in favor of making it easier for the poor, but good, student to secure a stipend. It recommended that all students be freed from paying tuition who entered the gymnasia from the "first" class of the common schools and who showed that they were needy. It further argued that the stipends should be divided into classes and given with more care. The Chancellery agreed with the suggestion of the Gubernium, and Leopold II did not countermand the order issued to put it into effect.[27]

Next the question came up as to the language to be used in instruction in the common schools, in the gymnasia, and in the theological seminaries. For opponents of Germanization this was of utmost importance. The Estates did not ask directly that Czech be the language of instruction in the common schools of Bohemia, but in their demands with regard to the gymnasia and especially with regard to the theological seminaries they hinted that Czech should be restored there, too. The Estates asked that Czech be restored in the gymnasia in Prague. They also asked that, where Joseph II had introduced German into the theological seminaries, it should be replaced by Czech so that in the future the languages of instruction in these institutions would be Latin and Czech, instead of German, with here and there a little Latin. The Estates—and this shows the power of the clergy—argued that in a short while the schools would be educating a clergy ignorant of the language which was used in the greatest number of parishes in Bohemia. "To fill such parishes, only those completely conversant in the Czech language were qualified."

The Gubernium advised that nothing should be done until the new plan of reorganizing the school system had been adopted by the State Council. It could not understand the desires of the Estates as to Czech and Latin. Was it not true, argued the Gubernium, that "no more purely Czech-speaking

---

[27] See Third Desideria: 15 Wunsch: Wegen Abstellung des Schulgeldes, M I Archiv, Carton 519; Gubernium Bericht, 18. Feb. 1791, *ibid.*, Carton 520. and fn. 1.

youth were allowed to attend the gymnasia, because none were admitted who did not have a knowledge of the German language? And was it not true that the three-year schools, where instruction was still given in Czech, were few in number, and that they decreased from year to year? The Gubernium further pointed out that the clerical candidate would under the present system know German without forgetting Bohemian, and would fit himself thereby for a parish in a German or Czech-speaking community. Furthermore, the Latin then in use was only "common cook and monk Latin anyway."

The Court Study and Censorship Commission stated that it expected that the new plan on which the State Council was working would make concessions to the Estates with regard to the use of "Latin and the provincial language" in the preparation of the youth designated for the clergy. But it staunchly maintained that the administration of schools should so much the more zealously look after the spread of the "General National Language," namely, German in a "German Empire." The downfall of German must follow, if, according to the suggestion of the Estates, it was to be banished just at the point of its spread. The Bohemian Estates had not been mindful of the fact that knowledge of the German language would assist the youth of their province to official position, i.e. to the bureaucracy, and that its disuse would lead to a deterioration of the German style in Bohemia. "Bohemia would be cut off from the progress which other provinces were making in improving the style of the German language." The new laws of Joseph II did not allow anyone to enter the gymnasia, who could not show that he had attended for three years a common school "where all teaching was in German." And now "all of a sudden at the end of the Eighteenth Century came the unexpected desire of the Estates to have priests who did not need to know German." Doubtless the reason for this was "to make the clergy inaccessible to the sources" from which they might be enabled to see through the "destructive educational ideas and the so-called enlightenment of the Estates." [28]

The Bohemian Estates further asked that the gymnasia and seminaries which were in existence before their suppression by Joseph II, be reëstablished. They pointed out that there were fifteen gymnasia in Bohemia, one less than one for each circle, but that there were then four in Prague, and none in seven circles. The cost of sending a child so far from home was an obstacle to education and many capable students had thereby been prevented from attendance at the gymnasia. The cities in which gymnasia had formerly existed lost much through their suppression. The Estates asked that there be at least one gymnasium for each circle.

The Gubernium pointed out that formerly the gymnasia had been supported partly out of the income of public city property and partly out of funded capital. The seminaries had been under the management of the orders and of the monasteries. Joseph II brought all of them under state control and support. He cut down the number of gymnasia to fifteen, and in the place of the seminaries erected three normal classes and several general seminaries. The Gubernium agreed with the Estates that the cities had lost through the suppression of the gymnasia and that "a few more gymnasia might be permitted; but, one must not increase the costs" for now the money came out of the Treasury. Latin schools, it argued, were falling behind the German, and seminaries were useless.

The Court Study and Censorship Commission did not agree with the Gubernium or the Estates on the question of the restoration of the gymnasia. They had been superfluous, "because they did not have enough students." The Court Chancellery also agreed with the Commission. [29]

The Estates asked also that the Count Straka Academy

---

[28] *Ibid.*, and Zum Studien Protokoll vom 6. April 1791. M I Archiv, Carton 519. All bureaucratic authorities speak of the suddenness of the Czech revival among the Estates in 1790. It was one of the hidden currents of the times.

[29] See fn. 27.

be restored to them, declaring that its administration rightly belonged to them by the will of Count Straka made out in 1720. It seems that he had entrusted the administration of his estates and the school to the old Statthalterei, and the "protection" of the entire legacy to the Estates. The Gubernium made the mistake of arguing that the old Statthalterei was the same as the Gubernium. That was not true. The Court Chancellery and Leopold II gave the Estates charge of the administration of the estates of Count Straka on promise that they report regularly to the government.

An interesting proposal of the Bohemian Diet was the plan of Count Francis Anton Kolovrat to found an academy for noble youth in Prague.[30] Here the children of the nobility were to receive instruction under the control of the Estates. Count Kolovrat believed that the education of the youths was too costly, and that the adolescent boy had no opportunity to learn "except in bad company, when he became a shame to his family and his kingdom." He planned to establish an academy after the pattern of the Theresian or Savoy academies in Vienna.

The government was to be asked to give a building, preferably one left vacant as a result of the Jesuit suppressions. The headmaster was to look after the entire school, while every ten or twelve boys were to come under the care of a submaster, who should be a retired military officer. Religious services were to be emphasized. Boys from ten years of age were to be accepted. They were to begin their studies in the humanity classes or Latin schools, and might continue to live in the academy until graduation from the university. Instruction in fencing and dancing was also to be given. French, Italian, and Czech languages were to be taught by special teachers. There was to be a "billiard" table in the recreation

---

[30] Vorschlag wegen einer in Prag zu errichtenden landständischen Akademie und des hierzu zu verwendenden General Seminariums. 2. Oktober, 1790-239 ex. Aug. 1791. M. I Archiv, Carton 518. See Chapter VII for details of Bishop Schulstein's proposition with regard to teachers of commercial subjects.

room. Boarding was to be supplied by contract and to consist of "six dishes at midday and four at night, including salads and fruit." There were provisions as to beer drinking, horse-riding, and the wearing of uniforms. It was estimated that training a student in such a school might cost about 600 florins yearly and so a fund of about 60,000 florins was necessary to insure the care of 100 students. One of the Counts Černín offered immediately to donate 10,000 florins to the fund.[31]

The Gubernium[32] considered the time ill advised to start such a foundation. If the sovereign would approve, the Council would recommend that the Straka Academy, the Ferdinand Academy, and the newly proposed one be united. It was inclined to think that Count Kolovrat painted the academy in too glowing colors and set himself up too much as a practical pedagogue. Leopold II's decision of October 21, 1791, postponed action until a fund was found for such a purpose.[33]

We have mentioned several times that a new plan of reorganizing the school system was under discussion before the State Council. Baron Martini, the tutor of Leopold II and long the opponent of Van Swieten, was the sponsor of the new plan. Its chief principle was to decentralize the system and to give to the teachers a certain amount of autonomy. The autonomy was to be exercised by provinces and by certain groups of teachers within these provinces. In each province there were to be six teachers' assemblies: the body of theological professors, the faculty of law, of medicine, of the gymnasia, and of the normal schools. School legislation was to begin in each of these assemblies where the teacher or professor had a right to express his opinion. In each province there was to be a study commission made up of laymen, who were to be assisted by a study committee of six assessors, one assessor being elected by each of the six groups. Each of the

[31] Č N M Archiv, Sternberg Diary, Oct. 30, 1790.
[32] M I Archiv, Carton 520: Bericht des böhm. Landes-Guberniums über den Wunsch der Stände dass hierlands eine Akademie zu Erziehung adliger Jungen errichtet wurde. Dec. 12, 1790.
[33] Decree, Okt. 28, 1791, M I Archiv, Carton 515: 936 ex Okt. 1791.

six groups in turn was to be under the "eye" of some higher institution. The theological faculty was to be under the care of the Ordinariate, the law faculty under the Justices; the faculty of philosophy was to look after the gymnasia, the gymnasia after the normal schools. The Committee of Assessors, the Study Commission, and the Gubernium were to coöperate in making laws for the schools. Teachers were urged to publish studies in order to prevent their own stagnation. Discipline was to be strict, and the exercise of religion duly looked after. There were to be two Masses daily, and Communion was to be reintroduced. Attendance at class was to be compulsory, and absences were to be reported. The libraries were to be put in order, and catalogues really to be made up. And finally, higher salaries were to be paid to the teachers and competitive examinations instituted. From this, one can see that the plan on the whole was an improvement and sought to remedy the most flagrant defects of the Josephinian system.[34]

Leopold II, who had approved of the main lines of the new plan early in 1791, issued several regulations in October 28, 1791,[35] whereby he granted some of the demands made by the Bohemian Estates. A chair of the Czech language was to be created at Prague University. An investigation was immediately started as to who among the officials in Bohemia could speak Czech. Preparations, concluded later by Francis II, were made for the teaching of Czech in the gymnasia at Prague.[36] Leopold II displayed his interest in the revival of the national language by attending a Czech play given during the coronation ceremonies. At this time more Czech was heard spoken by the Estates, who had carried on their debates

[34] H H S Archiv, Staatsrat Akten, 2548 in 1790, 1731 in 1791. See Adler, *Die Unterrichtsverfassung Kaiser Leopolds II*, pp. 30 ff.
[35] M I Archiv, Carton 515: 936 ex Okt. 1791. See also Kropatschek, *Gesetze*, III, 115, I, 37-39.
[36] See the news of joy in the *Krameriusowy Cýs. Král. Wlastenecké Nowiny*, January 21, 1792, on the report that Leopold II was planning to restore Czech in the common schools and gymnasia of Bohemia beginning with the next fall. See also June 30, 1792, when professors of Czech were wanted in Prague gymnasia.

in German, than at any time since the "age of enlightenment" had dawned upon Bohemia. The Czech revival was a reality.

We have seen that at the end of the third quarter of the Eighteenth Century both the educational system of the Jesuits and the language and culture of the Czechs were rapidly declining. The absolute monarchy brought on the dissolution of the Order of the Jesuits, and the facile ideas of political and economic centralization introduced official Germanization. Down to that time, let us say 1775, the Germanization of Bohemia had proceeded voluntarily and it is thought might even have led to a peaceful assimilation of the Czechs in the course of a little over a generation. But the economic reforms of Joseph II, such as the emancipation of "serfdom" (Leibeigenschaft) in 1781, the granting of toleration, the freedom from censorship, and the temporary suppression of robot, gave stimulus to the slowly awakening nation. The more that Joseph II Germanized, the more the nation, though grateful for his economic reforms, awoke. In 1790 the Germanization of Bohemia had been officially and nominally completed: by that same year the Czech nation had revived. The two movements had run parallel to each other, and in 1790 they clashed in the reaction which followed the death of Joseph II.[37]

That was why the Bohemian Estates—among whom from henceforth a few could be counted as Czech élite—"so suddenly" asked for the restoration of the Czech or provincial, or even "the national language," as it was called. Perhaps strongest in their desire to see the language revived in the schools were the clergy. They had already lost much through Joseph II's regulation of the system of education, but they were threatened with destruction as a result of his efforts at Germanization. According to his system priests would soon be

[37] For various views on this subject see Chapter X, fn. 9, especially the works of Hanuš, Kraus, Straka, Strakoš, Pekař, and Kleinschutz. Compare also Krofta, "Výjvoj českého národního vědomi" (Česká Revue, 1918), ibid., Čechy a Rakousko v minulosti (1526-1848), and Hassinger, Die Entwicklung des tschechischen Nationalbewusstseins und die Gründung des heutigen Staates der Tschechoslowakei, Chapters I-III.

educated who could not preach in Czech to two-thirds of the parishioners of Bohemia. And so in 1790 we witness the spectacle of the Roman Catholic Church staunchly defending the Czech language—the very language which they, led on by the Jesuits, had done their best to destroy after the Battle of White Mountain.

Leopold II and Francis II admitted the inevitability of the Czech revival, based as it was upon the Czechs' increasing knowledge of their history. The days of the Roman censorship were past. Thereafter strong impetus was given to the movement by Dobrovský, Kollár, and Šafařík. Meanwhile, the system of schools, shorn of its despotism and its mechanical features, cleansed by religious devotional exercises, nationalized by provinces, and reinvigorated by an active and more efficient teaching force, was an improvement over that of Joseph II. It answered the best maxims of wise statesmanship; it was best suited to Bohemia.

Joseph II had not really Germanized Bohemia: he had awakened the Czechs and made them more tenacious and conscious than ever before of their historical past and the possibilities of their future.

PART V
CONCLUSION

CHAPTER XII

CONCLUSION

THE interesting evolution which changed Bohemia from an independent feudal state of the Sixteenth Century to a province of a modern, highly centralized empire has been traced. In the course of this evolution the State of Bohemia not only lost its independence, but also its religion, and its national language. By 1790 its political structure had been profoundly changed, but the Estates still existed; society was still medieval. This was one of the decisive factors which determined the course of events in Bohemia and, in fact, elsewhere in the Monarchy. There was for this reason no revolution, in the modern sense of the word, for example, as in France. The Estates were too reactionary to give up their old privileges. They still lived in that narrowing medieval atmosphere in which they fought not only among themselves as members of an Estate, but also as an Estate against Estates. All the four upper Estates thought only of holding the peasantry down, instead of opening to it the gates of modern life by suggesting positive reforms. Hence the serf could not be on their side. The government by its reforming attitude had taken care to win the friendship of the peasants. And without the serf a revolution by the Estates alone was impossible.

The Bohemian Estates in 1790 were not statesmen enough to build for the future; they looked only to their medieval past. To them old Bohemia furnished a panacea for all ills. To this ancient source of their political thought they added a few new ideas such as Rousseau's theory of compact government, but only so far as it concerned the sovereign and themselves. They could grasp the value of freedom of con-

367

science, but not political religious liberty. And they talked vaguely of the common welfare, but did little in a practical way to promote it.

The Bohemian Estates demanded a new constitution which, on the basis of Rousseau's theory of social contract, could not be changed at the will of the sovereign. They wished a constitutional structure, such as had existed in the Sixteenth Century, yet they did not ask for the suppression of the great centralizations of Maria Theresa, which had led to the formation of the Court Chancellery and the Supreme Court. They did not see the contradiction in these two totally different bases. Doubtless the fact that the officials of the central government were members of the Diet had its influence on their decisions. The government, guided by Leopold II, gave the Estates the Constitution that was in effect in 1764, that is, after the great reforms of Maria Theresa. The Estates were to have a Diet and an Executive Committee, they were to meet annually, and all taxes were to be inserted in the royal Postulata laid before the Diet annually. Thus the reforms of Joseph II were swept away in matters pertaining to the structure of the Constitution.

The Estates did not demand the abolition of the Josephinian system of courts, but asked rather that they be allowed to incorporate themselves into the number of justices in the courts of the first and second instances in Bohemia. They demanded that the Josephinian Code of law so far as it pertained to the rights of Estates, property, inheritance, and marriage be suppressed. The government saved the Josephinian judicial system as it was and compromised on the Code of Joseph II. The Code of 1811, which is still law to-day in Austria, bears the earmarks of this compromise in the clauses on the inheritance of women of the nobility and of illegitimate children, in laws on usury, and in the regulations pertaining to trusteeship.

In the matter of economic changes the Bohemian Estates, except on the question of serfdom, took a position which was to their credit. They argued for a more liberal tariff policy to offset the excessive prohibitive tendencies of the central government. They demanded a friendlier policy toward neighboring States. They asked for a national bank so as to provide credit for landowners and keep money in Bohemia. And they were in favor of schools for the benefit of commerce and of industry. The government was decidedly in favor of retaining the protective tariff, although Leopold II himself hoped to reduce it somewhat. It was also not much inclined to enter into real negotiations with Prussia and Saxony, nor able to bring the war with Turkey to a speedy conclusion. By treaties with the former the Estates hoped to open up the Elbe, the Oder, and the Danube so as to offset the long haul to Trieste. Leopold II desired to live on friendly terms with Prussia but the State Council postponed the matter until one is almost forced to conclude that it opposed an *entente* with Prussia. The enmity with Prussia had been the cause of much economic woe in both Bohemia and Silesia.

The stand of the Estates on the question of the bank was a very good one. They also had a solid basis for their charges that the government had for twenty-three years misdirected over thirteen million florins of revenue which should have gone for the payment of debts. On this the government offered no answer, merely admitting the fact. The administration refused to give the Estates their old laws on usury and postponed a decision on the establishment of the bank, although Leopold II favored it in principle. The Bohemian Estates pointed out also that for forty-three years they had been paying taxes for 11,200 fictitious farmers who did not exist. This had amounted to a total of over twenty-eight million florins, which meant that besides paying its own enormous quota Bohemia was paying the taxes of other provinces by an amount annually of more than a half-million florins. A solution was finally found, but it was at the expense of the serf as in the past.

In respect to serfdom the Estates longed vaguely for a

"tighter bond" between them and the serf. They tried, but failed, to secure military rule in order to overawe the serf when the Josephinian system of taxation and serfdom was abolished. The position taken by the government during this time was very creditable. In the first place, it refused to declare martial law; in the second place, it prevented the Estates from changing the Josephinian Code for the punishment of peasants, and granted only a future change in its manner of execution; and it urged upon the Estates a uniform plan for the abolition of robot. It is to the great discredit of the Estates in matters regarding taxation and robot that they refused to prevent the government from heaping the 11,200 fictitious farmers back on the serf and that they obstructed and finally blocked all attempts to abolish robot. Their only proposal was that robot might be abolished by the individual landowner, but on his own terms—by right of free contract and without the interference of the officials of government. They won on this point because the ever-reddening course of the French Revolution made necessary to the central government the support of the Estates, in order that the serf should be held down. After 1792, in matters pertaining to serfdom, the alliance of the government and the Estates, which had been disrupted in 1775, was renewed. The reaction in Bohemia destroyed entirely the reform of the taxation system and the abolition of robot, but did not succeed in changing the tariff, nor in destroying the Patent which called for the emancipation of "Leibeigenschaft." It won in the matter of guilds and markets and in its refusal to abolish robot. It lost in its struggle to free itself from the chronic deficit of the central Josephinian government.

Leopold II saved the Patent for Religious Toleration which Joseph II had issued in Bohemia. The clergy wished to see it abolished, the Diet demanded that its political provisions be suppressed, but the government retained it as it was, with here and there a slight correction. Nevertheless, further at-

tacks on religion were prohibited. No more monasteries were
to be suppressed, and religious exercises were to be introduced
into the schools.

The forces which resulted in making Bohemia officially
German and in reawakening the sleeping Czech nation confronted each other in 1790. The Estates asked the restoration
of Latin and Czech in certain schools. The demand was
strongest among the clergy, who were fighting for their own
self-preservation. The trend of Josephinian Germanization
would have made the clergy German and two-thirds of the
inhabitants of Bohemia, atheists. The reaction secured the
withdrawal of official Germanization and the right to have a
chair of the Czech language at the University and in the gymnasia at Prague. The reaction was therefore of positive value
for the Czech revival and conclusively proved that Bohemia
was on the threshold of a new era.

Such were the victories and the defeats of the reaction in
Bohemia. Leopold II ruled in a firm but tactful manner.
He had come to Vienna from Florence revolving in his mind
how constitutional government might be linked up with absolute government. There is no doubt that he meant to realize,
should it some day prove expedient, the fruits of those long,
but able, years of governing and constitutional planning in
Tuscany. But the times were not propitious as yet in the
Habsburg Monarchy for an absolutism, mildly tempered with
constitutionalism and founded on some basis of the representation of the people. The Estates were medieval, and foreign
complications—especially the fear of contagion from the
French Revolution—prevented attempts to remake society in
the Danubian Monarchy.

In Bohemia the two positive facts which counted most were
the restoration of some of its constitutional rights and the
impetus which the Czech revival received in the schools.
These factors soon brought changes in that country's historical evolution. After 1792 Bohemia was no longer wholly abso-

lute in form of government or officially German. Henceforth, it had at least the semblance of a constitution, and as time went on it became more and more bilingual. The reign of Leopold II was marked by decisive events in the history of Bohemia.

PART VI

BIBLIOGRAPHY

BIBLIOGRAPHY

In discussing the literature of this subject, it seems most convenient to consider it under three headings: first, bibliographical guides and publications, second, sources, in manuscript and in print, and third, secondary authorities. In the third, at the very beginning a short historiography of the literature of the specific field of the study will be attempted.

I

BIBLIOGRAPHICAL GUIDES AND PUBLICATIONS

The standard bibliography of Bohemian history is Čeněk Zíbrt's exhaustive work, *Bibliographie České historie*, 5 vols. (Prague, 1900-1912). It is a monument of patient labor, handicapped somewhat by its system of cataloguing. It is one of the most important bibliographical guides for Central European history. Much important material may be found in F. Krones, *Handbuch der Geschichte Österreichs von den ältesten Zeiten*, 5 vols. (Berlin, 1876-1879) and *Grundriss der österreichischen Geschichte mit besonderer Rücksicht auf Quellen- und Literaturkunde* (Vienna, 1882). They are very serviceable for Austrian history. Richard Charmatz, *Wegweiser durch die Literatur der österreichischen Geschichte* (Berlin, 1912) is a useful handbook for the German literature on Austrian history. Unfortunately it contains no titles of books written in the Slavic or Hungarian languages, and its comments on the works cited are not always appropriate. Dahlmann-Waitz, *Quellenkunde der deutschen Geschichte* (Leipzig, 1912) will be found of some use, although it is subject to the same criticism as the work by Charmatz.

For current bibliography one must turn to scientific historical journals and society publications. The *Český Časopis Historický* (Prague, 1895 ff.) is the standard Czech historical quarterly. It has been ably edited, first, by Jaroslav Goll and now by Josef Pekař, and deserves a wider reputation than has hitherto been its lot. A bibliographical appendix has appeared annually with this publication since 1904 and is of great value for the current bibliography of the literature of Bohemian history in any language whatsoever. The *Mittheilungen des Vereins für Geschichte der Deutschen in Böhmen* (Prague, 1862 ff.) corresponds to the *Český Časopis Historický* for the Germans in Bohemia. It is edited by A. Horčička. The same group of scholars has published also the *Beiträge zur Geschichte Böhmens,* since 1864.

The *Časopis Musea Českého* is the official publication of the famous Bohemian Museum. The publication began in 1827. V. Schulz compiled an index (1827-76) in 1876 and indices have been compiled decennially since then. This journal contains much valuable material for the history of Bohemia and has had many noted editors and contributors. The Bohemian Society of Learning and Sciences (*Královská Česká Společnost Nauk—Die böhmische Gesellschaft der Wissenschaften*) has been issuing publications since 1785. The sets run as follows: 1785-1789; 1791-1798; 1802-1823; 1836-1866; 1867-1883. From 1881 the *Pojednání-Abhandlungen* have appeared while the Proceedings (*Zprávy o zasedání-Sitzungsberichte*) go back to 1859 in German, to 1873 in Czech. In 1886 the *Věstník-Jahresberichte* appeared. G. Wegner has compiled an appendix for the century ending in 1884 under the title of *Obecný rejstřík k spisum král. české společností nauk,* 1784-1884 (Prague, 1884). These publications are of great importance and contain countless monographs on the history of Bohemia and of Austria. The Francis Joseph Academy (*Česká akademie císaře Františka Josefa pro vědy, slovesnost, a umění—Die Gesellschaft zur Förderung deutscher Wissenschaft, Kunst, und Literatur in Böhmen*) has published almost in parallel order a long series of excellent historical, literary, and legal monographs since 1891.

At Vienna the Imperial Academy of Sciences (*Kaiserliche Akademie der Wissenschaften*) has published since 1848 an excellent series of publications which are of capital importance for the history of Bohemia, as well as for the empire. These publications consist of 1) Memoirs (*Denkschriften*); 2) Proceedings (*Sitzungsberichte*); 3) The Archive for the Study of the Sources of Austrian History, since 1865 entitled The Archive for Austrian History (*Archiv für Kunde österreichischer Geschichtsquellen—Archiv für österreichische Geschichte*); 4) the Notices (*Notizenblatt-Beilage zum Archiv*, bis 1860); 5) *Fontes Rerum Austriacarum* in two parts *a*) *Scriptores*, *b*) *Diplomataria et Acta*; and 6) an *Almanac*. There is a *Register* for the years 1847-1874, volumes 1-50; and in volume 80 for volumes 51-80. The Institute for Archival Research publishes a journal entitled: *Mittheilungen des Instituts für österreichische Geschichts-Forschung* (Vienna, 1880 ff.). The tone of these Vienna publications is in general scientific and void of chauvinism. They do not however escape the charge that their point of view is often imperial.

Moravia and Silesia are Lands which belonged to the Bohemian Crown and their history has often been one with that of Bohemia. Prominent among the publications in these Crown Lands may be mentioned: *Schriften der historisch-statistischen Sektion der k. k. mährisch-schlesischen Gesellschaft zur Beförderung des Ackerbaues, der Natur- und Landeskunde* (since 1851) and *Zeitschrift des Vereines für die Geschichte Mährens und Schlesiens* (since 1897). Both are German, and of importance in comparison with publications in Czech in Bohemia. There are other publications in the Lands of the Bohemian Crown and in such provinces as Galicia, Styria, Carinthia, and Carniola, but to name them here would be venturing too far afield.

In foreign publications notices on the bibliography of Bohemian history will be found from time to time in *Jahres-*

berichte der Geschichtswissenschaften and in the *Revue Historique.*

Among encyclopedias and biographical dictionaries should be mentioned, for Bohemia, *Ottův Naučný Slovník,* 13 vols. (Prague, 1888-1898), for Austria, Wurzbach, *Biographisches Lexikon des Kaisertums Österreich,* 60 vols. (Vienna, 1855).

II

SOURCES IN MANUSCRIPT AND PRINT

The archives used in preparation of this study are to be found chiefly in Prague and Vienna. At Prague there is what was formerly the Statthalterei Archive where repose all the acta of the central government such as court decrees, ordinances, regulations for the local government, reports of officers of the local government, and many other sources. It is the ancient archive of the king of Bohemia. The Land Archive (*Zemský Archiv-Landes-Archiv*) is the archive of the Estates —the Bohemian Diet. Much of its original material had been transferred to Vienna, but since 1918 copies of the transferred documents have been made and are now to be found in this archive. It has an excellent catalogue and an efficient staff. Other archives in Prague are of less importance for this study. The City Archive contained little or nothing, the Archive of the Cathedral of St. Vitus had a few documents, and so had that of the Abbey of Strahov. The Land Archive has copies of the manuscripts in the Lobkovic Library. The Archive and Library of the Bohemian Museum, besides having much contemporary printed material, contain the Sternberg Papers, the documents left behind by a member of the Diet. The archives in the country were not consulted because all the important material is at Prague, and because the archives of noblemen are generally still inaccessible for the Eighteenth Century.

At Vienna, the Archive of the Ministry of the Interior, *Haus-Hof- und Staats-Archiv,* and the Treasury Archive

(*Hofkammer*) were consulted. The first mentioned archive contains the papers of the monarch and the votes of the State Council, the second contains the papers of the Court Chancellery of 1790-1792, and the third contains the financial documents of the period.

The libraries in the former Austrian Empire still lag somewhat in the principles and practice of library science. The Library of the Bohemian Museum and of the University are the best in Prague. The Hof-Bibliothek and the University Library in Vienna have excellent books, but very poor service. In giving the present review of the source material used in the preparation of this study the following principle has been followed. Most of the legislation began at the bottom in the time of Leopold II. We shall therefore begin at the bottom. The two lowest sources on the list are the circles of the administration and the individual members of the Diet. From them material went in the case of the former to the Gubernium in Prague, in case of the latter into the Diet. From the Diet, documents were transmitted to the Gubernium and, if need be, were commented upon and sent to the Court Chancellery. If necessary, on any given subject, the Court Chancellery asked the opinion of the Supreme Court, the Court Treasury, or various Commissions such as those on Desideria, Religion, Study, etc. The Court Chancellery then gave its decision and transferred the matter to the State Council and that institution in turn to the monarch.

Let us turn first to the Diet. From the Sixteenth Century it had been the custom to publish after the close of the sessions of that assembly the conclusions or laws (*Landtagsschlüsse-Artikule*). In the Eighteenth Century there is a long series of them but they thin out toward the end. They contained at the close of the century only the barest skeleton of results. One cannot get from them just what took place in the Diet. Down to 1789 no Journal of the Diet had been kept, but after that a Protokoll was kept, and it is one of the important sources for the Diets under Leopold II. Count Francis

Sternberg kept a *Diary,* of which the original is in the Archive of the Bohemian Museum. It is at times even more useful between July 10, 1790, and January 29, 1791, than the Official Journal. Count Sternberg was fair-minded and in general careful about his facts. In the Archive of the St. Vitus Cathedral is a diary entitled *Kurze Anmerkungen* which runs through the same period beginning March 9, 1790. It gives more emphasis naturally to religious matters, for its author was doubtless a monk or a member of the clergy.

Under Leopold II the Diet produced the Three Desideria and many supplementary memoirs. It would be idle to record here in detail the full titles of the numerous documents which come under that name or were appended to them. There were the Three Desideria; the first on Taxation and Serfdom, the second on the Constitution, and the third on all other grievances. The originals are kept in the Archive of the old Court Chancellery, the Ministry of the Interior, in Vienna. The First Desideria was entitled "Vorschläge zu Berichtigung und Konsolidirung des Steuersystems, Nov. 23, 1790." It can be found in Carton 514 of the Archive of the Ministry of the Interior. The Second Desideria was entitled: "An seine Majestät, Bericht der treugehorsamsten böhmischen Stände mit den gnädigst geforderten Vorschlägen, wie die bestandene ständische Verfassung und ihre Wirksamkeit mit Rücksicht auf die gegenwärtigen Umstände auf die zweckmässigste Art wiederhergestellt werden könne, Sept. 4, 1790," Carton 517. The Third Desideria has the title: "An seine Maj., Bericht der treugehorsamsten böhmischen Stände mit den Vorstellungen im dritten Absatze des Reskripts vom Iten Mai, 1790 . . . Gegenstände. November 27, 1790," Carton 516. Each of these had many supplements such as minority opinions, statistical tables, and memoirs which have been mentioned in the text. Of the three Desideria the second has been published in the *Historische Aktenstücke über das Ständewesen in Österreich* (Leipzig, 1847). Some of the early, but less important, documents on taxation and serfdom were published in *Sammlung einiger Schriften welche von den königl. böhmischen Ständen über das neue Steuer- und Urbarial-System veranlasst worden* (Dresden, 1790).

The material then went to the Gubernium for an opinion. The Gubernium under Leopold II seldom agreed and there was generally a minority opinion in the Council. The Gubernium opinions were the "Berichte des böhm. Landes-Guberniums," now preserved in the Archive of the Interior, and were given on all of the Desideria and all of the memoirs.

When the material reached the Court Chancellery (*Hof-Kanzlei*) that council decided whether or not it could give a complete opinion of its own; if so, it was registered as a *Hof-Kanzlei Dekret* which resulted from a *Sitzung* (session) and often a Protokoll (*der Hof-kanzlei*) was kept. If the Chancellery needed further information or wished the advice of other institutions, it would send extracts of the Desideria and the opinions of the Gubernium to the Supreme Court (*Oberste Justizstelle*) or to the Commission für Religions-Sachen, or to the Hof-Studien und Censur-Commission. Records and returned reports of all of these matters can be found for Bohemia under *Ständische Desiderien,* Cartons 513-520, in the Archive of the Ministry of the Interior. When the matter was ready for a decision, then out of the Court Chancellery Council was created a Commission or Conference, because the heir to the throne, the Archduke Francis, and one or two other ministers attended. The documents left behind by this body are called Protokollen der Konferenzen (or über die Konzertazion) and are to be found in the same cartons. In the course of the preparation of this study naturally search widened the scope of the material used until cartons, other than those entitled *Desiderien,* were also used.

Thus for political matters, those cartons catalogued as Ständische Postulata and Ständische Verfassung were used; for economic conditions those entitled Volkszählung, Bauernunruhen, etc.; for social conditions, Religionssachen, Studien-Angelegenheiten. The numbers of the cartons are duly cited in the footnotes. See the *Inventar des allgemeinen Archivs des Ministeriums des Innern* (Vienna, 1909) for the organization of the old Archive of the Ministry of the Interior.

Having received the opinion of the Court Chancellery and of the Commission on Desideria the huge documents went to the State Council. Here they were passed around from member to member. The documents were generally given a number as "2530 in 1790" which explains itself. On each document the members of the council recorded their vote in handwriting. These were called the *Staatsrat Akten*.

When the votes of the councillors had been duly recorded the "Vortrag des Hofraths" went to the sovereign. From him issued the Court Decrees (*Hof-Dekreten*), the Patents, the High Resolutions (*Höchste Resolutionen*), etc. In the case of the Desideria, the First Desideria was ruled upon in the Court Decree of October 21, 1791, the Second on August 12, 1791, and the Third on October 28, 1791. The Decrees can be found in the Archive of the State, the Interior, the Gubernium, or the Land in Prague. Some of the decisions of the monarchs of Bohemia have been printed in collections which can never be complete, but which are serviceable nevertheless. J. Weingarten, *Codex Ferdinandeo-Leopoldino—Josephino-Carolino (1347-1717)* (Prague, 1720) explains itself. It can be supplemented by Franz Wekebrod, *Sammlung der seit dem Jahre 1600 bis zum Jahre 1740 ergangenen allerhöchsten Gesetze in chronologischer Ordnung* (Brünn, 1795). Then J. Kropatschek began a series of collections which are valuable. For Maria Theresa he collected: *Sammlung aller k. k. Verordnungen und Gesetze vom Jahre 1740 bis 1780, die unter der Regierung des Kaisers Joseph, theils noch ganz bestehen, theils zum Theile abgeändert sind*, 8 vols. (Vienna, 1789). He also arranged the *Handbuch aller unter der Regierung des Kaisers Joseph II für die k. k. Erbländer ergangenen Verordnungen und Gesetze in einer chronologischen Ordnung und systematischen Verbindung*, 18 vols. (Vienna, 1785-1790). He followed this up with *Leopold II, Franz II und Franz d. L.*

politische Gesetze und Verordnungen f. d. deutschen, böhm. und galiz. Kronländer von 1790-1829, 57 vols. (Vienna, 1791-1831). There are smaller sets like Kopetz's for industrial ordinances, Roth-Blasek's for serfdom, and another for schools, but in this study they have not been used owing to the fact that many of these decrees were at hand in the archives and can be cited more accurately this way.

Another class of printed sources is that of contemporaries who published either observations, statistics, or sources, or even wrote monographs. Thus J. A. Riegger, *Archiv der Geschichte und Statistik insbesondere von Böhmen,* 3 vols. (Dresden, 1792-1795) and *Materialien zur Statistik Böhmens,* 12 vols. (*ibid.,* 1789-99) are full of contemporary material. So, too, is H. Grellmann, *Statistische Aufklärungen über wichtige Theile und Gegenstände der öster. Monarchie* (Vienna, 1789, ff.). To this class of statistical, cultural, and political collections belong also: D. Kostetzky, *Die Verfassung des Königreichs Böhmen* (Prague, 1816), *Schematismus für das Königreich Böhmen* (Prague, 1789 ff.); and Schreyer, *Kommerz, Fabriken, und Manufakturen* (Prague, 1792). The last monograph is by a Josephinian protectionist, but interesting nevertheless. From the newspapers, *Krameriusowy Cýs. Král. Wlastenecké Nowiny, Prager Oberpostamtzeitung,* and the *Wiener Zeitung* one may get but little material. Journalism under Leopold II, as under Joseph II, amounted to very little. Nevertheless the first-named newspaper had a mission to nurture the Czech revival and for that reason it is interesting. No better account by a traveler in Bohemia during this time exists than *Beobachtungen in und über Prag* (1787) written by a German traveler who sympathized with conditions (as he found them) from a Josephinian point of view. His observations are not overdrawn and may be taken with little reservation. Perhaps in few countries does there exist as excellent a diary of the average agrarian life of the Eighteenth Century as the *Memoirs of Vavak (Paměti Vavakovo).* They exist in manuscript in the Bohemian Museum from 1775 to 1795 and have been pub-

lished under the title, *Paměti Františka J. Vavaka*, edited by
P. J. Skopec, 3 vols. (Prague, 1914-16). Vavak was a justice
of the peace, a staunch Catholic, and a loyal Czech. His views
are as interesting as they are important, and if he tells us how
the country looked in the last days of the Eighteenth Century,
Beobachtungen shows us how the people in the capital of
Bohemia lived. See also Stanislava Hájková, "Vavak a jeho
pojetí českých dějin" (*ČČH*, 1919, XXXV, Nos. 2, 3).

Besides these, it must be remembered that a large number
of monographs, hereafter to be cited, contain documentary
appendices of some value. The works of Kalousek, Grünberg,
Hock, Kink, Rieger, and others contain documents.

Hermengild Jireček published in Prague, 1888, the Land
Ordinance of 1627 under the title of *Die Verneuerte Landes-
Ordnung—Obnovené právo a zřízení zemské dědičného království českého*. Here both the German and the Czech texts
appear in parallel columns.

III

SECONDARY AUTHORITIES

A. HISTORIOGRAPHY

A life of Leopold II or a complete history of his reign in the
Austrian Monarchy is yet to be written. The early, almost
contemporary, literature about Leopold II was panegyric. One
may gather this from such puerile lines as those of Joseph
Oehler, *Skizze der Lebensbeschreibung Leopolds des Zweiten*
(Vienna, 1790); J. v. Alzinger, *Ueber Leopold den Zweyten*
(Berlin, 1792); *Biographie Kaiser Leopolds des Zweyten,
Königs von Ungarn und Böhmen, Erz-Herzogs von Österreich,
Grossherzogs von Toscana* (Vienna, 1792). Nor does Franz
Hegrab, *Versuch einer kurzen Lebensgeschichte Kaiser Leopolds II bis zu dessen Absterben* (Prague, 1792), depart from
the cheap, popular bookstall selling book of Prague or Vienna
of that day. All of these are poor and almost useless to the
historian. A pamphlet in German and Latin, hostile to Leo-

pold II, but laudatory of Joseph II, may be found under the title of *Gespräch zwischen einem durch Ungarn reisenden Fremden und einem unparteyisch denkenden Ungarn über das Ende der Regierung weiland Kaiser Josephs des Zweyten und über die damalige des Kaisers und Königs Leopold des Zweyten* (1791) (Library of the Abbey of Strahov). Sartori, *Leopold-inischen Annalen*, 2 vols. (Augsburg, 1792), is fuller but adds no real estimate. J. B. Schel, *Geschichte Österreichs unter der Regierung K. Leopolds II* (Vienna, 1837) is less panegyric and pays a great deal of attention in his pages to military history. Diplomatic history and internal history, while they receive better treatment here, were still in their infancy. And so one may conclude that before 1848 little had been published on Leopold II that is worth while for the serious historian, except panegyrics and the military accounts of the Turkish War. There were reasons for that. In the first place, the censorship still existed, and then Leopold II's reign was short and the internal history of his two years of rule was little known except to the living, then statesmen and members of Estates themselves.

The year 1848 brought the Revolution and with it the desire to know what had been done under Leopold II with the Bohemian Constitution. Under such circumstances Baron V. Adrian published the Second Desideria in the series which by name explains itself, *Historische Aktenstücke über das Ständewesen in Oesterreich* (Leipzig, 1848). There followed a live interest in the reforms of Maria Theresa, Joseph II, and Leopold II after the abject despotism of Francis II. I. Beidtel began to publish in the publications of the Vienna Academy (1851, 1852) a series of able monographs dissecting the internal history of the Monarchy, 1740-1792. They were published later under the title of Beidtel-Huber, *Österreichische Staatsverwaltung*, I (1740-1792), (Innsbruck, 1896). This was the beginning of serious historical work on the internal history of that epoch. He went at his subject coolly, though much like a bureaucrat.

From this time on monographs appeared usually on parts of the entire period of reforms, some on foreign policy, others on internal policy, most of them from the general Austrian point of view. A. Jaeger, *Kaiser Joseph II und Leopold II* (Vienna, 1867) looked at this period from a clerical point of view—all turned about what Joseph II or Leopold II did on the question of toleration. Then came a few works on Leopold II's Italian (Tuscan) reign such as A. V. Reumont, *Geschichte Toskanas seit dem Ende des florentinischen Freistaates* (Gotha, 1877), G. Capponi, *Storia di Pietro Leopoldo* (Firenze, 1877), and F. Hirsch, "Leopold II als Grossherzog von Toscana" (*Historische Zeitschrift*, 1878, XL) which illuminate fairly satisfactorily that part of his life, but do not go into his later career. The Wolf-Zwiedineck-Südenhorst publication, *Österreich unter Maria Theresia, Joseph II und Leopold II, 1740-1792* (Berlin, 1884), offers a well-rounded account of this period. It is impartial and pays equal attention to foreign as well as to internal problems. It is also well written. A good recent account of the period from Maria Theresa to 1849 is to be found in Karel Uhlirz (continued by Matilde Uhlirz), *Handbuch der Geschichte Österreichs und seiner Nachbarländer, Böhmen und Ungarn*. Vol. II, i (Vienna, 1930). Devoted particularly to the earlier part of the subject of this study is E. Guglia, *Maria Theresia. Ihr Leben und ihre Regierung* (Vienna, 1920).

For Bohemia no reasonably adequate account of Leopold II's reign existed until Justin V. Prášek published his *Panovaní císaře a krale Leopolda II* (Prague, 1904) in the series of Rezek's *Dějiny Čech a Moravy*. It is a popular history though not well-arranged, but on the whole remarkably well done for the sources used by Prášek. He depended chiefly on printed sources, leaving the manuscript material untouched. As a popular history it performs its task well. Like Südenhorst, Prášek rescues Leopold II from certain misconceptions now disproved by monographic work. To get an accurate inside view of conditions under that sovereign, one must turn to the manuscripts and to the monographs enumerated in the following pages.

In a study devoted to internal history it was thought unnecessary to analyze extensively foreign policy, except as it affected the internal situation. For this see Paul Mitrofanov, *Leopold II Avstriiskii, Vnieshnaia politika*, I, chast i (*Zapiski Istoriko-filologischeskago Fakulteta Imperatorskago Petrogradskago Universiteta*, 1916, erroneously numbered CXXXI, but which should be numbered CXXXII) and the discussion in footnotes pp. 55, 57, 84-5, and 99-101. The works of Ranke, Schultze, Adam Wolf, H. Schlitter, Huber and Beer have clarified Leopold's foreign policy, attacked as it was too vigorously by Herman and defended too liberally by Sybel.

Joachim Zimmermann, *Das Verfassungs-Projekt des Grossherzogs Peter Leopold von Toscana* (Heidelberg, 1901), has laid the basis for a new interpretation of Leopold's views on politics and constitutions. He began planning a constitution for Tuscany a few years after Virginia's Bill of Rights and Constitution in 1777 but did not promulgate it because he thought it was not expedient to do so. Paul Mitrofanov in his *Joseph II, seine politische und culturelle Tätigkeit* (Vienna, 1910) has rendered a real service to scholars. His work indicates how little really thorough research work has been done in the field, even though he himself has slighted many excellent monographs. It is to be regretted that he was unable to continue his work on Leopold II cited above, due to the outbreak of the war and his own ill health. Of the foreign writers worth mentioning there is also E. Denis, *La Bohême depuis la Montagne blanche*, 2 vols. (Paris, 1903). While devoting too little space to the reign of Leopold II, he has nevertheless pointed out that the Bohemian Diet of 1790 was of far greater importance than Springer and other German writers are willing to give to it.

So much of the history of Bohemia from 1620 to 1918 is interpreted in the light of the significance of the Battle of White Mountain that two accounts of the historiography of this event and its aftermath may be found of value: H. Opočenský, "Bíla Hora a česká historiografie" (*Pokrokovy Revue*, 1912, IX) and Jaroslav Werštadt, under the same title and in the same review (1913, X). In connection with this, the brilliant essay by the leading Czech historian, Joseph Pekař, *Po Bílé Hoře* (Prague, 1921), should be read. Břetislav Jelinek, *Die Böhmen im Kampfe um ihre Selbständigkeit, 1618-1648*. 3 vols. (Prague, 1916) deals with the period in greater detail.

B. POLITICAL

In general there are three tendencies in the writing of the constitutional history of Bohemia down to 1918. There is the German school which maintains that since the Battle of White Mountain (1620) and especially since the time of Joseph II Bohemia really had no constitutional history, but both Bohemia and Austria have been since Maria Theresa a part of a new state. Necessarily in interpreting the Land Ordinance of 1627 they agree that the famous "Jus legis ferendae" clause —"to change—to alter—to mend"—refers to constitutional, i.e. public law, as well as to private. Consequently the monarch was supreme, he could change the Constitution at will, and the great changes carried out by Maria Theresa and Joseph II were strictly within the letter of the law.

The Czech school maintains that the famous clause—best stated in the Patent of Promulgation, where it is inserted among references to private law—refers only to private law. In only that sense, they claim, can it be understood, because Ferdinand II would not have issued the Confirmation of Privileges, May 21, 1627, which, with certain exceptions, confirmed old rights. By means of this interpretation the Czechs maintain that the reforms of Maria Theresa and Joseph II, which really destroyed the Bohemian State, were unconstitutional—as much acts of force as Ferdinand II's Land Ordinance. They maintain therefore, that the Land Ordinance which preserved the statehood of Bohemia was the last depository of Bohemian rights.

The foreign or neutral school, made up mostly of writers foreign to Bohemia, tends to maintain a middle position. In general, these writers give the Czechs the credit for construing literally, the Germans for construing broadly and for taking into account the practice of sovereigns after 1627. That is, both are right. The Czechs interpret narrowly on the exact wording of the documents, the Germans broadly, and they bring forth later practice to support their views. Thus they give the Czechs the right in theory, the Germans the right in practice.

The German school bases its faith upon the interpretation by Anton Gindeley, "Vznik obnoveného zřízení zemského" (*Právník*, 1894, XXXIII) and in his *Geschichte der Gegenreformation in Böhmen* (Leipzig, 1894). The Czech school points to the works of Joseph Kalousek, *České státní právo*, 2d edition (Prague, 1892) and of J. Kapras, *Právní dějiny zemí koruny české*, 3 vols. (Prague, 1913-20). In this study, Kalousek is used more frequently than Kapras because of his very convenient documentary appendix. The foreign school is represented best by L. Eisenmann, *Le Compromis austro-hongrois* (Paris, 1904) and E. Denis, *La Bohême depuis la Montagne Blanche*, vol. I (Paris, 1903).

Glancing at the historiography of this subject it is to be noted that in 1790 the Bohemian Desideria accepted the fact that the king could change the Constitution at will. They wished to prevent his doing so and by advancing the Rousseau theory of compact government, by a Pragmatical, by new clauses in the Constitution, and finally by a new constitution, they hoped to set at rest any statement that the king could change the law of the Constitution at will. Joseph Veith, *Statistische Uebersicht der böhmische Staatsverfassung und Landeskultur von den ältesten Zeiten bis auf Ferdinand II* (Prag, 1798) and Kostetzky, *Die Verfassung des K. Böhmen*

(Prag, 1816) both accept the view that the Ordinance gave the sovereign the right to change the Constitution.

The troubles that followed and the Revolution of 1848 brought renewed interest in the subject. There were attempts to understand the action of the Diet of 1790 and so the *Historische Aktenstücke über das Ständewesen in Österreich* (Leipzig, 1848) and *Baron V. Adrian und der böhmische Landtag im Jahre 1847* (Hamburg) contained important documents on the constitutional history of Bohemia. The former included the Constitutional Desideria of 1790 and the latter the Deduction über der landesverfassungsmässigen Gerechtsamen und Freiheiten der böhmischen Stände. Both vividly recalled the past.

But the real discussion of constitutional questions did not begin until after the Prussians won at Königgrätz in 1866 and the Compromise with Hungary was being threshed out. Then it was that V. V. Tomek in his *Sněmy české dle obnoveného zřízení zemského Ferdinanda II* (Prague, 1868) first clearly stated the view of the Czechs. He was ably assisted by Max Wellner, *Beyträge zur Geschichte des böhmischen Staatsrechtes* (Vienna, 1868), and by Hugo Toman in his *Das böhmische Staatsrecht und die Entwicklung der österreichischen Reichsidee* (Prague, 1872), and his somewhat too sanguine *Die Schicksale des böhmischen Staatsrechtes in den Jahren 1620-1627* (Prague, 1870). He was answered caustically by Joseph Winter, "Die Ferdinandische Landes-Ordnung in Böhmen" (*MVGDB*, 1867, IV). Winter saw nothing but reaction in the policy of the Estates of Bohemia since 1627. Then Kalousek wrote the first edition of the fundamental work mentioned above. Kalousek was followed by the Czechs: Jaromir Čelakovský, *Povšechné české dějiny právní*, 2d ed. (Prague, 1900); Karel Kramář, *Das böhmische Staatsrecht* (Vienna, 1896, also in Czech); Bohumil Baxa, *K dějinam veřejného práva v zemích koruny české* (Prague, 1906); and Kapras, as indicated above. They have restated the Czech point of view. The German point of view has been maintained by Huber-

Dopsch, *Österreichische Reichsgeschichte,* ed. 2 (Vienna, 1901); and in similar works by Luschin von Ebengreuth (1895) and Adolph Bachmann (1904).

Additional light on these problems is to be found in J. Kapras, *Český stát a centralisace zemí habsburgských* (Prague, 1918), Joseph Salaba, "Pobělohorská ústava a zákonník" (*ČČH,* XXXV, no. 2), B. Mendl, "O poměru Čech k staré říši" (*Česká Revue,* 1917-18), and J. Demel, "O významu pragmatické sankce pro české státní právo" (*Sborník Věd, Právních a Státních,* 1914-15, XV). Jan Heidler, "Počátky našeho statoprávního boje" (*Česká Revue,* 1917-18), critically analyzes the origins of the constitutional struggle.

The period treated by this study has recently been used as the background of two able works: Hans Schlitter, *Aus Österreichs Vormärz,* 4 vols. Vol. II on Bohemia (Leipzig, 1920), and Viktor Bibl, *Der Zerfall Österreichs. Kaiser Franz und seine Erbe* (Vienna, 1922).

Those who wish to follow the course of events elsewhere in the Habsburg Monarchy should see, in addition to the works just mentioned, the able monograph by H. J. Bidermann, "Die Verfassungs-Krisis in Steiermark zur Zeit der ersten französischen Revolution" (*MHV Steiermark,* 1873, XXI). This is especially good for questions pertaining to taxation and the Constitution. Viktor Bibl, *Die Restauration der niederösterreichischen Landesverfassung unter k. Leopold II* (Innsbruck, 1902) is an excellent work written from materials in the archives. So is his *Die niederösterreichischen Stände im Vormärz* (Vienna, 1911). For Moravia and Silesia there is Christian d'Elvert, *Schriften der historischen-statistischen Sektion der k. k. mährisch-schlesischen Gesellschaft zur Beförderung des Ackerbaues, der Natur- und Landeskunde,* XIV (Brünn, 1865). Here are published the Moravian Desideria. For Tyrol, see Joseph Egger, *Geschichte Tirols von den ältesten Zeiten bis in die Neuzeit,* III (Innsbruck, 1880); for Carniola, E. H. Kosta, "Ein Beitrag zur Geschichte des Ständewesens in Krain" (*MHV Krain,* 1859, XIV); for Galicia. Stan. Starzyński, *Projekt Galizyjskiej Konstitutcyi 1790-91. Charta Leopoldina.* For Hungary and Belgium, see footnotes pp. 83-85. To study the Bohemian Estates one should turn to the following suggestive bibliography. A. Gindely, *Die Entwickelung des böhmischen Adels und der Inkolatverhältnisse seit dem 16. Jahrhundert* (Prague, 1866) is scholarly and traces this subject down to the Eighteenth Century where Boh. Baxa, *Inkolat (a Indigenat) v zemích koruny české* (Prague, 1908) takes it up. Both are scholarly and fair, their conclusions being based for the most part on the sources. For a general account of the Bohemian nobility see Anton Peter ritter von Schlechta-Wsserdsky-Wssehrd, "Die Entwicklung des böhmischen Adels" (*Österreichisch-Ungarische Revue,* 1890, NF IX, 81-114, 265-302), and for the old nobility see Franz Vlasak, *Der Ältbohmische Adel und seine Nachkommenschaft nach dem Dreissigjährigen Kriege* (Prague, 1866, also in Czech). Another general survey is by Rudolf graf Meraviglia, *Der böhmische Adel* (Nürnberg, 1866). For the legal position of the cities see Vincenz Falk, *Die landesverfassungsmässigen Verhältnisse der königlichen Städte als vierten Standes im Königreiche Böhmen* (Prague, 1847), a good work for that time and on the whole clear. On this subject see also Jaromir Čelakovský, "Postavení vyslaných král. měst na sněmech českých a spor měst Hory Kutné, Plzně, a Českých Budějovice o přednost' místa a hlasu na sněmě" (*ČMKČ,* 1869, 115, 243, 307).

The institution in which the Estates had the greatest interest was the Executive Committee of the Diet. Robert Flieder, *Zemský výbor v království českém. Jeho organisace v lectech 1714-1783* (Prague, 1917), has written the fundamental work on this subject. Glimpses of the struggles of political centralization may be seen in J. Prokeš, "Boj o Haugvicovo 'Directorium in publicis et cameralibus' r. 1761" and his "Instrukce vydana r. 1762 pro českou a rakouskou dvorní kancelář" (*VKSN,* 1926-27). Here the Court Chancellery is traced. The views of Eighteenth Century bureaucrats are analyzed in L.

Sommer, "Die österreichischen Kameralisten in dogmenge-schichtlicher Darstellung" (*Studien zur Sozial- Wirtschafts-und Verwaltungsgeschichte*, 1925, XIII, 2).

C. Law and the Judicial System

For general histories of law and the judiciary in Bohemia one should turn to J. Kapras, *Právní dějiny zemí koruny české*, 3 vols. (Prague, 1913-15), which supersedes Čelakov-ský's and Kalousek's works on this subject. Still valuable in parts is Johann F. Schmidt von Bergenhold, *Geschichte der Privatrechts-Gesetzgebung und Gerichtsverfassung im König-reiche Böhmen von den ältesten Zeiten bis zum 21. September, 1865* (Prague, 1865). A more recent work in German is by Otto Peterka, *Rechtsgeschichte der böhmischen Länder*. Vol. II (Reichenberg, 1928) which covers the period from the Fif-teenth Century to Maria Theresa. Still useful, though undi-gested, are the works by Christian d'Elvert, *Beiträge zur Geschichte des österreichischen Straf-, Polizei- und Bürger-lichen-Rechts* (Brünn, 1868), and *Weitere Beiträge zur öster-reichischen Rechtsgeschichte* (*ibid.*, 1894). A. von Domin-Petrushevecz, *Neuere österreichische Rechtsgeschichte* (Vienna, 1869), though old, is an excellent and capable work written in a very fair spirit.

Not a few monographs have been written in this field. J. L. Banniza, *Vollständige Abhandlung von den sämtlichen öster-reichischen Gerichtsstellen* (Vienna, 1767) is a contemporary manual containing some interesting sidelights on justice in the Eighteenth Century. A. Voigt, *Geist der böhmischen Ge-setze* (Prague, 1788) is an attempt to interpret old Czech law in the light of the teachings of Montesquieu. Emil Ott, *Bei-träge zur Receptionsgeschichte der röm.-canon. Processe in den böhm. Ländern* (Leipzig, 1879) traces excellently the infiltration of Roman canonical law into Bohemian jurispru-dence. Joseph Carl count Auersperg wrote *Geschichte des k. böhm. Appellationsgerichts* (Prague, 1805), not at all bad for a monograph at that time. It has been superseded by Schmidt in a work having the same title and published at Prague in 1850. M. baron Maasburg has written several scholarly monographs in this field which are to be highly recommended. *Geschichte der Obersten Justizstelle in Wien* (ed. 2; Prague, 1891) is, on the whole, his best work. It is the standard history of the great Supreme Court and contains many valuable biographical hints in addition to the exhaustive treatment of its own subject. His two other works, *Die Organisirung der böhm. Halsgerichte im Jahre 1765* (Prague, 1884), and *Die Processordnung für Böhmen von 1753* (Vienna, 1886) contain, besides the laws themselves, a scholarly historical introduction. Sigmund Adler has succeeded in writing perhaps the most valuable monograph in this field in his *Das adelige Landrecht in Nieder- und Ober- Österreich und die Gerichtsreformen des XVIII. Jahrhunderts* (Vienna and Leipzig, 1912). This is especially good for its use of the papers of the State Council and should serve as a model for future work done in this field. R. Bartsch, "Wiener Gerichte im Vormärz" (*Festschrift zum einundreissigsten deutschen Juristentag*, Vienna und Leipzig, 1912) is a brief, but serviceable, survey of the judicial organization in Austria, 1790-1848.

There is also a fairly extensive literature on the history of codification of law in Bohemia and in the Habsburg Monarchy. We shall mention here only a few types. For Bohemia, besides Kalousek and Kapras, see Jaromir Čelakovský: *O účasti právníkův a stavů ze zemí českých na kodifikaci občanského práva rakouského* (Prague, 1911), which contains the best history. Besides being a scholarly monograph it has an excellent bibliography and an appendix with a very useful document written up by the Estates in 1790. See the chapters on the Constitution (IV and V). Tilsch in *Österreichisches Zentralblatt f. d. jur. Praxis*, XXXI, Heft 6: "Die Entstehung und Entwickelung des österr. Zivil Rechts," published also in the *Revue de Droit international et de Legislation comparée*, March, 1911, gives a good account of the work of codification. Harras v. Harrasowsky, *Der Codex Theresianus und seine*

Umarbeitung, vols. I-V (Vienna, 1883-1886), has an excellent introduction to the text of the Theresian Code, and Leo. Pfaff und Franz Hoffmann, *Commentar zum österreichischen Allgemeinen Bürgerlichen Gesetzbuche,* 5 vols. (Vienna, 1877), contains much important material, as well as the code itself. The A B G, as the code is abbreviated in German, is dissected in a very scholarly way in the *Festschrift zur Jahrhundertfeier des Allgemeinen Bürgerlichen Gesetzbuches,* 2 volumes (Vienna, 1911). Of interest to us are especially the following monographs: Wollspacher, "Das Naturrecht und das A B G"; Koschenbahr-Lykowski, "Zur Stellung des römischen Rechts in A B G für K. Österreich"; and Binder-Suchomel, "Zur Lebensgeschichte des Hofrat Franz Georg Edlen v. Keesz." The first two are excellent, the last slightly too favorable to Keesz, who, however he may have worked toward the right end, had even more faults than Joseph II.

D. Economic

General works on the economic history of Bohemia have not as yet been written, but one may find many monographs —some of them of a very high order—which will help toward an understanding of some of the economic questions of that country in the Eighteenth Century.

Among the recent works on commerce and industry in Bohemia, for the period down to 1740 we have the excellent archival researches of Alfred Příbram, "Zur Geschichte des böhmischen Handels und der böhmischen Industrie in dem Jahrhundert nach dem Westphalischen Frieden" (*MVGDB,* XXXV, XXXVI) and published separately as *Das Commerz-Collegium und seine Thätigkeit* (Prague, 1898). It is written conscientiously and with a slight protectionist leaning. A work which casts much light upon the emperor's commercial dealings down to 1740 is the able monograph of Heinrich von Srbik, *Der staatliche Exporthandel Österreichs von Leopold I bis zu Maria Theresia* (Vienna and Leipzig, 1907). Useful for the Elbe outlet for the trade of the Habsburg

Monarchy is the monograph by A. Wieske, *Der Elbhandel und die Elbhandelspolitik bis zum Beginne des 19. Jahrhunderts* (Halberstadt, 1927). A general survey of the development of industry in Central Europe to 1792 may be found in Johann Slokar, *Geschichte der österreichischen Industrie und ihrer Förderung unter Kaiser Franz I* (Vienna, 1914). The researches of Adolph Beer, though very dry, are thorough and penetrating and show here and there the manner in which the extreme tariff policy of the Habsburgs reacted upon Bohemia. See his "Die Zoll-Politik und die Schaffung eines einheitlichen Zollgebietes unter Maria Theresia" (*MIÖG*, XIV, 237 ff.) for the manner in which a local and feudal tariff became an imperial modern protective law; his "Die österreichische Handelspolitik unter Maria Theresia und Joseph II" (*AÖG*, LXXXVI) and "Die handelspolitischen Beziehungen Österr. zu den Deutschen Staaten unter Maria Theresia" (*ibid.*, LXXIX) give the larger results of the economic policy of Maria Theresa and Joseph II and emphasize the importance of the neighboring states in this policy.

A. Fournier, in his "Handel und Verkehr in Ungarn und Polen um die Mitte des 18ten Jahrhunderts. Ein Beytrag zur Geschichte der österreichischen Commerzial-Politik" (*AÖG*, LXIX) reprinted and revised in his *Historische Studien und Skizzen* (Prague and Leipzig, 1885, also Vienna, 1898) under the title of "Maria Theresia und die Anfänge ihrer Industrie und Handelspolitik" casts much light upon the policy of the government between the second and third Silesian wars. Hock-Bidermann, *Der österreichische Staatsrath* (Vienna, 1868-78) contains much material and ought really to be considered an abridged source book. A Baldauf, *Beyträge zur Handels- und Zoll-Politik Österreichs in der zweyten Hälfte des 18ten Jahrhunderts insbesondere unter Joseph II* (Halle, 1898) is a work compiled from printed and secondary sources and deals wholly with the reign of Maria Theresa. It is, however, suggestive in parts.

Anton Gindely, in his little monograph, *Das Zunftwesen in*

Böhmen von 16ten bis 18ten Jahrhundert (Prague, 1884) describes the guild system in Bohemia up to 1740, on the whole in an able way. Karl Příbram in his *Geschichte des österr. Gewerbe-Politik*, I, 1740-1798 (Leipzig, 1907) has gathered together a vast amount of material of vital importance for the economic history of Austria in the Eighteenth Century. It is to be hoped that future economic historians of that country will pattern after this penetrating work. Arthur Salz, *Geschichte der böhmischen Industrie in der Neuzeit* (Munich and Leipzig, 1913) is a series of essays, picking up some odds and ends and doing well for pioneer work in the field. But it must be supplemented by a wider search for information in this field in monographs written in Czech on various details of Bohemian industrial history. A few introductory remarks on labor in Bohemia may be found in Cyril Horáček, "Počátky českého hnutí delníckého" (*Rozpravy, ČA*, 1896, I, 5, No. 3).

The literature on finance and taxation is likewise in the monographic stage of development. For the Sixteenth Century there is K. Oberleitner, "Finanzen und Kriegswesen unter Ferdinand I (1524-1564)" (*AKÖG*, 1860, XXII). It brings much new material on central finance, but wholly omits the evaluation of such a country as Bohemia. It is imperial—"all-Austrian"—in tendency. Anton Gindely, "Geschichte der böhmischen Finanzen von 1526 bis 1618" (*KAW*, 1868) presents a scholarly work coming to startling conclusions as to the financial rôle which Bohemia played in the first century of Habsburg rule in Bohemia. W. W. Tomek, *České sněmy dle obnoveného zřízení českého Ferdinanda II* (Prague, 1868) similarly to Gindely discusses the revenues of Bohemia between 1627-1740. It is a work of solid and patient scholarship based on the conclusions of the Diets (*Landtagsschlüsse*) and is authoritative for the period it covers. The royal income is not taken up by Tomek, and this can be got only from documentary sources. Gindely, Tomek, and even Oberleitner, were written at the time of the Austro-Hungarian Agreement of 1867-8. Supplementing all of these is Josef Pekař, "České katastry, 1654-1789" (*ČČH*, 1913-15, XIX-XXII) also as separate (Prague, 1915). These articles cast much light upon both the royal and provincial revenues of Bohemia down to 1740.

Franz baron von Mensi, *Die Finanzen Österreichs von 1701 bis 1740* (Vienna, 1890), gives on the whole a satisfactory and simple account of the general features of Austrian finances during this period, without going too deeply into the causes which led to the crises depicted or without giving sufficient regard to the condition of provincal finances. Srbik's *Export-handel* already mentioned points out the connection between central finances and government trade in metals. This practically disposes of monographs on the period down to 1740.

Christian d'Elvert, *Zur österreichischen Finanzgeschichte* (Brünn, 1881), contains much undigested material and an excellent bibliography. His tendency, when expressed, is centralist. Adolph Beer in "Die Finanzverwaltung Österreichs, 1749-1816" (*MIÖG*, 1894, XV) has written the most scholarly account of the central financial administration for that period. His "Die Staatsschulden und die Ordnung des Staatshaushalts unter Maria Theresia" (*AÖG*, 1895, LXXXII) and "Finanzgeschichtliche Studien" (*Sitzungsberichte, KAW*, 1903), should be used to supplement it. He is a conservative centralist. Besides the works of Paul Stiassny and Wilhelm König on the state bankruptcy of 1811, there are the two more recent monographs of Viktor Hofmann, "Die Devalvierung des österreichischen Papiergeldes im Jahre 1811" (*Schriften des Vereins für Sozialpolitik*, Munich, 1923) and of Johann Kraft, "Die Finanzreform des Grafen Wallis und der Staatsbankrott von 1811" (*Veröffentlichungen des historischen Seminars der Universität Graz*, 1927, V).

The two government publications, *Österreichischer Erbfolgekrieg*, 1740-1748 (Vienna, 1896) and *Krieg gegen die französischen Revolution, 1792-1797* (Vienna, 1905) contain tables on finances and are very suggestive. Boh. Baxa, *K dějinam veřejného práva* (Prague, 1906) discusses the constitutional aspects of Bohemian finances. Boh. Rieger, "Navrh české zemské banky r. 1790" (*Osvěta,* 1887) reviews the proposal of the Bohemian Estates to establish a national bank.

In general, it may be said future research should devote itself systematically to study the private, royal, and provincial revenues of the Habsburgs and this should be carefully collated with the details of the financial policy and revenues of the central government. Without that, our knowledge of the subject will continue to be incomplete.

The literature on the subject of taxation and especially land taxation is not very extensive. S. Lindner, *Grundsteuerverfassung in den deutschen und italienischen Provinzen,* 2 vols. (Vienna, 1840), is antiquated and gives little space to Bohemia. Vincenz Falk, *Die Grundsteuerverfassung von Böhmen von den ältesten Zeiten bis auf die gegenwärtige Zeit* (Prague, 1848), is very useful after 1748 because it reprints almost bodily the text of the patents. Before 1748 it should be used with caution. Alois Müller, *Geschichte des Grundsteuerwesens des Königreichs Böhmen seit der Urzeit bis zur Gegenwart* (Prague, 1880) repeats much of Falk, even with his mistakes. It is however suggestive in parts especially after 1748. Some insight into the system of taxation in Bohemia for the earlier period is to be found in Otto Plachta, *České daně, 1517-1652* (Prague, 1925) and, with especial reference to Bohemian cities, in Jaroslav Novotný, *Zdanění českých měst podle katastru z r. 1654-1757* (Prague, 1929).

For a competently written general survey of the history of the Bohemian peasantry see Kamil Krofta, *Přehled dějin selského stavu v Čechách a na Moravě* (Prague, 1919). František Vaček, "Selský stav v letech 1419-1620" (*Časopis pro Dějiny Venkova s přílohou Selský Archiv,* 1927, XIV) covers in more detail the two centuries before the Battle of White Mountain. Joseph Pekař, *Kniha o Kosti,* 2 vols. (Prague, 1909-11), and the series of articles by the same author under the title of "České Katastry, 1654-1789" (*ČČH,*

1913-15, XIX-XXII, also as separate, Prague, 1915) constitute research of a most thorough character in the agrarian
history of Bohemia. Pekař blames the government for the
ruin of the serf in Bohemia down to 1748.

On serfdom the general work by Samuel Sugenheim, *Geschichte der Aufhebung der Leibeigenschaft und Hörigkeit in
Europa bis um die Mitte des neunzehnten Jahrhunderts* (St.
Petersburg, 1861) is now antiquated. G. F. Knapp, the
founder of a school of agrarian historians, in his article on
"Leibeigenschaft in Österreich" (*Beilage zur Allgemeinen Zeitung*, July 3, 1892, 203) pointed out that Bohemia, Moravia,
and Silesia had serfdom similar to that found in the area east
of the Elbe to the boundaries of Poland. Karl Grünberg, *Die
Bauernbefreiung und die Auflösung des gutsherrlich-bäuer-
lichen Verhältnisses in Böhmen, Mähren, und Schlesien*, 2
vols. (Leipzig, 1894) is the standard work on Bohemian serfdom. He is a pupil of the Knapp school and has done his
work on the whole impartially. The second volume contains
valuable documentary material. The general tendency of the
book is to stress chiefly the legal aspects with emphasis on the
point of view of the government rather than the Estates and
the serf. Pekař's work mentioned above should be carefully
compared with it.

For those who are still interested in the degradation of the
serf there are J. Lippert, *Die Knechtschaft in Böhmen* (Prague,
1890), and its answer by John Peisker under the same title,
date and place, as well as the review by W. Milkowic in
MIÖG, 1894, XV, from which it is evident that the Bohemian serf, while oppressed, was not so badly off as has heretofore been pictured. It is difficult, however, to exonerate the
Habsburgs from their guilt in the oppression of the Bohemian
serf, and it is to the honor of Joseph II that he sought to do
him justice.

Shorter and more detailed studies on various aspects of this
subject are to be found in the following: J. V. Šimák, "Zpravy
o selské bouři r. 1680 z říšského válečního archivu" (*VČA*,

XXII), K. V. Adamek, "Království české v r. 1771" (*Památky Archaeologických a Místopisných*, XXV), František Roubík, "Relace císaře Josefa II o jeho cestě do Čech, Moravy, a Slezka r. 1771" (*Časopis pro Dějiny Venkova s přílohou Selský Archiv*, 1926, XIII), and J. Prokeš, "Memorially o hospodářskem stavu Čech před selskou bouři z r. 1775" (*ibid.*, 1924, XI, 1925, XII).

The enclosure movement and problems of land reform are treated in Václav Černy, "Dělení pastvin v zemích českých v. 1. 1768-1848" (*ibid.*, 1924, XI) and "Pozemkova reforma v XVIII. století" (*ibid.*, 1927, XIV), in J. Proházka, "Parcelování velkostatků (raabisace) za Marie Terezie v Čechách" (*Kapras Seminar*, Prace 10), and in J. Kapras, *Velkostatky a fideikomisy v českém státě* (Prague, 1918) and his "Fideikomisy" (*Česká Revue*, 1923, XVI). There is an analysis of research work done in these topics by J. Proházka, "Výsledky a úkoly historických praci o hospodářském vývoji zemí koruny české" (*Sborník prace z dějin práva československého*, Prague, 1930, a collection of essays in honor of J. Kapras, the successor of Kalousek and Čelakovský).

The political consciousness of the Bohemian peasantry during the French Revolution and on the occasion of the meeting of the Diet in 1792 is seen from J. Volf, "Vyšetřování vlivu novinářských zprav o francouzské revoluci na selský stav v Čechách r. 1789" (*Osvěta*, 1913) and František Roubík, "Sedlaci na zemský sněm do Prahy v lednu 1792" (*Časopis pro Dějiny Venkova s přílohou Selský Archiv*, 1929, XII).

E. SOCIAL

1. *Religion*

Accounts of the religious life of the peoples of the Habsburg Monarchy in the Eighteenth Century are few in number. E. Friedberg, *Die Gränzen zwischen Staat und Kirche und die Garantien gegen deren Verletzung* (Tübingen, 1872) is very general, but still serviceable in parts. It has the merit of being impartial. Sebastian Brunner, *Die theologische Dienerschaft am Hofe Josephs II. Geheime Correspondenzen und Enthül-lungen* (Vienna, 1868) is really a collection of documents and extracts, some of which are very important, all of which are interesting. Although clerical in point of view, he does not go out of his way to attack Joseph II, but tears down the veil with which the hero is draped. His *Die Mysterien der Auf-klärung in Österreich, 1700-1800* (Mainz, 1869) is also very suggestive, the greatest emphasis being put upon the Free-masons and their spread in the Habsburg Monarchy. The author maintains that toleration was ushered in largely by these lodges. Important in this connection is G. Holzknecht, "Ursprung und Herkunft der Reformideen k. Josefs II auf kirchlichen Gebiete" (*FIGÖ*, 1914, Heft II). Hans Schlitter, "Die Reise des Papstes Pius VI nach Wien und sein Aufent-halt daselbst. Ein Beitrag zur Geschichte der Beziehungen Josephs II zur Römischen Curie" (*Fontes Rerum Austria-carum*, 1892, XLVII) holds that Joseph II's policy was to correct real abuses and "destroy a state within a state." He finds the origin of Joseph II's toleration ideas in French phi-losophy. G. Wolf, *Josephinna* (Vienna, 1890) emphasizes reli-gion and the schools and is on the whole fairly written.

Gustav Frank, *Das Toleranz-Patent Kaiser Josephs II. Ur-kundliche Geschichte seiner Entstehung und Folgen* (Vienna, 1881) is a scholarly monograph, the standard work from a Prot-estant point of view on the subject. It should be used with Georg Loesche, *Von der Duldung zur Gleichberechtigung. Archivalische Beiträge zur Geschichte des Protestantismus in Österreich von 1781 bis 1861* (Vienna, 1911). Both, however, are Austrian in their point of view and omit important detail in the "provinces." Hock-Bidermann, *Der österreichische Staatsrath* (Vienna, 1868-1878) is full of suggestions. It can be used like a source book.

Of more general interest, yet touching on the condition of things in the Monarchy is S. Merkle, *Die Katholische Beur-theilung des Aufkärungs-Zeitalters* (Berlin, 1909). It is a polemical monograph, suggestive in parts however. For another general work see J. Küntziger, *Febronius et le Febronian-isme. Étude historique sur le mouvement réformateur pro-voqué dans l'église Catholique au XVIIIe siècle par Febronius et l'origine des réformes ecclésiastiques de Joseph II* (Brussels, 1889).

We come nearer to our subject when we consider the mate-rial on Bohemia alone. A. Frind, *Die Kirchengeschichte Böhmens im allgemeinen und mit besonderer Beziehung auf die Leitmeritzer Diözese*, 4 vols. (Prague, 1864-78) is old, but still serviceable. Bernhard Czerwenka, *Geschichte der Evan-gelischen Kirche in Böhmen*, 2 vols. (Prague, 1870), is on the whole good, but has only a few pages for the epoch after 1620. Exhaustive in its treatment and thoroughly scholarly on the history of the Bohemian Confession is F. Hřejsa, *Česká Confese* (Prague, 1912). But it will be noted that this covers only a part of the history of Czech Protestantism. No one can afford to omit reading A. Gindely, *Geschichte der Gegenreformation in Böhmen* (Leipzig, 1894) a scholarly work and on the whole fair to all sides. His "Die Processierung der Häretiker in Böhmen unter Karl VI" (*Abh. BGW*, 1887, VII F, 2 bd.), is very suggestive. The work of the Jesuits in Bohemia to 1635 has been discussed in Alois Kroess, *Geschichte der böhmischen Provinz der Gesellschaft Jesu*, vol. II, i. (Vienna, 1927). Further light on their activities and their views may be found in "Gutachten der Jesuiten am Beginne der kath. Gegenrefor-mation in Böhmen" (*Hist. Jahrbuch*, XXXIV, 1, 2) by the same author; in O. Flegl, "Relaci kardinala Harracha o stavu pražské arcidiecese do Říma" (*VČA*, 1914, XIII); and Fran-tišek Snopek, "Acta kardinala Ditrichštejna z let 1619-35" (*ČMM*, 1915, XL). The question of the publication of sources on the Counter-reformation in Bohemia has been dealt with by J. Borovička, "O výdavání pramenů k dějinam obnovy katoli-ckého náboženství v Čechách" (*VČA*, 1917, XXVI). Prob-lems connected with the patronate have been investigated by Jan Schlenz, *Das Kirchenpatronat in Böhmen* (Prague, 1928).

With the works of Gindely should be read the three monographs which follow: Antonín Rezek, *Dějiny prostonárodního hnutí náboženského v Čechách od vydání Tolerančního Patentu až na naše časy* (Prague, 1886). (Only the first part down to 1781 was completed.) The work, however, is a path-breaker in the field, treating the subject of the national religious movement and sectarianism in Bohemia with originality and vigor. Karl V. Adamek, *Listiny k dějinam lidového náboženského hnutí na českém východě v XVIII. a XIX. věku* (Prague, 1911), I (1750-1782) supplements especially T. V. Bílek, *Reformace katolická neboli obnovení náboženského katolického v království českém po bitvě bělohorské* (Prague, 1892).

2. Schools and Germanization

This field of research has long been unexplored and is too much open to national differences. Nevertheless, some excellent monographs have been written on various problems connected with it. W. W. Tomek, "Pamětí o školách českých z rektorských let M. Martina Bachačka, 1598-1612" (*ČMČ*, 1848, 340-397), and his *Geschichte der Prager Universität* (Prague, 1848), give an account of higher education in Bohemia, which is old, but still useful. Rudolf Kink, *Geschichte der kaiserlichen Universität zu Wien*, 2 vols. (Vienna, 1854), is a very capable work, the second volume of which contains valuable documents. It should be used along with Tomek, which it excels so far as solidity and general point of view are concerned. Joseph Alexander baron von Helfert, *Die Gründung der österreichischen Volksschule durch Maria Theresia* (Prague, 1860) has written a reliable work, fair to both nationalities, which is now supplemented by A. Egger, *Die Reform der österreichischen Volksschule unter Maria Theresia* (Brixen, 1912). G. Wolf, *Das Unterrichtswesen in Österreich unter Joseph II* (Vienna, 1880), is a short monograph including chiefly Sonnenfels' (1785) report on Austrian schools drawn up for Catherine II of Russia. See J. Šafránek, "O Josefínském popise škol v království českém" (*VČSN*, 1902) and his

"Pravda o školách v království českém za vrchní zpravy Kindermannovy" (*Osvěta*, 1907, I) for the Czech point of view on school questions. He criticizes especially the documentary publication—a valuable one though it is—of Anton Weiss, *Geschichte der theresianischen Schulreform in Böhmen*, 2 vols. (Vienna, 1908). Its introduction is entirely inadequate. See in this connection V. J. Nováček, "Ferdinand Kindermanns von Schulstein Promemoria: 'Über den Zustand der Seelsorge auf den Kammeralherrschaften in Böhmen'" (*VKČSN*, 1914). Very useful for the study of this period is Sigmund Adler, *Die Unterrichtsverfassung Kaiser Leopolds II und die finanzielle Fundierung der österreichischen Universitäten nach Anträgen Martinis* (Vienna, 1917).

The progress of Germanization is ably traced by Boh. Rieger in "Z germanisačního úsili 18. věku" (*Osvěta*, 1887) and in his capital work on local government, *Zřízení krajské v Čechách*, 2 vols. (Prague, 1889, 1893). He is fair to the Germans. The origin and course of the Czech national revival have been matters of much dispute among scholars. The elements of the controversy may be found chiefly in the writings of Joseph Hanuš: "Počátky král. české společností nauk" (*ČČH*, XIV, 141-152), "Dodatek k počátkum král. české společností nauk" (*ČČH*, XV, 277, 425), "Mikuláš Adaukt Voigt" (*Rozpravy, ČA*, 1910, no. 32), "František Martin Pelcl, český historik a buditel" (*Rozpravy, ČA*, 1914, III, no. 38), "František Faustin Procházka, český buditel a literární historik" (*Rozpravy, ČA*, 1915, III, no. 39) and "Autobiografie Gelasia Dobnera" (*ČČH*, 1917, XXIII, 129-138). For another view see Arnošt Kraus, "Pražské časopisy, 1770-1774, a české probuzení" (*Rozpravy*, ČA, III, no. 31), and his "Augustin Zitte" (*Sborník Filologické*, 1914, V, 140-161). See also Joseph Volf, "Zánik jediných českých novin na konci r. 1771" (*ČNM*, 1923, XCVII), Cyril Straka, "Reforma pražských zednářských lozi r. 1778" (*ČČH*, XXXI, 131-140), and Jan Strakoš, *Počátky obrozeného historismu českého v pražských časopisech a Mik. Ad. Voigt. Příspěvek k historii protisvicenské reakce v národ-*

ním obrození, vol. III (Prague, 1929). Joseph Pekař, "Naše šlechta a jazyk český v 18. století" (*ČČH*, XX, 80-82) adds a footnote on the use of Czech by the Bohemian nobility, and Flora Kleinschutz, "J. Dobrovského řeč 'Über die Ergenbenheit und Anhänglichkeit der slavischen Völker an das Erzhaus Östreich' " (*Listy Filologické,* 1918, XLV), throws light on Dobrovský's famous lecture before Leopold II.

In connection with this subject as a whole the brilliant and capable surveys of Kamil Krofta, "Vývoj českého národního vědomí" (*Česká Revue,* 1918), and *Čechy a Rakousko v minulosti* (1526-1848) (Vienna, 1923), from the Czech point of view, and H. Hassinger, *Die Entwicklung des tschechischen Nationalbewusstseins und die Gründung des heutigen Staates der Tschechoslowakei* (Kassel, 1927), from the German point of view, will be found suggestive.

INDEX